# DISEASING OF AMERICA

A barbarian . . . [is one who] thinks that the customs
of his tribe and island are the laws of nature.
—George Bernard Shaw, *Caesar and Cleopatra*

## Other Books by Stanton Peele

The Truth About Addiction and Recovery

Visions of Addiction

Love and Addiction (with Archie Brodsky)

*Published by Jossey-Bass:*

The Meaning of Addiction

# DISEASING OF AMERICA

How We Allowed Recovery Zealots and the
Treatment Industry to Convince Us We Are Out of Control

by

STANTON PEELE

*With a New Preface*

Jossey-Bass Publishers • San Francisco

Jossey-Bass books and products are available through most bookstores. To contact Jossey-Bass directly, call (888) 378-2537, fax to (800) 605-2665, or visit our website at www.josseybass.com.

Substantial discounts on bulk quantities of Jossey-Bass books are available to corporations, professional associations, and other organizations. For details and discount information, contact the special sales department at Jossey-Bass.

**Library of Congress Cataloging-in-Publication Data**

Peele, Stanton.
   Diseasing of America : how we allowed recovery zealots and the treatment industry to convince us we are out of control / Stanton Peele.
       p.    cm.
   Paperback ed. published: New York : Lexington Books, 1995.
   Includes bibliographical references and index.
   ISBN 0-7879-4643-5
   1. Substance abuse—Treatment—Social aspects.   2. Compulsive behavior—Social aspects.   3. Alcoholism—Social aspects.
   4. Recovery movement.   I. Title.
RC564.P43   1999
362.29—dc21                                                       98-30568

*PB Printing*        10 9 8 7 6 5 4

# Contents

*Preface to the Paperback Edition*      *vii*

*Preface and Acknowledgments*      *x*

1. Why Addiction Is Not a Disease
   *And Why We Should Care that It Not Be
   Treated as Such*      1

2. Alcoholism in America
   *How We Discovered that Alcohol Is Addictive
   and that So Many People Are Alcoholics*      31

3. Who Says What the Truths about
   Alcoholism Are?      55

4. Transforming the Addict into a Role Model,
   and the Person into an Addict      85

5. The Addiction Treatment Industry      115

6. What Is Addiction, and How Do People
   Get It?
   *Values, Intentions, Self-Restraint, and
   Environments*      145

7. How People Quit Addictions, Usually on Their Own — 173

8. Our Confusion over Law, Morality, and Addiction — 203

9. How We Lost Control of Our World — 231

10. Creating a World Worth Living In
*Community, Efficacy, and Values* — 259

*Notes* — 289

*Index* — 311

*About the Author* — 323

# Preface to the
# Paperback Edition

SINCE *Diseasing of America* first appeared, the problems I analyze have gained increasing recognition and some attempts at
amelioration—even while, in some ways, the diseasing trend has
continued and perhaps worsened. On the positive side:

- Many have joined my attack on the tendency to call every
human problem a disease, create a twelve-step group for each
"disease," and excuse criminal misconduct as the result of such
diseases. Books such as Wendy Kaminer's *I'm Dysfunctional, You're
Dysfunctional* and Charles Sykes's *A Nation of Victims* have focused
attention on how ludicrous and counterproductive the diseasing
of America has been.
- Insurers have greatly reduced the money they spend on for-
profit hospitalization for drug and alcohol treatment—as well as
that for compulsive gambling, love sickness, etc. The retrench-
ment in this area has been assisted by government and private
investigations and corruption charges against major hospital
chains such as Psychiatric Institutes of America and CompCare.
- Important government and private bodies (including the prestigious Institute of Medicine) have recommended a major revamp-
ing of the alcohol treatment system to eliminate the "one-size-
fits-all" disease model. This is the assumption that everyone who
has ever had a drinking problem has a disease that will inevitably
progress to death unless remedied by AA or the medical establishment. This reevaluation includes a growing recognition that most

people—particularly young people—who have periodically drunk too much may resume drinking at a reduced level.
• In the field of drug policy, a growing chorus of voices now wonders aloud whether hiring more police and building more prisons in order to arrest and house drug users is a costly mistake. We must cease the insanity of imprisoning otherwise lawful casual drug users while excusing heavy users and addicts from criminal responsibility for violent and destructive acts. In this vein, the recommendation that marijuana be legalized is one step in the right direction.

Nonetheless, much remains to be remedied. Thus, I continue to argue that:

• Criminals intoxicated on drugs and alcohol are not to be excused but should be penalized additionally for crimes against people and property. Typically, a young alcoholic argued in a New York court in 1994 that he was in a blackout when he murdered the physician couple living in his family's old house. But this man never notified the police of the killings in the years afterwards, not even as he told his AA colleagues about the crime.
• Otherwise sensible books such as *I'm Dysfunctional, You're Dysfunctional* fail to take on the alcoholism and AA industry, while attacking the easy targets of twelve-step groups for those who overindulge in eating, shopping, gambling, sex, and so on. If you can't explain why it is wrong and harmful to view overdrinking as an out-of-control medical or spiritual problem, then you can't explain why it is wrong to make compulsive gambling and shopping into diseases.
• We are accelerating the rate at which we medicalize our personal and social problems. Some may look askance at those who claim they have a disease like compulsive shopping, which makes them spend the family food budget on jewelry, clothes, cars, or other instant fixes for themselves. But, at the same time, we diagnose and treat with a growing pharmacopeia of antidepressant drugs more and more of our citizens whom we label as afflicted with diseases such as depression, PMS, CFS, or OCD (read the book if you don't already know what these acronyms mean).
• A growing majority of people receiving substance abuse treatment do so unwillingly. They are forced by courts, social agencies,

and employers to "admit" they have a disease and to get the "proper" treatment for it. Oddly, many progressive thinkers who recognize that we must cease throwing drug users in prison are enamored of twelve-step or disease treatments that are just as coercive and useless as incarceration. Despite the benefits such treatment supposedly offers substance abusers and victims of other behavioral and mood diseases, they must be pressured— including the threat of jail—into treatment.

Although many people now recognize this or that particular inanity or injustice in our addiction treatment system, *Diseasing of America* is just as necessary today as when I first wrote it. For we cannot reverse our misdirected policies—and our conceptions of ourselves as individuals and as a society—unless we can understand the cultural, economic, and psychological forces that drive the *Diseasing of America*.

# Preface and Acknowledgments

A RECENT network telecast of a pro football game included as a brief human-interest feature a morality play about the life of Bob Hayes: his great success in track and football, his descent into addiction and crime, his redemption through abstinence, faith, and service to others. The narrative stated that, along with his athletic ability, Hayes had inherited "the genes for alcoholism." For the hundredth time I marveled at the strange amalgam of religion and pseudoscience that constitutes the current dogma about alcoholism and other addictions. Naturally, no one had tested Hayes for "alcoholic genes," since there is no known genetic marker for alcoholism and it is clear that no such distinctive indicator exists. Yet this type of simpleminded supposition—presented as fact—is standard fare on TV and in newspapers and magazines. Meanwhile, as Americans are learning to accept this view of the nature and causes of addiction, drug and alcohol abuse continues unabated and even grows, along with a host of other problems we now call addictions.

I have written this book for those who (perhaps without knowing why) are as skeptical as I am when asked to accept the glib rationalizations about alcoholism and addiction shown on TV, who wish to have hard information on the topic readily at their disposal, and who think it is important to take an open-minded look at some of our most urgent social problems. These readers will find that what has been presented as straightforward data about alcoholism and addiction is in fact an implausible mélange of scientific, cultural, and historical prejudices. I have written this book to put on public record that which needs to be said, and which many people suspect—but which somehow never makes it to the level of cultural consciousness nor is considered when we make crucial public policy decisions.

Like everyone else, I am concerned about the lost and wasted lives associated with drug and alcohol abuse and other compulsive behavior. I lament the senseless deaths of people killed by drunk drivers, and the way some young people destroy themselves and others, cutting off life's potential, because they have learned only destructive ways of asserting themselves. I am distressed by the large and small depredations that people suffer when, in response to the imbalances and futilities of their lives, they lose themselves in overeating, gambling, smoking, or destructive relationships of any kind. Furthermore, I am personally repelled by the excesses of intoxication. When there is so much to do in life that is satisfying, challenging, and fun, I don't associate with people who regularly change their behavior and consciousness through drinking or drug taking.

*My* concern is simply that we examine these problems with common sense, with an awareness of people and culture, and with some knowledge of history. Instead of repeating superstitions and rituals that don't work, let's at least understand what it is we're actually dealing with and do things that really make a difference.

I feel obliged to explain my motives because I have been attacked (and will be again, in response to this book) by both sides of the polarized political climate in the United States on the issue of drugs. Several publishers to whom I submitted this book not only rejected it but also objected to its message. Many well-meaning people in publishing, and other concerned people, believe that my insistence on personal responsibility and the individual's capacity for choice as  essential elements for understanding and dealing with addiction precludes compassion toward alcoholics and addicts. As if it were compassionate to automatically label the teenage weekend drinker, the person caught using an illicit substance, or the drunk-driving offender as having a lifelong "disease" of "chemical dependency."

It is self-defeating, not compassionate, to tell the high school student who drinks in response to the pressures of adolescence that he or she is an alcoholic who can never drink again. It is stupid, not liberal, to tell a professional athlete who has been discovered using cocaine in the off-season that if he ever sips another beer he has embarked on the long slippery return to chemical dependence. It is disrespectful of human dignity and of human rights to force people into treatment in violation of both their own judgment and the United States Constitution. And it is useless and wasteful to require expensive pseudomedical therapies for all these cases when these treatments *have been shown* to be less effective than ordinary legal and community procedures—such as suspending a drunk driver's license or jailing a reckless driver—for correcting the behaviors in question. All of these mistaken efforts are based on misinformation and falsehood; they exacerbate the problems they ostensibly attack; and they are a step toward totalitarianism.

If the liberal responds to my rejection of the expedient labeling of misbehavior as disease by saying that I lack compassion, the conservative is alienated by my refusal to be swept away by the hysteria surrounding drug use. I spend no time in this book condemning the use of illicit drugs as inherently addictive and immoral, and I oppose the cryptoprohibitionism of the alcoholism movement. It is not that I welcome frequent or habitual intoxication by many young people and others; I detest it. Rather, I am convinced that people are best able to avoid or outgrow destructive habits through being provided with honest information as best we can discern it, through respect for variations in how individuals and cultural groups prefer to conduct their lives, through recognition of people's capacity to choose, to adapt, and to grow, and through the creation of a society that offers those prone to unhealthy involvements reasonable alternatives for accomplishment and self-respect. Underlying these accommodations to the less-than-ideal conditions that many people face, we all have a responsibility not to kill, maim, steal, or damage the lives of others, as well as a communal responsibility to restrain destructive behavior and to support others in realizing positive values in their lives.

Nearly all the supposedly modern, scientific views of and remedies for drug and alcohol misuse and other addictions are simply an old and familiar moralism, albeit dressed in contemporary medical garb. We need to lay out reasonable social policies with respect to all the behaviors—including sexual assault, crime, family violence, drug and alcohol use, and compulsive behavior of all kinds—that have been confused through our addiction experts' specious scientific analyses. Otherwise, we are in danger of being destroyed by our unresolved social problems. Our failure, however, will differ from that of previous civilizations that were crushed by their internal contradictions in that our demise will be sanctified and confirmed by the label *scientific*—which in most cases now means "inbred," "unchangeable," and "requiring medical treatment."

I grant that potential critics on both the left and right are correct about one thing: addiction is a political issue. It is political not just in the ways we choose to deal with it but in its very nature. We cannot understand addiction by trying to isolate it under the microscope in a biochemistry laboratory. Addiction takes on meaning only in the context of culture and society and of what people think and feel about themselves. In much of the world, addiction does not mean what it means to us, and nowhere in the world did it mean what it now does to us prior to about a century ago. Both individual addictions and America's preoccupation with addiction say something very crucial—and nonbiological—about our society as well as about addicted individuals.

This book is grounded in the belief that we cannot begin to confront the social problem of addiction unless we take account of what it says about us. The things we believe about addiction are a major contributor to the way we experience it—and thus to the incidence of addiction in our society. In other words, understanding the history, psychology, sociology, and economics of addiction is not a luxury, an idle interest to be indulged only after we have stamped out the drug trade and put everyone in treatment centers or support groups. It is a necessary first step toward realistic coping. One must keep in mind while reading my proposals that throughout Europe and the rest of the world outside the United States—most of which has fewer of the problems discussed here than does America—much of what I say is considered unexceptional. In this sense, this book could only have been written in America. At the same time, however, as the United States exports its ideas—rather perversely, one would think, in view of how poorly we are doing ourselves—what I say here can serve as a warning to other countries as they ponder how they should respond to American initiatives in the addictions. These are the stakes, then, as I analyze the ever-worsening impact of the addiction industry on our individual and social well-being.

I am indebted for their help in completing this book to the same two people who were most helpful to me in writing my first book, *Love and Addiction*, more than a dozen years ago—Archie Brodsky (who coauthored *Love and Addiction*) and my wife, Mary Arnold. Hopefully, this is a tribute to continuity in life and community spirit. I am indebted as well to a number of the researchers whose work I cite favorably here, many of whom took the trouble to keep me abreast of their thoughts and publications. I won't thank these people individually; instead, I rely on the strength of their ideas to shine through on their own, bespeaking both my thanks and the quality of their work and of their contributions to the field. I am also most grateful to the staffs of the Rutgers Center of Alcohol Studies library (particularly Penny Page), the Joint Free Public Library of Morristown and Morris Township (New Jersey), and the Alcohol Research Group (and most particularly Andrea Mitchell) for their continuing bibliographic assistance. I especially want to thank Lexington Books, my longtime publisher, and Margaret Zusky, my editor, for their loyal support. I owe my gratitude to all these people and others; however, the ideas in this book are solely my own responsibility.

# 1

# Why Addiction Is Not a Disease

## And Why We Should Care that It Not Be Treated as Such

Medical schools are finally teaching about alcoholism; Johns Hopkins will require basic training for all students and clinicians. . . . Alcoholism, as a chronic disease, offers "a fantastic vehicle to teach other concepts," says Jean Kinney [of Dartmouth's Cork Institute]. . . . William Osler, Kinney remarks, coined the aphorism that "to know syphilis is to know medicine," . . . . Now, she says, the same can be said of alcoholism.

—"The Neglected Disease in Medical Education," *Science*[1]

OCD (obsessive-compulsive disorder) is apparently rare in the general population.

—American Psychiatric Association, 1980[2]

The evidence is strong OCD is a common mental disorder that, like other stigmatized and hidden disorders in the past, may be ready for discovery and demands for treatment on a large scale.

—National Institute of Mental Health, 1988[3]

---

IN AMERICA today, we are bombarded with news about drug and alcohol problems. We may ask ourselves, "How did we get here?" Alternatively, we may wonder if these problems are really worse now than they were five or ten years ago, or fifty or one hundred. Actually, in many cases the answer is no. Estimates of the number of alcoholics requiring treatment are wildly overblown, and reputable epidemiological researchers find that as little as one percent of the population fits the clinical definition of alcoholism—as opposed to the 10 percent figure regularly used by the alcoholism industry. Meanwhile, cocaine use is down. All indicators are that very few young people who try drugs ever become regular users, and fewer still get "hooked."

Of course, we have real problems. The nightly news carries story after story of inner-city violence between crack gangs and of totally desolate urban environments where drugs reign supreme. The cocaine problem has resolved itself—not exclusively, but very largely—into a ghetto problem, like many that face America. A *New York Times* front-page story based on an eight-year study of young drug users showed that those who abuse drugs have a number of serious background problems, and *that these problems don't disappear from their lives when they stop using drugs.*[4] In other words, the sources—and solutions—for what is going on in our ghettos are only very secondarily a matter of drug availability and use.

America is a society broken into two worlds. The reality of the crack epidemic and of inner cities and poor environments sometimes explodes and impinges unpleasantly on our consciousness. For the most part, however, our reality is that of the middle class, which fills our magazines with health stories and warnings about family problems and the strivings of young professionals to find satisfaction. And for some time now, this other world has also focused on addiction. But this new addiction marketplace is only sometimes linked to alcohol and drugs. Even when it is, we have to redefine alcoholism as the new Betty Ford kind, which is marked by a general dull malaise, a sense that one is drinking too much, and—for many, like Betty Ford and Kitty Dukakis—relying on prescribed drugs to make life bearable.

However we define loss-of-control drinking, Betty Ford didn't experience it. But treating problems like hers and those of so many media stars is far more rewarding and profitable than trying to deal with street derelicts or ghetto addicts. At the same time, *everything can be an addiction.* This remarkable truth—which I first described in *Love and Addiction* in 1975—has so overwhelmed us as a society that we have gone haywire. We want to pass laws to excuse compulsive gamblers when they embezzle money to gamble and to force insurance companies to pay to treat them. We want to treat people who can't find love and who instead (when they are women) go after dopey, superficial men or (when they are men) pursue endless sexual liaisons without finding true happiness. And we want to call all these things—and many, many more—addictions.

Since I was part of the movement to label non-drug-related behaviors as addictions, what am I complaining about? My entire purpose in writing *Love and Addiction* was to explain addictions as part of a larger description of people's lives. Addiction is an experience that people can get caught up in but that still expresses their values, skills at living, and personal resolve—or lack of it. The label *addiction* does not obviate either the meaning of the addictive involvement within people's lives, or their responsibility for their misbehavior or for their choices in continuing the addiction. Forty million Americans have quit smoking. What, then, are we to think about the people who do not quit but who sue a tobacco company for addicting them to cigarettes after they learn they are going to die from a smoking-related ailment?

This discrepancy between understanding addiction within the larger context of a person's life and regarding it as an *explanation* of that life underlies my opposition to the "disease theory" of addiction, which I contest throughout this book. My view of addiction explicitly refutes this theory's contentions that (1) the addiction exists *independently* of the rest of a person's life and *drives* all of his or her choices; (2) it is progressive and irreversible, so that the addiction *inevitably worsens* unless the person seeks medical treatment or joins an AA-type support group; (3) addiction means the person is incapable of controlling his or her behavior, either in relation to the addictive object itself or—when the person is intoxicated or in pursuit of the addiction—in relation to the person's dealings with the rest of the world. Everything I oppose in the disease view is represented in the passive, *1984*-ish phrase, *alcohol abuse victim*, to replace *alcohol abuser*. On the contrary, this book maintains that people are *active agents* in—not passive victims of—their addictions.

While I do believe that a host of human habits and compulsions can be understood as addictions, I think the disease version of addiction does *at least* as much harm as good. An addiction does not mean that God in heaven decided which people are alcoholics and addicts. There is no biological urge to form addictions, one that we will someday find under a microscope and that will finally make sense of all these different cravings and idiocies (such as exercising to the point of injury or having sex with people who are bad for you). No medical treatment will ever be created to excise addictions from people's lives, and support groups that convince people that they are helpless and will forever be incapable of controlling an activity are better examples of self-fulfilling prophecies than of therapy.

What is this new addiction industry meant to accomplish? More and more addictions are being discovered, and new addicts are being identified, until all of us will be locked into our own little addictive worlds with other addicts like ourselves, defined by the special interests of our neuroses. What a repugnant world to imagine, as well as a hopeless one. Meanwhile, *all of the addictions we define are increasing.* In the first place, we tell people they can never get better from their "diseases." In the second, we constantly find new addicts, looking for them in all sorts of new areas of behavior and labeling them at earlier ages on the basis of more casual or typical behaviors, such as getting drunk at holiday celebrations ("chemical-dependency disease") or checking to see whether they locked their car door ("obsessive-compulsive disorder").

We must oppose this nonsense by understanding its sources and contradicting disease ideology. Toward this end I describe in the chapters that follow how the addiction movement has come to dominate American society. I detail the history of drinking in America—a history that has given America AA and all its myriad offshoots and that has produced the multimillion-dollar alcohol-as-a-disease treatment industry and now a host of new diseases, such as being the child-of-a-person-with-the-disease-of-alcoholism. In addition to the history of the disease movement, I review in highlight form the scientific research on addiction and alcoholism. I then describe in some detail what addiction is and how people become addicted; then how people get over addiction—as people so often do (or at least did in the past) with the help of family, friends, role models, work and social success—without turning to formal treatment or to specialized groups organized to help every variety of addict.

At the larger social level, I address how our society is going wrong in excusing crime, compelling people to undergo treatment, and wildly mixing up moral responsibility with disease diagnoses. Indeed, understanding the confusion and self-defeating behavior we display in this regard is perhaps the best way to analyze the failure of many of our contemporary social policies, as I attempt to do. Finally, I confront the actual social, psychological, and moral issues that we face as individuals and as a society—the ones we are constantly repressing and mislabeling through widening our disease nets. It is as though we were creating distorted microscopes that actually muddy our vision and that make our problems harder to resolve into components we can reasonably hope to deal with.

## What Are Real Diseases?

Most of this book deals with what it means to regard addiction as a disease. But if we are to distinguish between addiction and other diseases, then we first need to understand what have been called diseases historically and how these differ from what are being called diseases today. To do so, let us review three generations of diseases—physical ailments, mental disorders, and addictions.

The *first* generation of diseases consists of disorders known through their physical manifestations, like malaria, tuberculosis, cancer, and AIDS. The era of medical understanding that these diseases ushered in began with the discovery of specific microbes that cause particular diseases and for which preventive inoculations—and eventually antibodies—were developed. These maladies are the ones we can unreservedly call diseases without clouding the issue. This first generation of diseases differs fundamentally from what were later called diseases in that the former are *defined by their measurable physical effects*. They are clearly connected to the functioning of the body, and our concern is with the damage the disease does to the body.

The *second* generation of diseases are the so-called mental illnesses (now referred to as emotional disorders). They are not defined in the same way as the first generation. Emotional disorders are apparent to us not because of what we measure in people's bodies but because of the feelings, thoughts, and behaviors that they produce in people, which we can only know from what the sufferers say and do. We do not diagnose emotional disorders from a brain scan; if a person cannot tell reality from fantasy, we call the person mentally ill, no matter what the person's EEG says.

The *third* generation of diseases—addictions—strays still farther from the model of physical disorder to which the name *disease* was first applied by modern medicine. That is, unlike a mental illness such as schizophrenia, which is indicated by disordered thinking and feelings, addictive disorders *are known by the behaviors they describe*. We call a person a drug addict who consumes drugs compulsively or excessively and whose life is devoted to seeking out these substances. If an addicted smoker gives up smoking or if an habituated coffee drinker decides to drink coffee only after Sunday dinner, then each ceases to be addicted. We cannot tell whether a person is addicted or will be addicted in the absence of the ongoing behavior— the person with a hypothetical alcoholic predisposition (say, one who has an alcoholic parent or whose face flushes when drinking) but who drinks occasionally and moderately is not an alcoholic.

In order to clarify the differences between third-generation and first-generation diseases, we often have to overcome shifting definitions that have been changed solely for the purpose of obscuring crucial differences between problems like cancer and addiction. After a time, we seem not to recognize how our views have been manipulated by such gerrymandered disease criteria. For example, by claiming that alcoholics are alcoholics even if they haven't drunk for fifteen years, alcoholism is made to seem less tied to drinking behavior and more like cancer. Sometimes it seems necessary to remind ourselves of the obvious: that a person does not get over cancer by stopping a single behavior or even by changing a whole life-style, but the sole and essential indicator for successful remission of alcoholism is that the person ceases to drink.

Addictions involve appetites and behaviors. While a connection can be traced between individual and cultural beliefs and first- and second-generation diseases, this connection is most pronounced for addictions. Behaviors and appetites are addictions only in particular cultural contexts—obviously, obesity matters only where people have enough to eat and think it is important to be thin. Symptoms like loss-of-control drinking depend *completely* on cultural and personal meanings, and we will explore in subsequent chapters how cultural groups that don't understand how people can lose control of their drinking are almost immune to alcoholism. What is most important, however, is not how cultural beliefs affect addictions but how our defining of addictions as diseases affects our views of ourselves as individuals and as a society.

# How Far Can Hunting Microbes Get Us?

Each of the three types of diseases is associated with a revolution in medical practice. Being able to identify and combat individual microorganisms led to clear-cut advances in combating first-generation diseases such as anthrax, cholera, rabies, tuberculosis, yellow fever, and malaria. The technologies for preventing or limiting the damage done by these microbes signaled the advent of the modern era of medicine, when medical technology finally advanced beyond folk medicine and actually demonstrated effects better than those brought on by simple faith in a healer. Modern medical practice demands of an efficacious technique or medicine that, in a double-blind experiment (where neither healer nor sufferer knows whether a treatment is actually being administered), those receiving the treatment show significantly better outcomes than do those who do not receive it.

This approach has worked best in medicine with bacteria and some viruses in which a single disease agent could be identified and assaulted. Discoveries by such legendary microbe hunters as Robert Koch, Louis Pasteur, and Joseph Lister led to the rout of many long-standing disease scourges through the sciences of bacteriology and immunology and the techniques of vaccination and sterilization. But diseases that came to haunt us later in this century have proved much less susceptible to this medical arsenal. The example of the microbe hunters has thus far failed to halt the ravages of cancer, for example. Yet we cling to the microbe-hunter model in our approach to diseases of all kinds. Like some prescientific people, we genuflect to potent-seeming totems as a way of dealing with problems we cannot hope to control.

Nowhere is this failed model more apparent than in our efforts to deal with second- and third-generation diseases. Despite constant trumpetings of advances and successes, we have not been able to eliminate—or even to substantially reduce—the incidence of schizophrenia and depression or alcoholism and drug addiction. Indeed, *many peasant and premodern societies are notable for having fewer of these maladies than the United States and some other advanced societies.* According to Dwight Heath, America's leading anthropological investigator of drinking practices, "Drinking problems are virtually unknown in most of the world's cultures."[5] While we *dream* that we can isolate the physical causes of addiction and mental illness in order to prevent and treat them, we find it inordinately difficult to get beyond the level of untreated remission that occurs when we do nothing for these disorders and their sufferers. To the extent that we feel we are doing better than this, we are mainly reflecting propaganda from researchers and treatment personnel.

It would be wrong, of course, to say we have failed only at curing emotional disorders and addictions. In this century, as one after another of the infectious killers have been conquered (in 1900 the leading causes of death were influenza and pneumonia, followed by tuberculosis and gastroenteritis), other maladies have resisted our best medical efforts. Today, the leading killers in the United States are heart disease, cancer, and strokes (which together account for two-thirds of our deaths). While the overall death rate in the United States dropped steadily from the beginning of this century until 1950, it has leveled off since then. Cancer deaths have increased over the last twenty-five years. Moreover, our average life expectancy is no higher than that of Costa Rica or Puerto Rico and lower than that of Greece, Spain, Hong Kong, and a dozen other countries.

As a result of our failures in dealing with diseases like heart disease, cancer, and stroke (as well as some infectious diseases, such as AIDS), we have changed some of our basic disease-fighting tactics. When we finally made some inroads in combating these diseases (like heart disease), we did so more through changing individual habits of diet and exercise and through resisting habits like smoking, excessive drinking, and promiscuous sex than through direct medical interventions. That is, we focused more on how our behavior makes us susceptible to disease. Simultaneously, we focused on the environment—the presence of fatty foods in our diets and poisonous air—that fosters heart attacks and cancer.

Of course, the environment is important to infections also. Environmental interventions like eliminating the swamps where mosquitoes that carry yellow fever and malaria live have been tremendously effective. Yet we have not generalized this environmental approach very well in the later stages of disease control. For example, we don't fight mental illness by trying to create better communities, even though we know community support is a tremendous force for mental health. Our environmental approaches to drugs are of the most superficial kind—cutting off drug supplies. We fail entirely to ask which communities inspire the most drug abuse. Indeed, we argue (contrary to all common sense and epidemiological evidence) that community approaches don't make sense because drug addiction and alcoholism are diseases to which those in all communities are equally vulnerable.

Moreover, even in the case of cancer, we have remained stuck in our tendency to invest massively in frontal attacks against disease agents and mechanisms. Since 1971, when Congress declared an official war on cancer, we have exponentially increased our investment in finding the cause and cure for the disease. Almost twenty years later, having now spent billions of dollars, this attack has produced few benefits and no cures. Despite constant advertising that we are winning the war on cancer, a congressional investigation of progress in the war on cancer criticized the National Cancer Institute for overstating the gains: instead, the report noted, "For a majority of the 12 most common tumors there was little or no improvement from 1950 to 1982 in the rate at which patients survived their disease."[6]

Yet our primary search is still for the central mechanism or source of cancer and for a way to eradicate it, and any claim of a pharmacological breakthrough is scarcely restrained by the failure of previous efforts. Some notable recent episodes in the history of hysterical expectations that a cure for cancer had been found include premature announcements of success through the use of interferon and interleukin 2. In 1986, following a virtual interleukin craze in cancer treatment, the *Journal of the American Medical Association* published a sharply worded editorial indicating that "IL-2 therapy . . . is associated with unacceptably severe toxicity and astronomical costs. These are not balanced by any persuasive evidence of true net therapeutic gain."[7]

# Diseases as Failures of Human Agency

Of course, it is possible that someday one of these cancer-cure claims will be borne out. On the other hand, cancer's origin and growth are so complicated, involving an interplay among environment, host, and diseased tissue, that they present a whole new *image* of disease. They suggest an illness that engages all of our humanness; something about cancer—along with heart disease—seemingly connects them ineradicably to the world we inhabit and the lives we lead. Perhaps to have a substantial effect on either disease we would need to change the essence of modern life.

Many experts now recognize that mental states contribute to the onset and remission of illness, and a growing body of research suggests that particular personality outlooks make some diseases more likely and affect prognosis after the onset of the disease.[8] The best-known example of this is the suggested role of "type A" personality in the development of heart disease.[9] In addition, people with a generally pessimistic and hopeless outlook have been found both to be more susceptible to illnesses like cancer and to recover less readily from them. This has led a number of commentators (most notably author Norman Cousins) to recommend as a part of medical treatment encouraging a positive state of mind in patients. Those who can galvanize their emotional resources to fight their ailments, including their desire and hope for a cure, will do better than those who remain passive and pessimistic.

While individual outlooks may affect disease, it is perhaps a far broader cultural dimension that results in our epidemics and our failures to cure certain resistant killers. This is the argument Leonard Sagan makes in *The Health of Nations*. Taking a long-term epidemiological view (epidemiology is the study of the population characteristics of diseases—how they spread and whom they affect), Sagan has offered a radical vision of the whole human history of fighting diseases. Sagan points out that Western societies had reduced disease even before they introduced vaccinations or modern hygienic practices on a broad scale, and before nutrition improved and people had an abundance of food to eat. In this century, death from infectious diseases was substantially reduced *even before* the advent of modern antibiotics.

Rather, Sagan indicates, the extension of life span has been due to two key human factors. The first is community and family supports. Nurturant communities that protect and support the individual and family reduce the entire range of human killers, from famine and brutality to disease and mental illness. The second factor, Sagan finds, is the sense that people have developed that they can control their destinies, both as individuals and as communities or societies. This outlook, called self-efficacy, means that people believe they can bring about desired outcomes in life; the opposite of self-efficacy is hopelessness, or passivity and pessimism about affecting one's life. People and communities with a sense of self-efficacy both are more resistant to modern diseases and other killers and recover more successfully when injured or sick.

The Sagan argument, however persuasive, has not been acted on in any large-scale way. In the world at large—and in the United States in particular—we have found it infinitely easier to invest in medical technology than in community solutions and cures. It simply fits better with the American economy, research industry, and treatment apparatus to administer X rays and drugs than to clean our air and water. Furthermore, average Americans have in many ways given up on their communities as sources of nurturance, and people outside the home (and even families) have become sources mainly of anxiety and threat. Obviously, if people are so suspicious of those around them and feel they can't change their worlds for the better, their sense of self-efficacy has also suffered.

At the same time as our society has failed to attack social and community sources of first-generation illnesses, we are now claiming that second- and third-generation maladies are best fought by the medical technologies and treatments that succeeded best with infectious disease. We now look almost exclusively for sources of emotional distress and behavioral excesses in the chemistry of drugs and people's bodies. In seeking biological cures for emotional disorders and addictions, we are going in *exactly the opposite direction* we need to follow, not only with these maladies but even with the first-generation diseases that still elude our medical grasp.

# Convincing Ourselves of the Impossible—Medicine Can Cure Emotional Problems

The rapid advances brought on by bacteriology, especially at the turn of this century, led some thinkers to believe that similar advances

could be made in the areas of addiction and mental problems. Thus
began the effort to identify the second-generation and third-generation
diseases of mental illness and addiction: "Disease entities were being
established in definitely recognizable physical conditions such as
typhoid and cholera. The belief in scientific progress encouraged
medical intervention in less definable conditions."[10] The effort to
find physical sources for mental disorders has been a major theme
of twentieth-century psychiatry. However, the highly heralded treatment advances conceived along these lines have not stood up well
over time. For example, the originator of the lobotomy operation
won the Nobel Prize for medicine in 1949, although psychosurgery
and related techniques have today been thrown in medicine's scrap
heap.[11]

Nonetheless, the idea that mental problems are diseases was broadly
accepted in America by the 1950s. (This effort succeeded more rapidly with mental disorders than it did with addiction, even though
it began in the same era.) The 1961 *World Book Encyclopedia* listed
the following entry under mental illness:

> Mentally ill persons are sick people, just as persons suffering from
> sore throats or heart disease are sick people. Like other sick persons,
> the mentally ill need specialized treatment by a physician.
>
> No social or economic class of persons is free of it. . . . Medical
> science knows neither specific causes of all kinds of mental illness nor
> specific ways of preventing them.

This is the humane view that mental illnesses should be treated as
a medical problem, although—as yet—medicine does not know how
to treat or prevent them.

At the same time, categories of mental illness—even today—often
seem very large, vague, and moralistic. Neurosis is described as a
form of mental illness in the *World Book*. Nymphomania, homosex-
uality, and antisocial character disorders—including stealing and
other varieties of misbehavior—have commonly been diagnosed as
psychiatric disorders. Some "radical" critiques of the mental-illness
model have maintained the model is merely middle-class morality
dressed up in medical garb. French social historian Michel Foucault
argued in *Madness and Civilization* that modern conceptions of mental
illness arose when bourgeois society prevailed in the nineteenth cen-

tury and demanded greater conformity to behavioral norms. Modern notions of madness and increased institutional warehousing are the results of this decreased tolerance for deviance. European-born, American psychiatrist Thomas Szasz contested the entire analogy between mental and physical illness in *The Myth of Mental Illness*. Organic causes of mental disorders were presumed simply because the latter had been declared illnesses, Szasz insisted, rather than because such causes really existed. Like Foucault, Szasz claimed that the labeling and treatment of mental illness was a means for controlling behavior we didn't like.

Scottish psychiatrist R. D. Laing analyzed the inner experiences of the mentally ill in *The Divided Self*. Like Gregory Bateson before him, Laing found that psychosis is often the result of unresolvable claims about reality that were presented to people in vulnerable positions within the family. For example, a child might be told that his parents love each other even though they express only hatred for one another. The young person in this position is placed, in Bateson's words, in a double bind—he cannot reject his parents' version of reality, but this means his own impressions must be crazy. Such a child might develop an inner self that ignores or clashes with his outer world, and the clash between the two selves *is* in Laing's view the psychosis. Nonetheless, Laing felt, this conflict can be resolved through a spiritual struggle that should be permitted to unfold in a supportive setting.

The criticism of these radical theorists is that psychoses and other mental illnesses obviously exist, since people express deeply felt pain and confusion. To think of insane people as social outcasts or dissidents, as Foucault and Szasz view them, ignores the therapeutic needs these people have, as does Laing's view of psychosis as a spiritual journey. Both Laing and Szasz are psychiatrists, however, and each offers a method for dealing with psychosis. Followers of Szasz might confront patients with real-world demands and hold them responsible for their actions, including making them legally accountable for misbehavior. Someone hearing imaginary voices could be told, "Talk to them later; right now you have to go to the store." Laing pioneered therapeutic communities, where people can feel safe and be supported as they grapple with psychotic episodes.

By the end of the 1970s, the views of these radical critics had been pushed aside by enthusiasm over progress in the neurosciences. There was a renewed sense that insane behavior can be explained by brain and neurological functioning and that the promise of understanding and treating mental illness through biology was being fulfilled. In 1980, the American Psychiatric Association published the third and most ambitious edition of its *Diagnostic and Statistical Manual of Mental Disorders (DSM-III)*. The manual (revised as *DSM-III-R* in 1987) catalogs and describes disorders including manic-depressive illness, schizophrenia, sexual dysfunction, marijuana abuse, caffeine intoxication, and "conduct disorders" (for example, adolescent lying)— and creates the feeling that we have a firm grasp on emotional problems and their etiology, symptoms, and treatment.

How true is this today? How far have we progressed from the rather hopeful but unsubstantiated vision of the 1961 encyclopedia description of mental illness? In that *World Book*, the principal "mental illness terms" listed were Freudian, like *defense* and *sublimation*. Today the neurosciences have accumulated a large vocabulary and list of concepts and findings about the workings of the brain and the nervous system. Chemicals have been discovered in the body that activate the brain, and new electrical and chemical scanning techniques offer images of the brain at work. New families of drugs have been devised that mimic the effects of the brain's own chemicals. Antipsychotic drugs and antidepressants are today the major means for dealing with mental illnesses.[12]

Yet it has remained surprisingly difficult to translate these advances into improved prognoses for mental disorders such as depression and schizophrenia. Not only have we failed to eliminate depression and schizophrenia, but they have actually increased in the latter part of this century. Moreover, despite the feeling that mental patients are being much better managed through the use of drugs, systematic evaluations of drug therapy effectiveness have not been overly impressive. In 1986, early results from a massive National Institute of Mental Health study found that drug therapy did not help severely depressed patients any more than ordinary psychotherapy. This study continues, and the question is whether the effects of psychotherapy will last longer than drug therapy, as some suspect. Another finding of this study was that, for those with milder depression (but who nonetheless sought and were thought to need treatment), drug treatment and psychotherapy were not significantly better than placebo treatment—that is, treatment with drugs that have no significant biochemical effects but that patients believe are potent.[13]

It is fairly clear that medical and pharmaceutical breakthroughs on the level of the antibiotics in the case of first-generation diseases have not been forthcoming in dealing with our major mental illnesses. While *nearly all* physicians endorse the use of psychotropic drugs for these conditions,[14] *hardly any* regard them as a cure and nearly all recognize that they work only irregularly and produce serious side effects and few benefits for at least some patients suffering from the conditions under attack. What is more, there is a residual uneasiness about making patients depend on drugs (and the medical approach requires them to do so for the rest of their lives) when the benefits are so variable and when some people do as well without them.

Our limitations in dealing with the mental illness of schizophrenia are apparent in a major series of articles that appeared in the *New York Times* in 1986. The series summarized the state of knowledge about schizophrenia and the difficulties we have had in translating brain research into an improved prognosis for mental illness. For example, the title of the lead article in the series was SCHIZOPHRENIA: INSIGHTS FAIL TO HALT RISING TOLL. Successive articles covered the apparent rise in schizophrenia, the lack of success of treatment, the growing awareness that the condition often improves on its own, the involvement of family as a cause and a cure of the ailment, and new biological speculations about its etiology. The series found that schizophrenia is more apparent now than ever before. Either the disease is spreading, or else the populations that schizophrenia strikes most frequently are growing—for example, the underclass.

The *Times* series maintained that our understanding of the disease is growing, and that although effective treatments lag, new biological discoveries may be close to pinpointing organic causes of and cures for the disease. In an article on the biology of schizophrenia, the *Times*'s medical writer emphasized dramatic changes in the brain activity of schizophrenics being measured by new brain scanning techniques; these "abnormalities may be present in 5 to 15 percent of schizophrenics." However, some caution is indicated since "just how [brain function] aberrations account for hallucinations . . . and the schizophrenic's chaotic attitude toward the world . . . are still a mystery." Other researchers believe that viral infections in pregnant mothers may lead to the eventual development of schizophrenia in children. At least some investigators urge caution, however, and the need "to be respectful of the false starts made in the past."[15]

As yet, such research has not led to effective therapies. Indeed, the earlier optimism that drugs could counteract the biochemical changes that cause schizophrenia was refuted in the *Times* series, because of "the failure of powerful drugs to ameliorate some of the most prevalent symptoms." Previously, treatment had focused on the most obvious outward signs of the disease, like delusions and hallucinations. Today, such symptoms are dealt with as secondary to "less flamboyant symptoms, like apathy and inertia, [that] are now regarded by many experts as constituting the core of the disorder." Successful treatments have found it more important to help in enhancing the person's "simple management of daily life." As a result, "a 30-year study of hospitalized schizophrenics who had been given up as hopeless, but were released in a program that closely manages and monitors their lives, has found that two-thirds of them are now living normal lives . . . , half of them without any signs of the disorder."[16]

While schizophrenics have shown substantial progress with treatment geared toward improved management of daily life tasks, other findings indicate that people show similar improvement on their own, divorced from therapy. According to the series, "A recent long-term follow-up of 118 schizophrenics who were discharged from Vermont State Hospital 20 to 25 years earlier found that half to two-thirds had since achieved significant improvement or recovery. The improvements seemed to be spontaneous, for the most part coming well after treatment. Fully 45 percent had no psychiatric symptoms, and another 23 percent had lost all symptoms of schizophrenia while developing symptoms of other, more treatable mental disorders. The results corroborated similar results from three European studies and another American study over the past decade indicating that half or more of the schizophrenics eventually recovered or significantly improved."[17]

Many of us may find it hard to believe that people gradually evolve out of psychosis, especially if we encounter deranged people on the streets of New York. The case of Joyce Brown, aka Billie Boggs, is instructive in this regard. Brown was a random inductee in Mayor Ed Koch's plan to remove psychotic homeless people from the street to shelters. Although she defecated in the street and acted bizarrely when homeless, Brown came across in press conferences as she fought her hospital incarceration (during which she was medically judged insane) as an aware, self-controlled person, as though being offered respect and a facilitative environment could almost instantaneously eliminate her psychosis. On the other hand, after she was once again forgotten after this case and relegated to single-occupancy residences, she again developed problems and was arrested for possession of a hypodermic syringe and other drug paraphernalia.

Research findings demonstrating total remission of psychosis dispute *DSM-III*'s claim that "a complete return to premorbid functioning is unusual—so rare, in fact, that some clinicians would question the [original] diagnosis." Here is an example where American psychiatry has fooled itself through its own labels: if schizophrenia is an incurable disease, then those who get better had something else that at one point was indistinguishable from schizophrenia. That treatment of mental illness may not be substantially more effective than natural remission supports the radical positions Szasz and Laing mapped out two and three decades ago. Szasz's emphasis on ordinary social and behavioral responsibilities for patients and Laing's reliance on the person's natural strength and recuperative powers, along with supportive groups and environments, now have quite strong evidence in their favor. Despite this evidence, according to the *Times*, "Those tracing the causes of schizophrenia to family or childhood experiences . . . have faded in recent years. . . . Most scientists are focusing on possible biological or medical causes."

The *Times* series and other recent writing decry "the pain the earlier view [of family influences on mental illness] inflicted on the families of schizophrenics: adding guilt to the[ir] agony." Nonetheless, strong environmental influences are evident in the relationship between socioeconomic class and poverty and schizophrenia, while important family influences continue to be discovered. According to another *Times* article, schizophrenia is more often found in children of parents who "habitually gave children confusing and negative messages. This disordered communication was a strong predictor of which children in the study eventually showed signs of schizophrenia." The article reported that another study had found that those children who don't learn to socialize with others more often become schizophrenic.[18]

## PHIL DONAHUE SAYS IT ALL

The psychiatrist E. Fuller Torrey, who writes about schizophrenia as a disease,[19] is a regular guest on *Donahue*. On
December 8, 1988, he appeared with a number of schizophrenics arguing for treating schizophrenia as a purely biological disease. However, Torrey's version of the disease
was substantially different from that presented by another
guest, Joe Rogers of the National Mental Health Consumers' Association, a self-help group Rogers founded. This
group, in keeping with its emphasis on self-help, argues
that emotionally disturbed people can indeed improve.
Rogers himself had lived on the street for years after he
developed paranoid delusions, but then he outgrew his
symptoms; his chief encouragements for doing so, Rogers
indicated, were his marriage and other social supports.

Although Rogers once took medications for his condition,
he no longer does, and he emphasizes that medication *does
not cure* the condition, attacks only symptoms, and often
has side effects. In this and many other ways he disagreed
with Torrey, who strongly favors medication as the major
treatment for schizophrenia. While Torrey explained that
since the disease is biological, counseling does no good,
Rogers indicated that supportive counseling and other social services, along with independent living and work, are
the keys to improvement. While Torrey asserted that the
disease is biological and that its course cannot be influenced by human will or effort, Rogers described how patients—himself included—are often trapped by being told
that they can't get better, so that they might as well not
even try.

Incidentally, for those who don't believe that America is
being "diseased," consider that on the same day *Donahue*
had the schizophrenia show, Oprah Winfrey had a show
on obsessive-compulsive disorders. In an exact parallel to
the *Donahue* show, the *Oprah* show featured a psychiatrist
and a panel that claimed obsessive-compulsive disorders
are due to chemical imbalances, can't be affected by psychotherapy or by efforts of will, and require drug treatment.

### PRETTY SOON WE'LL FIND THE BIOLOGICAL CAUSES AND CURES FOR MENTAL ILLNESS

Our optimism about finding biological solutions for schizophrenia and other mental illnesses continues unabated despite our consistent failures to date. A front-page *Times* headline announced in 1987 that researchers had identified the gene that causes manic-depressive disorders among a group of Amish. But this article also pointed out that "the same issue of the scientific journal [announcing the discovery of this gene] carried another study showing that the gene was not associated with manic-depressive illness in *two* other populations that were studied" (emphasis added). Perhaps for this reason, "no one knows how useful the finding will be."[20]

When a new study on the genetic basis of schizophrenia was published in the journal *Nature* in 1988, the *New York Times* trumpeted the results in another front-page headline: SCHIZOPHRENIA STUDY FINDS STRONG SIGNS OF HEREDITARY CAUSE.[21] The researchers averred in the article that they had found "the first concrete evidence for a genetic basis to schizophrenia." This *Times* article too, however, reported that—in the same issue of *Nature*—an international research team had found no evidence, in another population of schizophrenics, of the genetic link identified by the first research team. The second group of researchers concluded that the failure to replicate the other team's results was due to the peculiar nature of schizophrenia: "schizophrenia is really a catch-all term for a biologically heterogeneous group of diseases that produce much the same symptoms." As a result, the schizophrenics in one study may have been suffering from a form of the disease related to the first genetic marker, "while the schizophrenics in the other study may be suffering from a form unrelated to that defect." It might seem we are not even clear on the integrity of the phenomenon being investigated, let alone finding clues to its sources.

This tendency to overstate positive disease findings and to ignore negative ones will be described throughout this book. Incidentally, one of my favorite negative find-ings about internal chemistry and psychosis stems from the classic research of Peter Witt, a physician and phar-macologist who has studied the effects of drugs on spi-ders' webs for forty years. Spiders are tremendously sensitive to psychotropic drugs and build bizarre webs when exposed to even the mildest traces of a psychoac-tive substance: for example, Witt found that spiders build altered webs when injected with the urine of psychiatric patients who are taking antipsychotic drugs. However, web tests of various body fluids from psychotic patients who aren't taking drugs do not affect the spiders, indi-cating for Witt the absence of any unusual chemistry in these patients. " 'If mental patients had such substances in their blood or urine, it's likely we would have found them,' Dr. Witt maintains."[22]

# The Third Wave of Diseases: When Behavior Is the Disease

Those who promote the third generation of diseases—addictive-behavioral diseases—typically describe them in the following ways:

- The disease is marked by loss of control of an involvement or behavior.

- The sufferer cannot recognize the disease in the absence of ed-ucation by disease experts, including especially other sufferers.

- The disease exists in and of itself and cannot be traced to child-rearing practices or other environmental causes.

- The disease will progress inexorably, no matter what efforts sufferers make or life changes they undergo, unless they receive treatment aimed at containing or eliminating the behavior that defines the disease.

- The disease is a permanent trait, and sufferers must accommodate to it for the rest of their lives.
- The disease responds to two quite different kinds of treatment:
  1. a support group organized by and for those who share the disease; and
  2. treatment according to a medical model, under the supervision of a physician or other trained specialist, involving private consultations and a medical-type regimen, preferably in a hospital setting.
- Sufferers ought not be held to ordinary moral standards and codes of community conduct in relation to behavior attributable to their disease.
- Because of the inherent tendency for sufferers and society to deny the presence of the disease, it is remarkably prevalent, yet frequently undetected, calling for more aggressive identification and treatment of sufferers.

The third generation of diseases embodies what is wrong in our approach to all diseases, while it elevates these errors in thinking, science, and social policy to new heights of futility. If readers wish to summarize the theme of this book in one simple message, it is that we will never, ever *treat* away drug abuse, alcoholism, and the host of other behaviors that are now called addictive diseases. The prototype for addictive diseases was originally heroin addiction. However, in America today, it is the alcoholism industry that has given us the model for what diseases *are* and how they *should be treated medically* (as in the opening quote in this chapter from an article in *Science*). Key in the development of third-generation diseases has been the rapid expansion of the alcoholism-as-disease model to such new areas as compulsive gambling. This expansion makes sense in that gambling, like any other compulsive problem behavior, cannot be distinguished in etiology, treatment, or outcome from alcoholism or drug addiction.

On the other hand, thinking about gambling in the context developed by the alcoholism movement—that alcoholism is a genetic, biological malady—lays bare just how wrongheaded third-generation disease assumptions are. The issue of whether alcoholism and other addictive diseases are special maladies or simply traditional bad habits appears throughout the history of the development of the concept of addiction. For the term *addiction* has been with us since antiquity, as have narcotic drugs and alcohol. Yet addiction was not applied especially to narcotics or alcohol until well into this century. Until the twentieth century, *addiction* simply meant liking to engage in a habit, and the term was applied equally to *all* popular medicinal bromides, as well as to habits unconnected with substance use. As one modern observer remarked on an earlier student of the effects of opium: he did not hold "any concept of addiction distinguishing addiction to opium from addiction to, say, sugar plums."[23]

The idea that narcotic addiction is a special disease arose only within the last hundred years in England, Germany, and the United States. It astounds us today to learn that narcotics (along with cocaine) were indiscriminately dispensed in the last century, and yet for the most part people in Europe and the United States did not consider these drugs dangerous or especially likely to provoke addiction. It was difficult to find people in the last century who didn't use—often quite regularly—the drugs we now consider to be the epitome of disease-causing, addictive agents. As late as 1906, Coca-Cola contained a very potent dose of cocaine,[24] while according to Virginia Berridge and Griffith Edwards (the former a social historian and the latter Britain's leading psychiatric addiction expert), narcotic consumption in Britain in the middle of the nineteenth century averaged 127 therapeutic doses a year for every man, woman, and child. (Dosing children with tincturated opiates was standard practice in Britain and the United States.)[25] Yet, according to Berridge and Edwards, the dominant nineteenth-century image of habitual narcotics use was of a person "indulging a self-regarding act which was mildly damaging to health and perhaps a little bit of a nuisance."

Several studies have found that there was in fact little drug addiction in Britain and the United States during this earlier period. Psychiatrist-historian David Musto discovered no indications that soldiers who received morphine during the Civil War returned home addicted. Rather, American social and political policies at the beginning of the twentieth century set in motion the definition of heroin addiction as a peculiarly American problem, and the disease grew to severe dimensions in the United States alone of all the countries in the world.[26] Berridge and Edwards noted that opiate addiction began to be reported in Britain only late in the nineteenth century, after general consumption of opiates had declined considerably, but when the medical profession began to regard it as a medical condition. Rather than finding that the medical approach proved especially helpful, Berridge and Edwards concluded instead that the medical "profession, by its enthusiastic advocacy of a new and more 'scientific' remedy and method, had itself contributed to an increase in addiction."[27]

The evidence until the present is that medical approaches to all the third-generation diseases we will discuss have done *at least as poorly* as medical treatment for schizophrenia and substantially worse than medical approaches to infectious diseases. As one example, Edward Brecher summarized the long-term results of treatment for narcotic addiction at the renowned public health hospital at Lexington, Kentucky, which had a largely black, inner-city population:

> At any time after being "cured" at Lexington, from 10 to 25 percent of graduates may appear to be abstinent, nonalcoholic, employed and law abiding. But only a handful at most can maintain this level of functioning throughout the ten-year period after "cure." Almost all become readdicted and reimprisoned early in the decade, and for most the process is repeated over and over again.[28]

In 1982, evaluating programs for heroin addiction in New York, Joseph Califano estimated that at least 90 percent of addicts were using heroin again soon after treatment. Substantial evidence seemed to be accumulating that addiction, as a fully behavioral malady, simply is not amenable to medical interventions.[29]

Why, then, did these programs persist and expand? Until the 1970s, drug addiction affected a limited group of people; as a society, we segregated this group and assumed most would never become functioning members of society. While different observers bought more or less of the idea that addiction is a treatable illness, most were nonetheless willing to leave the care and containment of addicts to the legal authorities. These officials arrested those they caught using and selling narcotics, often sending them for treatment to federal hospitals like Lexington that were not unlike prisons. But the 1960s began a period when drug use became a standard feature, first of college life and then of adolescence. At first, authorities continued to see this as a moral and an enforcement problem. But by the 1980s, the permanent presence of drugs on the American landscape had led to a broader application of the disease model to a much larger—and different—group of people than that found at Lexington.

Meanwhile, the alcoholism movement came into its own as an industry and a social force after Prohibition ended. Alcoholics Anonymous (AA), established soon after the repeal of Prohibition, became the major organization dealing with alcohol problems in the United States. For some time AA was a private fellowship of like-minded people who sought an understanding of what they regarded as their special drinking problem. This movement, however, was gradually co-opted by its own success and by its integration into mainstream medicine and psychotherapy. By the 1970s, AA had become the model for all treatment groups and a linchpin in the provision of services for drinking problems in the United States. At the same time, the National Council on Alcoholism (the public-relations arm of the AA movement) convinced Americans that there are millions of unrecognized and unacknowledged alcoholics who require immediate medical and group treatment.

As treatment for drugs and alcohol moved away from the self-help concept that AA originally endorsed, it became more coercive, more hospital-oriented, and more expensive. Medical treatment today retains AA's emphasis on the permanence of alcoholism and the need for the patient to assume a lifelong identity as an alcoholic—which means that alcoholism is never cured and that the person remains a potential patient forever. The supposed effectiveness of medical and AA techniques notwithstanding, a prominent psychiatrist announced in his well-known 1983 book, *The Natural History of Alcoholism*, that his hospital patients (who also attended AA) had not improved more than alcoholics who went completely untreated. Nonetheless, Dr. George Vaillant was quoted widely to the effect that it is imperative to get alcoholics into the medical system to be treated. Furthermore, the push has been to recruit into treatment younger patients and others with milder drinking problems, as well as the entire families of alcoholics.

Whatever its success rate, the AA-medical view of alcoholism is now so popular that it is applied to every kind of behavioral problem. AA-type groups have been created for overeaters, compulsive shoppers, gamblers, sufferers from agoraphobia and other severe anxieties, and those involved in compulsive sexual and love relationships. In response to the popularity of these self-help groups, medical treatments increasingly link themselves with AA and borrow elements of the AA experience. On the other hand, pharmaceutical companies have attempted to supplant Smokenders and other popular groups by claiming that people require medical interventions to wean them from their nicotine addictions. Similar competitions have arisen between commercial self-help groups and medical programs for weight loss. Despite all these efforts, the American Cancer Society still indicates that 95 percent of the 40 million people who have quit smoking did so on their own.

How many people are affected by all these diseases? Experts like Douglas Talbott claim that 20 or more million Americans are alcoholics. This means that in addition, as many as 80 million Americans suffer from the disease of *coalcoholism* and require treatment for being members of families with alcoholics. The National Council on Compulsive Gamblers maintains that 20 million Americans are addicted gamblers. Thirty million or more women could suffer from anorexia and bulimia, but if obesity is also counted, 80 million Americans have eating diseases. Following eating disorders in numbers is cigarette addiction, since 30 percent of adult Americans still smoke.

Estimates of the depressed and anxious include about one-fifth of Americans, meaning as many as 50 million additional disease-sufferers, mainly women. As these last examples indicate, many Americans now suffer from milder versions of diseases defined originally by the second-generation disease revolution as severe mental illnesses. These emotional disorders now have quite a bit in common with behavioral, addictive diseases; for example, they are frequently treated in AA-type support groups. Thus, in many ways, second-generation diseases have been folded into and subsumed by the third-generation disease revolution.

Women also suffer frequently from premenstrual tension and postpartum depression. Some claims imply that *all* women suffer from versions of these diseases! Other estimates offered by those who treat premenstrual syndrome (PMS) and postpartum depression claim that a third of all women suffer from severe varieties of these problems. Women also seem to suffer more from compulsive love affairs, while men more often become compulsive fornicators—leading to estimates of up to perhaps 25 million love and sex addicts.

Actually, when the National Institute of Mental Health conducted an epidemiological survey of mental disorders among the American population, *none* of the above was found to be the most common mental disorder. Rather, a whole, new previously unrealized epidemic was discovered—obsessive-compulsive disorder, or OCD. (This is the disease where people clean their houses compulsively, or constantly check to make sure they haven't left an appliance on, or have "persistent, unpleasant thoughts."[30]) Whereas previously American psychiatry found OCD to be rare, the latest survey found that it is twenty-five to sixty times as common as previously supposed, and it predicted that "like other stigmatized and hidden disorders in the past, [it] may be ready for discovery and demands for treatment on a large scale."

Children have become special targets for disease diagnoses, particularly around their drinking and drug taking. Since fully half of high school boys and male college students regularly get drunk and more than half use illicit substances, they are highly prone to be labeled as alcoholic or "chemically dependent." The frequent discovery of learning disabilities in children who have problems learning and behaving at school commenced in the 1970s and has continued to grow in the 1980s. At the same time, children's lives at home, in the neighborhood, and at day-care centers now seem alarmingly problematic, due to epidemics of sexual and other physical abuse. Here both culprit (or abuser) and victim have been called disease victims who need therapy.

The sheer number of these diseases suggests a very perilous world, one hard to negotiate without falling prey to one or another malady. What most distinctly marks this new phase in the history of diseases, with its emphasis on emotional/behavioral disorders, is their commonplaceness, the potential susceptibility of everybody, no matter how healthy, good, or seemingly in control of themselves they are. And although the diseases are often imagined to have biological bases, they are said to be incurable. Ubiquity and permanence mark the new diseases, even as we regard more and more habitual misbehaviors as disease symptoms and medical issues. Some of the other problems associated with the new diseases are:

• Disease conceptions of misbehavior are bad science and are morally and intellectually sloppy. Biology is not behavior, even in those areas where a drug or alcohol is taken into the body. Alcoholism involves a host of personal and environmental considerations aside from how alcohol affects the bodies of drinkers. Furthermore, once we treat alcoholism and addiction as diseases, we cannot rule out that anything people do but shouldn't is a disease, from crime to excessive sexual activity to procrastination.

• Disease categorizations fail at the central goal said to justify them—the possibility of ameliorating the problem behavior by medical therapy. Systematic comparisons indicate that treated patients do not fare better than untreated people with the same problems. This has been shown in the cases of alcoholism, drug abuse, smoking, overweight, and learning disabilities, but it is probably even truer of diseases like PMS and love addiction that to date have been examined mainly in self-help groups and courtrooms.

• People's belief that they have a disease makes it less likely that they will outgrow the problem. For this reason, disease approaches are most inappropriate and dangerous for the young. Treatment programs for chemical dependence stress to young substance abusers that they will always have a drug-taking or drinking problem. This almost *guarantees* that relapses will be frequent, when under ordinary conditions the vast majority would outgrow their youthful excesses. Treatment thus serves mainly as an impediment to the normal process of "maturing out" of addiction.

• Sanctioned by medicine and other benign institutions, disease treatments are regularly forced upon people, supposedly for their own good. Treatment is often imposed as an alternative to jail or losing a job. Patients are then persuaded that they have a disease, often through group-pressure techniques that closely resemble brainwashing. As a consequence, ordinary people are branded—and brand themselves—as sick and debilitated. Those who disagree with such diagnoses are told that this is a sign of their sickness that must be expunged.

• By revising notions of personal responsibility, our disease conceptions undercut moral and legal standards exactly at a time when we suffer most from a general loss of social morality. While we desperately protest the growth of criminal and antisocial behavior, disease definitions undermine the individual's obligations to control behavior and to answer for misconduct. Such disease defenses for murder lately have included overindulgence in junk food, too much

TV viewing, PMS, alcoholism, drug addiction and withdrawal, post-partum depression (used by women who kill their infant children), and the old standby for killing lent new validity by disease ideas—lovesickness and the inability to separate from a painful relationship.

• Disease notions actually increase the incidence of the behaviors of concern. They legitimize, reinforce, and excuse the behaviors in question—convincing people, contrary to all evidence, that their behavior is not their own. Meanwhile, the number of addicts and those who believe they cannot control themselves grows steadily.

• Disease conceptions now dominate major parts of ordinary experience, incorporating common problems associated with growing up or conducting ordinary relationships and family life. Less of our personal selves, our relationships with our children, and our private views of life remains our own, while normal joy and pain are denied us through being defined as clinical syndromes. The greatest casualty is the chance for young and old to come to grips with themselves and their weaknesses and to grow, to change, and sometimes to accept weakness and imperfection.

• Because internal (psychological) and external (environmental) factors are given short shrift in disease views, we lose hope of changing our worlds. In the diseased world, striving for personal and social goals becomes secondary to counteracting unchangeable, inbred maladies. Disease views in this way attack the human and social values that make our lives worth living. The whole focus of our society becomes more pessimistic and self-preoccupied, traits that (as we shall see) then contribute to the incidence of these diseases.

The pseudomedical inventions and treatments of new diseases increasingly *determine* our feelings, our self-concepts, and our world-views. Our emotional and behavioral diseases define our culture and who we are—this is the diseasing of America. As I hope to make clear, the promotion of these new diseases—as well as being ungrounded scientifically and worse than useless therapeutically—holds out the possibility for a totalitarianism similar to but more insidious than the one George Orwell imagined would occur through political means in *1984*. The new disease movement strikes at the very core of our individual selves and collective consciousness, attacking important elements of what it means for us to be human beings. And as we lose control of ourselves and our world, we become persuaded that we have more and more psychic diseases.

I propose in this book a vision of life opposed to the disease-infested one that we are being sold. In doing so, I discuss the scientific, psychological, and moral underpinnings of the two views of being human. I argue that human beings and society are self-correcting mechanisms, that knowledge and experience are the best ways people have for learning how to behave healthily, that interactions with parents are the most important influences on children, and that the best way to curb misbehavior is to insist on standards of decency. If we cannot persuade our children that they have the capacity to manage their lives and that the world is worth living in—and then work to create a world in which this is true—medical treatments will expand endlessly but will not be able to help us.

This enterprise is not an idealistic or quixotic one, because people all the time overcome formidable obstacles to achieve goals and to correct personal problems. People regularly quit smoking, cut back drinking, lose weight, improve their health, create healthy love relationships, raise strong and happy children, and contribute to communities and combat wrong—all without outside expert interventions. What is most striking about modern disease theories of behavior is that they militate against such human potentialities in favor of hypothetical disease mechanisms. In this perverted medical effort, more and more behavior is defined as being out of control, leading to more expressions of loss of control, which are then interpreted as justifying and proving the disease conceptions in the first place. It is as if, in the words of psychologist/physician Henry Murray, we were trying to "reduce the concept of human nature to its lowest common denominators," and then were "gloating over our successes in doing so." This book marshals the evidence for human potency and morality, a goal that I believe is at least equally defensible scientifically and considerably more worthwhile than the perverse psychology Murray decried.

# 2

# Alcoholism in America

*How We Discovered that Alcohol Is Addictive and that So Many People Are Alcoholics*

WOMAN IN THE BALCONY: Is there much drinking in Grover's Corners?
MR. WEBB: Well, ma'am, I wouldn't know what you'd call *much*. Sattidy nights the farmhands meet down in Ellery Greenough's stable and holler some. Fourth of July I've been known to taste a drop myself—and Decoration Day, of course. We've got one or two town drunks, but they're always having remorses every time an evangelist comes to town.

—Thornton Wilder, *Our Town*

Let's face it, pizza and a Sprite after games just don't get it.

—Carlton Fisk, Chicago White Sox catcher,
after his team banned beer in the clubhouse

## Overview: The Changing Tides of Drinking in the United States

*O*UR *TOWN* was published several years after the repeal of Prohibition (in 1933) and shortly before Alcoholics Anonymous published its bible, or "Big Book" (in 1939). At that time, most

Americans thought about alcoholism as Thornton Wilder did: it was a rare occurrence, something found among a few social pariahs. In addition, some lower types (like the farmhands down in Ellery Greenough's stable) were likely to get drunk on weekends and create a commotion. Most upstanding townspeople, like Mr. Webb, might be occasional drinkers, but they wouldn't make a regular habit of it.

Of course, people of different regions and religions felt differently about alcohol. Fundamentalist Protestants deplored all drinking; they—like rural Americans and those in the South and Midwest—had formed the backbone of the temperance and antisaloon movements. Women were prominent in these movements, although few joined because they themselves had a drinking problem; rather, as a group they suffered from men's drunkenness, especially in working-class families where men often wasted their time and wages on their visits to the saloon. For this reason, temperance was an important component in the Progressive movement's effort to improve the lives of the working class.

Yet most immigrants, city dwellers, and other elements of the liberal coalition in the United States felt quite differently about alcohol. For many immigrant groups, liquor was the glue of life, the spirit of any celebration, and the mild lubricant that aided digestion and accompanied every dinner. For these people and other cosmopolitan Americans, the temperance movement was a product of small-minded Americans and religious zealots. Nonetheless, in 1920, national Prohibition was enacted in the United States. Prominent liberals like Clarence Darrow, who were implacably opposed to Prohibition, railed against the moral crusaders who would impose their morality on everyone else in the country.

After Prohibition's repeal, it seemed as if the cosmopolitan attitude toward drinking represented by urban liberals like Darrow and the newer European immigrants had won out. The secular society at large accepted alcohol as a regular part of ordinary life. True, some people sometimes drank too much. For most people, however, such overimbibing was often excused as an acceptable excess on special occasions like New Year's Eve or the office Christmas party or the ethnic funeral, and for some—like high-spirited young men—as a stage they had to go through and grow out of. Toward some few others who habitually became drunk or who couldn't control their drinking, most people adopted an attitude between knowing condescension and outright scorn: why were these people so weak or immoral as not to know when enough was enough?

But Americans weren't preoccupied with alcoholics or with the negative potential of alcohol. Drinking—even periodic intoxication—was portrayed as innocent and normal in movies, television, novels, and plays. The "Thin Man" and his wife—played onscreen by William Powell and Myrna Loy—were tipplers, often portrayed as being "high," as were many other adorable American characters. Even the Walt Disney film *Fantasia* depicted the Greek god of revels, Bacchus, in an intoxicated but merry state. Consider the following baseball story:

> Kirby Higbe once recalled a game in the 1940's, when the Pirates were also-rans, in which he pitched against the Reds and "five of our regulars were plastered." They kept blowing plays. It was a close game, Higbe remembered, "and the bases were loaded, like our fielders." A fly ball was hit to the center fielder, who stumbled in as the ball flew over his head. "Everyone scored," he said. "I couldn't take it no more. I walked off the mound. Billy Herman, the manager, didn't know what I was doing. He said, 'What's wrong, Hig?'
> "I said, 'They're drunk.'
> "He said, 'Who's drunk?'
> "I said, 'Everyone!' "[1]

The stories of Babe Ruth entering the locker room after his all-night benders are legendary. This view of drinking continued well into the 1960s and early 1970s. Mickey Mantle revealed in his autobiography that he played important games with hangovers.

How differently we react to the same stories today! Tales of playing under the influence are now recounted by players who have entered treatment. Only these are regarded no longer as tales of athletic high jinks but as horror stories of the evils of addiction and alcoholism. Today we are most likely to hear about drinking and drunkenness in the context of people who are suffering from an inexorable disease and who need treatment that will aid them to recovery. We discover that stars like Elizabeth Taylor, Liza Minnelli, Mary Tyler Moore, and many others have been treated for alcoholism. Most go to the Betty Ford Center, named after the First

Lady who courageously admitted *her* alcoholism and who now stands as a model to all Americans to seek treatment for *their* drinking problems.

We hear constantly on television and radio—both from nonprofit organizations like the National Council on Alcoholism and from profit-making private treatment centers—that if we *think* we have a drinking problem, then indeed we *do*, and that this problem can only get worse unless we get help. We are told that there are from 15 to 22 million alcoholic Americans and that the families of such people are as disturbed as the alcoholic himself or herself, leading to estimates that as many as one in three Americans suffers as a result of alcoholism and requires treatment for this malady. We see frequent TV shows about families disrupted and almost destroyed by a family member's alcoholism and about the need for the family to overcome their denial that this person is an alcoholic so that all together can seek treatment.

And the children! Drunkenness has become a regular activity for high school students, to judge from national surveys. As a result, we are sending out a new brand of temperance lecturers, like David Toma, who often combine antidrug with antialcohol messages in the hope of discouraging young people from ever drinking. Alcohol (along with drug) education is now a part of *elementary* school curricula, and what children are told is that alcohol is bad, pure and simple. Only a decade and a half ago, the National Institute on Alcohol Abuse and Alcoholism attempted to get young people to learn responsible drinking habits at home and in college. Today, a more typical message is this one from an alcohol educator from Southern California: "A home instruction course in safe drinking makes as much sense as teaching your child to skin-pop heroin (the method of injecting heroin into the fatty tissue, rather than directly into the vein) in hopes that the youngster will not become addicted."[2]

What has happened here? Has our drinking really gotten this far out of control? Or were we in America always simultaneously enthralled and ravaged by alcohol, only we didn't know it (in a kind of national denial)? More important, where are we headed? Is it really true that we need massive alcoholism treatment, earlier and earlier interventions into the lives of young people, greater restrictions on our drinking behavior, and more coercive regulations both at work and in the courts to make sure that more people learn that they are alcoholics and must enter treatment? Will this then solve our problems with alcohol? Or if the malady is truly inbred, must a sizable portion of our population live with the constant awareness that a single drink will lead them into an alcoholic binge, while all the rest of us anxiously guard against tempting these ill people by serving liquor and enjoying it ourselves?

Just as there is a pluralism of political attitudes in a democracy, there remains a range of attitudes about alcohol and its effects and a considerable spectrum of views about what constitutes appropriate drinking. This is true both around the world and within the United States. However, this range has narrowed considerably in the United States in the last decade and shows signs of becoming even more constricted. How could attitudes not change, with the degree of public education on the dangers of alcohol that every American now receives from childhood on? While many people continue to teach their children to regard alcohol as a mild and enjoyable intoxicant, they face a growing tide of antidrinking sentiment.

# From the Colonial Tavern to the Temperance Lectern

The changing tides of opinion about alcohol and drinking in America began in colonial America. Colonial Americans were not concerned about their drinking—far from it! They believed alcohol to be a natural substance and imbibed it freely: "The 'liquor problem' was not a public issue or fact of consciousness in colonial America. In the 17th and 18th centuries alcoholic beverages, and especially rum, were highly esteemed and universally valued and were in no way stigmatized or regarded as tainted or evil. All liquor was regarded as good and healthy. . . . It was drunk at all hours of the day and night, by men and women of all social classes, and it was routinely given to children." The average colonial drank several times as much alcohol per year as the current American, and even the Puritans called liquor the "Good Creature of God."[3]

If so much liquor was drunk, why didn't people recognize alcoholism as a problem? In the first place, most people controlled their drinking most of the time. For example, the tavern was a social center in New England, where families joined together with their neighbors before a fire to discuss the news, enjoy hearty fellowship, and drink. In this setting, problematic drinking was rare, and the tavern keeper—a person of esteem and authority—made sure drinking did not get out of hand. On the other hand, when people did drink too much and behave violently, alcohol was not blamed. "Drunkenness was not so much seen as the cause of deviant social behavior—in particular crime and violence—as it was construed as a sign that an individual was willing to engage in such behavior."[4] The conventional punishments of the pillory and flogging were meted out to drunkards who could not control their behavior.

All of this changed dramatically in the fifty years dating roughly from 1785 to 1835. During this period, drinking became a disruptive force for many Americans. The tight-knit community tavern disappeared, and instead the new industrialized work force and the western ranch laborer went to boisterous saloons to get drunk. Imagine as a model of nineteenth-century male drinking the Dodge City dance hall—where the only women likely to be present were prostitutes and where gunplay and fights were common. Middle- and upper-class Americans cut back their drinking drastically because it was no longer considered appropriate for an industrious life. As alcohol was eliminated from the ordinary daily routines of the middle class, when people did drink, they were more likely to go on binges where they drank all out.[5] Drunkenness was defined as a time for letting go—"To get drunk was to abandon both respectability and self control."[6]

These changes in drinking habits and images of alcohol were part of a vast social and institutional revolution that was taking place in the United States. The country was expanding dramatically: Americans were leaving established communities to explore new territories, while older communities were being invaded by waves of new immigrants. Overall, the population of the United States nearly doubled, and growth was even more rapid in the West and in eastern cities. The fifty years between 1785 and 1835 marked the end of family and community regulation of social problems like poverty, crime, insanity, and alcoholism. In place of such community self-regulation, these problems were now handled by the poorhouse, prison, asylum, and sanitarium.[7] It was in this context that alcohol-related misbehavior grew out of hand and Americans became acutely conscious of the ravages of alcoholism.

The image of "demon rum" was born in the 1800s, the result of this new discovery of the dangers of drinking. Alcohol came to be seen as the root cause of modern evils, and the idea arose that America could be perfected if everyone ceased drinking alcohol (or, originally, distilled spirits). The temperance movement dates from the formation of the American Temperance Society in 1826; by 1835, more than a million merchants, lawyers, teachers, and others had promised not to drink distilled liquor; 500,000 had pledged not to drink alcohol of any kind. The temperance movement was strongly nativist, Protestant, and middle class, and new tides of European immigrants ran afoul of temperance when they insisted on continuing their European drinking habits. By the middle of the nineteenth century, drinking had declined per capita to about a third of its colonial level.

As people decided alcohol was evil, they also came to believe that liquor could enslave a person against his or her will. In 1784 Benjamin Rush (a physician and signer of the Declaration of Independence) first advanced the idea that habitual drunkenness is a disease. The temperance movement propagated and expanded this view during the next century: drinking was so dangerous, it said, people should not even sample a first beer, or else they would likely embark on an inevitable path toward alcoholism. When the drinker eventually became a drunkard (the word *alcoholic* did not become popular until this century), he simply could not control his drinking. Despite an ardent search, however, temperance adherents never identified an account of a drunkard before the 1800s who reported that he had lost control of his drinking. "The idea that alcoholism is a progressive disease—the chief symptom of which is loss of control over drinking behavior, and whose only remedy is abstinence from all alcoholic beverages—is now about 175 or 200 years old, but no older."[8]

The temperance ideology differed from the modern alcoholism movement in that it maintained that alcohol is inevitably dangerous and inexorably addictive for *everyone*. That is, some people might believe they can drink moderately, but it is only a matter of time before they encounter increasing problems and completely lose control of their drinking. As strange as it seems to us today, the temperance message thus was that alcohol is inevitably addicting, in the same way that we now think of narcotics. A regular part of temperance propaganda was newspaper cartoons, plays, songs, and articles that portrayed the innocent social drinker who gradually slid from casual drinking to tippling to inveterate drunkenness and ended up destroying himself and his family. The temperance movement was not nearly as antidrunkard as it was opposed to those who claimed to be happy moderate drinkers, and the term *intemperate* was applied equally to habitual drunkards and to those who drank with meals.

The key element in the temperance view of alcoholism was the drinker's *loss of control*, which rendered the inebriate incapable of making moral distinctions or of seeing the damage he was causing himself and those around him. The solution for this condition was a religious conversion that led the drinker to see the light and declare he would never drink again. Since alcoholism grew inevitably and inexorably from drinking, the only safe course was total abstinence. Abstinence, of course, actually belies the literal meaning of the word *temperance*—whose meaning is closer to "moderation"—and was only adopted as the official goal of the movement in 1836. Before this date, many—including Rush himself—thought that only distilled spirits led to the disease we call alcoholism and that people might still drink beer and wine moderately.

One group that became important within the temperance movement around the 1840s was the Washingtonians—a brotherhood of reformed drunkards who supported one another's abstinence and preached to other heavy drinkers to join them. Like other temperance associations, they followed the pattern of the Protestant revival meeting: the sinner—in this case, the inebriate—publicly and emotionally confessed his transgressions, sought and gained group acceptance and absolution for his sins, and was redeemed with a new identity and a vow forevermore to hew to a straight and godly path. At its peak, the Washingtonian movement had 600,000 members, perhaps 150,000 of whom remained totally abstinent.[9] After the Civil War, reformed drunkards joined the Women's Christian Temperance Union and other temperance and reform clubs, as well as forming their own organizations, such as the Oxford Group.

These reformed alcoholics (invariably men) became a mainstay on the American scene. Sharing the lecture circuit with the likes of Mark Twain, they reenacted the throes of their drunken degradation and eventual reclamation through God and good living, leading to the new sober selves that stood before the audience. (Observers noted that audiences seemed far more interested in the lecturers' stories about the former drunken lives.[10]) The reclamation of the alcoholic became a common tale in America, one regarded by many with cynicism, as in Wilder's description of the few town drunkards in Grover's Corners: "they're always having remorses every time an evangelist comes to town." Some insisted on seeing them and their spiritual mentors as hypocrites and on regarding their resolves to perpetual sobriety as temporary expedients to gain favor and attention.

One devastating portrait of this process is in Mark Twain's *Huckleberry Finn*, where Huck describes a judge's efforts to remake his father after Pap is sent to jail on one of his drunken binges. The judge and his wife welcome Pap into their home, feed and clothe him, and give him a temperance lecture. In a blubbery scene, Pap holds out his hand and swears:

> "Look at it gentlemen, and ladies all. . . . There's a hand that was the hand of a hog; but it ain't so no more; it's the hand of a man that's started on a new life, and'll die before he'll go back. You mark them words—don't forget I said them. . . ."
> So they shook it, one after the other; all around, and cried. The judge's wife she kissed it. Then the old man he signed a pledge—made his mark. The judge said it was the holiest time on record, or something like that. . . . In the night . . . [Pap] got powerful thirsty and clumb out onto the porch-roof and slid down a stanchion and traded his new coat for a jug of forty-rod, and clumb back again and had a good old time; . . . drunk as a fiddler, . . . [he] rolled off the porch and broke his left arm in two places and was froze most to death when somebody found him after sun-up. The judge he felt kind of sore. He said he reckoned a body could reform the old man with a shot-gun, maybe, but he didn't know no other way.

Mark Twain, needless to say, was not a temperance advocate; nor were many of those he met in his riverboat days, his time in the West in mining camps and as a San Francisco journalist, and his later years in the East among William Dean Howells and his other intellectual and business associates. For example, Twain published the highly successful memoir of one prominent heavy drinker, Ulysses S. Grant, who did not find it necessary to reveal and repudiate his drinking problems. These associations and locales produced people with a sense of drinking entirely different from that embodied by temperance. Indeed, to describe one's attitude toward alcohol was to make a major statement about oneself, as in the declaration "I'm a drinking man." Whether a person recognized drinking as a problem or felt that abstinence was likely to be a solution to the problem was often a matter of who he was and where he came from. People occupied different drinking worlds, and those in each viewed those in the other as inhabitants of a strange planet.

## Prohibition, Its Effects, and Its Aftereffects

These differences underlay the war between wets and drys in America—a battle whose ferociousness we might today find hard to comprehend. Following the Civil War, the temperance movement turned its sights toward the prohibition of alcoholic beverages. "The temperance movement was the largest enduring, secular mass movement in 19th century America."[11] At first, there was little opposition to temperance—since so much of nineteenth-century drinking revolved around abandoned drunkenness, the temperance argument seemed just good sense. A national Prohibition Party was formed, and the Women's Christian Temperance Union singled out the urban saloon as the seat of the evils of drinking. In the 1880s, prohibition was passed in several states, starting with Kansas. But the laws were ineffective and were repealed within a few years.

Carry Nation represented the growing militancy of the prohibition forces in Kansas and elsewhere after the failure of the prohibition laws of the 1880s. Her first husband died a drunkard (her second husband, the minister David Nation, eventually divorced her for desertion), and she began to see visions that dictated she destroy saloons. The prohibition struggle itself became more divisive and nativistic: it was heavily rural and Protestant, antiforeigner and anti-Catholic. When the Reverend Burchard denounced the Democrats in the late nineteenth century as the party of "rum, Romanism, and rebellion," he spoke for many Americans.[12] The National Anti-Saloon League was founded in 1895. It was the most effective force ever for prohibition and became a model for modern single-issue lobbying organizations.

Backed by powerful political, moral, nativist, and capitalist forces, prohibition became a movement for preserving the family and the nation and for eliminating sloth and moral dissolution. On the eve of national Prohibition in 1919, Billy Sunday lectured before a live audience of ten thousand people and a huge radio audience:

> The reign of tears is over. The slums will soon be a memory. We will turn our prisons into factories and our jails into storehouses and corncribs. Men will walk upright now, women will smile and the children will laugh. Hell will forever be rent.[13]

By the time national Prohibition finally went into effect in 1920, it was an accepted development across the country. (Thirty-one states were already dry or had passed the enabling legislation.) But this didn't mean that all people—or groups of people and regions—agreed to abstain. The strongest impact of Prohibition was felt by working-class people, who found alcohol harder to obtain (or at least to afford) and who drank considerably less. By several measures, such as cirrhosis deaths, alcoholic fatalities dropped for the nation as a whole during Prohibition.[14]

Home production and moonshine, however, reduced the impact of Prohibition for some rural areas and among urban ethnics. Some cities, like Detroit, hardly seemed affected by Prohibition at all, and alcohol was everywhere available. New York State repealed its enforcement laws because juries wouldn't convict Prohibition violators. Moreover, middle-class drinking actually increased during Prohibition, supplied both by domestic production and by the importation (mainly from Canada) of illegal liquor. Distilled spirits replaced beer and wine as the most popular drinks because they were more concentrated and easier to transport illegally. Illegal clubs or "speakeasies," where only "hard" liquor was served and intoxication was normal, became the principal drinking places for middle-class consumers.

Thus, the 1920s actually marked a heavy drinking period for many Americans, like those Diana Vreeland knew:

> What a generation that was! It was the martini era. In those days people would get out of the car to see you home, and they'd weave around a bit and fall down on the sidewalk. . . . It was so appalling, the martini of the twenties. If I gave you some gin with a drop of Vermouth that wouldn't cover the head of a pin, that would be the

martini. The people who drank them were carried home, usually unconscious. . . .

I fell in love with . . . a "bottle club". . . . you'd be admitted by someone looking at you through an eyehole in the door; you'd go down a long, very dark flight of stairs, bringing your own bottle, which would then be served to you in bouillon cups. People in those days drank bouillon by the *quart*.[15]

According to psychiatrist Norman Zinberg, the kinds of social sanctions that operated to prevent alcoholism in the colonial tavern were completely reversed in the Prohibition speakeasy and for other illicit drinking in that era. Families didn't drink together, food was not served with alcohol, and the whole point of going out to drink illegal (and expensive) liquor was to get drunk.[16]

It would be incorrect, however, to attribute the increase in middle-class drinking and problem drinking solely to Prohibition. Just as occurred during the rise of temperance and Prohibition itself, drinking attitudes and patterns were reactions to other, more fundamental social currents. The 1920s—paradoxically, the era of Prohibition— also marked the advent of the "flapper" and the death of Victorian standards for women and the middle class at large. A code of liberated personal behavior grew and with it the idea that drinking should accompany a full life: drunkenness was taken as a sign of personal freedom. Some influential examples of this code were the Hollywood film and the notorious bohemian lifestyle that grew up in Greenwich Village.[17]

Prohibition was repealed in 1933, and the idea that we should prohibit the sale, production, and use of alcohol disappeared from the American scene. In the first place, it became evident that Prohibition had failed to transform American society in the monumental way Billy Sunday and other temperance advocates had predicted. The Great Depression made clear that Prohibition was not an unmitigated economic boon, either. That is, influential businessmen had supported national Prohibition because they believed it would energize the work force. Now many felt that renewed liquor sales taxes would lower personal income taxes and stimulate the economy. Moreover, labor unrest and other social upheavals were being blamed on the general disregard for the law fostered by Prohibition.

Although Prohibition was finally and decisively rejected in the United States, American ambivalence about drinking persists. In the first place, prohibition remains a live issue in individual counties and even in entire states. Mississippi repealed statewide prohibition as recently as 1966, Oklahoma in 1959, and many American municipalities and counties remain dry to this day. In some places an active debate on sale of drinks by the shot continues: on July 1, 1987, Kansas enacted a constitutional amendment allowing liquor to be sold by the drink. Other nations such as Canada, Britain, and the Scandinavian countries have had important temperance and prohibition movements. These Northern European countries contrast with the lowland and Mediterranean European nations, which are among the wettest in the world and in which prohibition is unthinkable— imagine prohibition in Italy! However, even the European countries that have had their own temperance movements do not display the degree of repugnance that many Americans still feel toward alcohol and drinking. To this day, the percentage of abstainers in the United States—about one-third of the adult population—is, along with Ireland's, the highest among Western nations.

This number of abstainers might seem impossibly high in the experience of many readers who know hardly any abstainers: again, this is due to large variations in abstinence rates for different ethnic, religious, and regional groups. Some groups have hardly any abstainers, while almost half those in conservative Protestant sects abstain.[18] America is the most emphatic among Western nations in its emphasis on abstinence as the best—or more often the only—solution for the individual with a drinking problem. The United States is also singularly marked by its sense of the desperateness of the alcoholic's condition and the irreversibility of alcoholism. This outlook has been propagated consistently and successfully in the United States by Alcoholics Anonymous, a group that was born following Prohibition.

# The AA Credo Becomes National Dogma

Two alcoholics—Bill Wilson, a stockbroker, and Robert Smith, a physician—met in Akron in 1935 and agreed that they were powerless over their drinking. Out of this insight was created the AA fellowship, dedicated to the proposition that an alcoholic is unable to control his or her drinking and that only through the support and acceptance of those in the same condition can the person achieve sobriety (which requires total abstinence). Both AA's philosophy and its style closely resembled that of the Washingtonians and the temperance societies of the previous century. It seems that once national abstinence was rejected, a core group of Americans who are deeply ambivalent about their drinking reappeared. In tapping this ever-present group, the success of AA is not surprising. Indeed, in an earlier, less populous America, the Washingtonians obtained 600,000 sobriety vows from alcoholics within ten years of its founding; ten years after AA's founding, it had fifteen thousand members, and AA's American membership only reached the half-million point in the 1980s.

The chief innovation in the AA philosophy is the idea that alcoholics constitute a special group who are unable to control their drinking from birth—a condition that *Alcoholics Anonymous* (the so-called Big Book of AA) describes as an allergy to alcohol.[19] The alcoholic needs to forswear alcohol totally—a single taste is sufficient to set him or her off on an uncontrolled binge. Since alcoholism is inbred, it is also irreversible. As a result, alcoholics are obligated to think of themselves as having a lifetime condition. This notion is expressed in AA members' descriptions of themselves as "recovering," as opposed to "recovered." The process is carried forward "one day at a time," while alcoholics are taught to believe that they are exactly one drink away from total relapse and the need to start again at day one.

Although AA proposes a biological explanation for alcoholism, its climate is that of nineteenth-century revivalistic Protestantism. The twelve steps in the AA credo are an obeisance to God (God is mentioned six times) and the need for taking moral inventory and for contrition. The final two steps urge "prayer and meditation to improve our conscious contact with God . . . [and] knowledge of His will for us" and that alcoholics spread their "spiritual awakening" to all alcoholics. But primary in the AA liturgy—the first step—is the admission of being "powerless over alcohol," leading each participant at a meeting to declare "I am an alcoholic." The public confessional and repentance, the spiritual rebirth leading to a new identity, and the need to convert others are all part of AA's fundamentalist religious roots.[20]

While the Washingtonians had a meteoric rise and fall (the group had practically disappeared within two decades of its founding), AA has come to dominate the American alcoholism landscape completely. In part, AA has succeeded because it selected its battleground so well—it explicitly rejected universal prohibition and maintained that only the true alcoholic needs to abstain. This ostensible rejection of blue-nose moralism has been crucial for recruiting liberals into the movement to treat alcoholics as diseased, whether they want to be treated or not. AA also developed an excellent public-relations apparatus. In the late 1930s, the Yale Center of Alcohol Studies was established (its best-known member was Elvin Jellinek) and endorsed the disease view. In the 1940s, the center collaborated with prominent AA members like Marty Mann to create what eventually came to be called the National Council on Alcoholism (NCA). The NCA's aims were to convince Americans that alcoholism is a disease and the alcoholic a sick person who needs help and treatment. The NCA also wanted to alert America to the dangers of alcoholism as a major public health problem.

The NCA succeeded beyond any hopes it could originally have harbored. When the Big Book appeared in 1939, AA had approximately a hundred members. In 1941, a prominent member of the alcoholism movement claimed with alarm that over 100,000 persons were suffering from alcoholism in the United States, while in 1946, a Yale spokesman indicated that there were "more than a million excessive drinkers." In the 1950s, this number was placed at 5 or 6 million, and by the 1980s alcoholism was thought to be affecting ten to twenty million Americans. The NCA formed local chapters throughout the country, sponsored by public education programs, and took out advertisements to drive home its vision of alcoholism—that the alcoholic is a sick person and "is not responsible for his condition," that alcoholism can effectively be treated as a disease, and that the chief obstacle to progress against alcoholism is public apathy and lack of knowledge about the nature and prevalence of the disease.[21]

One reason for the Washingtonian movement's failure had been its hostility toward medicine and institutionalized religion. AA shared at least the former attitude: the Yale summer school almost never invited physicians to lecture in the 1940s, and even today AA members frequently attack physicians for their ignorance about alcoholism. The American Medical Association endorsed the idea that alcoholism is a disease only belatedly, in 1956. Although the relationship between AA and medicine remains uneasy, most medical treatment today typically functions as an adjunct to AA. Physicians conduct an initial examination and detoxify the alcoholic in the hospital, then turn the patient over to paraprofessional counselors who are themselves recovering alcoholics. As a part of treatment, the patient *must* attend AA meetings. Only in the United States has the sober alcoholic achieved such a prominent role in alcoholism treatment, and many of the field's leaders are treatment and AA veterans.[22]

The reasons for AA's success in selling the nation on its views of alcoholism include its remarkable appeal to the media. From the founding of the NCA, Marty Mann (a professional publicist) and others regularly presented the disease concept in magazine articles. NCA founders also consulted with the film industry in making motion pictures such as *The Lost Weekend* that presented the alcoholic's plight sympathetically. As a result of AA's popular success and the acceptance of the disease viewpoint, prominent alcoholics today do not place the emphasis on anonymity that AA officially demands of its members: many public figures have described their alcoholism and their treatment before the camera. Public information programs continually pronounce that alcoholism is a disease, while school counselors, personal advice columns, and medical figures regularly recommend AA and emphasize that medical treatment offers effective help for alcoholics. A 1987 Gallup poll found that almost 90 percent of Americans believe that alcoholism is a disease, and those who refuse to accept this view are often portrayed in the press as benighted and moralistic.

# The Expanding Marketplace of Alcoholism Treatment

In 1970, the government established the National Institute on Alcohol Abuse and Alcoholism (or NIAAA, within what is now called the Department of Health and Human Services), representing the growing success of the alcoholism movement. But when confronted by legislators with some fundamental questions, like how many alcoholics needed treatment, the movement was somewhat at a loss. Estimates based on deaths due to cirrhosis of the liver had placed the number of alcoholics at 5 or 6 million through the 1960s. Meanwhile, a group of researchers under the direction of Don Cahalan at Berkeley had been conducting a series of national surveys of America's drinking problems.[23] When asked how many alcoholics there were currently in the United States, the Berkeley investigators gave very approximate estimates of 9 or 10 million *problem drinkers*. Of this group, the NIAAA concluded, about half—or 5 million—were alcoholics. However, around this time the NCA began claiming there were 10 million alcoholics in the United States.

How many people with the extreme variety of alcoholism shown by early AA members and portrayed in movies like *The Lost Weekend* are there actually? Robin Room, an epidemiologist and current director of the Berkeley Alcohol Research Group, compared the drinking of those in alcoholism treatment with the drinking problems found in general population surveys in the 1970s. About 1 percent of the adult population, or around 1.5 million Americans, drank as much as the typical clinical alcoholic. Since there were already 1.7 million people in treatment in 1976, Room concluded that "the number of people in the general population who resemble those in clinical populations may be no larger than the number in treatment or recently out of it."[24] In other words, just before a tremendous growth spurt in alcoholism treatment and services in the mid-1970s, Room saw little evidence that there were scores of alcoholics who were going untreated.

Yet in the 1980s, even the 10 million figure for alcoholics—generalized from the number of problem drinkers estimated by the Berkeley group—seemed to many in the treatment industry far too small. According to G. Douglas Talbott, a physician and recovering alcoholic who now heads a drug and alcohol program:

The old figure was 10,000,000 alcoholics. I was interested in where that figure came from and found out it was thought up one night in Washington when the first alcohol support bill was presented to Congress . . . and that figure got frozen into literature. It is way beyond that now, and, as far as we are concerned, 22 million people have an alcohol problem related to the disease of alcoholism.[25]

Talbott here makes light of earlier alcoholism estimates, even though these data were originally heavily promoted by those in the alcoholism movement and by legislators. Ironically, the Berkeley researchers themselves all along gave these estimates reluctantly, because most of those who have a drinking problem are very far from qualifying for a diagnosis of alcoholism.[26]

The viewpoint of Cahalan, Room, and their coworkers is sociological—one that sees alcohol abuse in a social context. It finds alcohol abuse to vary widely for different ethnic groups, at different times of the individual's life, and with different drinking companions. This approach is at the opposite extreme from that of seeing alcoholism as an inbred disease. In contrast to the uniformity of AA accounts, the Cahalan group's research reveals drinking problems to be extremely variable. Problems in the national surveys range from frequent intoxication and binge drinking to marital, police, financial, and health problems due to drinking. People's drinking problems in these surveys appear very unlike the obligatory AA story of inexorable progression and inevitable loss of control.[27]

Only a small percentage of those who have had some kind of drinking problem who are sampled in general population surveys have been in treatment (although this number began to increase appreciably in Alcohol Research Group surveys in the late 1980s). Apparently, such surveys tap a largely different problem drinker from those who typically enter AA. Most of these people seem able to come to grips with their drinking problems on their own and in any case do not choose to label themselves as alcoholics who need treatment. These people are also likely to reduce their problem drinking rather than quit altogether. This is not to say that they even think of themselves as having a drinking problem. Their shifts in behavior stem mainly from maturation or other life changes that bring them into contact with different people and different environments and that encourage moderation.

The growth in alcoholism treatment has involved persuading the public that people like these problem drinkers require treatment as alcoholics. Here the ideology of AA and the alcoholism movement has shifted perceptibly. That is, if people are born alcoholics from their first drinks, then this group should be obviously identifiable as a distinct part of the population. Early AA members did not talk about denial— their alcoholism had been obvious, even to themselves. But this view has gradually shifted to emphasize the *progressive* nature of alcoholism (a view that, ironically, returns to the temperance view of drinking), one that means alcoholism often begins with subtle problems that will grow unless checked. Disease proponents now argue that someone with a milder drinking problem—a person earlier AA members would clearly distinguish from themselves—needs treatment to avoid getting worse. Thus, all drinkers who ever have had a problem are suitable for alcoholism treatment, and it is these "early-stage" alcoholics that treatment personnel most anxiously seek.

The number of alcoholics in treatment per capita in the United States multiplied twentyfold between 1942 and 1976, Robin Room has calculated. Since then, the number of people treated for alcoholism has continued to rise precipitously. (For example, AA membership doubled between 1977 and 1987.) Moreover, the shift from government funding of public facilities to support for third-party financing of alcoholism treatment created a tremendous expansion of private inpatient treatment. Between 1978 and 1984 the number of for-profit residential treatment centers increased by 350 percent and their caseloads by 400 percent.[28] Today most such therapy is paid for by insurers. In response, private hospitals and hospital conglomerates like Fair Oaks and CompCare have arisen to handle these patient loads through twenty-eight-day inpatient programs. These hospital stays cost from $7500 to $35,000, and the new alcoholics who fill these programs are quite different from the typical public inebriates who were shunted off to government hospitals.

Since the mid-1970s, the emphasis has been on recruiting prosperous, functioning individuals who do not appear to be alcoholics (the prototypical case being Kitty Dukakis). In fact, because these people are so unexceptional, they must often be persuaded of the potential severity of their drinking problems. Advertisements, educational programs, and the testimony of attractive notables like Betty Ford and Elizabeth Taylor are used to convince people that they should seek treatment for their disease, just as if they had diabetes or gout. However, since such alcoholics are often judged to be in "denial" and blind to the true nature of their problem, they often need to be forcibly confronted with their alcoholism by loved ones and treatment personnel. This contrasts with the early philosophy of Alcoholics Anonymous, which emphasized that the alcoholic needed to accept his condition voluntarily.

The change has meant that coercive tactics are now a regular part of the treatment arsenal. The main source of referrals for alcoholism treatment has become drunk-driving arrests. The arrestees—most often younger men—are given the choice of incarceration or submitting to treatment in which they are forced publicly to admit that they are alcoholics. But others besides drunk drivers are now often referred to treatment. Heavy drinkers convicted of felonies from writing bad checks to child abuse to rape have been placed in treatment rather than in prison—in several cases, murderers have been remanded for court-ordered alcoholism treatment.[29]

Rapidly growing employee assistance programs (EAPs) have the potential for reaching even more people. Here the same activist approach is followed of offering the problem drinker the choice of accepting treatment or losing his job. At the workplace, more young people are brought into the net through the discovery of their drug use. A young man found smoking marijuana in a company with a treatment program of this sort will be told he has a disease—chemical dependence—that he must confront. Although combining alcohol and drug treatment has presented problems for AA groups and remains an issue within AA, medical treatment programs and EAPs typically group drug and alcohol abusers together for diagnostic and treatment purposes.

When one considers that the 22-million figure cited by Dr. Talbott for alcoholism represents one in seven adult Americans and that over 60 percent of high school seniors use illicit substances, the phenomenal growth in chemical-dependence treatment in America is not surprising. Corporations have forged chains of such treatment centers, and the largest new category for hospitalizations has become chemical dependence. Between 1980 and 1984, for example, there was a 350 percent jump in the hospitalization of teenagers—at a time when hospitalizations overall declined. These figures were presented on the May 20, 1985, *CBS Evening News;* on the same show, a producer phoned a treatment center to say that he suspected his teenage daughter had used marijuana and that she was disrespectful and was dating an older boy. On this evidence, the girl was placed in a hospital. The girl wore a concealed microphone, and when she claimed she didn't have a drug problem, a counselor was heard saying that this is the response inmates always give (i.e., denial).

The hospital chain in question, CompCare, is among the most prominent in America. CBS interviewed CompCare's medical director, Joseph Pursch (the physician who treated Betty Ford) about this case. Pursch claimed that no one would be hospitalized without a medical examination (the girl received none). In fact, CompCare trains consultants to work with high school counseling staffs, teaching them how to run "interventions"—sessions in which students suspected of drug use are surrounded by family, friends, teachers, and others who insist the child enter treatment immediately. (Intervention protocol recommends that a cab be kept waiting for the moment the student admits his problem so that he can be rushed to a center before he changes his mind.)

Obviously, parents are terribly concerned lest their child be abusing drugs unbeknownst to them. They are warned in publications like those by Straight, Inc. that if they suspect a child has smoked marijuana, this "is probably only the tip of the iceberg." Salespeople for treatment programs encourage parents to make any financial sacrifice to get and keep their child in treatment—after all, parents are told, "this could be a matter of life or death." Straight publishes a newsletter called *Epidemic*—the first issue of which featured the banner headline DENIAL and the boldly printed Straight credo: "In understanding the drug problem and in understanding Straight's role in dealing with that problem, we must understand that the single, biggest problem we have to confront is denial." It is this denial that makes children and their parents claim that the kids are not addicts when Straight decides they are.

Actually, the intoxicating substance used most heavily by children is not an illicit drug, but alcohol. National surveys conducted at the University of Michigan among high school seniors find that about 40 percent of seniors overall (and half of high school senior boys) have had at least five drinks in a single sitting within two weeks of being interviewed.[30] A 1982 Gallup poll revealed that fully one in three American families suspect that one or more members have a drinking problem, perhaps reflecting the heavy drinking of so many teens. Special units based on AA ("Alateen") have now been set up for youthful children of alcoholics, often with the goal of alerting them to their own susceptibility to alcoholism. Indeed, the young have been the fastest growing segment of AA membership. In both AA and chemical-dependence treatment programs, youngsters are taught that they are alcoholics (or chemically dependent) and that they must commit themselves never again to drink or to use a psychoactive substance of any kind.

Yet the largest growth area of all in the field of alcoholism does not concern people who are active drug or alcohol abusers. This is the movement to bring "codependents" and "coalcoholics" (or spouses of addicts and alcoholics) and entire families into treatment. Al-Anon is the group created for spouses of alcoholics, overwhelmingly women. Because alcoholics are more likely to have drug- or alcohol-abusing children, treatment centers strive to recruit the "high-risk" children of alcohol abusers to therapy, often before they have drunk or taken drugs—sometimes as preschoolers. One strong message these children receive in therapy is that they are tremendously susceptible to alcoholism themselves, should they ever drink.

Moreover, children of alcoholics safely beyond the age of influence—labeled "adult children of alcoholics"—have been the most heavily recruited of all for therapy. According to a founder of the National Association for Children of Alcoholics, "Children of alcoholics deserve and require treatment in and of themselves," whether or not they have ever had a drinking problem. These "adult children" have been the focus of a string of best-sellers, national conferences, public service announcements, and new support groups. The rapid rise of this movement is described by one of its leaders: " 'The wounded are everywhere,' said Sharon Wegscheider-Cruse. . . . 'In a sense, our movement is a social revolution.' "[31]

## America the Addicted

From the time in the recent past when Americans were blithely unaware of alcoholism as a significant social problem, we have come to feel that alcohol and related drug problems are epidemic. The new temperance lecturers speak to parents and children in packed audiences around the country about the need never to consume any type of drug or alcohol. Alcoholism treatment is mandated for large—and growing—numbers of people. This treatment conveys the idea of uncontrollable substance abuse as a regular feature of contemporary life, and as a permanent characteristic of innumerable Americans. The way out is treatment—expensive treatment, but treatment that is necessary if people are to avoid the inexorable descent into alcoholic or addictive hell. A new vision of alcohol and alcoholism is upon the land.

This chapter has reviewed the history of attitudes toward drinking and alcohol abuse in the United States. America has had many different images of this one substance, beverage alcohol. Changing images of drinking and its dangers are *not* clearly related to *levels* of consumption. For example, colonial Americans drank three times as much as contemporary Americans but worried less about drinking and seemed actually to have fewer drinking problems. Consumption dropped precipitously in America between 1835 and 1845, never again to return to colonial levels. Yet although drinking was greatly reduced, alarm about the dangers of alcohol continued to grow. National Prohibition actually went into effect at a time when drinking and drinking problems were far from their peak nineteenth-century levels.

The image of alcohol with which I am most concerned is that it is addictive, that it makes drinkers "lose control." If alcoholism is a biological imperative beyond conscious control, then it is wrong to hold alcoholics accountable for their drinking style or for their behavior when drunk. Disease proponents maintain that this model eliminates the moral stigma many erroneously attach to chronic drunkenness and alcoholic misbehavior. In fact, the contemporary alcoholism movement preserves temperance's moral baggage. It views alcoholism as an evil reaction set off in the body and soul by alcohol, one that demands that the drinker swear off alcohol at all costs. To an unrecognized extent, we are living today with nineteenth-century ideas about drinking presented as if they were modern scientific discoveries. The dominant approach to drunkenness in America continues to be a religious one, steeped in American Protestant revivalism and accompanied by the sense of alcohol as a looming evil.

The primary additions to the disease model of alcoholism in the twentieth century have been the view that alcoholism is an inbred trait for some and the view that the neurosciences can explain why people drink too much. These ideas underlie much scientific research on alcoholism in the second half of this century; in this way, the disease theory was successfully merged with modern medical and scientific belief. As a result, organized medicine has become a strong voice added to AA's in proselytizing for the disease view of alcoholism. This urge to reduce moral problems to biological dimensions

goes back a long way: Benjamin Rush, the eighteenth-century founder of the disease concept of alcoholism, also thought that lying,
murder, and political dissent were diseases.

Today, no other country in the world has as active an alcoholism
establishment as the United States, treats as many people for alcoholism, commands as much media attention for the problem, or has
gained such wide acceptance for the conception that alcoholism is a
disease. Moreover, no other nation has taken the implications of
disease theories of behavior as far as the United States or applied
the disease model to as many new areas of behavior. America has
elevated the alcoholism movement to the status of a national icon;
in the United States the diseases of alcoholism and addiction have
become national themes. The issue that remains is whether this
actually ameliorates alcoholism and related problems—or, indeed,
exacerbates them.

# 3

# Who Says What the Truths about Alcoholism Are?

AA, treatment centers and alcohol counseling are the only known successful methods of arresting the compulsion to drink or take drugs. Alcoholism was totally untreatable and fatal until 1935, when AA was founded.

—Ruth Harris, WomenSpace Shelter Project, Cleveland

---

WHAT WE "know" about alcoholism, like the points in Ruth Harris's quote above, has been determined by an active group of proselytizers for AA and the alcoholism movement, most of whom are alcoholics. These advocates have had very specific experiences with drinking. At the same time, many of their experiences and views were distinctive even *before* they became alcoholics and were in fact quite different from those of people *less* likely to become alcoholics. Nonetheless, public opinion surveys show that Americans at large have accepted all or most of the contentions of the modern alcoholism movement. Still, not everyone agrees.

The core beliefs that the alcoholism movement has successfully promulgated are:

1. Alcoholics don't drink too much because they intend to, but only because they can't control their drinking.

2. Alcoholics inherit their alcoholism and thus are born as alcoholics.

3. Alcoholism always grows worse without treatment, so that alcoholics can never cut back or quit drinking on their own.

4. Alcoholism as a disease can strike any individual—it is an "equal-opportunity destroyer"—and respects no social, religious, ethnic or sexual bounds.

5. Treatment based on AA principles is the *only* effective treatment for alcoholism—in the words of one proponent, a modern medical "miracle"—without which no one can hope to arrest a drinking problem.

6. Those who reject the AA approach for their drinking problems, or observers who contradict any of the contentions about alcoholism listed here, are practicing a special *denial* that means death for alcoholics.

These keynotes to the AA and National Council on Alcoholism perspective existed before any research had been conducted to verify them—they represent folk wisdom. This folk wisdom has come to be accepted by most Americans. For example, according to a 1987 Gallup poll, 87 percent of Americans endorse the idea that alcoholism is a disease (although only 68 percent express *strong* agreement with this idea). This figure has increased steadily, jumping from 79 percent who agreed in 1982, as Americans are told they must accept the "truths" of alcoholism, which are said to represent modern scientific breakthroughs in our understanding of drinking problems. For example, Gallup presented Americans' growing acceptance of the disease viewpoint under the heading "Misconceptions About Alcoholism Succumb to Educational Efforts."[1]

The actual scientific evidence, however, strongly *contradicts* the contentions of the alcoholism movement. For example, the standard wisdom is that AA is unmatched in effectiveness for dealing with alcoholism and that alcoholism would be licked if only everyone joined AA. Certainly, many people who belong to AA tell us that AA stopped them from drinking. However, this no more demonstrates the general effectiveness of AA than testimony that some people decide not to kill themselves after they discover Christ is evidence that Christianity is the cure for suicide. In fact, research has not found AA to be an effective treatment for general populations of alcoholics. Consider the following summary by researchers at the Downstate (New York) Medical Center Department of Psychiatry:

> The general applicability of AA as a treatment method is much more limited than has been supposed in the past. Available data do not support AA's claims of much higher success rates than clinic treatment. Indeed, when population differences are taken into account, the reverse seems to be true.[2]

Not one study has ever found AA or its derivatives to be superior to any other approach, or even to be better than not receiving any help at all for eliminating alcoholism when alcoholics are assigned to different kinds of treatment. At the same time, other methods that have regularly been found superior to AA and other standard therapies for alcoholism have been completely rejected by American treatment programs. To preview the startling proposition that therapies that are universally advocated have already been shown to be ineffective and that more effective approaches are available, consider the prevailing approach to drunk-driving convictions in America—remanding drinking drivers for treatment. Advocates of a humane, informed approach to the problem continually plead for more such referrals and bemoan primitive programs that simply arrest, imprison, or place on probation those caught driving while intoxicated (DWI). Meanwhile, *comparative studies of standard treatment programs versus legal proceedings for drunk drivers regularly find that those who received ordinary judicial sanctions had fewer subsequent accidents and were rearrested less.*[3]

While standard disease treatments and education programs for drunk drivers have conclusively been shown to fail at their mission, nondisease rehabilitation programs—such as those teaching DWIs social skills (like those needed to reject additional drinks), enhanced personal responsibility in decision making, and methods for drinking moderately—*have* shown beneficial results.[4] Yet almost no such nondisease programs for drunk drivers remain in the United States, and these few are under strong attack. In 1985, the attorney general of New York and the State Division of Alcoholism and Alcohol Abuse attempted to close such a program in Rochester, although the program had operated successfully for years under the auspices of the county DA's office. (Eventually, the New York State Supreme Court ruled in favor of the program, Creative Interventions, mainly on technical grounds.[5])

AA's undeserved status as a universal cure for alcoholism and the beleaguered state of skill-training approaches for drunk drivers are some of the many indicators that alcoholism practices are based on the prejudices of a few rather than on scientific data. That this situation prevails in the United States is clear in a remarkable quote from the current director of the National Institute on Alcohol Abuse and Alcoholism, Enoch Gordis:

> In the case of alcoholism, our whole treatment system, with its in- numerable therapies, armies of therapists, large and expensive pro- grams, endless conferences . . . and public relations activities is founded on hunch, not evidence, and not on science. . . . Yet the history of medicine demonstrates repeatedly that unevaluated treat- ment, no matter how compassionately administered, is frequently useless and wasteful and sometimes dangerous or harmful. The lesson we have learned is that *what is plausible may be false, and what is done sincerely may be useless or worse.* (emphasis in original)[6]

While alcoholism movement experts strive to declare that the dom- inant American approaches to alcoholism represent the end point of a long process of scientific discovery, other countries have repudiated the disease approach entirely. Consider this quote from British psy- chiatrist Robin Murray:

> There can be no doubt that current British and American perspectives on alcoholism differ widely. . . . Even R. E. Kendell, one of the British psychiatrists most interested in categorical diagnostic systems, states that for alcoholism it is "increasingly clear that most of the assumptions of the 'disease model' are unjustified and act as a barrier to a more intelligent and effective approach to the problem."[7]

The following is a list of some of the widely promulgated and gen- erally accepted ideas about the disease of alcoholism, along with the research that contradicts them.

# Loss of Control

The core idea of the AA version of the disease of alcoholism is that alcoholics cannot cease drinking once they start. The first step of AA, admitting that the alcoholic is "powerless over alcohol," means that alcoholics simply cannot regulate their drinking in any way. According to AA, even a single taste of alcohol (such as that in an alcoholic dessert) sets off uncontrollable binge drinking. Alcoholism professionals have attempted to translate AA's view into scientific-sounding terms. For example, in a popular book on alcoholism, *Under the Influence*, James Milam claims: "The alcoholic's drinking is controlled by physiological factors which cannot be altered through psychological methods such as counseling, threats, punishment, or reward. In other words, the alcoholic is powerless to control his or her drinking."[8]

In fact, this statement has been demonstrated to be false by every experiment designed to test it. For example, alcoholics who are not aware that they are drinking alcohol do not develop an uncontrollable urge to drink more.[9] Psychologist Alan Marlatt and his colleagues found that alcoholics drinking heavily flavored alcoholic beverages did not drink excessive amounts—as long as they thought the drinks did not contain alcohol. The alcoholics in this experiment who drank the most were those who believed they were imbibing alcohol—*even when their beverage contained none.*[10] From this study, we see that what alcoholics believe is more important to their drinking than the "facts" that they are alcoholics and that they are drinking alcohol.

Rather than losing control of their drinking, experiments show, alcoholics aim for a desired state of consciousness when they drink.[11] They drink to transform their emotions and their self-image—drinking is a route to achieve feelings of power, sexual attractiveness, or control over unpleasant emotions.[12] Alcoholics strive to attain a particular level of intoxication, one that they can describe before taking a drink. Nancy Mello and Jack Mendelson of Harvard Medical School and McLean Hospital—the former a psychologist and the latter a physician—found that alcoholics would continue working to gain credits with which to buy alcohol until they could stockpile the amount they needed to get as drunk as they wanted. They continued to work for credits as they were undergoing withdrawal from previous binges, even though they could stop and turn in their credits for drink at any time.[13]

Alcoholics are influenced by their environments and by those around them, even when they are drinking and intoxicated. For example, researchers at Baltimore City Hospital offered alcoholics the opportunity to drink whenever they wanted in a small, drab isolation booth. These street inebriates curtailed their drinking significantly in order to spend more time in a comfortable and interesting room among their companions. In these and other studies, alcoholics' drinking behavior was molded simply by the way the alcohol was administered or by the rewards alcoholics received or were denied based on their drinking styles.[14]

What does this research prove? *Alcoholism* is the term we use to describe people who get drunk more than other people and who often suffer problems due to their drinking. Alcoholism exists—overdrinking, compulsive drinking, drinking beyond a point where the person knows he or she will regret it—all these occur. (In fact, these things happen to quite a high percentage of all drinkers during their lives.) But this drinking is *not* due to some special, uncontrollable biological drive. Alcoholics are no different from other human beings in exercising choices, in seeking the feelings that they believe alcohol provides, and in evaluating the mood changes they experience in terms of their alternatives. No evidence disputes the view that alcoholics continue to respond to their environments and to express personal values even while they are drinking.

# The Genetics of Alcoholism

AA originally claimed that alcoholics inherit an "allergy" to alcohol that underlies their loss of control when they drink. Today this particular idea has been discarded. Nonetheless, a tremendous investment has been made in the search for biological inheritances that may cause alcoholism, while many grandiose claims have been made about the fruits of this search. In 1987, almost two-thirds of Americans (63 percent) agreed that "alcoholism can be hereditary"; only five years earlier, in 1982, more people had disagreed (50 percent) than agreed (40 percent) with this statement. Furthermore, it is the better educated who agree most with this statement.[15] Yet widely promulgated and broadly accepted claims about the inheritance of alcoholism are inaccurate, and important data from genetic research call into doubt the significance of genetic influences on alcoholism and problem drinking. Moreover, prominent genetic researchers themselves indicate that cultural and environmental influences are the major determinants of most drinking problems, even for the minority of alcoholics who they believe have a genetic component to their drinking.

Popular works now regularly put forward the theory—presented as fact—that the inherited cause of alcoholism has been discovered. In the words of Durk Pearson and Sandra Shaw, the authors of *Life Extension*, "Alcohol addiction is not due to weak will or moral depravity; it is a genetic metabolic defect . . . [just like the] genetic metabolic defect resulting in gout." One version of this argument appeared in the newsletter of the Alcoholism Council of Greater New York:

> Someone like the derelict . . . , intent only on getting sufficient booze from the bottle poised upside-down on his lips . . . [is] the victim of metabolism, a metabolism the derelict is born with, a metabolic disorder that causes excessive drinking.[16]

Is it really possible that street inebriates are destined from the womb to become alcoholics? Don't they really have a choice in the matter, or any alternatives? Don't their upbringings, or their personal and social values, have any impact on this behavior?

Several well-publicized studies have found that close biological relatives of alcoholics are more likely to be alcoholics themselves. The best-known research of this kind, examining Danish adoptees, was published in the early 1970s by psychiatrist Donald Goodwin and his colleagues. The researchers found that male adoptees with alcoholic biological parents became alcoholics three to four times more often than adoptees without alcoholic relatives. This research has several surprising elements to it, however. In the first place, only 18 percent of the males with alcoholic biological parents became alcoholics themselves (compared with 5 percent of those without alcoholic parentage). Note that, accepting this study at face value, the vast majority of men whose fathers are alcoholics do not become alcoholic solely because of biological inheritance.[17]

Some might argue that Goodwin's definition of alcoholism is too narrow and that the figures in his research severely understate the incidence of alcoholism. Indeed, there was an additional group of problem drinkers whom Goodwin and his colleagues identified, and many people might find it hard to distinguish when a drinker fell in this rather than in the alcoholic group. However, more of the people in the problem drinking group did not have alcoholic parents than did! If alcoholic and heavy problem drinkers are combined, as a group they are not more likely to be offspring of alcoholic than of nonalcoholic parents, and the finding of inherited differences in alcoholism rates disappears from this seminal study. One last noteworthy result of the Goodwin team's research: in a separate study using the same methodology as the male offspring study, the investigators did not find that daughters of alcoholic parents more often became alcoholic themselves (in fact, there were more alcoholic women in the group *without* alcoholic parents).[18]

Other studies also discourage global conclusions about inheritance of alcoholism. One is by a highly respected research group in Britain under Robin Murray, dean of the Institute of Psychiatry at Maudsley Hospital. Murray and his colleagues compared the correlation between alcoholism in identical twins with that between fraternal twins. Since the identical pair are more similar genetically, they should more often be alcoholic or nonalcoholic together than twins whose relationships are genetically equivalent to ordinary siblings. No such difference appeared. Murray and his colleagues and others have surveyed the research on inheritance of alcoholism.[19] According to a longtime biological researcher in alcoholism, David Lester, these reviews "suggest that genetic involvement in the etiology of alcoholism . . . is weak at best." His own review of the literature, Lester wrote, "extends and . . . strengthens these previous judgments." Why, then, are genetic viewpoints so popular? For Lester, the credibility given genetic views is "disproportionate with their theoretical and empirical warrant," and the "attraction and persistence of such views lies in their conformity with ideological norms."

Several studies of male children of alcoholics (including two ongoing Danish investigations) have not found that these children drink differently as young adults or adolescents from their cohorts without alcoholic relatives.[20] These children of alcoholics are not generally separated from their parents, and we know that for whatever reason, male children brought up by their alcoholic parents more often will be alcoholic themselves. What this tells us is that these children aren't born as alcoholics but develop their alcoholism over the years. In the words of George Vaillant, who followed the drinking careers of a large group of men over forty years:

> The present prospective study offers no credence to the common belief that some individuals become alcoholics after the first drink. The progression from alcohol use to abuse takes years.[21]

What, then, do people inherit that keeps them drinking until they become alcoholics? Milam asserts in *Under the Influence* that the source of alcoholism is acetaldehyde, a chemical produced when the body breaks down alcohol. Some research has found higher levels of this chemical in children of alcoholics when they drink[22]; other research (like the two Danish prospective studies) has not. Such discrepancies in research results also hold for abnormalities in brain waves that various teams of researchers have identified in children of alcoholics—some find one EEG pattern, while other researchers discover a distinct but different pattern.[23] Psychiatrist Marc Schuckit, of the University of California at San Diego Medical School, found no such differences between young men from alcoholic families and a matched comparison group, leading him to "call into question . . . the replicability and generalizability" of cognitive impairments and neuropsychologic deficits "as part of a predisposition toward alcoholism."[24]

Washington University psychiatrist Robert Cloninger (along with several other researchers) claims that an inherited antisocial or crime-prone personality often leads to both criminality and alcoholism in men.[25] On the other hand, antisocial acting out when drinking, as well as criminality, are endemic to certain social and racial groups—particularly young working-class and ghetto males.[26] The Cloninger view gets into the slippery realm of explaining that the underprivileged and ghettoized are born the way they are. In addition, Schuckit has failed to find any differences in antisocial temperament or impulsiveness to differentiate those who come from alcoholic families and those without alcoholic siblings or parents.[27] Instead, Schuckit believes, one—perhaps *the*—major mechanism that characterizes children of alcoholics is that these children are born with a diminished sensitivity to the effects of alcohol[28] (although—once again—other researchers do not find this to be the case[29]).

In Schuckit's view, children of alcoholics have a built-in tolerance for alcohol—they experience *less* intoxication than other people when drinking the same amounts. (Note that this is the opposite of the original AA view that alcoholics inherit an allergy to alcohol.) In the Schuckit model, alcoholics might unwittingly drink more over long periods and thus build up a dependence on alcohol. But as a theory of alcoholism, where does this leave us? *Why* do these young men continue drinking for the years and decades Vaillant tells us it takes them to become alcoholics? And even if they *can* drink more without experiencing physical effects, why do they tolerate the various drinking problems, health difficulties, family complaints, and so on that occur on the road to alcoholism? Why don't they simply recognize the negative impact alcohol is having on their lives and resolve to drink less? Certainly, some people do exactly this, saying things like "I limit myself to one or two drinks because I don't like the way I act after I drink more."

One insight into how those with similar physiological responses to alcohol may have wholly different predispositions to alcoholism is provided by those who manifest "Oriental flush"—a heightened response to alcohol marked by a visible reddening after drinking that frequently characterizes Asians and Native Americans. Oriental flush has a biochemical basis in that Asian groups display higher acetaldehyde levels when they drink: here, many believe, is a key to alcoholism. But individuals from Asian backgrounds who flush do not necessarily drink more than—or differ in their susceptibility to drinking problems from—those who don't flush.[30] Moreover, groups that show flushing have both the *highest* alcoholism rates (Native Americans and Eskimos) and the *lowest* rates (Chinese and Japanese) among ethnic groups in the United States. What distinguishes between how people in these two groups react to the same biological phenomenon? It would certainly seem that Eskimos' and Indians' abnegated state in America and their isolation from the American economic and achievement-oriented system inflate their alcoholism rates, while the low alcoholism rates of the Chinese and Japanese must be related to their achievement orientation and economic success in our society.

Not even genetically oriented researchers (as opposed to popular-izers) deny that cultural and social factors are crucial in the devel-opment of alcoholism and that, in this sense, alcoholism is driven by values and life choices. Consider three quotes from prominent medical researchers. Marc Schuckit: "It is unlikely that there is a single cause for alcoholism. . . . At best, biologic factors explain only a part of" the alcoholism problem[31]; George Vaillant: " 'I think it [finding a biological marker for alcoholism] would be as unlikely as finding one for basketball playing.' . . . The high number of children of alcoholics who become addicted, Vaillant believes, is due less to biological factors than to poor role models"[32]; Robert Clon-inger: "The demonstration of the critical importance of sociocultural influences in most alcoholics suggests that major changes in social attitudes about drinking styles can change dramatically the preva-lence of alcohol abuse regardless of genetic predisposition."[33] In short, the idea that alcoholism is an inherited biological disease has been badly overstated, and according to some well-informed observers, is completely unfounded.

## Alcoholic Progression—A Drinking Problem Can Only Get Worse

The nineteenth-century view of alcoholic progression—that occa-sional drinkers become regular drinkers become alcoholics—is alive and well in the modern alcoholism movement. Now the idea is that anyone who ever has any problems with their drinking must either seek treatment or progress to inevitable, life-threatening alcoholism. "The ultimate consequences for a drinking alcoholic," Dr. G. Doug-las Talbott says, "are these three: he or she will end up in jail, in a hospital, or in a graveyard."[34]

Of course, when you talk to alcoholics, you discover that they were early problem drinkers before *they* progressed to alcoholism. But the fact is, the large majority of problem drinkers outgrow their drinking problems, according to the national surveys conducted by Don Cahalan and his associates. Men often go through problem drinking periods, depending on their stage in the life cycle and the people they associate with, only to emerge from these when their life circumstances change. Incidentally, the large majority of these untreated former problem drinkers do not choose to abstain but continue drinking while diminishing or eliminating their problems. The largest group of problem drinkers is young men, but young drinkers show the highest rate of natural remission as they age.[35]

Several surveys conducted by Kaye Fillmore, of the Institute for Health and Aging (University of California, San Francisco), indicate that drinking problems that appear in college and late adolescence— problems up to and including blackout—*rarely* persist through middle age.[36] Exactly similar data pertain to youthful drug abuse, and all research shows the tendency to use, to use regularly, and to be addicted to drugs drops off after adolescence and early adulthood.[37] Apparently, as people mature they find they can achieve more meaningful rewards than those offered by drugs and overdrinking. These rewards are generally the conventional ones of family life and accomplishment at work that dominate adult life for most people, even most of those who had a drinking or drug problem earlier on.

Nor are children of alcoholics destined to progress to alcoholism when they drink. A large, long-term study of Tecumseh, Michigan, residents conducted by epidemiologists at the University of Michigan found that children of heavy-drinking parents most frequently choose to drink moderately themselves. Although alcoholics have more alcoholic offspring than average, the researchers noted, "alcoholic parental drinking only weakly invites imitation."[38] It seems that people are quite capable of *learning* from observing a parent's alcoholism to avoid such problems themselves. In doing so, the researchers found, children are helped when the heavy drinker is the parent of the opposite sex. In addition, there was *less* imitation in this study of a heavy-drinking parent when the children as adults recalled the parent as having drinking problems.[39] Finally, several studies of children of alcoholics have shown that, even after they themselves develop a drinking problem, they do better in treatment aimed at moderating drinking rather than at abstinence than do other problem drinkers.[40]

Although by far the largest percentage of those who outgrow a drinking or drug problem without treatment are younger, natural recovery in alcoholism and addiction is not limited to the young or to those who fall short of developing severe alcoholism.[41] Those who have progressed to definite alcohol dependence also regularly escape from alcoholism on their own; indeed, natural remission for alcoholics may be more typical than not. In the words of British physician Milton Gross, who has focused on the biological aspects of alcohol dependence:

> The foundation is set for the progression of the alcohol dependence syndrome by virtue of its biologically intensifying itself. One would think that, once caught up in the process, the individual could not be extricated. However, and for reasons poorly understood, the reality is otherwise. Many, perhaps most, do free themselves.[42]

A number of studies have now documented that such self-cure among alcoholics is common. These untreated but recovered alcoholics constitute, according to researcher Barry Tuchfeld, a "silent majority."[43] Based on his research in Australia, psychiatrist Les Drew has described alcoholism as a "self-limiting" disease, one that creates pressures for its own cure even in the absence of outside interventions.[44] In the words of Harold Mulford, "Contrary to the traditional clinical view of the alcoholism disease process, progress in the alcoholic process is neither inevitable nor irreversible. Eventually, the balance of natural forces shifts to decelerate progress in the alcoholic process and to accelerate the rehabilitation process."[45]

# Alcoholism Isn't Due to Anything but Alcoholism—Alcoholism as a "Primary Disease"

Members of AA and representatives of the alcoholism movement argue that alcoholism is not the result of other problems that the alcoholic drinks to forget or disguise. Rather, they claim, alcoholism is a self-contained disease that exists independent of other aspects of the alcoholic's life and personal functioning. In this view, alcoholics have no special difficulties other than those produced by their drinking, and improving their lives in any other way aside from getting them to stop drinking will not affect their disease.

At this point, I introduce the personage of George Vaillant, the psychiatrist and author of *The Natural History of Alcoholism*, to whom I have already referred. (Vaillant is now at Dartmouth Medical School.) Vaillant is a remarkable figure in the modern history of alcoholism research. He is actually one of the first epidemiologists to investigate the sources of alcoholism from a disease perspective, as opposed to the social perspective used by the Berkeley Alcohol Research Group. Vaillant emphatically endorses the disease model of alcoholism and of medical treatment for it. He sees alcoholism as a primary disease that has "a life of its own and is not a moral or psychological problem." However, Vaillant's claims are frequently contradicted by his own data.

For example, while Vaillant repeatedly stresses that alcoholism is an independent disease and not a response to some other set of problems, he reports the following research results from his own and other studies:

> The most important single prognostic variable associated with remission among alcoholics who attend alcohol clinics is having something to lose if they continue to abuse alcohol. . . . Patients cited changed life circumstances rather than clinic intervention as most important to their abstinence. . . . Improved working and housing conditions made a difference in 40 percent of good outcomes, intrapsychic change in 32 percent, improved marriage in 32 percent, and a single 3-hour session of advice and education about drinking . . . in 35 percent.[46]

In other words, people get over alcoholism because of changes in other parts of their lives that make it worthwhile to quit, that counterbalance their urge to drink, or that remove the stresses (such as marital problems) that led them to drink alcoholically. Vaillant urges those who want to help alcoholics to "learn to facilitate natural healing processes" since these processes are the key to alcoholic recovery. Yet Vaillant seeks mainly to warn these helpers "*not to interfere* with the recovery process," because his research shows that "it may be easier for improper treatment to retard recovery than for proper treatment to hasten it." More than anything, Vaillant's actual findings are that the course of alcoholism depends mainly on how well people can resolve their life problems. (This was the theme of Vaillant's previous work, *Adaptation to Life*, written before he got into the alcoholism field.)

# Alcoholism, the "Equal-Opportunity" Disease

One of the most popular items produced by the alcoholism movement is a poster entitled "The Typical Alcoholic American." It depicts a range of people from different ethnic, racial, and social groups, of different ages, and of both sexes. The point of the poster is that anyone from any background may be alcoholic—a point often driven home in educational programs about alcoholism. Strictly speaking, this idea can be true (although there are virtually no cases of adolescents who demonstrate a physical dependence on alcohol). But there are demographic categories that enhance the possibility of becoming alcoholic so significantly that it is hard to imagine that someone experienced with alcoholism would fail to notice these. Indeed, were it possible to isolate a measurable biological factor that distinguished those at risk for alcoholism as well as the drinker's sex, social class, ethnic background, and disadvantaged minority status, the discoverer of such a mechanism would win the Nobel Prize.

Epidemiologists such as Cahalan and Room have been able to predict extremely well which American men will develop drinking problems based purely on demographic categories: those who live in disadvantaged social settings, blacks and Hispanics, specific religious and ethnic groups, and certain social groups like young working-class men are highly predisposed to problem drinking. Sociologist Andrew Greeley led an investigation at the National Opinion Research Center into "ethnic drinking subcultures" around the country. He found that "there is overwhelming evidence of differences among American ethnic groups and drinking patterns, particularly among Italians, Jews, and Irish."[47] George Vaillant found that the Irish subjects in his study were *seven times* as likely to become alcoholic as their Italian neighbors. Moreover, Italians were more likely than others to moderate their drinking—rather than to abstain—after they *developed* a drinking problem. Vaillant described this Italian-Irish difference as follows: "It is consistent with Irish culture to see the use of alcohol in terms of black or white, good or evil, drunkenness or complete abstinence, while in Italian culture it is the distinction between moderate drinking and drunkenness that is most important."

Others, like James Milam in *Under the Influence*, have proposed farfetched racial theories to account for why the Irish, Indians, and other high-alcoholism groups more often become drunkards. Here, of course, the disease theory—developed to remove the stigma from alcoholism—starts sounding a lot more invidious. Are blacks and Hispanics and Indians and Eskimos in the United States really alcoholics more often because of inherited racial differences? Are lower-class or ghettoized or non-college-bound people really in these positions because of genetic differences that make them prone to drunkenness or criminality? Although proponents do not intend harm, such racial interpretations of human differences can be and have been used in prejudicial and very damaging ways.

Along with social and ethnic differences, gender differences in the incidence of alcoholism are monumental. In every type of measure, from drunk driving to treatment referrals to consumption levels, women display from one-third to one-tenth or less the drinking problems of men. No epidemiological research has ever disputed this fact. Yet contemporary alcoholism specialists frequently bemoan the large number of "hidden" women alcoholics who refuse to seek treatment because of the greater stigma attached to female drunkenness. In this view, *apparent* gender differences in alcoholism rates are the result of women and other groups with a reputation for fewer drinking problems underreporting their drinking problems because they are too ashamed to acknowledge their alcoholism.

Research has established that women with drinking problems are actually *more* likely to seek treatment than men, just as they seek more psychotherapy of every kind. In addition to the lower alcoholism rates for women in general, research finds that alcoholism occurs for middle-class women even less frequently. Once again, any summary of actual findings of research in an area of alcoholism reveals conclusions exactly the opposite of those presented to the public and maintained as gospel by the alcoholism movement. According to Barbara Lex, of the Harvard Medical School, in her exhaustive survey of alcoholism in special populations:

> The stereotype of the typical "hidden" female alcoholic as a middle-aged suburban housewife does not bear scrutiny. The highest rates of problem drinking are found among younger, lower-class women . . . who are single, divorced, or separated.[48]

Without an awareness of such fundamental ethnic, social, and gender differences, it is hard to imagine how a researcher or clinician can make sense out of the most elementary aspects of alcoholism.

Jews have been the object of a similar campaign to uncover hidden alcoholics, marked by the special shame they carry because they belong to a group that is not *supposed* to be alcoholic. Programs like the Chemical Dependency division of Jewish Family Services of Cleveland have energetically mounted campaigns "to deal with whole community denial and to emphasize that the disease can strike any member of the community."[49] In 1980, two sociologists—convinced that the number of Jewish alcoholics was increasing—conducted a survey of Jewish drinking in an upstate New York city. They found no sign that any of their eighty-eight respondents had ever abused alcohol. Following up leads from doctors, alcoholism counselors, and rabbis about Jewish alcoholics, the sociologists never actually located one. Nearly all these informants claimed to know of at most one or two Jewish alcoholics, and one—who reported, "There is an alarming problem with alcoholism in the Jewish community"—claimed that there were five in this city with about ten thousand Jews. In other words, the most dire, unsubstantiated claim was that the Jews in the city had an alcoholism rate of one-twentieth of one percent, or perhaps 0.1 percent of adults.[50]

Interviews by these researchers reveal that Jews have an extreme aversion to problem drinking and problem drinkers. They avoid people who drink too much and/or become obstreperous when they drink, and they make jokes about non-Jews' excessive drinking, embodied in the phrase "*shikker* [drunk] as a goy." What is more, non-Orthodox Jews in this study did not accept the disease theory of alcoholism. (It was actually Orthodox Jews, generally lower in socioeconomic status, who were more willing to believe in this disease.) In the words of the authors, "Reform and nonpracticing Jews define alcoholism in terms of psychological dependence and view suspected alcoholics with condemnation and blame."[51] If they suddenly were to accept the idea that problem drinking is the result of an unavoidable, inbred biological mechanism, one wonders if they would then begin to show the rates of alcoholism common to other ethnic groups in the United States!

The modern alcoholism movement insists that all people recognize that alcoholism is a disease, and it emphasizes the need for a value-free view of alcoholism. Jews and other groups with extremely low alcoholism rates (like the Chinese) avoid alcohol problems within a very different social context. These cultures divest alcohol of its magical powers and instead incorporate drinking in a low-key way in a family context where the young drink mild alcoholic beverages in the company of parents and older relatives. They disapprove strongly of overdrinking, especially when it leads to inappropriate behavior. There is a strong moralism here, but the moralism is not toward alcohol as evil incarnate; it is toward larger values of community, proper deportment, and self-control. Sociologist Milton Barnett describes the drinking in New York City's Chinatown:

> They drink and become intoxicated, yet for the most part drinking to intoxication is not habitual, dependence on alcohol is uncommon and alcoholism is a rarity. . . . The children drank, and they soon learned a set of attitudes that attended the practice. While drinking was socially sanctioned, becoming drunk was not. The individual who lost control of himself under the influence of liquor was ridiculed and, if he persisted in his defection, ostracized.

Barnett examined the police blotters in the Chinatown police district between the years 1933 and 1949; among 15,515 arrests, not one involved drunkenness.[52]

It's hard to understand what people mean when they discount cultural differences in alcoholism and insist that those groups with apparently low alcoholism rates are merely disguising their drinking problems out of shame. Sometimes they argue that they know an Italian alcoholic, or that there are French alcoholics in the Paris subways and Jewish alcoholics in Tel Aviv, or that some Jews have joined AA. *Yet there is no aspect of drinking and alcoholism more self-evident than that it varies tremendously across groups, particularly ethnic groups*. Indeed, Jellinek himself, in *The Disease Concept of Alcoholism*, was convinced that cultural differences are fundamental, major, and crucial to the nature of alcoholism.

When one sees a film like *Moonstruck*, the benign and universal nature of drinking in New York Italian culture is palpable on the screen. If one can't detect the difference between drinking in this setting, or at Jewish or Chinese weddings, or in Greek taverns, and that in Irish working-class bars, or in Portuguese bars in the worn-out industrial towns of New England, or in run-down shacks where Indians and Eskimos gather to get drunk, or in Southern bars where men down shots and beers—and furthermore, if one can't connect these different drinking settings, styles, and cultures with the repeatedly measured differences in alcoholism rates among these same groups, then I can only think one is blind to the realities of alcoholism.

# The Infallibility of AA and Medical Treatment for Alcoholism

Although alcoholism is billed as an *incurable* disease, we are told that there *is* effective medical treatment for it. Private treatment centers claim remarkable remission rates of 70, 80, and 90 percent. Meanwhile, Father Martin, the lecturing alcoholic priest, calls AA a "modern medical miracle," and one often hears claims that *everyone* who *seriously* embarks on an AA program will become sober. Along with television specials about the treatability of alcoholism, we now have a popular feature-length film, *Clean and Sober*, that trumpets the success and importance—the essentialness—of getting treated for alcohol and drug abuse.

Yet the research on treatment paints a very different picture. It has been remarkably hard to find systematic proof that treatment for alcoholism and other addictions accomplishes *anything at all*. The discrepancy between grandiose claims by treatment centers and the research results occurs because treatment centers cannot be counted on to do assessments of their programs that truly take into account the number of people who drop out of their programs; whether patients remain sober after leaving the treatment center; how different their patients are from average alcoholics (since well-off, employed, and middle-class patients have a superior prognosis under any circumstances); and how often people cut back or stop drinking on their own even if they don't enter treatment.

When researchers trace every case that enters treatment (including those who drop out) and compare treated populations with comparable groups of untreated alcoholics, the results often surprise even the treatment advocate. Consider George Vaillant's reactions to his research results for the patients he treated in Cambridge Hospital with an AA-based program:

It seemed perfectly clear that by meeting the immediate individual needs of the alcoholic . . . , by disregarding "motivation," by turning to recovering alcoholics rather than to Ph.D.'s for lessons in breaking self-detrimental and more or less involuntary habits, and by inexorably moving patients from dependence upon the general hospital into the treatment system of AA, I was working for the most exciting alcohol program in the world.

But then came the rub. Fueled by our enthusiasm, I . . . tried to prove our efficacy. Our clinic followed up our first 100 detoxification patients . . . every year for the next 8 years. . . . After initial discharge, only 5 patients in the Clinic sample *never* relapsed to alcoholic drinking, and there is *compelling evidence that the results of our treatment were no better than the natural history of the disease.* (emphasis added)[53]

What Vaillant did was to compare his treatment results over eight years with remission rates in "natural history" studies of alcoholics, in which drinking alcoholics were simply followed in their natural settings for a number of years. Certainly, a percentage of Vaillant's treated patients were not actively alcoholic when followed up eight years later. Only this percentage was not significantly different from that for untreated alcoholics. Remarkably, in this book that is cited as a beacon of defense for the often-assailed efficacy of medical treatment for alcoholism, the author—a research psychiatrist—reveals that alcoholics who are left to their own devices do about as well as did those in his expensive treatment program! Why, we may wonder, did Vaillant begin his book by indicating that "in order to *treat* alcoholics effectively we need to invoke the model of the medical practitioner"? (We may also wonder if Vaillant is any more skeptical about "turning to recovering alcoholics for lessons in breaking self-detrimental and more or less involuntary habits.")

Why does everyone believe AA and related treatments for alcoholism are so tremendously successful? The universal praise for AA focuses on its successes and disregards its failures, while we hear little about the successful recovery of those who don't attend AA. People who overcome drinking problems on their own, despite their numbers, are not an organized and visible group on the American alcoholism landscape. For example, George Vaillant found that many of his alcohol abusers cut back their drinking—nearly all without treatment. But even a solid majority of those among Vaillant's subjects who quit drinking altogether did not join AA. Yet not one of the successful cases of remission Vaillant highlights in his book involves a person who quit a drinking problem without AA or treatment—Vaillant simply ignores the bulk of his data when it comes to his case studies.

In order to evaluate a treatment's *general* effectiveness, research must assign patients randomly to different treatments and/or to a group that receives no treatment (called a control group). Two psychologists, William Miller and Reid Hester, reported every controlled study of alcoholism treatment—that is, studies that employed various treatment and no-treatment comparison groups.[54] These researchers discovered only two controlled studies of AA's effectiveness. Keith Ditman, a physician and head of the Alcoholism Research Clinic at UCLA in the 1960s, studied outcomes for three groups of alcoholics—those assigned by a court either to AA, to an alcoholism clinic, or to an untreated control group.[55] Forty-four percent of the control group were not rearrested in the follow-up period, compared with only 31 percent of AA clients and 32 percent of clinic clients. In the other controlled study of AA, Jeffrey Brandsma and his colleagues reported in 1980 that those randomly assigned to AA engaged in binge drinking significantly more frequently at three months than those assigned either to the nontreatment control group or to other therapies. (At twelve months they did as well, but no better, than the other groups.)[56]

Nor does comparative research find that group counseling sessions, such as those portrayed in the film *Clean and Sober*, are better for recovery than doing nothing. Three researchers have evaluated the most popular group technique in alcoholism and addiction treatment, confrontation therapy, in comparison with other group therapies, from transactional analysis to T-groups. Confrontation therapy is based on the Synanon "game," in which one member of the group at a time is put on the hot seat and has all his or her defenses shot down by other group members. While all the other group therapy techniques in this study came out even in the evaluations, confrontation therapy was found to produce the most significant negative outcomes, requiring psychiatric treatment for some group members.[57]

In addition to AA, group, and confrontation therapy, Miller and Hester found that alcoholism education, drug therapy, and individual alcoholism counseling have not shown positive results in controlled studies. However, the standard treatments for alcoholism in the United States consist entirely of these therapies for which Miller and Hester found no evidence of effectiveness! In the researchers' words, "American treatment of alcoholism follows a standard formula that appears impervious to emerging research evidence, and has not changed significantly for at least two decades." Miller and Hester's survey also showed that hospital (or inpatient) treatment is no better than far less expensive outpatient treatment.[58] As a 1987 *Science* article also indicated, a large body of research has established that intensity of treatment has no bearing on results. Instead, the *Science* article summarizes, the best predictors of patient outcome are the characteristics of the patient who enters the treatment.[59]

Miller and Hester did find a number of therapies that have shown better results than chance or natural recovery: therapy that conditions aversive reactions to drinking, behavioral self-control training, marital and family therapy, social skills training, and stress management. A therapy that showed particular effectiveness with a group of hospitalized alcoholics was the community reinforcement approach, which offered training in problem solving and job skills, behavioral family therapy, and social skills training. The community reinforcement approach would seem to address the natural processes that Vaillant found were the keys to remission in alcoholism. Yet the therapies that have been shown to be effective, like the community reinforcement approach, exist only in research studies and are not used as standard treatments practically anywhere in the United States.

In addition to the most effective types of treatment, another question is how we should measure the results of treatment. And the most controversial question of all in the alcoholism field is whether alcoholics can or should drink again, perhaps with the goal of moderating their drinking. In the United States (unlike most other countries), virtually no treatment centers allow nonabstinence alternatives. Nonetheless, all systematic treatment assessments (like Vaillant's) have found that nearly all alcoholics drink again following treatment and that some can sustain moderate drinking for long periods when they do drink again. At the same time, most alcoholics who drink again return to their previous levels of alcoholism. Is there some way to build upon the group who manages to continue drinking at less severe levels to get more of the alcoholics who perpetually relapse to moderate their drinking?

Dr. Edward Gottheil (who holds both an M.D. and a Ph.D. in psychology) of Jefferson Medical College reported that 33 to 59 percent of patients engaged in some moderate drinking during a two-year follow-up of alcoholism treatment at a VA hospital. Moreover, only 8 percent of this hospitalized group actually abstained throughout the two years. Gottheil commented:

> If the definition of successful remission is restricted to abstinence, these treatment centers cannot be considered especially effective and would be difficult to justify from cost-benefit analyses. If the remission criteria are relaxed to include . . . moderate levels of drinking, success rates increase to a more respectable range. . . . [Moreover] when the moderate drinking groups were included in the remission category, remitters did significantly and consistently better than non-remitters at subsequent follow-up assessments.[60]

Although Gottheil's findings about abstinence following treatment are typical, his conclusions are anything but acceptable in American alcoholism treatment. That is, studies that find hardly any remission due to strict abstinence criteria still refuse to consider the possibility that patients might improve while continuing to drink. One remarkable illustration of this is a highly publicized study by John Helzer, of the Washington University Department of Psychiatry, and his colleagues.[61] The most notorious result of this study, published in the prestigious *New England Journal of Medicine* and widely quoted in newspapers around the country, is that a minuscule *1.6 percent* of the alcoholics treated at a hospital subsequently became moderate drinkers.

In addition to the 1.6 percent of alcoholics who drank moderately and regularly throughout the three years of this study, an additional 4.6 percent of treated alcoholics drank moderately for up to thirty of those thirty-six months and abstained the rest of the time. In other words, these treated alcoholics drank moderately but not in *every* month of the three years; Helzer et al. therefore did not categorize them as moderate drinkers. Furthermore, the researchers discovered that 12 percent of treated alcoholics reported that they had had more than six drinks three times in one month in the previous three years but had had no drinking problems. The investigators were very careful to scrutinize any claims by patients that they had drunk without problems—the researchers questioned those who knew such

patients and checked hospital and police records. Nonetheless, despite the absence of information to contradict these former patients'
claims, the investigators decided that they were denying their continued alcoholic drinking.

Consider the overall results of the Helzer et al. study: 6 percent
of treated alcoholics never got drunk but drank lightly over the
previous three years; another 12 percent sometimes drank heavily
but reported no dependence symptoms and were not discovered to
have alcohol problems. Yet the researchers indicated that moderate
drinking by former alcoholics was next to impossible to attain. Clearly,
one might give these data a different cast. One could say that 18
percent of these hospitalized alcoholism patients drank sometimes
but were no longer drinking alcoholically (compared with the 15
percent who abstained). When the notorious Rand Report presented
almost exactly the same results in two studies in 1976 and 1980,[62]
the National Council on Alcoholism attempted to suppress the report
before publication and viciously attacked it in the press after it
appeared.[63]

Of course, we need to know what is best for the alcoholic patient
in assessing these data. That is, how well did these alcoholic patients
do, once these investigators discarded the possibility of moderate-
drinking outcomes? The overall prognosis for alcoholics treated in
the hospitals Helzer et al. studied was shockingly bad following
treatment. Before reciting these statistics, we must keep in mind that
not all alcoholic patients in Helzer et al.'s study actually received
alcoholism treatment; in fact, only one of four groups did. This group
had the lowest remission rate of the four! Twice as many alcoholic
patients treated in a medical-surgical ward were in remission from
alcoholism when assessed after treatment as those who actually received alcoholism treatment: only 7 percent of those in the alcoholism
treatment unit survived and were judged to be in remission from
five to eight years after treatment.

Thus, in a study widely taken to legitimize standard alcoholism
treatment in America, *less than 10 percent of those treated specifically for
alcoholism survived and were not drinking alcoholically five to eight years
after receiving treatment.* The percentage of alcoholics aided in recovery by the hospital treatment in this study is actually far smaller
than those Vaillant found when he examined natural-history studies
of alcoholism. In this sense, the parading of minimal moderate-

drinking outcomes in a setting where people were discouraged from believing they could moderate their drinking seems almost bizarre, as though the researchers and hospital staff were proud of eliminating one category of remission while finding they could not encourage any other. This is not the stuff of which announcements of great medical breakthroughs of the past were made.

# The Catch-22 of Denial

What if you are told you are an alcoholic and that you must abstain for life, and you don't agree? Then you are, according to treatment wisdom, practicing denial. Many, many people have been told they drink too much or that they are alcoholic. Scott Peck, a psychiatrist and author of the book *The Road Not Taken*, once remarked in an interview in *People* magazine that he regularly drank at home in the evening and that as a result he had had to deal with accusations that he was an alcoholic. After careful consideration, Peck rejected this idea. Many people without Peck's confidence, however, may eventually accept others' characterizations of their drinking or drug use. If, on the other hand, they continue to disagree with such diagnoses, this denial can then be used as *evidence* that they are really alcoholic or addicted. Modern treatment philosophy insists that denial is a keystone of alcoholism and must be attacked before recovery can occur.

Yet we have seen that people from different cultural backgrounds and with varied personal experiences may view drinking and alcoholism very differently. The picture of different views of alcoholism does not indicate that those who don't accept that they have a "disease" should be attacked and converted to a particular treatment's point of view. Nonetheless, the standard approach in the alcoholism movement is to bombard problem drinkers with the disease message until their previous beliefs are exorcised and, thus purified, they can join the movement. Often this approach backfires, since people tend to reject communications that attack their existing self-conceptions. But if people should refuse or drop out of or fail at treatment, then the supposedly benign model that alcoholism is a disease blames the drinkers for their failures—after all, they were told not to drink.

A group of studies have questioned people about their beliefs about drinking problems for which they are seeking treatment and their goals for treatment. In direct opposition to the denial hypothesis, three research teams in Britain have all found that problem drinkers' beliefs that they are capable of moderating their drinking and their lack of involvement in previous abstinence training are crucial factors in managing to control their drinking.[64] Those more oriented toward abstinence succeed better at totally abstaining. These British findings held for drinkers *no matter how dependent on alcohol they were.* In other words, people respond best to treatment that builds on their existing perceptions and experiences. This model applies as well, of course, to the people who are comfortable in AA.

Whether people seek help at all for a drinking problem is another decision steeped in people's views of themselves and the world. Barry Tuchfeld interviewed former alcoholics who had quit or reduced their drinking on their own.[65] Most had simply refused to seek help from some outside agency like AA or a therapist:

I'd never consider going to a doctor or minister for help. Good Lord, no! That would make me drink twice as much.

The one thing I could never do is go into formal rehab. For me to have to ask somebody else to help with a self-made problem, I'd rather drink myself to death.

I would sit there and listen to their stories . . . and I couldn't fit myself into their patterns.

Certainly there are people who say they are going to improve on their own and don't do so. But in the cases Tuchfeld investigated, people found their own routes to recovery and made them work. On the other hand, there are also those in treatment who claim they are trying to abstain or that they are abstaining but who are not. One cannot compare the imperfections of those rejecting treatment or trying to cut back their drinking with some rose-colored idea that all those who *go* to treatment are successfully abstaining. As Griffith Edwards, Britain's leading addiction researcher, asserts: "the number of times members have 'slipped' since joining AA [the majority of his AA subjects had done so] serves to emphasize that AA is as much a society of alcoholics who are having difficulty in remaining sober as it is one in which they are staying off drink."[66]

## And Researchers Who Deny the "Truths" of Alcoholism Must Be Crazy Too

While problem drinkers may be assailed for denying the "truths" about alcoholism—particularly that they need treatment—researchers in the field who deny these truths can encounter even more trouble. (I think I can speak from personal experience about this.) Psychologists and psychiatrists who have practiced controlled-drinking therapy and sociologists who report moderate drinking by hospital patients who have been *told* to abstain have had their funding suspended, have been castigated and vilified in the press, and have been accused by treatment spokespeople of causing the deaths of many alcoholics.[67] When a study was published by the Rand Corporation reporting that a strong minority of treated alcoholics return to drinking but reduce or eliminate their drinking problems, one critic reported that he had "learned that some alcoholics have resumed drinking as a result of . . . the Rand study" and that "this could mean death or brain damage for these individuals."[68] The implication was that perhaps such researchers should be jailed.

Consider, on the other hand, the following description of the Rand results in the 1985 book *Alcohol Use and Abuse in America* by Jack Mendelson and Nancy Mello:

> There have been an increasing number of clinical reports that some former alcoholics can drink socially and function well for periods of two and one-half to eleven years. Many clinicians have reported that alcoholics who drink moderately are better adjusted and have better social functioning than ex-alcoholic abstainers. Despite this gradually accumulating data base, the 1976 publication of . . . the Rand Report was responded to with outrage by many self-appointed spokesmen for the alcoholism treatment community. . . . When this national sample was followed again after four years, there were no significant differences in relapse rates between alcohol abstainers and nonproblem drinkers. . . .

It is of some interest to compare the presumed data base for Jellinek's original formulation of the notion of "craving" and "loss of control" [with that of the Rand study]. . . . Jellinek was an American pioneer in alcoholism studies. In 1946, Jellinek analyzed responses to a questionnaire circulated by Alcoholics Anonymous and concluded from the 98 responses received that "loss of control means that as soon as a small quantity of alcohol enters the organism . . . the drinker has lost the ability to control the quantity [he will drink]." . . . [In comparison, researchers] at the Rand Corporation chose a representative random sample of 14,000 clients . . . of geographically and demographically diverse patients.[69]

Yet the Rand data are disregarded and Jellinek's work is gospel in the alcoholism field. Mendelson and Mello are preeminent alcoholism researchers and editors of the most important journal in the alcoholism field (the *Journal of Studies on Alcohol*). However, few lay people or treatment professionals know of their views. For reasons that may by now be clear, those sympathetic to nondisease viewpoints in the United States present their ideas gingerly. As a result, the dogma that alcoholism is a disease goes unquestioned. George Vaillant, despite his own contrary data, simply quotes another disease-theory spokesperson:

The American Medical Association, American Psychiatric Association, American Public Health Association, American Hospital Association, American Psychological Association, National Association of Social Workers, World Health Organization, and the American College of Physicians have now each and all officially pronounced alcoholism as a disease. The rest of us can do no less.[70]*

Where has all this unanimity about alcoholism led us? We certainly don't seem to be eliminating alcoholism, despite multiplying again and again the money, effort, and people we invest in treatment and education. For one thing, many people refuse or drop out of treatment or relapse (like Joan Kennedy, who is far more typical of outcomes from treatment than Betty Ford). We rarely hear from the many people who fail at conventional treatments. Nor do we hear

---

*This statement is wrong in at least one particular: although the National Council on Alcoholism regularly reports that the American Psychological Association (APA) has taken the position that alcoholism is a disease, the APA has in fact never done so.

from those who refuse to enter treatment—except as dreaded examples of the phenomenon of "denial." We also don't hear much on public service announcements from those who moderate their drinking or, heaven forbid, their drug use. When Kareem Abdul Jabbar mentioned in his 1983 autobiography, *Giant Steps*, that he used drugs in college, reviewers were highly critical. But if he had lost control, become addicted, and been suspended from basketball while he entered treatment, he could have become a role model for our children.

# 4

# Transforming the Addict into a Role Model, and the Person into an Addict

[I was] a high-risk person out of an alcoholic family system and an uncomfortable person, somebody without self-esteem and lots of guilt and lots of anger. Alcohol relieved that discomfort and a process began that eventually developed into the disease of alcoholism. As a high-risk person that became a victim of the disease of alcoholism I was interested in other people that became alcoholics. I married an alcoholic. We created an even worse family system than the one I had come out of because neither of us were suitable as parents. We knew nothing about parenting, we knew nothing about developing a good relationship with one another, we knew nothing about trust. We knew no way to handle our confusion and our anger and anxieties except to drink.

—Monica Wright, director,
Breakthrough Alcoholism Treatment Program

## *Who* Is Denying the Truth?

M ONICA WRIGHT'S story would not seem to be much of a recommendation for a person who educates people about dealing with alcoholism and who directs an alcoholism treatment center. The television program on which she described her drinking introduced Monica in this way:

This woman spent almost 20 years of her life as an alcoholic. Her father and both grandfathers were alcoholics. Four out of six [of her] children once had drug or alcohol problems. Is alcoholism inherited, is it a chemical addiction and what's the best way to treat an alcoholic? How do you get someone to acknowledge he or she is an alcoholic in the first place?[1]

In the view of this program, Monica Wright's alcoholism was an unavoidable inheritance. Once she acknowledged she was an alcoholic (unfortunately, only after she had completed much of her adult life as a wife and parent), she had her alcoholism treated and now could lead other people in the right direction. She has been transformed in a way that makes her a role model for anyone else who has a drinking problem or worries about a loved one with a drinking problem.

Yet we have seen that the views of alcoholism put forward by this well-meaning TV program are dubious in every regard. They cannot in any case account for how Monica Wright became an alcoholic: even the genetic theories this TV program endorsed do not propose that women can inherit alcoholism (in the genetic sense) from their fathers and grandfathers. What are the consequences of this view of alcoholism for Monica Wright and other alcoholics, for people who listen to her, and for the society at large? Herbert Fingarette, a legal and moral philosopher, has written about the disease theory of alcoholism:

Instead of encouraging those concerned to see the drinking in the context of the person's way of life, and thus to discern what role or roles it may play for that person in coping with life, the logic of the disease concept does the contrary. It leads all concerned, including the drinker, to deny, to ignore, to discount what meaning that way of life may have. Seen as an involuntary symptom of a disease, the drinking is isolated from the rest of life, and viewed as the meaningless but destructive effect of a noxious condition, a "disease."[2]

What the disease theory does accomplish is to excuse—for herself and others—the guilt and anxiety that Wright's drunken career engenders. This excuse making may help someone tolerate the consequences of her behavior which otherwise she could not endure and may help her pull a life together (often, as in Monica Wright's case, one gone very far down the road). This is different from saying that the disease model is an accurate, scientific, or helpful description of alcoholism. For subscribing to the disease concept also has negative consequences.

The disease model has been sold, through treatment and the media, to drinkers and drug users with problems of all degrees of severity, until the expenditures on advertising and treating alcoholism and drug abuse are several billion dollars a year. Nonetheless, all indicators are that drug and alcohol problems have worsened in this time, that treatment has as many negative effects as positive, and that most people do not respond well to the kinds of messages the disease theory lays on them. In addition, despite its drawbacks, the disease model of addiction has been generalized to entirely new areas of behavior, behaviors that have nothing to do with drugs or alcohol; at the same time, the disease model is increasingly forced on people. This is necessary, in the view of the disease theory, because so many people "deny" their alcoholism and other addictions.

In fact, the unbelievability of the disease theory may be the biggest reason it is so often denied. One man, a physicist, told me about a trip he went on with a group of people, including a new AA indoctrinee. The alcoholic told his companions that tasting alcohol—even if it were in a rum cake—would lead him to an alcoholic binge. The other members of the party didn't believe him and mixed some liquor in his soft drink, a deception of which he never became aware! Of course, this deception replicates actual experiments and proves that lay people who don't believe popular claims about alcoholism are simply displaying good sense. At the same time, these "experimenters" also played a cruel hoax, and the alcoholic might well have drunk more if he had found out what his cohorts had done, since it is awareness of drinking, rather than alcohol, that causes such relapse.

The father of a family of three girls got drunk regularly throughout the girls' childhoods. They all dreaded the fights that broke out between their parents while their father peered out the windshield as he drove home down some country road at fifteen miles an hour. As adults, the women entertained their father at their homes and found that they could give him a few drinks at dinner and keep him happy, as long as they kept the bottle at their end of the table. Controlling their father's drinking in this artificial way proved to them that their father couldn't be an alcoholic, since they knew that alcoholics can't control their drinking! By taking seriously the alcoholism movement's message, these women misdiagnosed what would clearly be called alcoholism by any reasonable judgment.

Of all the ideas presented by the alcoholism movement, that of denial—which means that the drinker doesn't agree with what the alcoholism movement or treatment personnel tell him or her—has the most malicious potential. The concept of denial has been applied in very broad ways to explain nearly every failure of people to conform to the diagnosis or prognosis laid out for them. To consider just one remarkable case: Janet Woititz, whose book *Adult Children of Alcoholics* became a publishing phenomenon, conducted her Ph.D. research on the treatment of children of alcoholics. What Woititz actually discovered was that children of alcoholics who attended Alateen had *lower* self-esteem that those who did not attend. Woititz explains:

> Thoughtful analysis of the data and an understanding of the alcoholic family pattern can help explain this result. Denial is a part of the disease both for the alcoholic and his family. . . . This researcher suggests that the non-Alateen group scores significantly higher than the Alateen group scores because the non-Alateen children are still in the process of denial.[3]

According to Woititz, it only *seems* that children of alcoholics have higher self-esteem when they don't enter treatment, but they are actually *denying* their low self-esteem. Woititz is confident, however, that the children will be better off when this artificial self-esteem is stripped away.

# Becoming an Alcoholic: How People Learn What Is Wrong with Them

Since problem drinkers deny things that in fact are mostly untrue (for example, that they can never control their drinking), their denial is entirely justified. What is actually more remarkable is that people become convinced that the disease theory is true, given their own disconfirming experiences. Most people must be converted to the treatment and AA view in order to discount their previous perceptions and identities and to learn that they are alcoholics and (after they stop drinking) recovering alcoholics. They then become the very visible group of people we see on TV or lecturing at schools that alcoholism is a disease, that this knowledge saved their lives, and that everyone else with drinking problems must enter treatment to learn what they have discovered.

How do people become convinced about things that they didn't believe about themselves until they came to treatment? David Rudy, a sociologist, participated as a nonalcoholic observer in AA meetings for over a year. His investigation revealed

> that how AA members came to define themselves as alcoholics, how they talk about their alcoholism, and how alcoholic designations organize and give meaning to their lives are all important in becoming alcoholic. AA members are different from other alcoholics, not because there are more "gamma alcoholics" or "alcohol addicts" in AA, but because they come to see themselves and to reconstruct their lives by utilizing the views and ideology of AA.[4]

For example, disease-theory pioneer Elvin Jellinek proposed that blackout is an essential early sign of alcoholic drinking. Yet as Kaye Fillmore has shown, college drinkers who black out most often keep drinking but stop blacking out as they emerge into the adult world. Other research has shown that many hospitalized alcoholics have never experienced a blackout and that those who had usually did so well after they had become alcoholic, and not en route.[5]

Rudy described new AA members exploring the question of whether they ever blacked out. At AA,

> members learn the importance of blackouts as a behavior that verifies their alcoholism, and an indeterminable number of members who may not have had blackouts report them. When newcomers to AA claim that they cannot remember if they had any blackouts or not, other members use this claim as evidence of the event in question. As one member put it to a newcomer: "The reason you can't remember is because alcohol fogs your brain."

This is one example of the catch-22s of AA and alcoholism treatment. Another is the person who claims in treatment that he or she is not an addict or alcoholic and who thus proves that he or she is "in denial." Those in AA who refuse to acknowledge they are alcoholics are hooted down or else treated with a kind of knowing condescension until they get their views of themselves and alcoholism straightened out. As described by irrepressible *San Francisco Chronicle* columnist Charles McCabe, a friend of his from San Carlos went to an AA meeting to find out what it had to offer:

> The first thing that impressed him was this routine, which is by now familiar even to non-alkies. A guy gets up and says, "My name is Harry, and I'm an alcoholic." The faithful say, "Hi, Harry." He then goes into a little number about how he ruined his life, the life of his wife, mother, father, sons and the people who worked for him.
>
> "I was the last one in the circle," my friend said. "I couldn't say THAT, because it would be a lie. And then the answer came to me. When it came my turn I said: 'My name is Herb,' and before they could say anything I continued: 'And I am NOT an alcoholic, I am an Episcopalian drunk.' "
>
> Herb thought it was funny. He still does. But THEY didn't. With perhaps a bit of hyperbole he says, "I consider myself lucky to have got out of there alive."[6]

Rudy noted a speech given by a member to new affiliates at AA:

> If you think you have a problem, or if you think you are an alcoholic, I assure you that you are. You wouldn't be thinking about it and you wouldn't be here if you weren't an alcoholic.

The author commented, "Moderate drinkers, individuals with problems in living, and the present author have been offered or have qualified for the alcoholic role." Typical ads for treatment claim, "If you think you have a problem then you have one," and, "a drinking problem can only get worse"—both of which translate into "you are an alcoholic, you need treatment or AA to be saved, and you must never drink again." By these criteria, a remarkable number of people can be classified as alcoholics.

Yet many people with drinking problems refuse to believe they are alcoholics or seek treatment. In good part this is because they simply do not have the extreme drinking problems that are sometimes portrayed as the hallmark of alcoholism—the kind of complete abandonment of control that the Ray Milland character displayed in *The*

*Lost Weekend,* for example. We saw in chapter 2 that Robin Room and other epidemiologists have found that about 1 percent of the general population drinks as much as those in treatment.[7] However, Room's estimate was based purely on high levels of consumption. When researchers at the Alcohol Research Group examined instead the percentage of respondents in general surveys who had the kinds of drinking problems typical of clinical alcoholics, the apparent number of alcoholics in the general population dropped dramatically. Indeed, almost no drinkers in surveys show the alcoholism syndrome reported by those who come to treatment.

If it is almost exclusively those who are *already* in treatment who state that they have had the full array of alcoholic symptoms—like blackouts, loss of control, and progressively worsening drinking problems—then not much effort has to be put into recruiting new alcoholics. Early AA members did not believe an active campaign to convince people they were alcoholics was necessary.[8] They recognized that only a very small group of people shared their drinking problems. Today, those who have been in treatment or in AA are likely to claim that so few people with drinking problems report all the symptoms of alcoholism because these people are in denial (as were they themselves before they entered treatment). Yet the problem drinkers interviewed in the surveys Room reviewed confessed to all sorts of drinking problems, including wife beating (the single most common problem—reported by 14 percent of men—was frequent intoxication; the most common problem for women was impaired health—reported by 4 percent of female respondents). Why did they admit to these problems but not to the consistent list of symptoms the disease theory says they must have had?

Is it really possible that many alcoholics and addicts have to learn their symptoms in treatment? In fact, treatment programs make no bones about the need to educate addicts and alcoholics about the nature of their disease. The treatment *is* learning the disease viewpoint, combined with group sessions in which people describe their problems and are applauded when they admit these are signs of their disease. Successful completion of treatment means accepting that they are addicts or alcoholics and vowing never to drink or take a drug again. We read every day about recent graduates of such programs who tell how they learned to recite the disease theory, even when it doesn't make sense to them. Gary McLain, a basketball player who made the cover of *Sports Illustrated* when he was caught stealing and then confessed to his cocaine use, describes his disease education (one that closely parallels the nineteenth-century temperance lecture "The Fatal Glass of Beer"):

> I was shocked. . . . I'd have to give up *everything*. I did enjoy my beer every now and then. . . . It was easier to accept this after I learned about what they called progression. Someone treated for cocaine addiction might drink a beer because he thinks that's okay. But progression—beer first, then hard liquor, maybe marijuana next—will eventually lead the person back to the drug of choice. That made a lot of sense. The people at White Deer had seen enough relapses to make me believe it.[9]

In this description, McLain indicates that he was never a problem drinker, but that now he has learned that drinking is actually part of his disease. The proof is that so many people in his treatment program relapsed after they had a beer. Here, the very failures of disease treatment are cited as proof of the effectiveness of its prescription. In other words, when people who have been in treatment drink again (as they do far more often than not), they often experience a full-fledged relapse. Yet McLain never had this problem *before* he entered treatment. If McLain, now in his early twenties, does drink a beer following treatment, he is likely to relapse *to the extent that he accepts* the disease message he has learned. Disease treatment in this way actually *attacks* patients' existing feelings of self-control.

## The Drawbacks of Deciding One Is an Alcoholic or an Addict

Other famous athletes have been more reluctant to take on the disease message. Dwight Gooden, the Mets' star pitcher, was sent to a residential program when he tested positive for cocaine at the beginning of the 1987 season. After he was released, Gooden indicated that he was not actually addicted and that he never took the drug while pitching. "When he was asked how he could regulate the use of cocaine after taking it in the winter, he said: 'I wasn't addicted, so I was able to lay off it during the baseball season.' " Meanwhile,

A MODERN TREATMENT ANTI-MIRACLE—TURNING BREAD INTO
STONE: HOW KITTY DUKAKIS BECAME AN ALCOHOLIC AFTER A
LIFETIME OF MODERATE DRINKING

In February 1989, three months after he lost the presidential election, Michael Dukakis announced in a press conference that his wife, Kitty, was entering the Edgehill-Newport hospital in Rhode Island for treatment for alcohol abuse. His wife, he reported, clearly had drunk too much "two or three times" since the election in November. In March, when she left the hospital, Kitty Dukakis gave a press conference in which she declared herself an alcoholic while repeating the essential facts about her drinking that her husband had reported. The Dukakises and their friends and political associates all noted that Kitty had drunk lightly—typically wine with meals—her entire life.

How did a woman who got drunk several times at the age of fifty-two discover she was an alcoholic? In 1982, Kitty Dukakis had been treated at Hazelden in Minnesota for her addiction to prescribed amphetamines, which she used for weight control. (Kitty Dukakis provided this information in a press conference during the campaign.) At the point when his wife's subsequent treatment began, Michael Dukakis said that her previously diagnosed chemical dependence meant that Kitty could not control her drinking. When she left the hospital, Kitty—who had lectured widely about chemical dependence based on the success of her treatment at Hazelden—now said she had failed to learn one thing when she was treated seven years earlier: being chemically dependent meant she could never drink again.

Thus a woman who had drunk moderately all her life found out in treatment that she couldn't drink without losing control. This claim was based on the evidence that she drank excessively after an exhausting, negative political campaign in which her husband was successfully portrayed to the American public as, among other things, stiff and unfeeling. Having now learned *everything* about her chemical dependence, Kitty Dukakis promised to write an autobiography and continue lecturing to others about how they should deal with their drug and alcohol problems.

Despite the confidence they now express in their complete understanding of their situation, the Dukakises have revealed substantial gaps in their self-knowledge in their various press conferences. For one thing, that Kitty was addicted to amphetamines for twenty-six years without her husband's knowledge suggests a certain lack of communication or awareness in the marriage. Was Kitty afraid to tell her husband that she felt it necessary to diet constantly in order to share the public limelight with him? What anxieties made her feel too fat, made her afraid she couldn't control her eating on her own, and made her afraid to discuss all these things with her husband for over two decades?

Likewise, Kitty Dukakis seemed to be reeling after the election—as most of us would after what she went through—while her husband returned to work the day after his loss. As a result, Kitty grieved alone, and drinking was one way she used to allay her pain. It is uncomfortable to point out the flaws in troubled public figures like the Dukakises, but we must question their public-relations announcements about their lives. To accept these self-congratulatory, self-deceptive messages is to undermine an individual's or couple's ability to come to grips with both substance abuse and relationship problems.

---

Gooden did learn in treatment that "once you take it the first time, you're starting to be addicted." In other words, treatment in this case was administered for "starting to be addicted" (for which all the 25 million Americans who have taken cocaine are presumably liable). Gooden reported, "I cried a lot before I went to bed at night. It was embarrassing because whether you had a problem or not, you're there."[10]

The center at which Gooden was treated (the Smithers Alcoholism Center) was featured in an article in the *New York Times*.[11] Inmates regularly attend confrontation groups at Smithers. (Recall that no study has shown the benefits of such groups to be better than not receiving treatment, and that one study found significant negative outcomes resulted from group confrontation therapy.) The article described how inmates whose stories seemed too tame were "immediately upbraided by other members of the group." A training tape for staff members showed one inmate who listed some pale symptoms. The man was remonstrated by other members of the group: "If that was all that happened to me, I wouldn't be here." The same thing happened to Gooden, who could only describe using cocaine at parties. "My stories weren't as good. . . . They said, 'C'mon, man, you're lying.' They didn't believe me."

Gooden's failure to accept the party line (the way Gary McLain claimed to have) led to subsequent headlines like GOODEN IS FOCUS OF CONCERN: DRINKS BEER DESPITE ADVICE.

> "I take a couple of beers," Gooden said, when asked about his personal habits. "Not every day. I know the people at Smithers tell you to stay away from everything—beer, whiskey, chewing tobacco, everything. But beer's not a problem with me."[12]

This led to a rather remarkable analysis by Gooden's psychiatrist, an associate director of the Smithers program who sometimes accompanied Smithers's star patient on Mets road trips:

> The AA program at Smithers favors abstinence. But you don't find it that way all the time. You'd have an easier time if you did. But you cope if you don't.

This man seems to recognize controlled drinking and substance use, even by those who have been in treatment!

Those who are converted wholly to the AA disease view, on the other hand, have decided that everything associated with their lives while they were drinking or taking drugs was wasted and bad. They may try to give up all these things, including jobs, friends, and wives. In this way, they hope to eliminate the stress points in life.

Such life problems, however, very often resurface. At these times, of course, recovering drinkers rely on group support. Many feel they can never leave the group, and they attend meetings so frequently that involvements with people other than fellow addicts are almost impossible. With their lives rigidly arranged in this fashion, they are indeed highly susceptible to relapse whenever they encounter the slightest disruption of their routine. The *cure* for alcoholism or addiction can thus come full circle—limiting the person's activities and acquaintances just the same as when he or she drank or took drugs constantly.

Those in recovery don't recognize such problems. Now that they have understood their alcoholism or addiction, they feel their lives are better in every way. This is certainly a convenient set of beliefs for those who have accepted the new identity, but it is one not always supported by the evidence. Since 1980 a number of professional athletes have either entered treatment or testified about their drug use—for example, at the trial of Curtis Strong, a caterer who supplied baseball players like Keith Hernandez and Dave Parker with drugs. The stories told by various ball players are interesting because baseball, a game of statistics, allows us to check these tales against actual numbers.

A central figure in the baseball cocaine case was Lonnie Smith, who turned himself in for treatment for cocaine addiction in 1983. Although Smith made a strong comeback in the major leagues in 1989, it seemed as though he had to overcome his treatment in order to do so. His descriptions of how bad his life had been before treatment, and how good immediately afterward, were not borne out by the statistics. Smith batted .321 in the year he sought treatment. He explained, however, that this was misleading: "Look at my defense. It seemed like I was averaging two or three errors a game. I was getting picked off. Everything I swung at was away."[13] Smith hit more pitches, "away" or not, than at any other time in his career. He did make a lot of errors in 1983, although not two or three a game. He made fifteen in 130 games, or one in every nine games he played, which led the league. However, this statistic must be placed in context: Smith made a lot of errors and got picked off a lot throughout his career. The next year, when he was presumably free from drugs, Smith tied for the league error lead. Indeed, up to that point, Smith had never played a full year in the minor or major leagues without leading or tying for the error lead. (He held a total of seven such titles.)

In 1985, after being traded to Kansas City, although he did not play a full year for the team, Smith led the league in being picked off. But what was worse was his drop in batting performance. After batting .321 during his drug-addicted year and over .300 in his previous three years in the majors, Smith dropped to .250 the year after he was treated (1984). He had problems recovering his batting eye and dropped to the minor leagues before returning to the majors in 1989. This has occurred for other treated stars, such as Alan Wiggins of the San Diego Padres, who relapsed after being treated and never regained his previous level of performance, at either San Diego or Baltimore, where he was subsequently traded. Steve Howe, the Los Angeles Dodger pitcher, relapsed several times after treatment and couldn't stick with the Dodgers or with Minnesota.

What makes the indifferent careers of these players after treatment more notable is the continued star performance of several players who had stopped taking drugs on their own. At drug dealer Strong's trial, Keith Hernandez and Dave Parker reported that they had used cocaine heavily but had stopped. Both of these players continued to perform at or near their previous levels. In 1985, for instance, the year of the Strong trial, Parker batted .312 with 125 RBIs and 34 homers, and he had 116 RBIs and 31 homers in 1986. Hernandez batted .309 in 1985 and .310 in 1986, while leading the New York Mets to a World Championship. In one case, the Yankees dropped a pitcher who at the time had successfully completed treatment— Rod Scurry (Scurry has since been arrested for drug use)—in favor of Al Holland, whose previous untreated cocaine use came out in testimony during the Strong trial.

These statistics and anecdotes do not bear out the morality tale that those who seek treatment invariably succeed and those who do not invariably fail. And those who go untreated improve at much less cost to themselves and their teams. What, then, is the purpose of treatment? It is a way for management to deal with players who take drugs (and no matter what it is called, being put in treatment and forbidden to play is a punishment), it provides the team and the player an excuse for the player's misconduct, and it allows everyone to go back to business after a respectable time, when treatment is over. If the player doesn't quit drugs or booze until after disappearing from sports, like Thomas "Hollywood" Henderson (football) and Derek Sanderson (hockey), graduating treatment gives them post-athletic careers as drug and alcoholism experts.

Meanwhile, some players, such as Howe in baseball, Micheal Ray Richardson in basketball, Bob Probert in hockey, and Stanley Wilson in football, become constant recidivists, even after repeatedly undergoing treatment. Just as many players relapse—and relapse regularly—as stay off alcohol or drugs after treatment. Yet those who relapse are never calculated as treatment failures or give pause to anyone about whether the treatment is effective and perhaps some other approach should be tried—at least for these particular individuals. Meanwhile, those who succeed at treatment give speeches and write autobiographies to describe the incredible miracle of treatment, while relapsers who haven't been to treatment—like footballer Lawrence Taylor—then blame not having been to treatment for their failures.

Of course, we hear little about the success Parker, Hernandez, and others had in quitting drugs on their own; these stories are almost completely ignored. Indeed, Hernandez testified in court *that 40 percent of major league baseball players were using cocaine in 1980, almost none of whom needed treatment or came to the attention of the authorities.* Obviously, such players are not overeager to inform the public that they took drugs and then quit, and so we'll never hear their stories. Unsaddled with a public and self-image as alcoholic or addict, they are free to rejoin the normal world of unlabeled people—many far better off for being allowed to resume this role of normalcy. Keith Hernandez—although reporting that he "went crazy" on cocaine in the early 1980s—strongly rejected the contention in court that "once an addict, always an addict."[14]

Thus Keith Hernandez could happily down champagne after winning his World Series with the Mets. Darrel Porter presents an alternate image when, after being treated for alcohol and drug abuse, he shrank away from the alcohol his Cardinal teammates were splashing around during their 1982 League Championship and World Series celebrations. (Hernandez was also drinking in those locker rooms.) Porter, incidentally, is a case of retrogression following treatment as bad as Smith's, only Porter's performance never recovered. He batted .291 with twenty home runs for Kansas City in 1979, before seeking treatment in the spring of 1980. In the 1980 season, Porter batted

.249 with seven homers, and the next year, after joining the Cardinals, he batted .224 and had six homers. Although Porter had a good World Series in 1982, he never came close to his 1979 season achievements once he was treated.

# The Addicted Self-Image

Porter and others illustrate another facet of the limitations of treatment. Even when they don't relapse after treatment, they often seem burdened with their alcoholic or addicted self-image to a degree that hinders their functioning. Treatment and lifelong abstinence often take a toll on people's lives. George Vaillant found that most men achieve abstinence by adopting other compulsions—some benign, but others habits that can be as consuming and destructive as drinking. AA meetings are notorious for their smoke-filled atmosphere and the amount of coffee that members consume. Moreover, as in the case of Lonnie Smith, reformed alcoholics and addicts are able to use their addicted identity to explain all their previous problems without actually doing anything concrete to improve their performance. Others, like McLain, can excuse their misconduct—stealing, in McLain's case, or in Hollywood Henderson's, statutory rape.

There are benefits if the person can avoid this lifelong albatross of considering himself an alcoholic or explaining or excusing all misconduct as being due to an addiction. Steve Martin, the comedian, described on the *Tonight Show* how he began drinking heavily in his early years as a comedian, when he was having trouble getting an audience. He even started downing a number of glasses of gin during his act! He then described how he stopped this habit and now drank only wine at meals and on special occasions. We don't see Martin at alcoholism testimonials or in ads for treatment centers. In his hit movie *Roxanne*, Martin comfortably showed alcohol being consumed moderately in group celebrations and meals where people shared positive feelings about one another and the occasion.

Why do those who have been through treatment uncritically acclaim their therapy, even though they know the limitations of such treatment and even though many people with the same problems succeed without treatment? To understand this phenomenon, consider a man who licked another drug addiction—smoking—through the Smokenders program. Following treatment, he formed a support group with three other graduates to maintain their abstinence. After two years, all but this one man had started smoking again. But the man was adamant: joining Smokenders was the only way to quit smoking and anybody who tried to quit on his own was a fool! Yet even his own data are that three out of four of those who successfully completed the program relapsed. What is more, 40 million Americans have now quit smoking, and *95 percent have done so without treatment*; surely this man had run into *one* smoker who quit on his or her own.[15]

Of course, the man condemned those who would try to quit by themselves because this fact challenged his personal cure. The ideas that people can't quit drugs, drink, or cigarettes on their own and that a particular program is fantastically successful are not statements of fact. These are statements about people's own experiences: *they couldn't quit*—or, more accurately, didn't quit—until they entered the program. Quitting the habit thus is inextricably connected in their minds with a particular program's methods; belief in these methods seems to them essential for quitting. To accept that many people use other means to quit an addiction, or that they themselves might have quit some other way, or that many who have been through the same program as they have did not stay off drugs or cigarettes could endanger their *own* cures.

## A Special Case: The Young

All these factors make the remarkable growth in disease identification among the young especially disturbing. The young are a special target for drug and alcohol treatment. Generally, this treatment is initiated involuntarily, based on the discovery—or suspicion—that the child has used drugs. CompCare and other organizations teach school counseling staffs how to conduct "interventions" with such children, during which the children are surrounded by counselors, parents, teachers, and cooperative friends who convince them that they are dependent and must immediately seek treatment.

Based on such coercive and self-serving "diagnoses" of dependence, children enter a program whose entire basis is to convince them they suffer from a permanent malady that makes them forever different from everybody else. Although, in fact, most would quit drugs or cut back their drinking on their own, they are saddled with a lifetime identity of addict or alcoholic, one that—to the extent they believe it—they cannot escape. This indoctrination process has been used frequently by religious and political groups, but only now is it appearing as a regular tool in modern therapy for young people. An enormous number of children are now undergoing experiences like these; hospitalization of adolescents increased 350 percent between 1980 and 1984 due to drug referrals,[16] and the fastest growth in AA membership is among the young. Between 1968 and 1986, the percentage of AA members under age thirty (including substantial numbers of teens) tripled, until they are now between a fifth and a quarter of all members.[17]

Treatment personnel are not the least bit self-conscious about recommending that young people be forced into treatment, often on the vaguest diagnoses and flimsiest evidence. The following case is one of several presented as illustrations in the Alcoholism Council of Greater New York's *Update* magazine for treatment professionals. The article celebrates the new discovery that parents' drinking problems affect their children, so that unwilling children must themselves be placed in treatment:

> Jason, a sixteen-year-old boy with serious motivational problems, was brought in by his parents because of failing grades. His alcoholic father was sober one year, the approximate length of time his son had begun experiencing school problems, including cutting classes and failing grades. The boy was aloof and closed off to his feelings. The counselor suspected some drug involvement because of his behavior. It was clear the boy needed immediate help. He was referred to an alcoholism clinic offering specific help for young children of alcoholics, as well as to Alateen. He balked at the idea, but with pressure from his parents he accepted an intake appointment at the clinic. He will need a lot of help to recognize and accept his feelings and reverse his compulsive behavior.[18]

This teenager's problems accelerated *after* his father had entered treatment, and the boy became reluctant to enter the program when he observed its effects on his father. Nonetheless, backed by the ubiquitous concept of denial, the article assumes that the solution is to place the child in treatment over his objections.

 ˙What happens to children in treatment? The accelerated conversion experience promoted by residential treatment is often even more brutal for children than for adults. "Tough love" and other programs take it as their task to strip children of their previous identities and to rebuild them into new, more constructive identities. According to Gary Melton, a psychologist who has wide experience with such programs,

> Programs intended to "resocialize" troubled or troubling youth sometimes have resorted to holding youth incommunicado, refusing to allow them to wear street clothes, keeping them in isolation for prolonged periods of times, or forcing them to wear self-derogatory signs, engage in other humiliation rituals, or submit to intense and prolonged group confrontation.
>
> Such "treatments," which have been all too common in juvenile justice and substance abuse programs, are based on dubious psychological theory. . . . attempts to strip away a supposedly "missocialized" or antisocial character structure through intense confrontation or humiliation may destroy the youngster's already fragile self-esteem. The effects of such treatment are thus much more likely to be iatrogenic than ameliorative.[19]

Most children are sent to such programs with their parents' consent—albeit sometimes very reluctant consent. A number of parents have afterward publicly repudiated such treatment programs, however, both because of the abuse their children underwent and because they found that the children very often relapsed when they left the confinement of one of these completely enclosed communities. Other parents simply accept frequent relapse as a cost of doing business with tough love. One woman told me her two sons had been enrolled in treatment programs a number of times but that both were home and "using" again. While she had forced one son into treatment on a counselor's advice after she found some marijuana in the boy's backpack, both boys now accepted their treatment and agreed that they were addicts. As both boys continued to take drugs—with their mother's knowledge—they waited for beds in a hospital program in which they wanted to enroll because they had heard its success rate was so high.

One famous mother who forced her daughter into a tough love program is Carol Burnett, who now frequently lectures with her daughter, Carrie Hamilton, about the need for emergency measures to deal with a child's drug abuse. Together, mother and daughter traveled to the Soviet Union in 1988 to proselytize for AA and tough love programs, for which the Russians have no native equivalent. The younger Burnett, now recovered (although she did relapse after her first stay in treatment), began each talk to Russian audiences by announcing she was chemically dependent, hoping to encourage more Russians to reach similar conclusions about themselves. Burnett and Hamilton's visit is part of a larger effort by American experts to introduce AA and other American disease concepts to Russia and most other European countries, presumably based on the view that the United States has such an excellent handle on the problem.

# Let's Convince Him
# He's Addicted for Life

Parents consent to their children's treatment for diseases other than taking drugs. One of the most common groups of childhood diseases is "learning disabilities," including especially hyperactivity. Are such learning disabilities permanent? One piece of research showed that, "Contrary to the expectations of many experts, . . . boys who are hyperactive do not always have emotional or intellectual difficulties when they grow up." Half of the boys in the study who were diagnosed as hyperactive between the ages of six and twelve "were perfectly normal by the time they reached late adolescence and early adulthood." Even though these boys continued to be restless and distractible, they did as well in school and achieved as many academic honors as ordinary children.[20]

Parents are naturally concerned when children don't perform well in school despite being otherwise bright and able. Sometimes a problem in school performance is diagnosed as "dyslexia" or "hyperkinesis." What should parents do? Even if the child's problem will eventually diminish, parents and child are distressed by it. What is crucial is that children whose development is slower than hoped not become discouraged or demoralized and that their self-esteem be protected as they have the chance to mature. But most of the treatments for learning disabilities—like those for substance abuse—take a different approach entirely. Their aim is to convince children they are *perpetually* debilitated. Only *after* making this concession, treatment personnel contend, can children begin to make progress through life, albeit now convinced that they can never really be whole or lead a normal existence.

Some parents, like Mary and Bob, have rejected this approach, however. Mary and Bob told me that they battled the school system for years over the diagnosis that their son Timothy was hypoglycemic ("that meant the sugar he ate made him hyperactive and a poor listener") and dyslexic and had poor motor control. What most struck Mary and Bob was the difference between their impressions of Timothy and what they heard about him at school. "They didn't seem to know the Tim we knew, the active kid we saw at home who was a neighborhood go-getter and leader."

From third grade to high school, based on his learning disabilities, Tim was assigned a separate homeroom with three to five other kids. Once or twice during the day he was taken out of regular classes to attend special ed. Yet, Mary and Bob worried, Tim showed little improvement over the years. Worse, he deeply resented his special classes. "We saw a happy and contented kid become unhappy and filled with self-doubt," Mary laments. "His schoolwork didn't improve, and the other kids knew he was going off to this program because supposedly he couldn't do the regular work. This bright child began to see himself as dumb. These kids were put in a little box early on, and they never had a real chance to become 'normal.' Finally, at the end of middle school, we asked that Tim be taken out of the program and allowed to enter high school like every other freshman."

Flashing with resentment, Mary and Bob describe how they met with the entire counseling staff at Tim's school: "They even brought in someone from the high school." In Tim's parents' view this was "to make sure the high school counselor would see Tim the same way they did. Then one of the counselors at this meeting had the nerve to tell us we were setting Tim up for failure." Mary and Bob stood fast, and they have been glad of the results. "Tim isn't doing much better at his bad subjects, but he's not doing any worse. And his attitude is a hell of a lot better. We've always felt his academic aptitude is adequate, and that all he needs to do is stick to his work without getting discouraged." Still, the parents sense the school's disapproval, and they feel that now the biggest obstacle to Tim's success is the resistance of school personnel. "The school counselor sees Tim once or twice a semester for five or ten minutes. But we *know* this child. And more important, we're the ones who are responsible for how he turns out. We won't sit back and ten years later say we let someone destroy our son's life."

It is not surprising that few parents summon the fortitude Bob and Mary needed to get their child out of special ed, even when they share Bob and Mary's doubts. One set of parents who did and lived to tell about it are Lori and Bill Granger. Perhaps because Lori was a political consultant and Bill a newspaper columnist, they were more skeptical of their Chicago school's treatment of their son and were better prepared to fight the school's diagnosis and plans for the child. In addition, they wrote a book—*The Magic Feather*—describing their experiences and the rush to special education nationwide. For the Grangers, "special education teaches kids how to be failures."[21]

One consequence of the whole special ed experience for Mary is her realization that "everyone has a disability of one kind or another. I remember arguing with them at school that just because Tim had trouble with languages didn't mean he was dyslexic; I couldn't learn a language in school. We know he has limitations. But what is important is that he feel good about himself and that he become a productive, well-adjusted adult, which we know he will be. It seems as though the school and special education people related best to Tim in terms of his weaknesses. I think they've lost sight of the goal: they think primarily about special diagnoses and education programs instead of about the child and the life he leads." Instead of the education program working to support the child's ego, it operates primarily to limit the child's self-conception and life.

As children learn to think of themselves as diseased, they also learn to seek out and associate with others who share their maladies. Being a member of Alateen, for example, often guarantees that children will reject relationships and activities except for those involving other alcoholics or addicts. While it is considered a sign of sickness that some women consistently end up with alcoholic mates (this is the disease of codependence), young people who constantly attend AA meetings will most likely have mainly alcoholic friends and dates. They may also select as their role models not accomplished people but others who are preoccupied with their diseases—perhaps those who excuse their failures or misconduct as results of these diseases.

The AA system offers them as role models people who clearly have the most limitations in life and the most closed perspectives.

## Following the Blind: Is This Science, or Is It Religion?

Disease conceptions condition in people a blindness to life opportunities and to the variety of elements in their own experience and life history. Such a blindness is perhaps understandable in the cases of people desperate to give up an addiction with which they have been saddled for a lifetime. The problem is that these people then become the exclusive spokespeople for beating addictions. They swear to high heaven that the group or therapy changed their lives immeasurably for the better, that if they were to fall away from the group or treatment they would instantaneously return to their former, despised state, and that everyone with similar problems who doesn't follow their example is doomed to continue in a destructive and iniquitous path. The imagery of religious salvation derives not only from the roots of groups like Alcoholics Anonymous; it is a natural dynamic in this kind of conversion experience.

Nowhere but in the Untied States is a personal history of addiction considered essential for helping others combat the same problem.[22] In the United States, most treatment facility staffs are filled with reformed addicts who have few options. These jobs are not attractive or well-paying ones. While treatment centers and supervising physicians may make money, frontline staff are chronically underpaid. (I frequently ask counselors at conferences where I lecture how much they make. Under $20,000 is the usual answer, while I often meet young counselors who earn less than $15,000 a year.) The breakdown rate among these staff is particularly high, so much so that "burnout"—often referring to a return to drugs or other misbehaviors—has become a major new disease specifically affecting treatment personnel.

Recovering alcoholics and addicts often move directly from the patient to the therapist role because the treatment setting is the only one with which they are comfortable and familiar aside from a drug-using or drinking one. And the pay they receive may be—or may seem to be—the best they can do. Of course, we need to distinguish the puny salaries of these field workers from those of the media stars who promote their life stories as object lessons in addiction. Often, treatment centers 'and "star" patients make profitable deals for the recovered patient to tout the center in ads and speeches. Other ex-addicts go out on the lecture circuit on their own—a quite profitable enterprise for people whose earlier, colossal salaries in sports, music, and entertainment had disappeared.

> When former Miami Dolphins running back Eugene "Mercury" Morris was convicted of trying to sell cocaine to an undercover policeman in 1982, he was indigent. The court appointed two public defenders and Dade County paid Morris' legal fees of $8,600.
> Since then, Morris has hit the anti-drug lecture circuit and co-authored a book, *Against the Grain*. When the Metro Dade Commission learned in 1986 that Morris was expected to earn $100,000 annually from his lectures, it filed a lien to collect the $8,600.

Morris didn't have to repay the money, but instead made speeches against drug use at schools, businesses, and treatment centers.[23]

Morris's lecture fees are not as high as those of some stars in the field. When Toma came to the town in New Jersey where I live, I was told by the organizers of his presentation that he was paid a one-day fee of $5,000 (from a grant from a local church foundation) for a show he puts on literally hundreds of times a year around the country. Betty Ford, of course, receives considerably more than Toma for her speeches as an addiction expert. If Betty Ford hadn't discovered and revealed that she was a tranquilizer addict and an alcoholic, on what basis could she be an expert? What bodies of special knowledge or insight could she claim? Why would people listen to her speeches—what would she speak about?

Despite all the claims of biological discoveries about alcoholism, audiences still want to hear the testimony of addicts and alcoholics rather than learned tales of genes and neurochemistry. Addicts and alcoholics are qualified as experts in the first place because they developed noteworthy addictions and then quit them. Then, by claiming they had an uncontrollable disease, they cloak their recitations about their addicted lives and their disease and treatment in modern medical clothing. For example, when the Boston Museum of Science mounted an exhibit on alcoholism, it relied on Derek Sanderson as an adviser. Sanderson, a hockey player who was one of the earliest beneficiaries of sports free agentry, blew his fortune and quickly ran himself out of sports, after which he discovered he was an alcoholic and became a lecturer and consultant.

Reformed addicts and alcoholics present the only messages we hear about the nature of and solutions for addiction. Their personal and collective histories are ubiquitous on television and in schools. Young people whose difficulties do not resemble in the least the problems of Derek Sanderson, John and MacKenzie Phillips, or Monica Wright are thus supposed to learn from people like these who have ruined their lives and the lives of those around them. Betty Ford, on the other hand, serves as a gentler symbol for the new middle-class and female alcoholism patient. A prominent speaker at alcoholism conferences and before mass audiences, Mrs. Ford explains that alcoholism isn't what people think it is:

> The reason that I rejected the idea that I was an alcoholic was that my addiction wasn't dramatic. . . . I never drank for a hangover. . . . I hadn't been a solitary drinker . . . and at Washington luncheons I'd never touched anything but an occasional glass of sherry. There had been no broken promises . . . and no drunken driving. . . . I never wound up in jail.[24]

Indeed, by most diagnostic criteria Mrs. Ford was not an alcoholic, however much she felt she had a drinking problem she wanted to change. Betty Ford is such a model alcoholism patient because her drinking levels were low and she had so much family and financial support (which allowed her to pay substantial sums for private psychiatric treatment). She had gotten in trouble initially in good part because she was so comfortable and well supported by physicians. When she became First Lady, Betty gave interviews in which she readily confided she used tranquilizers regularly: "Valium three times a day, or sometimes Equagesic. That way I'm more comfortable. Otherwise, I find that I become tense when I realize how much there is to do in one day." It is ironic that the same Betty Ford who trusted her physician to overmedicate her now places so much faith in physicians to treat drug and alcohol abuse.

Really, the question is how Mrs. Ford was so blind as not to be able to sense that her constant reliance on drugs—albeit prescribed medications—was a problem in the first place. The basic problem is that some people, while failing so badly at coping, instead rely on mood modifiers to remedy their bad feelings about themselves and their situations. One important aspect of these people's behavior *is* their blindness in doing this, a blindness often labeled "denial." But what if we discovered that their blindness is not *due* to alcoholism or drug abuse as much as it is a *precondition* for it? This would mean that Derek Sanderson, Hollywood Henderson, Betty Ford, and Monica Wright are notable for their *obtuseness*, both before and after their addictions, rather than for being especially insightful about the human condition.

Those who spread the notion that alcoholism and addiction are diseases and who wish to force people to acknowledge and be treated for these diseases are the very people who have been the most out of control. This peculiarly American passion play is supported by Americans' fascination with self-destruction, combined with a special American version of the penitent sinner. The nineteenth-century temperance lecturer was a popular entertainment figure, one whose tales of degradation and ruin attracted and appalled people in equal measure. The part of the story in which the reformed drunkard described how he wallowed in filth, abused his family, committed unspeakable crimes, and consorted with the devil always took up the lion's share of his speech. But at the end he could reveal he had seen the light and been saved—a ritualized ending that excused everything that came before, since the fatal drink had led him astray originally.

The contemporary American has the same mixed feelings as did many who heard the reformed drunkard's temperance lecture. Uneasy with these displays and yet drawn to them, Americans love to read stories such as John Phillips's. A founder of the folk-rock group The Mamas and the Papas, Phillips entered an eclipse that included massive drug use, complete abdication of his role as a parent to his daughter MacKenzie (who became a drug abuser as well), completely irresponsible financial and business behavior, and so on. Readers of *People* magazine and Phillips's autobiography, *Papa John*, could find out how his veins collapsed so that he had to search out new routes for putting drugs into his body, how he betrayed friends and family, how he periodically got on the wagon (sometimes with the help of other rock stars), only to return to new and more prodigious bouts of drug use.

When Phillips entered the drug program at Fair Oaks Hospital under the care of celebrity doctor Mark Gold, his story became public property. Afterward, Phillips embarked on a new career, forming an antidrug band and becoming a leader in the reformed addict movement. Of course, Phillips had quit drugs any number of times before. Only this time, adopted (along with his daughter, Mac-Kenzie) by Dr. Gold as a symbol of the efficacy of Gold's program and with all the media hype and speaking engagements on the line, Phillips apparently stayed clean. After divorcing his second wife (the one he had been addicted with and had come clean with and had had a child by), he became a regular figure on the oldies music trail and the drug crusaders' podium. Some people, however, remain skeptical about what John Phillips's story tells us. One reviewer of Phillips's autobiography notes:

> [John] Phillips is not altogether realistic about himself. He recalls that when he was a postman, he threw mail away because his mailbags were too heavy; as a graveyard plot salesman, he received down payments, pocketed the money and never recorded the transactions. Still, on page 297 of a 444-page book, in reporting how he skipped out on a $2,000 hotel bill, he writes, "My values were beginning to corrode under the prolonged influence of hard drugs."[25]

For some, like this reviewer, the whole conversion experience—whether to God or to abstinence—seems too pat, too convenient, too self-serving. What qualifies these people to help and lecture to others? At the same time, we reject as messengers those who tell us they took drugs (or drank) without getting in trouble. When basketball great Kareem Abdul Jabbar revealed in his autobiography that he took psychedelic drugs with his teammates in college, he was chastised and his revelations ignored. Instead of learning what non-addicted users (the vast majority) have to tell us, we are fed the morality play of the reformed sinner. While children will never be told how Jabbar controlled his drug use within an exceptional and accomplishment-filled life, they may hear from athletes like Hollywood Henderson and Derek Sanderson, who ruined their careers:

> Thomas (Hollywood) Henderson, the former Dallas Cowboy linebacker who has been jailed in California since 1984 on sex charges involving two teen-age girls, will be released this week and has already

been scheduled for a paid speaking tour to talk against drug and alcohol abuse. Henderson was an admitted drug user.[26]

Rather than teaching children coping skills and providing models of how best to succeed, we rely instead on the passion-play approach: we will show them those who were tempted and fell from grace. Criticism seems almost like picking on the helpless, or in some cases like picking on a saint. (Isn't Betty Ford almost sacrosanct?) Yet comparative data show that the kinds of lectures given by these ex-addicts—filled with "information" and moralizing—comprise the least-effective prevention programs *and may actually lead to increased drug use among youthful audiences.*[27]

Despite this, recovered addicts and alcoholics, like the editor of a journal called *Professional Counselor*, are often quite critical of those who hold different views. This editor had entered the field "soon after embarking on his own recovery":

> I would find a way to take up the banner against the forces of wealth and cunning who promote behavioral retraining as a means to avoid the "penalty" of abstinence borne by those of us who have chosen the "traditionalist" route to recovery—the only known route, by the way. . . . The most effective means of spreading truth and enlisting soldiers to fight the wars against incompetence and deception is the mass media.[28]

Here is a man who isn't interested in any complexity and debate about definitions, data, and cultural perspectives. But he *is* editor of a magazine that reaches many professionals, and he stands as a spokesman for the field. As such, he has entered the world of scientific, clinical, and political debate. He does so militantly—brooking no opposition. (Imagine how he would react to this book!) What range of articles does he accept in his journal? What kind of teacher would he be? He himself received alcohol/drug studies and counseling skills certificates at UCLA. What kind of reasoned examination of the issues is he capable of conducting? While this man and others like him may be sincere, well-intentioned counselors, their overall impact is to prevent the field from escaping its limitations. As alcoholism studies and counseling programs have been entrenched in American universities, they translate the practitioner's intolerance of disagreement and open discussion into academic curricula.

# Conclusions: Recovery as the Route to God

Alcoholics and other former addicts undergo a conversion experience in treatment or in AA in which their previous identities are subsumed in a new one—that of recovering alcoholic or addict. All their experience is reinterpreted to concur with this new self-image. The drawbacks to this process, for the addict, for society, and for target drug users or drinkers who have not yet been converted are:

1. The conversion experience colors the former addict's vision so completely that he or she can offer only the standard line promoted by his or her therapy or support group.

2. The converted addict loses track of the meanings and motivations in his life, including the significance of his drinking or drug taking and other misbehavior.

3. The new limitations in the person's life—including continued unhealthy behavior (such as heavily addicted smoking and coffee drinking) and other compulsions, association only with other former addicts and alcoholics, and ideological blinders—may at times be as problematic as the former addiction.

4. The person is now convinced that a single slip will mean a complete return to the addiction or to alcoholism—a fate that befalls many "successful" graduates.

5. All of these pitfalls are *especially* problematic for young people who are convinced that their addictions or other limitations are lifelong and who thus learn to *define* themselves by their problems—problems they would more often than not otherwise outgrow.

6. Ex-addicts and recovering alcoholics as therapists are incapable of accepting clients or scientific data that disagree with the tenets of their own therapy.

7. Our society, searching for role models and teachers, increasingly turns for leadership to those least in control and aware of themselves.

Once addicts and alcoholics were ashamed of their behavior. They are now full of pride. Not pride in having been addicted; in the disease view that was unavoidable. But proud of discovering they were addicted, of their confession and contrition, and now of having taken up the banner of the recovered, to save and convert others. This scenario certainly indicates that everything in the universe comes full cycle: who would have believed fifty or twenty-five years ago that alcoholics and addicts would appear continuously on television, in schools, in print; that they would control the dissemination of information about drugs and alcohol; and that any who would oppose them—those who had never abused drugs or alcohol and who referred to solid scientific evidence—would run scared, afraid of accusations that they were antiscientific, antihumanitarian, even prodrug and prointoxication! And who, in God's name, can—or would want to—halt progress in treatment?

# 5

# The Addiction Treatment Industry

The nineteenth-century discovery that the [opiate] addict is a suitable case for treatment is today an entrenched and unquestioned premise, with society unaware of the arbitrariness of this come-lately assumption. . . . Any suggestion that the current model is fundamentally mistaken in its assumption, that the treatment enterprise should be closed down and people with bad habits left to their own devices, would be dismissed only as outrageous and bizarre.

          —Virginia Berridge and Griffith Edwards[1]

    Goodwin said that "all the stuff" that has been written in recent years about adult children of alcoholics has been, in his judgment, something akin to a hoax. Adult children of alcoholics are about like adult children of everybody else with a problem, he said, and it's hard to build a reasonable case for giving them extraordinary attention.
    Then why are they getting so much attention?
    Goodwin's answer: Therapists "invented" the concept that adult children of alcoholics have special problems that can be treated through therapy. They were able to sell this concept to the public and now they are eligible for reimbursement from insurance companies. In short, said Goodwin, it was a way for therapists to tap into a new market and make money.

          —Interview with Donald Goodwin, pioneering
          researcher in the inheritance of alcoholism[2]

Ten percent of the adult population has a sexual addiction that requires treatment. The extreme figures in the field say that a quarter of the population needs help in some area [of sexual addiction].

        —Dr. Edward Armstrong, Executive Director, National
        Association on Sexual Addiction Problems[3]

H ow HAS the addiction treatment industry grown, and how does it continue to grow? How big is it, and how big can it become? Why do we accept the industry and all its self-serving claims, sometimes eagerly signing on for our own groups and treatment, even when the evidence is that these groups and this treatment do little to help us as individuals and as a society? Clearly, the treatment industry must successfully address feelings and problems we have, even if it addresses these at an emotional rather than at a practical level, and even if its solutions give us the illusion of progress at the cost of a further worsening of our problems.

## How People Benefit from Treating Addictions as Diseases

Treating alcoholism and other addictions as diseases offers benefits both for health care providers and for the addict or problem drinker. The "patient's" drinking problem or other problem behavior is explained and justified, while help—on disease terms—is readily available. People can turn themselves over to the medical system for diagnosis and treatment and have a reassuring sense that progress is being made. The treatment specialists, meanwhile, have their own set of benefits. *Their* special expertise is appreciated and rewarded. In the case of alcoholism treatment, the search for respect and approval has been a long time coming. For other "diseases," newly discovered and unappreciated even as was alcoholism several decades earlier, the success of the alcoholism movement is an ideal to be emulated.

Alcoholism treatment differs significantly from that for traditional medical ailments. The disease of alcoholism is *defined* by people's behavior, and the treatment is to get people to stop drinking. Obviously, as a behavior, alcoholic drinking can be reinstated at any time (although many people grow weary of their alcoholism and really lose the stomach for heavy drinking). This imminent return of the disease—and the alcoholism movement proverb "one day at a time"—are hallmarks of the disease approach to alcoholism. Relapse is so common that it is used to justify the disease idea. Failures are not evidence of the futility of treatment; they simply indicate that, as the treatment personnel assert, people can never fully recover from the disease. Hence organizations like Hazelden lobby for medical insurance to cover unlimited bouts of treatment, one for every drinking bout.

Alcoholism not only offers the opportunity for unlimited, never-ending therapy for a group of problem drinkers that has constantly expanded (until it includes Betty Ford, drunk drivers, and young weekend drinkers). It draws into the disease net whole new areas of behavior. The very notion of illnesses based on behavior—albeit "uncontrollable" behavior—suggests a myriad of potential new diseases. There are an awful lot of things that people do that they know they shouldn't or that they regret doing more of than they want to. Once this pattern has been defined as a disease, almost anything can be treated as a medical problem. Jules Masserman, a past president of the American Psychiatric Association, pointed out, "Addiction to drink is a 'disease' only in the sense that excessive eating, sleeping, smoking, wandering, or lechery may also be so classified."[4]

# Beyond Alcoholism: The New Diseases

Masserman, writing in 1976, offered these analogies to show how ridiculous it is to treat alcoholism as a disease. Turning this logic on its head, however, disease treatments have been developed for all the things Masserman listed, as well as for stealing, overwork, worrying, sadness, fear, incompetence, procrastination, anger, child abuse, forgetfulness, murder, premenstrual tension, television viewing, gambling, shopping, and on and on. Consider the grounds on which one British psychologist explained overeating as an addiction: "The evidence [that overeating is an addiction] is overwhelming. . . . millions of people feel that their eating is excessive, would like to control it better than they do, but find great difficulty in so doing."[5]

Overeating and smoking are popular candidates for addiction treatment because so many people engage in them and because—like drug addiction—they involve excessive substance use (of food and nicotine). Several pharmaceutical companies and many medical programs now make use of the idea that smoking is an addiction to warn smokers that they can never possibly quit without medical help, since smoking—like drug addiction—involves physical dependence

on a drug. Merrell Dow Pharmaceuticals mounted a massive advertising campaign admonishing, "If you want to quit smoking for good,
see your doctor. . . . Now your doctor can provide a treatment to
help control nicotine withdrawal symptoms." The smoking industry
is too vast and the number of smokers wishing to quit too lucrative
for smoking to be overlooked as a medical problem.

Merrell Dow markets Nicorette, a chewing gum widely prescribed
to help people quit smoking. Thus the company was upset when
psychiatrist John Hughes published a study in 1989 in the *Journal
of the American Medical Association* that found that 10 percent of the
smokers who received the drug quit smoking over the long run,
compared with 7 percent who were given a placebo gum. This difference was not significant, and Dr. Hughes indicated that the use-
fulness of Nicorette in helping people quit smoking is either "small
or nonexistent." A company spokesperson countered that Nicorette
works, but that calling the product a failure because people smoke
a year after using the product "is like blaming an antidepressant
[drug] if a person gets depressed again a year after discontinuing the
drug." Apparently, then, Nicorette's manufacturer doesn't mean actually to wean people from a nicotine addiction, but only to provide
a nonsmokable substitute to which people can stay addicted.[6]

It is harder to describe obesity as a physical dependence on eating,
but it is nonetheless dealt with as an addiction, both in self-help
groups based on AA (such as Overeaters Anonymous) and in a host
of medical programs. A physician at Mt. Sinai (Cleveland) Hospital
described obesity in this way in the hospital magazine, *Caring* (Fall
1985):

> "Obesity is an incurable disease," stated Dr. Hazelton. "We don't
> know its complete etiology. We can, however, put a patient into
> remission for a lifetime through our weight-loss program. . . . We
> try to make our patients aware that their obesity is a disease, that it
> is incurable, and that they will need maintenance assistance for the
> rest of their lives."

Of course, the ironies of smoking and overeating as treatable illnesses
are that smoking is a habit widely encouraged by advertising and
eating is an activity in which everyone engages. Eating is perhaps
the ultimate disease in being not only legal but essential, completely
approved, and everywhere around us encouraged and invited.

# Selling Addiction/Selling Addiction Treatment

For this reason, obesity is the addictive (also called "appetitive") problem with the most victims; it is a malady that has spawned several million-dollar industries. The best known is the never-ending march of diet books. An industry that has grown rapidly in recent years is the medical and chemical treatment of obesity. If, however, a drug eliminates the causes of overeating or makes people less dependent on eating as an activity, can the replacement drug itself be addictive? This has always been the issue with methadone treatment for heroin addicts. The standard medical prescription for overweight has been amphetamines, to which many people become addicted. One such addict was Kitty Dukakis, wife of the Massachusetts governor, who began using diet pills when she was nineteen and, with the aid of a succession of doctors, continued using the drug for twenty-six years.

Mrs. Dukakis finally entered the Hazelden treatment center. Although she, like Betty Ford, had been introduced to and maintained on her addictive drug by a series of doctors applying standard medical practice, she now turned to doctors for treatment for her addiction. Reading medical journals, one finds a high percentage of ads devoted to antidepressant, antianxiety (tranquilizer), and antiobesity (stimulant) drugs. In other words, drug advertising, like food and cigarette advertising, is a principal element in creating the addictions for which treatment is then marketed. First people are offered emotional relief in a capsule; then they are treated for becoming dependent on a capsule for relief.

The media have been essential in the creation of the addiction treatment industry. Of course, this is a great tradition in the United States: in the nineteenth century, "temperance supporters turned out an enormous quantity of . . . pamphlets, articles, books, novels, short stories, plays, poetry, and songs, and major newspapers and magazines lent editorial support to the temperance line."[7] The modern alcoholism movement, as keynoted by Marty Mann and the National Council on Alcoholism (NCA), has used much the same approach. Mann (who worked as a public-relations flack) and other important figures in the movement understood that the media are the key to the acceptance of the new concept of alcoholism as a medical disease. We may be amazed to reflect today that, before AA and the NCA were established, the term *alcoholism* was practically unknown. (*Chronic inebriate* and *drunkard* were the standard terms for those who habitually drank too much.) Mann herself was not familiar with the word until she read AA's Big Book in 1939.[8]

In addition to writing for popular magazines such as the *Saturday Evening Post*, Mann and her colleagues frequently consulted with Hollywood producers to make sure films reflected the NCA's point of view. The acclaimed 1945 film *The Lost Weekend* (starring Ray Milland and Jane Wyman, directed by Billy Wilder) was the first motion picture to portray alcoholism as a medical illness, although some alcoholics criticized the film because the Milland character did not join AA. Later films on alcoholism, like *Come Back Little Sheba* and *The Days of Wine and Roses*, uniformly portrayed AA as the sole solution for alcoholism. Most people had no reason to dispute the ideas in these films as applied to extreme alcoholism, since neither they nor anyone they knew drank like Jack Lemmon and Lee Remick in *Wine and Roses* or Ray Milland in *The Lost Weekend*.

Disease advertising has progressed dramatically since the 1940s and 1950s, however, when the NCA was attempting to gain acceptance for the idea that alcoholism is a disease afflicting a relatively few unfortunate people. The modern disease message is that many people are in the dark not only about their alcoholism but about a host of similar diseases. People are alerted to be ever-vigilant toward their own behavior and that of those closest to them for signs of these diseases and possibly to confront unsuspecting victims with their need to be treated. This campaign never flags, fueled by television series and special-feature shows about alcoholism, drug addiction, and bulimia; public service announcements; and advertisements by private hospitals and other facilities about their programs for treating these diseases.

To accept what one sees on television now is to be overwhelmed by the range of potential diseases that can affect one's life. We are inundated almost exactly as the nineteenth-century American was with temperance imagery. Specials about alcoholism and literally scores of diseases are regular parts of every television season. Both documentaries and fictional accounts describe compulsive gamblers, shoppers, bulimics, child abusers, alcoholics, cocaine addicts. TV pundits have even given a name to the phenomenon—"the disease of the month." The programs on alcoholism and other diseases now especially emphasize the impact of the disease on the diseased person's family and children. One of the most heralded of these programs, *Shattered Spirits*, aired on ABC in January 1986 and starred Martin Sheen as the alcoholic. The National Association for Children of Alcoholics served as consultants to the film.

Serial dramas regularly feature segments on various characters' addictions. *Hill Street Blues* had two regulars whose alcoholism was an ongoing story line, along with a compulsive eater and gambler; *St. Elsewhere* had a bulimic, an alcoholic, and *several* drug addicts; even a comedy show, *Cheers*, had as its lead character an alcoholic. This same actor, Ted Danson, played a character on a separate television special who received treatment because he had a sexual relationship with his daughter. Meredith Baxter Birney (star of the comedy series *Family Ties*) starred in a highly publicized drama about bulimia distinguished by its realistic vomiting sound effects. In a remarkable case of life imitating fiction, Sharon Gless entered alcoholism treatment after her character's alcoholism was depicted on the TV show *Cagney and Lacey* (in a 1987 episode that was awarded an Emmy). By 1988, it seemed almost obligatory for lead characters in a series to have an addiction: *Murphy Brown* (played by Candice Bergen) was revealed in her first episode to be freshly returned from the Betty Ford Clinic, while George Segal introduced alcoholism as the key element in the personality of his character in the show *Murphy's Law*.

The number of shows on alcoholism and drug addiction themselves simply cannot be counted. David Toma, for example, developed a weekly TV show in which he lectured to kids about the dangers of drugs. Toma is a by-product of the addiction phenomenon of our time, a return to the old temperance revivals of the previous century. A former cop and the model for the television series *Baretta*, Toma rails against drug use and drinking of any kind. (He contemptuously spits out the phrase "moderate drinker.") His lectures at schools around the country, like his television show, consist of long monologues about his conversations with kids and the dire consequences that befall those who drink or take drugs. Oddly, in speeches and programs based on children's stories with audiences filled with children, Toma never shares the stage or allows a child to speak *except* to have them endorse what he has just uttered—a more controlling, anti-intellectual environment would be hard to devise.

Toma holds forth for upwards of four hours in his public talks. His speeches are filled with the most horrible and graphic descriptions of the consequences of substance abuse, the names of media stars he knows, the authorities and experts who have ignored him or tried to put him down, and his own unswerving devotion to children. Toma does little to promote local treatment facilities; nor does he encourage communication with parents as much as he puts down the ignorance and permissiveness of parents for letting their children run wild and go unloved. Instead, Toma relies on stirring accounts of how children bare their souls to him and tell him they wish he could be their parent. Indeed, in a 1986 CBS special about his career (entitled *Drug Knot*), Toma mentioned with tears in his eyes the number of students who committed suicide "after I left the school."

Publishing is just as assiduous as television in driving home disease messages. First-person accounts of drunken careers—so-called drunkalogues—have long been staples of the American publishing scene. But these have accelerated in the 1970s and 1980s, with more modern and appealing characters, many in midcareer. Some notable examples of this genre have been Jill Robinson's *Bed Time Story*, Barbara Gordon's *I'm Dancing as Fast as I Can*, and—the most significant of all—Betty Ford's *The Times of My Life*. Betty Ford's description of her disease is striking for its tone of normalcy, almost complacency. Not only are her drinking problems tame, but she never confronts negative emotions or describes anything but apple-pie feelings about her family—her marriage and everything else about her life is okay, especially now that she has graduated treatment.

The author of a syndicated household hints column, Mary Ellen Pinkham, has also striven to bring alcoholism into mainstream Americans' lives with a book, *How to Stop the One You Love from Drinking*, describing her discovery that she and her husband were alcoholics. (This was not her first behavioral disease book: in 1982, she wrote the *Help Yourself Diet Plan: The One That Worked For Me*.) Because ordinary, average suburbanites enter the alcoholic cycle without their knowledge, Pinkham favors confronting others about their alcoholism, as she had to do with her husband. Pinkham believes that treatment succeeds almost every time and that the many unknowing sufferers need only to be forced into treatment in order for them and their families to regain their health. Like Betty Ford's story, Pinkham's warns middle-class people of the danger that alcoholism can appear in average people's lives without their recognizing it. These cautionary stories certainly don't resemble the degraded drinking of the one hundred AA members who told their stories in the first Big Book put out by AA in 1939 or Ray Milland's drinking in *The Lost Weekend*.

Dennis Wholey, the PBS talk-show host, recounted his own admission of alcoholism and his recovery along with those of a number of prominent personalities in a 1986 best-seller, *The Courage to Change*. The group includes Grace Slick, Doc Severinson, Billy Carter, Jerry Falwell, Sid Caesar, Jason Robards, and others. The book tells how people from the very ordinary to the very famous are affected by alcoholism—many more than we can imagine. Altogether, "there are 20 million alcoholics in the United States. Half are women; many are teenagers and even younger. Counting friends, family, and other loved ones, 80 million Americans, one in three, are directly and tragically affected by this insidious disease."[9]

Having an alcoholic spouse or parent is, in and of itself, now considered a disease. Codependence is a condition for which groups organized like AA (called Al-Anon) are provided and about which best-sellers are written. The National Association for Children of Alcoholics (NACoA), meanwhile, was organized in 1983. NACoA was formed on the premise, according to its founders, that "children of alcoholics require and deserve treatment in and of themselves, not as mere adjuncts of alcoholics." This multiplier effect has had a remarkable impact on the treatment industry, as in the estimate that one in three Americans now requires treatment because he or she is directly affected by alcoholism. Indeed, more than an industry, the children of alcoholics have become, in the words of one proponent, "a social movement."

One publishing phenomenon was *Adult Children of Alcoholics* by Janet Woititz, which—despite being published by a small press in the alcoholism field—sold 300,000 books between 1983 and 1986 and continues to head the best-seller list. As the book's publisher remarks, "We think the book helped define this as a problem for a large group of folks who weren't really aware of it."[10] Innumerable books on this topic are now available, and the children of alcoholics movement has become the single hottest theme on the alcoholism and addiction-conference circuit. At the same time, the movement has spread well beyond professionals to reach the general public as the result of best-sellers, television specials, and magazine stories. Millions of Americans have now discovered that a key failure in their lives has been not coming to grips properly with an alcoholic parent.

In 1987–88, books and magazine articles detailing young celebrity drug and alcohol abuse abounded. Suzanne Somers made the talk-show circuit with her alcoholic father and siblings, talking about her book—*Keeping Secrets*—about her family's alcoholism. Books by musicians Judy Collins and Graham Nash, actress Carrie Fisher, and footballers Thomas Henderson and Lawrence Taylor described their drug and alcohol problems. Their and other people's faces (like Margaux Hemingway's and Drew Barrymore's) have graced covers and been mentioned in stories on alcoholism, alcoholics and addicts, and families of alcoholics and addicts in *Newsweek*, *U.S. News & World Report*, *Sports Illustrated*, and *People*. The 1988 movie *Clean and Sober* depicted a young man (Michael Keaton) who enters treatment to escape the sticky circumstances of his life but gradually realizes that he is addicted to alcohol and drugs and recovers. The therapy program Keaton undergoes—the confrontation, group, individual counseling, residential detoxification, and AA therapy—illustrates the feel-good techniques that no study has shown actually have more impact than simple lived experience.

Alcoholism and other diseases are promoted by regular advertising slots. Some ads are by nonprofit organizations whose mission is to encourage acceptance of certain diseases—such as depression. In one such ad, a boy is shown trembling in his bed. The ad lectures, "Learn to see the sickness." During mental illness week, full-page ads headlined MENTAL ILLNESS IS CURABLE describe mental illness as "Real biological diseases . . . [like] cancer."[11] Ads about drug and alcohol abuse as diseases are, of course, ubiquitous, promoted by government agencies and programs such as the Partnership for a Drug-Free America, by the national and state Councils on Alcoholism, and by private treatment centers. CompCare, the treatment chain, is the largest advertiser in the drug and alcohol field: it spent $5.8 million on TV ads in the first half of 1988.[12]

Ads on drug and alcohol abuse combine the direst possible predictions—if you think you have a drinking problem, you do; a drinking problem can only grow worse; a drinking alcoholic ends up either dead or institutionalized—with deprecations of any individual efforts to change and with images of the incredible guilt those close to the victim will feel if they don't seek treatment. One such ad likened trying to stop drinking on one's own to operating on oneself. An ad by a New York City treatment center showed an actor physically disintegrate in a series of harrowing shots—this is what will happen if you don't insist that a friend seek treatment. These ads are particularly effective when they concern children, like one showing a parent dialing frantically around to her daughter's friends while the daughter is shown taking a bus out of town, or another showing a man at a cemetery who cries that he didn't understand his son's depression and didn't get the child treated.

A full-page ad in the *New York Times* spoke to parents' concerns:

"If we had only known what to look for our child might still be alive."

In neighborhoods across America, teenagers are dying from illnesses their parents never knew they had.

Drug Abuse, Depression and Eating Disorders are dangerous and deadly disorders that can strike any adolescent. Yet most parents are unaware of the warning signs. Or what to do if they think their child has a problem.

That's why Regent Hospital is holding a series of evening seminars. Because an informed parent can intervene in time. And possibly save a life.[13]

An executive at an ad agency for a major treatment center explains the tendency to run more sensationalistic and frightening ads: "We have to run ads like this to get market share up. The marketplace is so competitive that it takes nearly constant advertising to keep the telephones ringing."[14]

When four teens committed suicide in New Jersey, the Fair Oaks Hospital held a press conference to promote its nationally renowned programs for adolescent depression and chemical dependence. Fair Oaks runs ads showing dangers to the lives of teens from a variety of problems that they treat. A newsperson in the audience pointed out that one of the dead youngsters had recently been treated at Fair

Oaks for drug and alcohol abuse! The nonplussed physician conducting the conference carefully intoned that this shows exactly how
difficult such problems are.

# Who Will Pay for Our Disease
# Treatment Binge?

There is a great deal of money tied up in the addiction treatment
industry. Private treatment centers have become important operations
for many hospitals, and numerous specialty hospitals and chains—like
CompCare—devote themselves to the treatment of alcoholism, chemical dependence, obesity, and assorted new maladies like compulsive
gambling, compulsive shopping, PMS, and postpartum depression. As
we saw in chapter 2, the number of such centers more than quadrupled
and the number of patients treated in them for alcoholism alone quin-
tupled between 1978 and 1984. A single thirty-day stay in a private
hospital for alcohol and drug abuse (like the one Michael Keaton enters
in *Clean and Sober*) costs between $7500 and $35,000. Total expenditures
for drug and alcohol treatment in the United States are now around
$2 billion: private hospitals generate a billion dollars annually in rev-
enues, while the federal and state governments spend another billion
dollars. These numbers are ever-increasing: Congress approved $4 bil-
lion for antidrug efforts for fiscal year 1989 (about 50 percent of which,
or $2 billion, were earmarked for drug abuse prevention and treatment).
For fiscal year 1990 Presidents Reagan and Bush have asked for more
than $5 billion, while congressional leaders have proposed $6.5 billion
(which, by the same formula, would translate to $2.5 to $3 billion for
drug abuse prevention and treatment).

This is the first time the federal government has invested massive
sums of money in drug treatment, based on persistent frustration
over our inability to curtail runaway inner-city drug use through
interdicting drug supplies (although the United States continues to
increase its investment in police and interdiction efforts as well).
This frustration is understandable; however, the failure of one long-
standing set of government policies does not mean that a whole other
set of bureaucratic solutions will succeed. We must keep in mind
that the United States *already* spends massive sums—in New York

State and elsewhere—to treat and prevent addiction and that this has not been enough to prevent the rise of a new and larger group of young crack addicts.

While we rush to spend money in new ways to attack the drug addiction in our ghettos, advertising also convinces people that they have other addictionlike diseases that medicine can treat. Again, the question is who will pay. The primary goal for the care provider is to have insurers and government (which ultimately pays the bill) accept the new diseases. The aim has been to argue in court—largely successfully—that insurers must cover alcoholism treatment because it is an illness like any other covered by insurance. Minnesota has pioneered in declaring alcoholism a treatable illness in this fashion. Likewise, employees found to be unable to perform their jobs because of drunkenness cannot be fired by Minnesota law (or by that of a majority of states) but must be treated at the employer's or insurer's expense.

Similar cases have also been mounted for employees fired for obesity. The possibilities are limitless: Riley Regan, director of the New Jersey State Division of Alcoholism, has complained, "Most of the insurance companies still have their heads in the sand when it comes to the treatment of the illness of compulsive gambling,"[15] although a number of forward-looking institutions—both private and government VA hospitals—have begun inpatient programs for compulsive gamblers. Yet these gambling and other inpatient programs for addictions are modeled on hospital programs for alcoholism that have failed to justify their costs. Instead, "the financial interests of alcoholism treatment providers . . . run precisely counter to the directions that seem wise and prudent in light of current research evidence."[16] The Canadian experience has been that even "the great majority of alcoholics seeking treatment for alcohol withdrawal can be safely detoxified in non-hospital-based units . . . at one tenth the cost."[17]

Because the length and intensity of therapy do not affect outcomes, the U.S. government has tried to rein in the costs of alcoholism treatment through limiting hospital stays. In 1983, Medicare attempted to limit reimbursement for alcoholism treatment to hospital stays of eight days (as opposed to the arbitrary but standard thirty-day program). This effort immediately led to protests from the National Council on Alcoholism, the National Association of Alcoholism Treatment Programs, the American Medical and American

Psychiatric Associations, the Joint Commission on the Accreditation of Hospitals, the Alcohol and Drug Abuse Association, and the government's own National Institute on Alcohol Abuse and Alcoholism. The eight-day limit was accordingly rescinded. (Betty Ford's appeal to her old friend Margaret Heckler, then secretary of the Department of Health and Human Services, was said to have been especially effective in this campaign.)[18] By 1986, the reimbursable stay was practically doubled, to fifteen days—a figure still termed "insupportable" by industry spokespeople—and no limitations have yet been placed on the hospital treatment of alcoholism for which the government and insurers regularly pay.[19]

## Controlling Childhood "Diseases"

Childhood is a special ground for fighting battles about behavioral diseases, since so many children are so prone to misbehave or to adjust slowly to adult demands and expectations. And drug and alcohol abuse are at the forefront of these adolescent diseases. A majority of young people have used an illicit drug, while many high school and college students drink excessively—almost half of male high school seniors and more than half of male college students get drunk regularly, along with a third of female students.[20] Periodically, events impinge on this world of youthful drinking and drug use, like the death of University of Maryland basketball star Len Bias while snorting massive doses of cocaine. The result is intense agitation to reduce drug and alcohol use, education programs to warn young people about drug and alcohol use as diseases, and more coercive treatment referrals.

The hospitalization of young people—often through involuntary referrals or due to intense, coercive group interventions—rose sharply through the 1980s. In chapter 2, we reviewed the 1985 *CBS Evening News* report of the case of a girl who was forcibly hospitalized at a CompCare facility when her "father" (who, like the girl, was a CBS employee) told hospital officials he suspected the girl used marijuana. In an interview with CBS, Joseph Pursch, CompCare medical director, claimed that no such incarceration could ever have occurred, given the strict medical controls CompCare imposed. One might think that CompCare would have been apologetic or defensive about this case. Quite the opposite occurred. CompCare vice president Ed Carels attacked those involved in the CBS program, including Ira Schwartz, director of the Center for the Study of Youth Policy of the University of Minnesota:

> I don't know why you think that when you're done, the mafia, NORML and all those supporting drug abuse in the world won't have Mr. Schwartz as their champions. Someone ought to ask Mr. Schwartz what is going to be done about the problems created by adolescents who are abusing these drugs—the unborn babies deformed by these drugs—the countless kids dying—the dollars that are used to support terrorism in other countries.

Carels noted that parents aren't concerned "about treatment professionals doing something wrong with their child. They are worried about their kid dying because of lack of professional help."[21] Clearly, opposing the treatment industry can be a perilous business.

Why do coercive programs for children remain so popular? They apparently convince parents and officials that something substantial is being accomplished in problem areas that confound and frighten us. Consider the bizarre case of *Scared Straight!* This film depicts the Lifer's Juvenile Awareness Program, in which recidivist criminals in Rahway Prison in New Jersey harangue youngsters about crime and delinquency. The first *Scared Straight!* won a special Academy Award for its depiction of criminals screaming at and threatening children, who often broke down on camera. A follow-up of the program entitled *Scared Straight! Ten Years Later*, shown on national television in 1987, was advertised as follows: "If you resist, you will be raped. If you report us, they'll put you in solitary. If they let you out, we'll kill you."

The films made outlandish claims of success rates for the program of "over 90%." In fact, no study has ever established the efficacy of these programs, even though quite a few such studies have been undertaken. Indeed, earlier evaluations of similar "prison awareness" programs had shown that delinquents who had *not* participated had fewer arrests, leading to the elimination of the programs in states such as Illinois and Michigan. When a sociology professor at Rutgers University, Edward Finckenauer, conducted a controlled evaluation of the Lifer's program in New Jersey, the results were that *twice* as many delinquent children who went through the Lifer's program committed a crime in the following six months as those in a comparable group who had not received the training. Even studies favorable to the program discovered an 80–90 percent rate of continued delinquent acts among participants.[22]

Nonetheless, the popularity of the Lifer's program remains high nationwide. The substance of the program—convicts physically intimidating children—is really an expression of the type of behavior that got the lifers where they are today, while one might expect that the principal result of such a program would be to teach delinquent children to emulate the swaggering lifers' aggressiveness and brutality. Meanwhile, the audience masks its own feelings of ineffectuality with a moralistic faith that browbeating children will bring them to their senses—even as most such supporters could never imagine acting this way toward their own children. Do the film's producer and onscreen stars (Peter Falk and Whoopi Goldberg) humiliate and threaten to maim their own children when these youngsters do something wrong?

While we seem to feel that large numbers of children are misbehaving, we are at a loss about how to change these children's behavior in constructive ways. This may be a very old story, but what is new is our eagerness to decide that children are born with medical problems that explain their difficulties or misconduct. Special education for learning-disabled children is an example of a primary effort to combat this new category of medical problems. These programs have grown enormously in the United States over the past ten years. For example, New York City now spends one-fifth of its education budget—over $1 billion a year—on special education.[23] Between 1977 and 1983, the number of special ed students in New York City jumped from 41,000 to 111,000. Despite these programs, the educational performance of city schools continued to deteriorate and reading levels and other school achievement tests plummeted.

At a 1984 conference with parents, the then-chancellor of the New York City schools, Nathan Quinones, decried the explosion in special education programs in his own school system. He claimed that they made it "extremely difficult to provide consistently high-quality educational services," and he recommended a drastic reduction in special education referrals. Mayor Edward Koch likened the situation in New York to having "two separate education programs. I believe this separateness is bad for schools and bad for education in this city." The president of the United Parents Association, Agnes Green, also viewed this growth as unhealthy, saying it was caused "by operating in a 'child deficit mode.' If something is not right in the classroom with this student, there must be something wrong with the child."[24]

If all parties in the New York City educational system are against these programs, why do they continue to grow? Perhaps it is because we can think of no more creative way to tackle the depressing inner-city cycle of declining school performance and worsening economic conditions. Unlike the politicians and educators directly responsible for New York schools who expressed dismay at the growth of such programs, educational specialists love the programs and clamor to expand them. At the same time that the 1984 conference deploring the explosion in special education was being held in New York City, the *Times* annual educational supplement appeared with the headline LEARNING DISABLED: A NEW AWARENESS. This highly respected survey presented articles that lauded the growing awareness that so many children are learning disabled and the expansion of special education programs.[25]

While New York City has placed more students in special education, other school systems have taken an even more medical approach to the problem of learning disabilities by widely prescribing Ritalin, a stimulant drug given to children who have difficulty concentrating on schoolwork (and who are frequently diagnosed as hyperactive). The use of this drug rose dramatically in the mid-1980s. (Production of the drug doubled between 1985 and 1987.) Some states use the drug far more frequently than others—Utah, for example, has *four times* the national level of consumption and nearly twice that of the state that uses the drug next most frequently. Interestingly, Utah also has the largest average class size among the states, leading some to believe Ritalin is a convenient way for teachers to control unmanageable numbers of students.[26]

# Childhood as a Marketplace for Diseases

The tremendous growth in the diagnosis of learning disabilities and in special education programs calls into question exactly how we decide exactly what is or is not normal in childhood. Whether a behavior is defined as a problem—and especially whether it is labeled a permanent disease or a "handicap"—has tremendous implications for the future of individual children and for the society as a whole. The trend is constantly upward in the discovery of new childhood maladies that are purportedly due to brain malfunctioning and that require special treatment, even though these problems are typically said to be uncorrectable.

Consistently, while working-class and inner-city parents are suspicious of special education programs, middle-class parents tend to welcome learning-disability diagnoses to explain their children's poor performance in school. For example, the Orton Society is an organization of parents and professionals who seek to gain recognition for the disorder of dyslexia. The society claims that dyslexia is a "hidden disease" because it isn't obvious, even though it is common. The society insists that dyslexia is a neurological malady so as to give legitimacy to the idea that it is a disease, but the society's professional staff makes clear that the nature of the disease is not yet understood. What is understood is that dyslexia makes it difficult for children to learn—no matter how high their IQ—in the standard educational environment. Of course, the anguish of parents with children who have problems at school is very real, and many—particularly middle-class parents—have found it reassuring to consider these problems the results of a disease. But does conventional treatment and education for the dyslexic child actually help?

Melvin Levine, a physician and researcher at the University of North Carolina School of Medicine, views learning disabilities—including dyslexia—in a different way. Rather than seeing them as "hard-wired" in the brain, Levine finds that maladies such as "dyslexia," "minimal brain dysfunction," and "hyperactivity" are actually "exceedingly variable" conditions—and that "in reality, no two people with learning disabilities are ever alike." For Levine, "a more useful approach is to describe in detail the strengths and deficiencies of a child (or adult), rather than to paste a broad diagnostic label on him" or her. In other words, disabilities are more aptly regarded as examples of individual variations in learning styles.

For Levine, learning disabilities are both universal and largely irrelevant to people's adult lives. He finds these disabilities to be the results of the rigid demands that school makes on everyone, no matter what their skills or what they intend to do in life. "Remember, when you're an adult, if you can't dance you don't go to dances. All too often, when you're a child, they'll push you into the middle of the dance floor." Thus, the disability often seems to diminish with age, because people either learn to compensate for their deficiencies or else they gravitate to those areas to which they are best suited and at which they are most successful. For example, dyslexia is most notable in children who are unable to focus on their assignments. Yet "attentional deficits" of this type generally improve as children get older. Some claim that children's nervous systems mature, but it may be that many simply become more engaged as they start to study things they like better or that are more connected to their lives.

Levine cautions that, if those identified as learning disabled "can survive schooling without being demoralized, they can go on to exploit their special talents in ways that are both personally satisfying and socially invaluable. After all, people with learning disabilities are simply extreme examples of our natural human diversity." Unfortunately, although Levine outlines this generally sensible approach to childhood learning disabilities, he also indicates that "Youngsters with attention deficits [so clearly] benefit from low dosages of stimulant medications . . . that it's virtually unethical not to use the drugs." He adds, "using them may be little different in spirit from an adult's taking an extra cup of coffee to get through a difficult task."[27]

I think that telling children they need a stimulant to get through a task is unethical and that it guarantees a warped sense of self— one likely to lead children to decide, exactly as Levine decries, that they have a permanent disease. Hyperactive children who have normal days may come to believe that they achieved normality because of their Ritalin. The tendency for children to attribute agency and responsibility to forces outside themselves is a side effect of all disease diagnoses and treatments. For example, children who stop abusing drugs or alcohol after they are treated are likely to believe their recovery is due to their group or to the treatment. More children are being persuaded at earlier ages that they have a disease and that this diseased person is *who* they are. We seem rapidly to be creating a future world of people who identify themselves primarily in terms of their diseases.

# The Most Common Disease—Eating?

It often seems that we might all find a disability or disease that typifies our lives and for which we could seek treatment or join a group. Among the potentially most common such disorders are those connected with eating, such as obesity, anorexia, and bulimia—all problems that are increasingly being approached as diseases. Obviously, in deciding how many people have the disease of obesity, one important issue is how much overweight qualifies one for the disease. Considering Americans who are 50 percent or more overweight, there are 15 million potential obesity patients (about 5 percent of the population). About a third of all Americans—approximately 70 million—consider *themselves* fat enough to diet or potentially to require treatment. On the other hand, by the standard of being 10 to 15 percent overweight, half of all Americans or more qualify as obese.

Anorexia (pathological thinness) and bulimia (cycles of binge eating followed by self-induced vomiting) have joined obesity as eating problems in the 1980s, fed by admissions by Jane Fonda and other celebrities of their eating disorders. The hospital ad about teen illnesses described above places the percentage of adolescent girls with such eating disorders at 15 percent. The ad also describes how, if left "untreated, anorexia and bulimia ravage the body—in many cases causing irreparable damage, and in some cases, death." The 15 percent figure is not the largest estimate of this phenomenon. An article in the *American Journal of Psychiatry* reported that some estimates indicate that as many as "one-half or more [of all] young women suffer from eating disorders" such as bulimia.

Where does the truth lie? To determine the actual incidence of bulimia, the authors of the journal article conducted a general survey of college and young working women. Forty-one percent of the working women and 69 percent of the college women reported binge eating ("eating an enormous amount of food in a short period of time").[28] In this sense, many young women (more than two-thirds of the college students) could be diagnosed as bulimic. However, the researchers did not find very many other signs of bulimia in their study. Only 9 percent of the working women and 17 percent of the college students feared they would lose control and not be able to stop eating voluntarily during a binge. Finally, incorporating the crucial criterion of purging (regular use of laxatives or vomiting), only *one* percent of the working women and 5 percent of the college women qualified as bulimic.

It is therefore inaccurate to combine the estimated prevalence of eating disorders among young women of from 15 percent to 50 percent with alarming public accounts of near-fatal and fatal anorexia and bulimia. In this sense, data about eating disorders are extremely similar to those about alcoholism and all the maladies discussed here. Very few members of the general population display the full-blown symptoms that appear in reports about the relatively small percentage of cases who seek clinical treatment. Yet more and more people consider themselves to have these disorders, even if their symptomatology doesn't measure up to what they read about in magazines or see on television. At the same time, more seek treatment for the disorder and identify in themselves more of the disease's symptomatology.

## Rating the Most Common Diseases— Do We All Have One or More?

Obviously, it all depends where you draw the line in deciding who has a disease, in eating or in any other area. Just as obviously, the tendency has been to expand these boundaries, to label more and more people as diseased. This tendency originates in part from treatment personnel and specialists in each disease area. But contrary to the disease notion of denial, many people seem eager to claim a disease for themselves. Having a disease is apparently so appealing that people stretch the criteria in order to include themselves, or perhaps even expand their behavior to meet the criteria. Whatever the reasons, very many Americans now fall within the defining limits established by experts for various diseases.

Since from 15 percent to 50 percent of Americans (or more) are potentially diagnosable as obese or suffering from an eating disorder, eating might be considered the most diseased activity that Americans engage in. Compared with eating disorders, far fewer people can be treated for alcoholism. However, if we accept the claim that children of alcoholics and those who marry or date alcoholics, or codepend-

ents, also suffer from a disease, the 20 million Americans alleged in
*The Courage to Change* to have the disease of alcoholism are then
multiplied into 80 million. Among the young, chemical dependence
(combining drug use and drunkenness)—which involves more than
half of teenagers—could be considered the most common disease.
At the same time, about 30 percent of adult Americans still smoke,
and nearly all of them—unlike illicit drug users—can probably be
said to be addicted. And, while alcoholism is said to affect 10 percent
of Americans, the National Council on Compulsive Gambling maintains that 12 percent of Americans are diseased gamblers.

While compulsive gamblers are nearly always men, women are
more often among the addicted shoppers who have begun forming
AA-type support groups, although compulsive shoppers also join
Debtors Anonymous, which enrolls as many men as women. For
those who see these ailments as slightly fatuous, disease experts and
counselors hasten to make clear the truly painful, compulsive, and
addictive nature of the problems: " 'shopping addiction . . . is a
compulsive disorder—it's a syndrome much like gambling and alcoholism,' says Janet Damon, a Brooklyn psychotherapist who
specializes in compulsive disorders"[29]; "Dr. Marilyn Jacovsky, a psychotherapist who specializes in dependency, says: 'The compulsion
to use debt and credit is just like any other compulsion—the compulsion to overeat, for example. It is progressive, and it finally gets
out of the individual's control.' "[30]

The point is, of course, that once we start viewing drinking as a
disease rather than a human weakness, shopping and spending are
no less eligible to be labeled diseases. We have seen, primarily, that
loss of control defines alcoholism and that loss of control is a subjective experience. People can certainly feel out of control of their
spending and therefore label it a disease. Indeed, those scientists who
want to establish the biological basis for alcoholism must deal with
the heartfelt pleading and suffering of compulsive gamblers. Many
of these same people are also alcoholics who claim they experience
no difference in the addictiveness of the two compulsions. On what
grounds can a scientist claim that one type of compulsion is biological
and genetic and that the other is not?

Aside from the laundry list of addictive and appetitive disorders,
two maladies that many Americans—and particularly women—say
they suffer from are anxiety and depression. Although these con-

ditions have long been around, we have returned to them in the 1980s as primarily biological and inbred maladies, and we often approach them like addictions—for example, by creating AA-type support groups for sufferers. According to Mark Gold, "Between 20 and 30 million people are plagued by an illness commonly called depression," and, "1 in 4 of all Americans will have a significant depressive illness in their lifetime."[31] In *The Anxiety Disease*, Dr. David Sheehan finds anxiety to be more prevalent than depression, and that eighty percent of those who suffer from it are women.[32] Putting these estimates together, "affective" diseases like depression and anxiety may claim one-third or more of women.

Yet anxiety and depression are not the most common emotional disorders (discounting entirely the addictive and appetitive disorders, from smoking to obesity to alcoholism to drug addiction to gambling to shopping). When the National Institute of Mental Health (NIMH) published the results of its survey of Americans' mental disorders in the fall of 1988, an emotional disorder largely unknown to the public—and unsuspected by the psychiatric researchers—was revealed to be most prevalent.[33] This is obsessive-compulsive disorder (OCD), in extreme cases of which people spend nearly all their time preoccupied by rituals such as washing their hands. Less severe cases include people who must return to their house to check whether they have left any appliances running or who clean their homes daily. The NIMH survey discovered that OCD is twenty-five to sixty times as common as previously supposed, and the researchers predicted that "like other stigmatized and hidden disorders in the past, [OCD] may be ready for discovery and demands for treatment on a large scale."[34]

In discovering all at once that a major mental disorder such as OCD has appeared in our midst, we see how such diseases are a matter of fad and fashion. In some cases, OCD reminds us of agoraphobia, a disease that prevents primarily middle-class women from leaving their homes to enter public places—for example, OCD and agoraphobia both describe the case of the woman who cleans her home constantly instead of venturing outside. When a 1987 PBS drama entitled *Dottie* dramatized agoraphobia, an accompanying press release indicated that millions of Americans with the disease never leave their homes. It might seem that agoraphobia will be supplanted by obsessive-compulsive disorder as the illness used to describe, among others, those preoccupied with their chores at home.

What diseases loom next on the horizon? One candidate, perhaps, is Cyclothymia. *McCall's* magazine warns that "one to two percent of American adults are affected by constant, sudden shifts in mood to such a degree that it can devastate their lives and those around them."[35] Apparently, from this article, most of the sufferers are women. We can compare the one to two percent rate *McCall's* claims for Cyclothymia to the two to three percent rate the NIMH discovered for obsessive-compulsive disorder that qualifies OCD for epidemic demands for treatment and support groups. In Cyclothymia, we may see the anatomy of a building epidemic.

If women in our society are most often the victims of all these diseases of emotional tension and suppression, the diseases we discover in men more often take the form of antisocial acting out. Alcoholism and gambling are examples of the latter. Conditions tied to violence, most often by men, that are said to be epidemic (but also to be hidden) are spouse and child abuse, which are now often regarded and treated as illnesses. If being abused creates a disease state, consider that 38 million Americans have had some form of sexual contact with adults when they were children.[36] Another disease affecting men that often has violent manifestations and that is frequently featured in the media is post-Vietnam stress. War trauma is part of a larger category called post-traumatic stress disorder, found in women as well as men who have lost babies or spouses or have been crime or accident victims.

Peculiar to women, of course, is premenstrual syndrome (PMS). Hazelden's July, 1983, *Professional Update* magazine for counselors called PMS "The Disease of the 80's." A wide variety of drug (along with hormone and vitamin) therapies, as well as psychological counseling, are now actively marketed for relieving PMS symptoms. Later in the 1980s, PMS has been joined in popularity by postpartum depression (PPD). At the International Congress of Psychology in Australia in the fall of 1988, I (along with all other attendees) was presented with a packet including an advertisement from a private treatment center saying a third of mothers suffer from PPD. What is interesting about PMS and PPD is the frequency with which they appear as defenses for women's violence against their mates or children. Women who *accept* being brutalized, on the other hand, are said to suffer from the battered woman syndrome. But this syndrome has also, paradoxically, become the standard defense to explain why women may eventually kill their husbands, or why (à la Hedda Nussbaum) they tolerate or cooperate in violence by their spouses against their children (see chapter 8).

The American family seems to be an increasingly dangerous place, and violence often characterizes intimate relationships. But psychiatry and other helping professions now often regard *intimate relationships themselves* as diseased, whether or not anyone is physically maimed. Several books in the 1980s sought to describe how some women are *biologically* driven to repeatedly form inappropriate and destructive relationships with men.[37] The misdirected, compulsive drive for love has formed the basis for a myriad of best-sellers along the lines of Robin Norwood's *Women Who Love Too Much*. Books like Norwood's are directed specifically to women. Men are more likely to suffer from "sexual addiction"—compulsive sexual contact with numerous women—which has prompted the creation of a Sexaholics Anonymous movement based on the AA twelve-step approach.[38]

*Time* magazine, *60 Minutes*, and the *New York Times* science section, to name a few, have run stories on sexual and love addictions. One pamphlet describes sexual addiction counseling as follows:

> Almost daily, newspapers across the country carry seamy accounts of sexual misbehavior. Congressman, clergy, and professionals get the most press, but the addiction traps people of all pursuits—white collar workers, blue collar workers, and homemakers. Their sexual compulsiveness ruins their lives and careers. For many of these people, those who want to stop but cannot, it is an addiction which falls like a shadow over all those who are affected. It penetrates and influences every aspect of their lives. Often the addiction is handed down from generation to generation and becomes the family's best kept secret. But the shadow deepens as the addictive behaviors escalate. . . .
>
> Sexually addictive behaviors range from the need to have constant affairs or masturbate, on one end of the spectrum, to incest and rape on the other end. Addicts, on the average, have at least three behaviors over which they have no control. With support and help, sexual addicts can integrate new beliefs and discard dysfunctional behaviors. Without help from others, the addict cannot regain control because the addiction feeds itself.[39]

According to the quote from the National Association on Sexual Addiction Problems at the front of this chapter, perhaps 10 percent—

or as many as *one quarter*—of all adult Americans suffer from sexual addiction problems. Sexual addiction as described in the advertising pamphlet has all the traits that characterize the diseases popularized by the alcoholism movement and the addiction treatment industry— loss of control that often serves as an excuse for misbehavior (according to this pamphlet, a sexual addiction could be used to defend rapists); the inherited, possibly biological nature of the malady; the ever-deepening addictive progression that can only be interrupted by treatment. The bottom line for this and other discoveries of new diseases is increased counseling services. Treatment corporations, private hospitals, and other institutions are hungry to expand the net for addictions and compulsive behaviors in this way. Alcoholism treatment provides the model for these new services, while the new diseases allow alcoholism treatment groups to expand their client base and to sustain their growth. CompCare and Hazelden are two organizations that have thrived by building from their roots in alcoholism first into the area of drug dependence and then into such areas as obesity, PMS, and sexual addiction.

In discussing sexual addictions and compulsive love affairs, I am obligated to mention my own role in the movement. I wrote (along with Archie Brodsky) the book *Love and Addiction*, which appeared in 1975 and which most works on love and sexual addictions use as a primary source. I concentrated on two goals in *Love and Addiction*. First, I wanted to make clear that drug addiction is not a medical disease, since it has the same compulsive profile as many behaviors we regard as quite ordinary and nonbiological, like love affairs. My aim there was turned on its head when subsequent writers agreed that compulsive love and sex were like drug addictions; therefore, they *also* were diseases. Second, *Love and Addiction* was a social commentary on how our society defines and patterns intimate relationships. But all of this social dimension has been removed, and the attention to love addiction has been channeled in the direction of regarding it as an individual, treatable psychopathology.

In calculating all the diseases I have listed in this section (and there are others), it seems that each American must have at least one such disease and, in addition, must know many people who altogether have a score of other diseases. It is hard to escape the conclusion that ownership of an emotional-behavioral-appetitive disease is the norm in America. And in the cases of PMS, postpartum depression, and love addiction, we see the ultimate definition of the ordinary discomforts and challenges in life as diseased events. To summarize the points of this chapter—the exaggerations and dangers inherent in the massive disease industry—I want to give some feeling for how shocked ordinary people, scientists, and public commentators typically are when one of these diseases is first explained to them.

In 1986, a physician wrote in the *Wall Street Journal* about the pervasiveness of PMS and the enormous costs it exacted of the work force[40]; the article provoked four letters that were published in the *Journal:*[41]

> I can scarcely believe my eyes! Premenstrual tension is a disease. How about that! It's even been given a label. The biological phenomenon that heralds a girl's coming of age into womanhood—all girls, all women—is a disease.
>
> It just goes to show. Here I always thought my monthly periods indicated that all was right with me and my world, that I was functioning normally and that, in time, as indeed happened, I would be able to have children.
>
> Sylvia Hornstein, Encino, Calif.

> In your article a physician estimates that "the illness costs U.S. industry 8% of its total wage bill." Let us ignore arguendo the facts of lower female participation in the work force, the wage differential between working men and women, and the proportion of the female workforce that is post-menopause, and assume for the sake of simplicity that: (1) 50% of the labor force is female; and, (2) women's wages are at parity with men's. . . . One is then forced to the conclusion that each woman worker, on average, loses 16% of her productive time due to PMS, or approximately 35 workdays per year. This is utterly preposterous.
>
> Steven S. Bremner, Seattle

> As PMS has been the basis for a growth industry, it is entirely appropriate for the *Journal* to report on it. In recent years, a number of therapists have devoted their practices to this presumed ailment, and pharmaceutical companies have made money from drugs developed to treat it.

There is, however, a growing uncertainty on the part of researchers about exactly what PMS is, as well as considerable skepticism about the extent to which it exists as a definable ailment. . . .
Prof. Cynthia Fuchs Epsteiny, Russell Sage Foundation

In my 77 years I have known only one, possibly two, such cases, although I have lived in a college dormitory and worked in a school teaching seniors. PMS is an abnormality that does not affect most young women, and it usually improves after a woman becomes sexually active (mine did with marriage). It *affects no woman past middle age* [emphasis added]. If PMS affects a woman at all, the effect is for hours not days.

Your story indicated great concern that women get a fair shake: Executives should make allowances for their special problems, and so on. But once employers had thought all that through, maybe, just maybe, they'd conclude they'd be better off to hire a man. . . .
Florence Wagner, Gainesville, Fla.

Here a group of readers of the *Wall Street Journal* have ably outlined the following problems with new disease diagnoses:

1. A normal experience for approximately half the population is declared an illness.
2. The disease is being blown out of proportion, and the preposterous inflation of its ubiquity and severity concocted for national media consumption is deflated by the most straightforward of calculations.
3. Those who profit from the new illness are disingenuous in raising these alarms—they make money from them.
4. The scientific community fails to agree on the basic premises of the illness, including whether it can actually be identified and separated from normal experience.
5. Typical observations by people well familiar with supposedly high-risk populations (in this case, all women, or all young women) are that the problem is rare, variable, and disappears almost entirely as people mature.

The last sardonic observation about PMS by Florence Wagner is the most biting and double-edged. She points out that PMS, defended in the name of helping women, actually dredges up harmful images of women that have traditionally been used to debilitate them. This debilitation is external in that it reinforces among employers hoary stereotypes of female inferiority and unreliability. More crushing, however, is the personal temptation for women to impose this diagnosis on *themselves*. For example, Bernadette Peters—while appearing in the Broadway production *Song and Dance*—announced to a national television audience on *Late Night* (the David Letterman show) that she suffered from PMS and would not be at her best because her period was coming on. Viewers might have tried to calculate when Peters's PMS would interfere with her performances, so as to avoid attending her show on those dates.

Disease theories of life have struck on a fundamental truth: everything that humans do—eating, drinking, sleeping, drug taking, loving, raising children, learning, having sex, having periods, feeling, thinking about oneself—has a healthy and unhealthy side, sometimes both at the same time or often alternating with one another. By elevating the unhealthy side of normal functioning to the status of disease state, therapists and others who claim the mantle of science now *guarantee* the preeminence, pervasiveness, and persistence of sickness in everyday life.

# 6

# What Is Addiction, and How Do People Get It?

## Values, Intentions, Self-Restraint, and Environments

Theories of drug dependence ignore the most fundamental question—why a person, having experienced the effect of a drug, would want to go back again to reproduce that chronic state.

—Harold Kalant, pioneering psychopharmacologist[1]

I never had a drug problem. I never had a drinking problem. I just had a winning problem. If some of the players had standards, they wouldn't be on dope.

—Fred Dryer, former L.A. Rams defensive end and star of TV series *Hunter*[2]

---

WHILE individual practitioners and recovering addicts—and the whole addiction movement—may believe they are helping people, they succeed principally at expanding their industry by finding more addicts and new types of addictions to treat. I too have argued—in books from *Love and Addiction* to *The Meaning of Addiction*—that addiction *can* take place with any human activity. Addiction is *not*, however, something people are born with. Nor is it a biological imperative, one that means the addicted individual is not able to consider or choose alternatives. The disease view of addiction is equally untrue when applied to gambling, compulsive sex, and everything else that it has been used to explain. Indeed, the fact that people become addicted to all these things *proves* that addiction is not *caused* by chemical or biological forces and that it is not a special disease state.

# The Nature of Addiction

People seek specific, essential human experiences from their addictive involvement, no matter whether it is drinking, eating, smoking, loving, shopping, or gambling. People can come to depend on such an involvement for these experiences until—in the extreme—the involvement is totally consuming and potentially destructive. Addiction can occasionally veer into total abandonment, as well as periodic excesses and loss of control. Nonetheless, even in cases where addicts die from their excesses, an addiction must be understood as a human response that is motivated by the addict's desires and principles. All addictions *accomplish something for the addict*. They are ways of coping with feelings and situations with which addicts cannot otherwise cope. What is wrong with disease theories as science is that they are *tautologies*; they avoid the work of understanding *why* people drink or smoke in favor of simply declaring these activities to be addictions, as in the statement "he drinks so much because he's an alcoholic."

Addicts seek experiences that satisfy needs they cannot otherwise fulfill. Any addiction involves three components—the person, the situation or environment, and the addictive involvement or experience (see table 1). In addition to the individual, the situation, and the experience, we also need to consider the overall cultural and social factors that affect addiction in our society.

## The Individual

Addiction follows all the ordinary rules of human behavior, even if the addiction engages the addict in extraordinary activities and self-destructive involvements. Addicts—like all people—act to maximize

## Table 1

| The person | The situation | The addictive experience |
|---|---|---|
| Unable to fulfill essential needs | Barren and deprived: disadvantaged social groups, war zones | Creates powerful and immediate sensations; focuses and absorbs attention |
| Values that support or do not counteract addiction: e.g., lack of achievement motivation | Antisocial peer groups | Provides artificial or temporary sense of self-worth, power, control, security, intimacy, accomplishment |
| Lack of restraint and inhibition | Absence of supportive social groups; disturbed family structure | |
| Lack of self-efficacy, sense of powerlessness vis-à-vis the addiction | Life situations: adolescence, temporary isolation, deprivation, or stress | Eliminates pain, uncertainty, and other negative sensations |

the rewards they perceive are available to them, however much they hurt and hobble themselves in the process. If they choose easier, powerful, and more immediate ways of gaining certain crucial feelings such as acceptance by others, or power, or calm—this, then, is a statement that they value these feelings and find in the addiction a preferred way to obtain them. Simultaneously, they place less value on the ordinary ways of gaining these feelings that most other people rely on, such as work or other typical forms of positive accomplishment.

Addicts display a range of other personal and situational problems. Drug addicts and alcoholics more often come from underprivileged social groups. However, middle-class addicts also usually have a range of emotional and family problems even before they become addicted. There is no "typical" addicted personality or emotional problem—some people drink because they are depressed, others because they are agitated. But as a group, addicts feel more powerless and out of control than other people even before becoming addicted. They also come to believe their addiction is magically powerful and that it brings them great benefits. When the addiction turns sour, these same addicts often maintain their view of the drug or booze as all-powerful, only they do so now as a way of explaining why they are in the throes of the addiction and can't break out of it.

Simply discovering that a drug, or alcohol, or an activity accomplishes something for a person who has emotional problems or a particularly susceptible personality does not mean that this individual will be addicted. Indeed, most people in any such category are *not* addicts or alcoholics. Addicts must *indulge* in their addictions with sufficient abandon to achieve the addicted state. In doing so, they place less value on social proprieties or on their health or on their families and other considerations that normally hold people's behavior in check. Think of addictions such as overeating, compulsive gambling and shopping, and unrestrained sexual appetites. Those who overeat or who gamble away their families' food budgets or who spend more money than they earn on clothes and cars or who endlessly pursue sexual liaisons do not necessarily have stronger urges to do these things than everyone else, so much as they display less self-restraint in giving into these urges. I always think in this connection of the Rumanian saying my in-laws use when they see an extremely obese person: "So, you ate what you wanted."

It takes more than understanding what a particular drug does for a person to explain why some individuals become addicted to so many things. If alcoholics are born addicted to booze, why do over 90 percent of alcoholics also smoke? Why are compulsive gamblers also frequently heavy drinkers? Why do so many women alcoholics also abuse tranquilizers? Tranquilizers and alcohol have totally different molecular properties, as do cigarettes and alcohol. No biological characteristic can explain why a person uses more than one of these substances excessively at the same time. And certainly no biological theory can explain why heavy gambling and heavy drinking are associated.[3]

## The Experience

People become addicted to drugs and alcohol because they welcome the sensations that alcohol and drug intoxication provides for them.

Other involvements to which people become addicted share certain traits with powerful drug experiences—they are all-encompassing, quick and powerful in onset, and they make people less aware of and less able to respond to outside stimuli, people, and activities. In addition, experiences that facilitate addiction offer people a sense of power or control, of security or calm, of intimacy or of being valued by others; on the other hand, such experiences succeed in blocking out sensations of pain, discomfort, or other negative sensations.

## Life Phases

Everyone knows people who drink or take drugs too much during a bad phase in their lives—for example, after a divorce, or when their careers have taken a bad turn, or some other time when they seem to be without moorings. The life phase in which people most commonly are rudderless and willing to try anything is when they are young. For some groups of adolescents and young adults, drug or alcohol abuse is almost an obligatory rite of passage. But in most cases, no matter how bad the addiction seems at the time, people recover from such a phase without mishap when they move on to the next stage in their lives. It is customary for those in the addiction treatment industry to say that such individuals were not really alcoholics or chemically dependent. Nonetheless, any AA group or treatment center would have accepted these people as addicts or alcoholics had they enrolled during their peak period of substance abuse.

## The Situation or Environment

Life stages, like adolescence, are part of a broader category in the addictive matrix—the situation or environment the individual faces. One of the most remarkable illustrations of the dynamics of addiction is the Vietnam war, an illustration to which I will return throughout this chapter. American soldiers in Vietnam frequently took narcotics, and nearly all who did became addicted. A group of medical epidemiologists studied these soldiers and followed them up after they came home. The researchers found that most of the soldiers gave up their drug addiction when they returned to the States. However, about half of those addicted in Vietnam did use heroin at home. *Yet only a small percentage of these former addicts became readdicted.* Thus, Vietnam *epitomizes* the kind of barren, stressful, and out-of-control situation that encourages addiction. At the same time, the fact that some soldiers became addicted in the United States after being addicted in Asia while most did not indicates how important individual personalities are in addiction. The Vietnam experience also shows that narcotics, such as heroin, produce experiences that serve to create addictions only under specific conditions.

## The Social and Cultural Milieu

We must also consider the enormous social-class differences in addiction rates. That is, the farther down the social and economic scale a person is, the more likely the person is to become addicted to alcohol, drugs, or cigarettes, to be obese, or to be a victim or perpetrator of family or sexual abuse. How does it come to be that addiction is a "disease" rooted in certain social experiences, and why in particular are drug addiction and alcoholism associated primarily with certain groups? A smaller range of addiction and behavioral problems are associated with the middle and upper social classes. These associations must also be explained. Some addictions, like shopping, are obviously connected with the middle class. Bulimia and exercise addiction are also primarily middle-class addictions.

Finally, we must explore why addictions of one kind or another appear on our social landscape all of sudden, almost as though floodgates were released. For example, alcoholism was unknown to most colonial Americans and to most Americans earlier in this century; now it dominates public attention. This is not due to greater consumption, since we are actually drinking *less* alcohol than the colonists did. Bulimia, PMS, shopping addiction, and exercise addiction are wholly new inventions. Not that it isn't possible to go back in time to find examples of things that appear to conform to these new diseases. Yet their widespread—almost commonplace—presence in today's society must be explained, especially when the disease—like alcoholism—is supposedly biologically inbred.

# The Addiction Experience

Consider one strange aspect of the field of pharmacology—the search for a nonaddictive analgesic (painkiller).[4] Since the turn of this century, American pharmacologists have declared the need to develop a chemical that would relieve pain but that would not create addiction. Consider how desperate this search has been: *heroin* was originally marketed in this country by the Bayer company of Germany as a nonaddictive substitute for morphine! Cocaine was also used to cure morphine (and later heroin) addiction, and many physicians (including Freud) recommended it widely for this purpose.

Indeed, every new pharmaceutical substance that has reduced anxiety or pain or had other major psychoactive effects has been promoted as offering feelings of relief without having addictive side effects. And in every case, this claim has been proved wrong. Heroin and cocaine are only two obvious examples. A host of other drugs— the barbiturates, artificially synthesized narcotics (Demerol), tranquilizers (Valium), and on and on—were welcomed initially, only to have been found eventually to cause addiction in many people.

What this tells us is that addiction is *not* a chemical side effect of a drug. Rather, addiction is a direct result of the psychoactive effects of a substance—of the way it changes our sensations. The *experience itself* is what the person becomes addicted to. In other words, when narcotics relieve pain, or when cocaine produces a feeling of exhilaration, or when alcohol or gambling creates a sense of power, or when shopping or eating indicates to people that they are being cared for, it is the *feeling* to which the person becomes addicted. No other explanation—about supposed chemical bondings or inbred biological deficiencies—is required. And none of these other theories comes close to making sense of the most obvious aspects of addiction.

One of the key dynamics in the alcoholism or addiction cycle is the repeated failure of the alcoholic or addict to gain exactly the state he or she seeks, while still persisting in the addicted behavior. For example, alcoholics (in research, these are frequently street inebriates) report that they anticipate alcohol to be calming, and yet when they drink they become increasingly agitated and depressed.[5] The process whereby people desperately pursue some feeling that becomes more elusive the harder they pursue it is a common one, and appears among compulsive gamblers, shoppers, overeaters, love addicts, and the like. It is this cycle of desperate search, temporary or inadequate satisfaction, and renewed desperation that most characterizes addiction.

How do people become addicted to powerful experiences such as gambling? Actually, gambling may be far more addictive than heroin. More people who gamble have a sense of loss of control than have this feeling with narcotics: very few people who receive morphine after an operation in the hospital have even the slightest desire to prolong this experience. It is the *total nature* of the gambling experience (as practiced in Atlantic City casinos, for instance) that promotes this sense of addictive involvement. The complete focusing of attention, the overriding excitement of risk, and the exhilaration of immediate success—or usually, the negative sensations of loss—make this experience overwhelming for even the strongest among us.

Any experience this potent—alluring and at the same time holding out the possibility of serious disturbance to one's life—has great addictive potential. Gambling uplifts one and then can make one miserable. The temptation is to escape the misery by returning to the ecstasy. People for whom gambling serves as a major source of feelings of importance and power are quite likely to become addicted to gambling, at least for a time. When thinking of who becomes addicted to gambling, we should also keep in mind that heavy gamblers are frequently also heavy drinkers. In other words, those who seek power and excitement in the "easy," socially destructive form of gambling are very often those prone to seek such feelings in alcohol.[6]

Many of us, on the other hand, have had addictive gambling experiences. We did so when we were young and went to a local carnival for the promise of easy and exciting money. Plopping down our quarters at the booth where the man spun the wheel, we became increasingly distressed as our anticipated winnings did not materialize. Sometimes we ran home to get more of our savings, perhaps stealing from our parents to get money. But this feeling rarely continued after the carnival departed. Indeed, when we got older and gambled in a small-stakes pinochle or poker game with friends, we simply did not have the same desperate experience that gambling had led us to under different circumstances at a different time in our lives. Just because people have had acute—even addictive—experiences with something by no means guarantees that they will always be addicted to this activity or substance. Even when they are addicted, by no means is every episode of the experience an out-of-control one.

---

## Who Becomes Addicted?

Two questions then are "Why do some people become addicted at some times to some things?" and "Why do *some* of these people persevere at the addiction through all facets of their lives?" The study we previewed of U.S. soldiers' drug use in Vietnam and after they returned home gives us good answers to both these questions. This study—based on the largest group of untreated heroin users ever identified—has such major ramifications for what we know about addiction that it could revolutionize our concepts of treatment for addiction—if only people, particularly scientists, could come to grips with its results. For example, Lee Robins and John Helzer, the principal investigators in this research, were shocked when they made the following discovery about veterans' drug use after leaving Asia: "Heroin purchased on the streets in the United States . . . did not lead [more] rapidly to daily or compulsive use . . . than did use of amphetamines or marijuana."[7]

What does it prove that people are no more likely to use heroin compulsively than marijuana? It tells us that the sources of addiction lie more in people than in drugs. To call certain drugs addictive misses the point entirely. Richard Clayton, a sociologist studying adolescent drug abuse, has pointed out that the best predictors of involvement with cocaine among high school students are, first, use of marijuana and, third, smoking cigarettes. Adolescents who smoke the most marijuana and cigarettes use the most cocaine. The second-best predictor of which kids will become cocaine abusers does not involve drug use. This factor is truancy: adolescents who cut school frequently are more likely to become heavily involved with drugs.[8] Of course, truant kids have more time on their hands to use drugs. At the same time, psychologists Richard and Shirley Jessor found adolescents who use drugs have a series of problem behaviors, place less value on achievement, and are more alienated from ordinary institutions such as school and organized recreational activities.[9]

Do some people have addictive personalities? What might make us think so is that some people do many, many things excessively. The carryover from one addiction to another for the same people is often substantial. Nearly every study has found that overwhelming majorities (90 percent and more) of alcoholics smoke.[10] When Robins and her colleagues examined Vietnam veterans who used heroin and other illicit drugs in American cities following the war, they found:

> The typical pattern of the heroin user seems to be to use a wide variety of drugs plus alcohol. The stereotype of the heroin addict as someone with a monomaniacal craving for a single drug seems hardly to exist in this sample. Heroin addicts use many other drugs, and not only casually or in desperation.

In other words, people who become heroin addicts take a lot of drugs, just as kids who use cocaine are more likely to smoke cigarettes and use marijuana heavily.

Some people seem to behave excessively in all areas of life, including using drugs heavily. This even extends into legal drug use. For example, those who smoke also drink more coffee. But this tendency to do unhealthy or antisocial things extends beyond the simple use of drugs. Illicit drug users have more accidents even when not using drugs.[11] Those arrested for drunk driving frequently also have arrest records for traffic violations *when they aren't drunk*.[12] In other words, people who get drunk and go out on the road are frequently the same people who drive recklessly when they're sober. In the same way, smokers have the highest rates of car accidents and traffic violations, and are more likely to drink when they drive.[13] That people misuse many drugs at once and engage in other risky and antisocial behaviors at the same time suggests that these are people who don't especially value their bodies and health or the health of the people around them.

If, as Lee Robins makes clear, heroin addicts use a range of other drugs, then why do they use heroin? After all, heavy drug users are equally willing to abuse cocaine, amphetamines, barbiturates, and marijuana (and certainly alcohol). Who are these people who somehow settle on heroin as their favorite drug? The heroin users and

## WHY DO SOME PEOPLE—AND THEIR FAMILIES AND EVERYONE THEY KNOW—DO SO MANY THINGS WRONG?

### *Lions' Rogers Out To Prove Himself*

Reggie Rogers, the Detroit Lions' top draft pick last year, doesn't want to fan the flames of a disastrous rookie season. "I think I was just burnt out on football, to be honest with you."

[His football] problems paled in comparison to those off the gridiron. Two months after being selected first by the Lions, Rogers was devastated when his older brother, Don, a defensive back with the Cleveland Browns, died of a cocaine overdose. During the season, Reggie Rogers was charged with aggravated assault, he was sued by two former agents, and his sister disappeared for several days. (July 31, 1988.)[14]

### *Obituaries*

A semicircle of caskets flanked a Berkeley minister Saturday as he looked out over a chapel of tearful mourners gathered for the funeral of three teens who were killed when their car was broadsided by Detroit Lions football player Reggie Rogers.

Rogers has been charged in warrants with three counts of manslaughter for driving under the influence of alcohol, speeding through a red light and colliding with the teens' car. (October 23, 1988.)[15]

---

addicts among the returned veterans Robins studied came from worse social backgrounds and had had more social problems before going to Vietnam and being introduced to the drug. In the words of Robins and her colleagues:

> People who use heroin are highly disposed to having serious social problems even before they touch heroin. Heroin probably accounts for some of the problems they have if they use it regularly, but heroin is "worse" than amphetamines or barbiturates only because "worse" people use it.

The film *Sid and Nancy* describes the short life of Sid Vicious of the British punk rock group The Sex Pistols. All in this group came from the underclass of British society, a group for whom hopelessness was a way of life. Vicious was the most self-destructive and alcoholic of the group. When he first met his girlfriend, Nancy—an American without any moorings—her main appeal was that she could introduce Sid to heroin, which Nancy already used. Vicious took to the drug like a duck to water. It seemed the logical extension of all he was and all he was to become—which included his and Nancy's self- and mutual absorption, their loss of careers and contact with the outside world, and their ultimate deaths.

## Are Addicts Disease Victims?

The development of an addictive life-style is an accumulation of patterns in people's lives of which drug use is neither a result nor a cause but another example. Sid Vicious was the consummate drug addict, an exception even among heroin users. Nonetheless, we need to understand the extremes to gain a sense of the shape of the entire phenomenon of addiction. Vicious, rather than being a passive victim of drugs, seemed intent on being and remaining addicted. He avoided opportunities to escape and turned every aspect of his life toward his addictions—booze, Nancy, drugs—while sacrificing anything that might have rescued him—music, business interests, family, friendships, survival instincts. Vicious was pathetic; in a sense, he was a victim of his own life. But his addiction, like his life, was more an active expression of his pathos than a passive victimization.

Addiction theories have been created because it stuns us that people would hurt—perhaps destroy—themselves through drugs, drinking, sex, gambling, and so on. While people get caught up in an addictive dynamic over which they do not have full control, it is at least as accurate to say that people consciously select an addiction as it is to say an addiction has a person under its control. And this is why addiction is so hard to ferret out of the person's life—because it fits the person. The bulimic woman who has found that self-induced vomiting helps her to control her weight and who feels more attractive after throwing up is a hard person to persuade to give up her habit voluntarily. Consider the homeless man who refused to go to one of Mayor Koch's New York City shelters because he couldn't easily drink there and who said, "I don't want to give up drinking; it's the only thing I've got."

The researcher who has done the most to explore the personalities of alcoholics and drug addicts is psychologist Craig MacAndrew. MacAndrew developed the MAC scale, selected from items on the MMPI (a personality scale) that distinguish clinical alcoholics and drug abusers from normal subjects and from other psychiatric patients. This scale identifies antisocial impulsiveness and acting out: "an assertive, aggressive, pleasure-seeking character," in terms of which alcoholics and drug abusers closely "resemble criminals and delinquents."[16] These characteristics are not the *results* of substance abuse. Several studies have measured these traits in young men *prior* to becoming alcoholics and in young drug and alcohol abusers.[17] This same kind of antisocial thrill-seeking characterizes most women who become alcoholic. Such women more often have disciplinary problems at school, react to boredom by "stirring up some kind of excitement," engage in more disapproved sexual practices, and have more trouble with the law.[18]

The typical alcoholic, then, fulfills antisocial drives and pursues immediate, sensual, and aggressive rewards while having underdeveloped inhibitions. MacAndrew also found that another, smaller group comprising both men and women alcoholics—but more often women—drank to alleviate internal conflicts and feelings like depression. This group of alcoholics viewed the world, in MacAndrew's words, "primarily in terms of its potentially punishing character." For them, "alcohol functions as a palliation for a chronically fearful, distressful internal state of affairs." While these drinkers also sought specific rewards in drinking, these rewards were defined more by internal states than by external behaviors. Nonetheless, we can see that this group too did not consider normal social strictures in pursuing feelings they desperately desired.

MacAndrew's approach in this research was to identify particular personality types identified by the experiences they looked to alcohol to provide. But even for alcoholics or addicts without such distinct personalities, the purposeful dynamic is at play. For example, in *The Lives of John Lennon*, Albert Goldman describes how Lennon—who was addicted over his career to a host of drugs—would get drunk when he went out to dinner with Yoko Ono so that he could spill out his resentments of her. In many families, drinking allows alcoholics to express emotions that they are otherwise unable to express. The entire panoply of feelings and behaviors that alcohol may bring about for individual drinkers thus can be motivations for chronic intoxication. While some desire power from drinking, others seek to escape in alcohol; for some drinking is the route to excitement, while others welcome its calming effects.

Alcoholics or addicts may have more emotional problems or more deprived backgrounds than others, but probably they are best characterized as feeling powerless to bring about the feelings they want or to accomplish their goals without drugs, alcohol, or some other involvement. Their sense of powerlessness then translates into the belief that the drug or alcohol is extremely powerful. They see in the substance the ability to accomplish what they need or want but can't do on their own. The double edge to this sword is that the person is easily convinced that he or she cannot function without the substance or addiction, that he or she requires it to survive. This sense of personal powerlessness, on the one hand, and of the extreme power of an involvement or substance, on the other, readily translates into addiction.[19]

People don't manage to become alcoholics over years of drinking simply because their bodies are playing tricks on them—say, by allowing them to imbibe more than is good for them without realizing it until they become dependent on booze. Alcoholics' long drinking careers are motivated by their search for essential experiences they cannot gain in other ways. The odd thing is that—despite a constant parade of newspaper and magazine articles and TV programs trying to convince us otherwise—most people recognize that alcoholics drink for specific purposes. Even alcoholics, however much they spout the party line, know this about themselves. Consider, for example, the quote at the beginning of chapter 4 in which Monica Wright, the head of a New York City treatment center, describes how she drank over the twenty years of her alcoholic marriage to cope with her insecurity and with her inability to deal with her husband and children. It is impossible to find an alcoholic who does not express similar reasons for his or her drinking, once the disease dogma is peeled away.

# Social Groups and Addiction

In the study of bulimia among college-age and working women, we saw that while many reported binge eating, few feared loss of control and fewer still self-induced vomiting.[20] However, twice as many of the college students as working women feared loss of control, while *five* times as many college women (although still only 5 percent of this group) reported purging with laxatives or through vomiting. Something about the intense collective life of women on campus exacerbates some women's insecurities into full-scale bulimia, while college life also creates a larger, additional group that has unhealthy eating habits that fall short of full-scale bulimia. Groups have powerful influences on people, as this study showed. Their power is a large part of the story of addiction. In the case of college women, the tensions of school and dating are combined with an intensely held social value toward thinness that many are not able to attain.

Groups certainly affect drinking and drug abuse. Young drug abusers associate primarily with drug abusers, as Eugene Oetting has clearly discerned in a decade's work with a wide range of adolescents. Indeed, he traces drug use and abuse primarily to what he calls "peer-group clusters" of like-minded kids. Naturally, we wonder why adolescents gravitate to such groups in the first place rather than joining, say, the school band or newspaper. But undoubtedly, informal social groups support and sustain much teen behavior. And some of these peer groups tend to be involved in a variety of antisocial activities, including criminal misbehavior and failure at school, as well as encouraging substance abuse.

One of the burdens of the disease movement is to indicate that it doesn't matter what social class one comes from—drug abuse and alcoholism are equally likely to befall you. Oetting disagrees strongly with this position. His opinion matters because he has studied fifteen thousand minority young people, including a great number of Hispanic and Native American youths. This is in addition to some ten thousand nonminority young people. Commenting on research that claims that socioeconomic status does not influence drug use, Oetting notes: "These studies, however, focus on middle and upper class levels of socioeconomic status and disadvantaged populations are underrepresented. Where research is conducted specifically among disadvantaged youth, particularly minority youth, higher rates of drug use are found."[21] These differences extend as well to legal drugs—18 percent of college graduates smoke, compared with 34 percent of those who never went to college.[22]

Middle-class groups certainly drink, and some quite heavily. Yet the consistent formula discovered in surveys of drinking is that the higher a person's social class, the more likely the person is both to drink and to drink without problems. Those in lower socioeconomic groups are more likely to abstain, and yet are much more often problem drinkers. What about drugs? Middle-class people have certainly developed broad experience with drugs in the last three decades. At the same time, when they do use drugs, they are more likely to do so occasionally, intermittently, or in a controlled manner. As a result, when warnings against cocaine became commonplace in the 1980s, cocaine use shrank among the middle class, while cocaine use intensified in ghetto areas, where extremely disruptive and violent drug use has become a major feature of life.

## Those with Better Things to Do Are Protected from Addiction

My point of view, however logical, goes so much against standard antidrug crusade wisdom that I hasten to defend my assertion about controlled drug users. It is not that there is any *question* that the data I cite are correct. Rather, I have to explain why so much of the information presented to the public is misinformation. For example, we hear constantly that the 800-Cocaine hotline reveals great numbers of middle-class addicts. In fact, examining the rolls of facilities for cocaine addicts reveals everything we have already reviewed— that nearly all cocaine addicts are multiple-substance users with long histories of drug abuse. Whatever greater rates of middle-class "stockbroker" addicts there are now, these are dwarfed by the typical cocaine abusers, who resemble other contemporary and historical drug abusers by being more often unemployed and socially dislocated in a number of ways.

What about the masses of cocaine users who appeared in the 1980s? The Michigan group studying student drug use found that high school grads in the early 1980s had a 40 percent chance of using the drug by their twenty-seventh birthday. Yet, most middle-class users use the drug only a few times; most regular users do not show negative effects and only a few become addicted; and most who have experienced negative effects, including problems of controlling their use, quit or cut back without treatment. These simple facts—which run so counter to everything we hear—have not been disputed by any investigation of cocaine use in the field. Ronald Siegel followed a group of cocaine users from the time they began use in college. Of the 50 regular users Siegel tracked for nearly a decade, five became compulsive users and another four developed intensified daily usage patterns. Even the compulsive users, however, only "experienced crisis reactions in approximately 10 percent of their intoxications."[23]

A more recent study was published by a distinguished group of Canadian researchers at the Addiction Research Foundation (ARF) of Ontario—Canada's premier drug addiction center. This study amplified Siegel's U.S. findings. To compensate for the overemphasis on the small minority of cocaine users in treatment, this study chose middle-class users through newspaper ads and by referrals from colleagues. Regular cocaine users reported a range of symptoms, most often acute insomnia and nasal disorders. However, only twenty percent reported frequently experiencing uncontrollable urges to continue use. Yet even in the case of the users who developed the worst problems, the typical response of the problem user was to quit or cut back without undergoing treatment for cocaine addiction![24] How different this seems from the advertisements, sponsored by the government and private treatment facilities, that emphasize the incurable, irresistible addictiveness of cocaine.

Where do these media images come from? They come from some extremely self-dramatizing addicts who report for treatment, and who in turn are extremely attractive to the media. If, instead, we examine college-student drug use, we find (in 1985—a peak year for cocaine use) that 17 percent of college students used cocaine. However, only one in 170 college-student users took the drug on as many as twenty of the previous thirty days.[25] Why don't all the other occasional users become addicted? Two researchers administered amphetamines to students and former students living in a university community (the University of Chicago).[26] These young people reported enjoying the effects of the drug; *yet they used less of the drug each time they returned to the experimental situation.* Why? Simple: they had too much in their lives that was more important to them than taking more drugs, even if they enjoyed them. In the words of a past president of the American Psychological Association Division of Psychopharmacology, John Falk, these subjects rejected the positive mood effects of the amphetamines,

> probably because during the period of drug action these subjects were continuing their normal, daily activities. The drug state may have been incompatible either with the customary pursuit of these activities or the usual effects of engaging in these activities. The point is that in their natural habitats these subjects showed that they were uninterested in continuing to savor the mood effects [of the drugs].[27]

Going to college, reading books, and striving to get ahead make it less likely that people will become heavy or addicted drug users or alcoholics. Having a good-paying job and a good social position makes it more likely that people can quit drugs or drinking or cut back when these produce bad effects. No data dispute these facts, even among those claiming that alcoholism and addiction are medical diseases that occur independent of people's social status. George Vaillant, for example, found his inner-city sample of white ethnic groups were three to four times more likely to become alcoholic than were the college students his research tracked over forty years.

The truth of the commonsense notion that people who are better off are less likely to become addicted, even after using a powerful psychoactive substance, is amply demonstrated by the fate of the cocaine "epidemic." In 1987, epidemiological data indicated, "The nation's cocaine epidemic appears to have peaked. Yet within the broad trend runs a worrisome countertrend." Although American cocaine use has stabilized or diminished, small groups within the larger group seem to have intensified their use. What is more, "cocaine use is moving down the social ladder." David Musto, a Yale psychiatrist, analyzed the situation:

> We are dealing with two different worlds here. The question we must be asking now is not why people take drugs, but why do people stop. In the inner city, the factors that counterbalance drug use—family, employment, status within the community—often are not there.[28]

Overall, systematic research finds cocaine to be about as addictive as alcohol and less addictive than cigarettes. About ten to twenty percent of middle-class repeated cocaine users experience control problems, and perhaps five percent develop a full-scale addiction which they cannot arrest or reverse on their own. As for the newest crisis drug, crack, a front-page *New York Times* story (August 24, 1989) carried the subtitle "Importance of users' environment is stressed over the drug's attributes." Jack Henningfield of the National Institute on Drug Abuse indicated in the article that one in six crack users becomes addicted, while several studies have shown that addicts find it easier to quit cocaine—"either injected, sniffed or smoked"—than to stop smoking or drinking. Those who become addicted to cocaine have generally abused other drugs and alcohol and are usually socially and economically disadvantaged. Certainly some middle-class users become addicts, even some with good jobs, but the percentage is relatively small and nearly all have important psychological, job, and family problems that precede addiction.

# Values

Although addicts are often impulsive or nervous or depressed and find that drugs relieve their emotional burdens, this does not mean that all people with these traits are addicts. Why not? Primarily because so many people, whether nervous or impulsive or not, refuse to use a lot of drugs or otherwise succumb to addiction. Consider a worried father who gets drunk at a party and feels tremendous relief from his tension. Will he start getting drunk after work? Far from it; when he comes home from the party, he sees his daughter sleeping, immediately sobers up, and plans to go to work the next morning so as to maintain the path he has selected as a family man, father, husband, and solid citizen.

The role of people's value-driven choices is ignored in descriptions of addiction. In the disease way of thinking, no human being is protected against the effects of drugs and alcohol—anybody is susceptible to addiction. But we find that practically all college students are disinclined to continue using amphetamines or cocaine or anything that gets in the way of their college careers. And hospital patients almost never use narcotics once they leave the hospital. *The*

### WHAT DO WE LEARN FROM JOHN BELUSHI'S DEATH?

Probably the single most shocking drug death in recent memory was John Belushi's in 1982. Since Belushi was a superstar (although after he left *Saturday Night Live,* only one of his films—his first, *Animal House*—succeeded), his death from overdose seemed to say that anyone could be destroyed by cocaine. Alternatively, people saw in it the message that heroin, which Belushi had only started injecting (along with cocaine) in the preceding few days, was the ultimate killer drug. However, we still must consider that almost the entire Hollywood and entertainment community Belushi knew took drugs (Belushi had snorted cocaine with Robert De Niro and Robin Williams the night before he died), and they didn't kill themselves. What is more, while Belushi had only just started taking heroin, his accomplice—Cathy Smith, who was injecting him with drugs—had been taking heroin since 1978. Was Belushi a worse addict than Smith?

Belushi's death was more a statement of the gargantuan nature of his binges, along with his overall self-destructiveness and bad health. Belushi died in the midst of his first serious binge in half a year. When he died, his body was filled with drugs. Over the previous week, he had been continuously injecting heroin and cocaine, had been drinking heavily, popping Quaaludes, and had smoked marijuana and taken amphetamines. Moreover, Belushi was grossly overweight (he carried over 220 pounds on his squat frame) and had a serious respiratory problem, compounded by his heavy cigarette smoking. Like most drug overdose cases, Belushi died in his sleep of asphyxiation or pulmonary edema (fluid on the lungs), having failed in his deep unconsciousness to clear the mucus from his asthmatic lungs.

Why did Belushi act this way? Belushi was deeply troubled by the state of his career and his relationships, yet he seemingly could not get a handle on either through constructive action. He considered himself unattractive and seemed to have few if any sexual relationships; he was rarely with his wife, whom he had dated since high school, but whom he frequently deserted, often in the middle of an evening. Belushi was living off the success of the film *Animal House,* while his last five films had failed. He was anxiously vacillating between two film projects when he died—one a script he had written (his first) in a feverish, drugged haze with another comedian, the other a project that had been offered to Belushi after floating around Hollywood—and interesting no one—for years. In contrast, Dan Aykroyd, Belushi's partner with whom he often took drugs, was in the midst of writing *Ghostbusters, Spies Like Us,* and another script. For Belushi, it is clear, risk factors that fed his massive drug use and that led to his death were bad work habits and insensitivity to his wife.[29]

---

*reasons that these and other people don't become drug addicts are all values issues—the people don't see themselves as addicts, don't wish to spend their lives pursuing and savoring the effects of drugs, and refuse to engage in certain behaviors that might endanger their family lives or careers.* Without question, values are *crucial* in determining who becomes and remains addicted or who chooses not to do so.

Actually, most college students indicate that they find amphetamines and cocaine only mildly alluring in the first place, while patients often dislike the effects of the powerful narcotics they receive in the hospital. Really, many more people find eating, shopping, gambling, and sex to be extremely appealing than find drugs so. Yet although more people respond with intense pleasure to hot fudge sundaes and orgasms than to drinking or drug taking, only a small number of people pursue these activities without restraint. How do most people resist the allure of constant snacking and sexual indulgence? They don't want to get fat, die of heart attacks, or make fools of themselves; they do want to maintain their health, their families, their work lives, and their self-respect. Values such as these that *prevent* addiction play the largest role in addictive behaviors or their absence; yet they are almost totally ignored.

For example, a typical *New York Times* story about the addictive effects of crack describes an adolescent girl who, having run out of money at a crack house, stayed at the house (she didn't go to school or work) having sex with patrons to get more money for drugs. The point of this tale is ostensibly that crack causes people to sacrifice their moral values. Yet the story doesn't describe the effects of cocaine or crack—for which, after all, most people (including regular users) don't prostitute themselves. This simpleminded mislabeling of the sources of behavior (that taking drugs must be the reason she had sexual intercourse with strangers for money) passes for an analysis of drug effects and addiction in a reputable national news publication. Similarly, prominent spokespeople lecture us that cocaine is a drug with "neuropsychological properties" that "lock people into perpetual usage" so that the only way people can stop is when "supplies become unavailable," after which "the user is then driven to obtain additional cocaine without particular regard for social constraints."[30]

What, inadvertently, the *New York Times* story actually provides is a description of this girl's life and not of cocaine use. Some people do indeed choose to pursue drugs at the cost of other opportunities that do not mean as much to them—in this girl's case, learning, leading an orderly life, and self-respect. The absence of such values in people's lives and the conditions that attack these values—especially among young, ghettoized people—may be expanding. The environments and value options people face do have tremendous implications for drug use and drug addiction, as well as for teen pregnancy and other social disabilities and problems. But we will never remedy either these conditions or these problems by considering them as the results of drug use or as drug problems.

## Life Situations

Although I have presented information that some people form addictive relationships in many different areas of their lives, I don't endorse the idea that people are permanently saddled with addictive personalities. This can never account for the fact that so many people—most people—*outgrow* their addictions. For example, problem drinkers as a group are younger drinkers. That is, the *majority* of both men and women outgrow their drinking problems as they grow up and become engaged in adult roles and real-world rewards, like job and family. Even most younger adults with antisocial tendencies learn to regulate their lives to bring about some order and security. No researcher who studies drug use throughout the life span can fail to be impressed that, in the words of one such researcher, "problem drinking tends to be self-correcting and [to] reverse well short of clinical syndromes of alcoholism."[31]

What about those who do not reverse their problem drinking or drug use and who become full-blown alcoholics or addicts? In the first place, these are most often people with the fewest outside successes and resources for getting better—in the words of George Vaillant, they don't have enough to lose if they don't overcome alcoholism. For these people, less success at work, family, and personal resolutions feeds into greater retreat into alcohol and drugs. Sociologist Denise Kandel, of Columbia University, found that young drug abusers who did not outgrow their problems became more and more absorbed in groups of fellow drug users and further alienated from mainstream institutions like work and school.[32]

Still, even though they are likely to outgrow problematic drug use and drinking, we must consider adolescents and young adults a high-risk group for drug and alcohol abuse. Among other life situations that predispose people to addiction, the most extreme and best-documented example is the Vietnam war. A large number of young men used narcotics in Asia. Of those who used narcotics five or more times there, *almost three-quarters* (73 percent) became addicted and displayed withdrawal symptoms. American authorities were terrified that this signaled a wholesale outbreak of drug addiction stateside for these returned veterans. In fact, what occurred stunned and baffled authorities. Most of those addicted in Vietnam got over their addictions simply as a result of returning home.

But this isn't the end of this amazing saga. Half of these men who were addicted in Vietnam used heroin when they returned to the United States—*yet only one in eight (or 12 percent) became readdicted here*. Here is how Lee Robins, John Helzer, and their colleagues who studied this phenomenon described all this:

It is commonly believed that after recovery from addiction, one must avoid any further contact with heroin. It is thought that trying heroin even once will rapidly lead to readdiction. Perhaps an even more surprising finding than the high proportion of men who recovered from addiction after Vietnam was the number who went back to heroin without becoming readdicted. Half of the men who had been addicted in Vietnam used heroin on their return, but only one-eighth became readdicted to heroin. Even when heroin was used frequently, that is, more than once a week for a considerable period of time, only one-half of those who used it frequently became readdicted.[33]

How to explain this remarkable finding? The answer is not a lack of availability of the drug in the United States, since the men who sought it found heroin to be readily available on their return home. Something about the environment in Vietnam made addiction the norm there. Thus, the Vietnam experience stands out as an almost laboratorylike demonstration of the kinds of situational, or life-stage, elements that *create* addiction. The characteristics of the Vietnam setting that made it a breeding ground for addiction were the discomfort and fear; the absence of positive work, family, and other social involvements; the peer group acceptance of drugs and the disinhibition of norms against addiction; and the soldiers' inability to control their destinies—including whether they would live or die.

These elements combined to cause men to *welcome* the lulling, analgesic—or painkilling—effects of narcotics. The same men who were addicted in Vietnam, given a more positive environment, did not find narcosis to be addictively alluring even if they sometimes took the drug at home. If we can only disregard what we "know" about addiction and its biological properties, we can see how completely logical addictive drug use is. If someone who knew nothing about addiction were asked to predict how people would react to the availability of a powerful analgesic drug when they were stuck in Vietnam, and then whether they would *regularly* seek out such a debilitating substance when they had the chance to do better things in the United States, average, nonexpert people could have predicted the Vietnam addiction scenario. Yet the leading addiction specialists in America have been perplexed by all this and still cannot come to grips with these data.

# Cultural Beliefs and the
# Addiction Splurge

It's truly remarkable how differently people in previous eras reacted to the situations we deal with as diseases as a matter of course today. When Ulysses S. Grant's periodic drinking binges were described to Abraham Lincoln, Lincoln is reputed to have asked which brand of liquor Grant drank, so that he could send it to his other generals. Lincoln was apparently untroubled by Grant's drinking, since Grant was successful as a general. He even toasted Grant when they met and watched Grant drink. What would happen to a general who had drinking binges today? (Grant, incidentally, drank excessively only when he was separated from his wife.) We would hospitalize him. Let's not imagine the results of the Civil War if Grant had been removed from service. Of course, Lincoln himself would be disqualified from the presidency on the grounds of what today would be called his manic-depressive disorder.

But now we know that alcoholism is a disease, just as—more recently—we have learned that sexual compulsions and child abuse are diseases that require therapy. Strangely, these realizations have come at times when we seem to be discovering more and more of each of these—and other—diseases. This brings up another remarkable aspect of alcoholism—the groups with the highest rates of alcoholism, such as the Irish and Native Americans, readily acknowledge that drinking easily becomes uncontrollable. These groups had the most diseaselike image of alcoholism *before* the modern disease era commenced. Other groups with abnormally low rates of alcoholism, such as the Jews and Chinese, literally cannot fathom the disease notion of alcoholism and hold all drinkers to high standards of self-control and mutual policing of drinking behavior.

Craig MacAndrew and sociologist Robert Edgerton surveyed the drinking practices of societies around the world.[34] They found that people's behavior when they are drunk is socially determined. Rather than invariably becoming disinhibited, or aggressive, or sexually promiscuous, or sociable when drunk, people behave according to the customs for drunken behavior in their particular cultural group. Even tribal sexual orgies follow clear-cut prescriptive rules—for example, tribe members observe incest taboos during orgies, even when the family connection among the people who will not have intercourse is incomprehensible to Western observers. On the other hand, those behaviors that are permitted during these drunken "time outs" from ordinary social restrictions are almost uniformly present during the orgies. In other words, societies define *which* kinds of behaviors are the result of getting drunk, and these behaviors become *typical* of drunkenness.

Consider, then, the impact of labeling an activity a disease and convincing people that they cannot control these experiences. Cultural and historical data indicate that believing alcohol has the power to addict a person goes hand in hand with more alcoholism. For this belief convinces susceptible people that alcohol is stronger than are they, and that—no matter what they do—they cannot escape its grasp. What people believe about their drinking *actually affects how they react to alcohol*. In the words of Peter Nathan, director of the Rutgers Center for Alcohol Studies, "it has become increasingly clear that, in many instances, what alcoholics *think* the effects of alcohol are on their behavior influences that behavior as much as or more than the pharmacologic effects of the drug."[35] Alan Marlatt's classic study—in which alcoholics drank more when they believed they were drinking alcohol than when they actually drank alcohol in a disguised form—shows that beliefs are so powerful that they actually can *cause* the loss of control that defines alcoholism.[36]

Obviously, beliefs affect all the behaviors that we call addictions in the same way that they affect drinking. Charles Winick is the sociologist who first described the phenomenon of "maturing out"— or natural remission—of heroin addiction. Indeed, Winick discovered, maturing out of addiction is more typical than not even on the harsh streets of New York City. Winick did note, however, that a minority of addicts never outgrow their addictions. These addicts, Winick observed, are those "who decide they are 'hooked,' make no effort to abandon addiction, and give in to what they regard as inevitable."[37] In other words, the readier people are to decide that their behavior is a symptom of an irreversible addictive disease, the more readily they fall into a disease state. For example, we *will* have more bulimia now that bulimia has been discovered, labeled, and promulgated as a disease.

Treatment in particular has a powerful influence on people's beliefs about addiction and themselves. And, as we have noted in the case of baseball players and others, this impact is not invariably positive. In their study of Vietnam veterans, for example, Robins and her colleagues offered a surprising glimpse of the world of addicts who did not seek treatment, including the remarkable ability to resist addiction even after having slipped back to using heroin for a time. Anxious about what they found, the researchers concluded their report with the following paragraph:

> Certainly our results are different from what we expected in a number of ways. It is uncomfortable presenting results that differ so much from clinical experience with addicts in treatment. But one should not too readily assume that differences are entirely due to our special sample. After all, when veterans used heroin in the United States two to three years after Vietnam, only one in six came to treatment. [38]

If they had looked only at addicts in treatment, the researchers would have had a very different view of addictive habits and of remission (or cure) than they developed from looking at the large majority who eschewed treatment. The nontreated even had better outcomes in the Vietnam study: "Of those men who were addicted in the first year back, half were treated and half were not. . . . Of those treated, 47 percent were addicted in the second period; of those not treated, 17 percent were addicted." Robins and her colleagues pointed out that treatment was sometimes helpful and that the addicts who were treated had usually been addicted longer. "What we can conclude, however, is that treatment is certainly not always necessary for remission."[39]

Although we in the United States spend considerable effort in the strange feat of convincing ourselves that we cannot control the activities so many of us choose to become involved with, the good news is that very few people accept all of this propaganda. As yet, apparently, not everyone believes they can't quit smoking or lose weight without a doctor's directions, or that—if they want to revamp their finances—they need to join a group that regards their overspending as an addiction. The reason disease beliefs are not more generally held is that so many people have personal experiences that

contradict disease claims and people tend to believe their own experience rather than disease advertisements.

For example, while every public announcement about cocaine, or
marijuana, or adolescent drinking is of negative, compulsive, self-
destructive behavior, most people control their use of these substances, and most of the rest figure out that they need to cut back
or quit on their own. Most of us between the ages of thirty-five and
forty-five know scores of people who took a lot of drugs in college
or high school but who are now accountants and lawyers and who
are worrying about whether they can afford to send their kids to
college. Let us now turn to the numerous examples that are available
of people who have changed significant habits in their lives. Indeed,
just as we may all consider that we have an addiction—whatever
that means to us—we can all probably equally well reflect on how
we overcame an addiction, sometimes without even consciously plan-
ning to do so, sometimes through concerted individual efforts, but
in either case relying on ourselves and those around us rather than
on the professional cadre of helpers who have appointed themselves
our saviors.

# 7

# How People Quit Addictions, Usually on Their Own

I couldn't go on saying, "Let's get a couple of grams of blow (cocaine) and write a song. Let's get stoned before the gig. Let's get stoned after the gig. I'm in town, where are the girls?" I was living the classic wild style, and that was no longer working for me. I'm not AA or anything. My ethic is that I work hard, do what I do under my own power, and at the end of the day, like everybody else in the world, I do what I can get away with.

—Iggy Pop, rock singer

We are here to drink beer . . . and [to] live our lives so well that Death will tremble to take us.

—Charles Bukowski, former alcoholic and poet-author of "Barfly," on the meaning of life

## Maturing Out of Drug Addiction and Alcoholism

THE ADDICTION treatment market is built on allegations like these that have been reported throughout this book: "If you *think* you have a drinking problem, then you need treatment. . . . Any drinking problem you now have can only grow worse. . . . Trying to deal with your own addiction is like trying to operate on yourself. . . . You can never escape an addiction; the best you can hope for is to arrest the progress of the disease for as long as you stay in treatment—therefore, treatment should be lifelong. . . . Alcoholism (or addiction) is a progressive disease with three possible outcomes: jail, hospital, or the cemetery. . . . Anyone who refuses to accept treatment is practicing denial and requires a loving—if forceful—intervention."

I debated an official of the southeastern California affiliate of the National Council on Alcoholism on a radio call-in show. The very first call was from a man who described his severe drinking problems and said he was an alcoholic, but he refused to believe that alcoholism is a disease. The man had not drunk for a number of years. My debate partner readily accepted that the man was an alcoholic but said that, in her experience, "99.9 percent of alcoholics cannot quit without an outside intervention." I said that either we were extremely lucky to hear on our first phone call from that one case in a thousand or else her statistics were wrong. Of course, this woman, recognized as an alcoholism expert, had made up these statistics—they're completely inaccurate, although statements like hers are regularly presented as factual information.

Let me contrast another image with the set of claims made by disease-theory proponents. When I speak before groups of addiction counselors (many of whom are recovered alcoholics) and other audiences, I ask which is the most difficult addiction to quit. The response is overwhelmingly "Smoking." I then ask how many people have quit smoking—usually from a third to close to half of the audience respond affirmatively. I then ask how many of these quit because of Smokenders or any other treatment program. The greatest percentage I ever got was 10 percent once; more often, *no one* had quit through treatment, even in audiences with 50 or more ex-smokers.

These audience surveys I conduct are consistent with an American scene in which 40 million Americans have quit smoking. The Office on Smoking and Health indicates that 45 percent of all Americans (and *60 percent* of all college graduates) who have ever smoked have quit. A full 30 percent of adult Americans are now former smokers.[1] Statistics further indicate, according to the American Cancer Society, that 95 percent of ex-smokers quit on their own. Presenting these data gives my audiences pause—remember, alcoholics and drug addicts have uniformly told me that smoking is the most difficult addiction to quit. Furthermore, a survey of drug addicts and alcoholics entering treatment published in the *Journal of the American Medical Association* verified my informal research—most said it was harder to quit cigarettes than drugs or alcohol.[2] Nonetheless, my addiction audiences don't change their beliefs that all alcoholics and addicts need to be treated. While most smokers quit on their own, they tell me, they are certain this doesn't apply to drug addicts and alcoholics.

From the opposite direction, the 1988 Surgeon General's report, entitled *The Health Consequences of Smoking: Nicotine Addiction*, makes clear that cigarettes are as addictive as heroin, cocaine, and alcohol. Many interpret this to mean that people therefore can't give up smoking, since surely heroin addicts can't just give up their habits. I watched, for example, as Jane Pauley interviewed two smoking experts after the 1988 report was released. Pauley insisted that if people claim they are trying to quit but then don't enter a treatment program, this means they aren't really serious and are bound to keep smoking. In this case at least, the experts (unlike typical alcoholism spokespeople) demurred from Pauley's wrongheaded conclusion.

In fact, data similar to those on smoking remission apply to drug and alcohol addictions. Let's return to George Vaillant and his re-markable *The Natural History of Alcoholism*. Vaillant found that among the alcohol abusers his research followed for over forty years, the majority had overcome their alcohol problem either by cutting back their drinking or by quitting altogether. Hardly any of those who licked a drinking problem had sought formal treatment, and certainly not those who became controlled drinkers. Moreover, *even among those who chose to abstain, more than 60 percent had no contact with AA.* Research has appeared regularly to indicate that alcoholics can out-grow alcoholism or stop drinking on their own.[3] But the idea that people actually can clear up a drinking problem without AA or therapy becomes more and more remote in our current milieu.

It turns out that natural remission is equally possible for the pro-totypical drug abuser—the heroin addict. In the 1960s, Charles Win-ick noted that most adolescent and young adult heroin addicts in New York outgrew their addiction by their mid-thirties.[4] Winick used the term *maturing out* to characterize this phenomenon. In doing so, he merely introduced to the research literature a term that was already used in the streets by addicts themselves. In the 1980s, a series of research studies by West Coast investigators detailed the cases of many untreated former heroin addicts and the varieties of methods they took to quit narcotics.[5] This research, for those who are interested in reality, should certainly enhance our respect for the human potential for change, as well as provide an antidote to long-indoctrinated images of the ever-deepening spiral of heroin addiction.

One other addiction that people certainly want to know whether they can quit is overeating, along with the resulting condition of obesity. The standard wisdom was expressed by distinguished obesity researchers Stanley Schachter and Judith Rodin in 1974: "Almost any overweight person can lose weight; few can keep it off."[6] Then, in 1982, Schachter announced the results of a study in two settings—a Long Island town where he had a summer home and the psychology department at Columbia University—that indicated that long-term weight loss was "a relatively common event." Sixty-two percent of his ever-obese subjects in the two communities who had tried to lose weight had succeeded and were no longer obese, having taken off an average of 34.7 pounds and kept the weight off for an average of 11.2 years. Another noteworthy finding in this study was that those who had never entered weight loss programs showed better long-term weight loss.[7] In the same research study, Schachter also discovered that people regularly quit smoking on their own. Once again, Schachter found better results for those who never entered a treatment program.

Overall, then, whether in connection with familiar or exotic (at least from a middle-class standpoint) addictions, self-cure is common, perhaps standard. This is part of the larger process of coming to grips with oneself that seems to characterize the human animal. For example, even in the wide-ranging NIMH survey cited in chapter 1 that found a high level of emotional disorder in the American population (including a strikingly high incidence of obsessive-compulsive disorder), every one of the frequently identified emotional and behavioral problems decreased after the age of forty-five, with the one exception of Alzheimer's disease. If you have to bet your money, then, bet that people will get better over time, usually on their own.

# How Well Do Adolescent Problems
# Predict Adult Maladjustment?

In a national survey of men aged twenty to twenty-nine conducted in the 1970s, Jack O'Donnell—another distinguished drug researcher—found that of all who had ever used heroin, less than a third had taken the drug in the previous year.[8] Most people who take drugs, even the "heaviest" drugs, stop by the time they become adults. Youth is a major predictor of substance abuse; growing up is a major indicator that people will cease using drugs. In the words of Richard Jessor, who has spent over a decade investigating adolescent problem behaviors (particularly drug and alcohol abuse):

> Development, at least in the mid- and later twenties, appears to be in the direction of greater personality, perceived environment, and behavioral conventionality. That direction may well follow from the assumption of new life roles in work and family and the occupancy of new social contexts other than that of school, both factors constituting conventionalizing influences.[9]

To put it more positively (and simply), most people become better with age at dealing with their problems and tensions and at gaining enough satisfaction from life to reject drugs. At the same time, think of Enos Cabell, one of the number of baseball players who testified before a federal grand jury that they had quit heavy cocaine use without treatment. Cabell explained that he had quit using cocaine because "I got older and I had more to lose."

We have created a number of industries—for example, children of alcoholics, early learning disabilities—that require forceful interventions into the lives of children so that their problems will be remedied and they can grow successfully into adulthood. How well can we identify young people who will have problems in the future? I should say that I am a strong believer in the continuity of personality—that people have consistent traits that link the adult with the child. But this continuity turns out not to predict extremely well who will successfully marry, work, amuse themselves, integrate their lives, give up addictions, and so on. In particular, adolescent problems are generally overstated by clinicians, at the same time that psychiatrists and others grossly overestimate how well they can diagnose who will successfully navigate adolescence into successful adulthood.

Young people who undergo clinical interviews often don't come out very well. For example, psychiatric interviews with a random group of young people brought in for ordinary medical visits revealed that *between a fifth and a quarter* "suffer from psychiatric problems serious enough to impair their lives," but that most are not receiving treatment for these problems. This may mean, according to some experts interviewed in the *New York Times*, that these young people will be particularly susceptible to similar emotional problems later in life. Other researchers, however, emphasize that children will outgrow many of their anxieties and phobias (the most common mental disorders of childhood).

Along with phobias, the chief disorders identified in the *Times* story were "conduct" and "oppositional," together affecting more than 10 percent of children. (These disorders are associated with juvenile acting out and conflict with parents.) The chief investigator of the primary study on which the *Times* article was based noted that "conduct problems are counted as psychiatric in the United States, but that is not the case in Europe, England or even in Canada," where "it's regarded more as a case of naughty children than as an emotional disorder." This psychiatrist thinks that overlooking these problems is a mistake, however, since she believes "a large proportion of adults with serious psychiatric problems showed emotional problems in childhood, while many adults who are lawbreakers had conduct disorders as children."[10] I have also noted in this book that antisocial young people more often abuse drugs as adolescents and more readily grow into adult alcoholism or drug abuse. However, as I pointed out in an article in *Pediatrician*, "it would be extremely misleading and dangerous to infer from the above findings that high school students and others who do not become positively engaged in school or who show other traits such as alienation and antisocial acting out are preordained to become alcoholics or addicts."[11]

Psychiatric interviews do not give even very successful young people a good shake or make accurate predictions about their adult states of mind. Between 1946 and 1949, for example, psychiatrists intensively examined and made predictions about more than two hundred first-year medical students. The interviews detailed an alarming number of psychological dysfunctions among this group, often of quite a severe nature. Yet hardly any of the psychiatrists' negative expectations for this group were realized when these medical students were assessed thirty-five years later. According to C. Knight Aldrich, a physician who followed up the predictions, "The psychiatrists appeared to have overemphasized the significance of the psychopathology they discovered and to have underestimated the potential of many of these young adults for spontaneous personality change."[12] In other words, clinicians exaggerate young people's problems along with the benefits of therapy while very much underestimating people's ability to improve on their own.

Consider, finally, children diagnosed as learning disabled or hyperactive. As described in a study in the *Archives of General Psychiatry*, many such children do not have emotional or intellectual difficulties when they grow up. This is so startling a finding that the researchers felt obligated to indicate that their results ran contrary to the beliefs of most experts. The study found that half of a group of 101 boys who were diagnosed as hyperactive between the ages of six and twelve were perfectly normal by the time they reached late adolescence and adulthood. "The common belief among clinicians and educators has been that hyperactive kids will do less well in later life than other kids," according to Salavatore Mannuzza, one of the investigators. However, Dr. Mannuzza found "that when they reached adulthood, half of the hyperactive boys were indistinguishable from a comparison group that had not been hyperactive."[13]

## The Changing Adult—The Elderly

Obviously, change is not limited to children. Indeed, one other group (in addition to adolescents) that has been singled out for its special problems actually demonstrates human resilience—the elderly. Simply arriving at old age is now often considered tantamount to having a psychological problem. Those problems most often mentioned in connection with the elderly are suicide and alcohol and drug abuse. Yet in fact, most people drink less when they become older. Certainly, Cicero—as he described in the Latin classic *De Senectute*—drank (and also ate) less in his old age: "I am very grateful to old age because it has increased my desire for conversation and lessened my desire for food and drinking."

While drinking problems drop off after adolescence and early adulthood, a residual group of heavy drinkers increases their drinking through their fifties. *This* group then shows a steady decline in drinking from their sixties on. For example, a typical study found that a quarter of men aged fifty to fifty-nine were heavy drinkers, but only 10 percent of those aged sixty to sixty-nine, and 4 percent of those above the age of seventy.[14] Only a small portion of the successive halving of the heavy-drinking population after sixty and seventy could conceivably occur due to a higher death rate for heavy drinkers. Edith Gomberg, director of the University of Michigan Institute of Gerontology, notes that while men's drinking declines for the most part around retirement age, for women the most precipitous drop in heavy drinking occurs after age fifty. In a national survey, 10 percent of women aged forty-five to forty-nine were heavy drinkers, but *only 1 percent* of those over fifty were. The drop in heavy drinking for women at this age is closely paralleled by a drop in suicide.[15]

Gomberg calls for a reevaluation of standard wisdom on the trauma of retirement and other events in later life. Apparently most people find retirement to be relaxing rather than stressful. In addition, men drink less as senior citizens, Gomberg reports, because they have less money and because they are less able to tolerate the effects of alcohol. Ron Stall describes a variety of cases of changing drinking patterns in a study in which 18 percent of men reported increasing their drinking with age, 27 percent drank at the same levels, and 55 percent said they reduced their level of drinking. The small group who increased their drinking often said that, because of changes in their family lives, they lost the social restraints that had curtailed their drinking. For the majority who drank less, a number felt that as their careers advanced and they acquired more responsibilities, they needed clearer heads to function. After retirement, many simply realized that they couldn't continue what they were doing and survive:

A group of men experienced a growing disdain for problem drinking as they aged. Many of these men had themselves been heavy drinkers and felt that they could no longer continue drinking problematically. One man, a self-identified alcoholic, felt that he and his wife could not continue drinking and expect to be able to take care of themselves in old age. He wanted "a future life, my health, money in the bank. So we got together and decided to quit."[16]

Nor does research indicate that old people indiscriminately consume mind-altering prescription drugs, such as tranquilizers.[17] Rather, older people in good economic shape and good health for the most part resist suppressing their consciousness in this way.

The large drop-off in heavy drinking (along with suicide and drug taking) that Gomberg identified among women at age fifty is especially interesting because it seems to fly in the face of the trauma of the "empty-nest syndrome." Apparently, more often than not, women adjust quite well to their children leaving home. Monica Wright, the director of the New York Breakthrough Treatment Center quoted in chapter 4, was inclined to drink heavily when confronted with the daily demands of child-rearing, but was able to quit drinking as her six children grew up. It seems that most parents find it more stressful to deal with an adolescent or young adult *in* the home. (My father described this process for me when I noted that his health had improved between the ages of sixty and seventy. He told me, "Yes, and I felt better when I was sixty than when I was fifty, and I looked and felt worst of all when I was forty. You know why? That's when you and your brother were still living at home.")

The bottom line to all this might not be surprising, were it not so strenuously denied by the disease industry: (1) people respond to positive options with healthy behavior; (2) people strive to right their lives and to overcome problems and frequently succeed over time; (3) age is an important ingredient in determining people's habits, in the large majority of cases leading to improved coping and self-contentment. Consider one typical example: everyone changes their eating behavior as they age. Even when we don't keep pace with our changing needs and do gain weight, we nonetheless cut out the nightly sundaes, daily candy bars, and after-school or after-work burgers and french fries favored by teens and twenty-year-olds. It is actually quite remarkable—although we take it for granted—that nearly everyone has such capacity to modify a basic behavior with changing life stages and physical needs.

There is a fourth deduction to make: people make decisions about their lives based on their assessments of their needs. As a part of the current trend toward identifying and attacking other people's addictions (especially "helpless" old people), one doctor described how he was asked by his family to speak to his grandfather, a European immigrant who was then over one hundred! The doctor's teetotaler aunt was worried about the old man's drinking whiskey "three to four times a day." When the younger man told his grandfather that sometimes older people drink too much, the older man agreed whole-heartedly. Finally, the doctor blurted out that he feared the grand-father drank too much. The old man replied bemusedly, "Watch your own health. . . . There are a lot more old drunks than old doctors." This physician promptly quit his intervention efforts, in-dicating that his grandfather "continued to drink what he wanted and never did become an alcoholic" until he died at 111.[18]

People do drink too much and do many other things that aren't good for them; occasionally, or periodically, such self-destructive behavior reaches life-threatening proportions. Changing this behav-ior is a legitimate concern of loved ones and helping professionals. But we must at the same time remember that people come to grips with life in their own ways. The grandfather in the previous story, who had emigrated from Russia as a youth to establish a hardware store that became a Toronto landmark, announced the key to long life was to "never get excited, go for a walk"—and perhaps to have a drink. To help someone change first requires that we respect and appreciate the way they are. Even severely disabled people (like diagnosed psychotic Joyce Brown, whom Mayor Koch tried to force into a homeless shelter) or people about whom we are deeply worried (like many adolescents) often have more personal resources and re-cuperative power than we imagine.

## How Do People Quit Addictions?

What lesson do we learn from people who grow up and shed their problems, particularly from those who quit addictions? Can we im-itate those who lose weight, to take the exact steps they took to quit an addiction? For example, if 95 percent of the considerable number of people who quit smoking do so on their own, do *they* have an infallible method that the rest of us can follow? If more people lose weight successfully by methods they devise themselves than through diets and weight-loss programs, maybe *they* have the key we can all follow. It is amusing that as soon as a Hollywood star like Elizabeth Taylor loses weight, she tells everyone else how to do it the way she did. Yet in many cases, self-curers can't actually describe any special methods they have used.

In the Schachter study, the formerly obese and reformed smokers could not give succinct pictures of how they managed to lick their addiction. A *Psychology Today* writer examined the research interviews and concluded in a sidebar entitled "(No) Accounting for Results":

> It seems that these people lost weight when they made up their minds to do so, and managed to drop substantial poundage by eating smaller portions and less fattening food. People made comments like: "I just cut down, just stopped eating so much." To keep the weight off, they stuck to their regimens of eating less. . . .
>
> The techniques of the 38 heavy smokers who quit smoking for [on average] nearly seven years were less varied. Roughly two thirds reported that their only technique was deciding to stop. "I took the cigarettes out of my pocket," one said, "threw them away, and that was it." Another explained: "I said 'the hell with it,' and never smoked again."[19]

The alternative to learning specific techniques may be that people attain a position in life in which smoking becomes less necessary or desirable. In one study, for example, blue-collar workers were able to quit when they achieved a degree of job security and experienced less anxiety at work.[20] In a broader sense, one researcher summarized the results of a survey of 2,700 British smokers as showing that people quit smoking when they "lose faith in what they used to think smoking did for them" while creating "a powerful new set of beliefs that non-smoking is, of itself, a desirable and rewarding state."[21] On the one hand, this can come about because people have changed their lives in ways that make smoking seem passé. When they see themselves as mature and self-controlled and when they associate mainly with nonsmokers, smoking no longer seems appropriate to them.

At the same time, people may be able to quit because they no longer feel they *need* the addiction in order to function. And of course, people often make a specific resolution to quit the addiction. After all, one day they must decide to throw the cigarettes away, to lose weight, and so on. What techniques do people design? If they're smart, the techniques they design fit best with their feelings and their worlds. Instead of reading magazine articles and books about how Elizabeth Taylor, or Cheryl Tiegs[22], or Judith Light, or Lynn Redgrave, or Dolly Parton, or Joan Rivers lost weight—or joining groups created by people who lost weight on their own, like Jean Nidetch and Richard Simmons—people do better to consider their own realities and do it themselves.

# A Moment of Truth—Or Quitting as an Apotheosis

In order to qualify for AA membership as the group was originally conceived, an alcoholic had to have "hit bottom." That is, his drinking had to have become so severe that it could never be ignored again. For example, he might have publicly embarrassed himself and his family beyond the point of toleration. But things, especially in AA as currently constituted, do not necessarily follow such a neat path. Some alcoholics, of course, regularly experience such nadirs without joining AA or quitting drinking. On the other hand, some who do fail to quit at such a bottoming-out moment end up quitting at some later point. AA members are *required* to describe such rock-bottom moments and, as a rule, they get better at doing so the longer they attend AA. As a result, AA confessions become standardized around identifying a specific moment when they saw the light and finally converted fully to the AA philosophy.

Barry Tuchfeld and his colleagues at Texas Christian University interviewed alcoholics who had quit or cut back drinking on their own—a group Tuchfeld has accurately categorized as the "silent majority" of alcoholics.[23] Tuchfeld placed the following advertisement in a local newspaper: "have you licked a drinking problem without treatment?" and selected fifty-one of the 162 people who answered the ad on the basis of the severity of their former alcohol dependence and the certainty of their current recovery. Forty-two of these fifty-one subjects had had memory loss or blackout; all fifty-one identified themselves as alcohol abusers *and* had had a family member seek treatment for them. Forty-four of the fifty-one reported having had trouble stopping once they had started to drink. Of the fifty-one subjects, forty now abstained, and the other eleven drank occasionally.

What are their accounts like? In some cases, they were indeed bottoming-out sorts of stories. One man used a built-in fan in his home as a commode: "What really shocked me, what made me continually think about it, was that supposedly my daughter . . . was up and saw me in that condition." Another man lay in the hospital after attempting suicide: "I think this is the first time in my whole life that I ever thought whiskey . . . had . . . caused all this problem I was having." On the other hand, the majority of circumstances were unexceptional—events that struck the narrator as important but that were entirely undetectable to some outside observer. Tuchfeld remarked that an outsider often couldn't make out the connection between the event and the alcoholic's resolution, yet "to the respondent the logical connections were evident."

One such man in Tuchfeld's study met a woman on a trip, one whom he would never meet again. "I kinda wished she would like me," but he was worried because "I had never been free of alcohol on this whole Goddamn three-day time out here. If she likes me, she likes somebody that isn't me." Very often, reasons like these for quitting or cutting back represent powerful ongoing concerns that suddenly surface at an unlikely moment. One man told me that he joined AA but continued drinking. One day, in a bar after a business deal, he saw an older man he respected and imagined what that man thought of him, just then starting to get drunk. He had already had two drinks; but he decided then to quit and this time maintained his sobriety.

The man worrying about the woman he met on the trip and the man in the bar stopped drinking to protect their self-concepts. They didn't like what they saw when they looked at themselves—as mirrored by how they imagined others saw them. People often don't have to go so far afield to find people whose opinions of them they are concerned to maintain or upgrade. Thus, an extremely typical reason for quitting is the feelings of a family member or loved one:

I was dancing with this little blond girl, and I looked at my wife and she didn't look too happy. So I went over and I asked her, "Do you want the rest of this beer?" and she said, "No, I don't believe so—

but *you* sure don't need it." . . . I said, "This is the last time I'm ever going to drink."

An often remarkable tale by women alcoholics, heroin addicts, and smokers is that they quit taking drugs or drinking during their pregnancy. In some cases, they may resume the addiction after the baby is born; in others, they remain clean after pregnancy:

> I was drinking [with a hangover from a previous night's drinking]. . . . I felt the baby quiver and I poured the rest of the beer out and I said, "God forgive me, I'll never drink another drop," and from that day to this I haven't.

Besides family and loved ones, health is a frequent impetus for change:

> I got up one Monday morning and I was completely able to go to work, but . . . I just felt hungover, and I told myself, "I'm not going to drink any for a while," and that was it.

Perhaps, the reader thinks, this man hadn't really been drinking long or did not have a serious enough problem. I spoke to the daughter of a man in his eighties who had been alcoholic throughout the woman's youth and adult life. (She was nearing forty.) Her father was shocked into sobriety in his late seventies when William Holden died after a fall when drinking alone at home one night. The father resolved never to allow this to happen to him, and the woman told me her father either stopped drinking at home or limited himself to a drink or two. "How do you know he really kept his resolution?" I asked. "I call him every Sunday night, and these last few years he has always been sober"—unlike any Sunday in the previous decades that she had been calling.

Think about smoking in this regard. Jerry Lewis and Governor John Y. Brown of Kentucky both say they knocked off four-pack-a-day cigarette habits after open-heart surgery. As Lewis puts it, all he needs to do when he feels like a smoke is to look at the gigantic incision running the length of his chest. Or there is my friend, editor Jeremy Tarcher, who told me he quit smoking when, during a visit to a friend in a hospital, a doctor took him aside to show him something—the cancer ward. That did it for Jeremy. But obviously it doesn't do it for everyone, or it might not have done it for him at some other time. Indeed, at another time he may even have had an exactly comparable experience, promised to quit, and failed.

A man with whom I coached Little League baseball told me that he quit smoking because he decided he hated how his father-in-law's clothes were full of holes from his cigarette ashes. I asked, "So you quit smoking then?" "No," he answered. "I quit a year later when I was in the service in Europe. I was flicking my cigarette ashes out the window and one was blown back into the car and burned my uniform, which was lying on the back seat. All of sudden I remembered my father-in-law." "So you quit then?" I asked. "Well, not totally. I started again a couple of months later, but I quit again for good later that year. Except I smoke a cigar now and then when I play poker." This on-and-off-again quitting process often makes quitting something that a person prepares for and accomplishes over a period of years, whether on their own, through treatment, or both.

## What Do These Stories Mean?

One really can't tell whether a story a person tells is the "real" explanation for why he or she quit or cut back a habit. Jean Nidetch says she started Weight Watchers after a friend thought she was pregnant. (Incidentally, *she* lost weight without Weight Watchers.) But surely Nidetch had encountered other people who had been startled by her obesity earlier. Really, when people tell stories like these, they are saying something like, "This is an example of something that really bothered me—a violation of my most basic values—that eventually caused me to change." The question actually is, does the person have values that are stronger than that of continuing the addiction? In fact, nearly every addict has one such value or set of values and has quit the addiction for a time.

I am reminded of an earlier study by Stanley Schachter—before he found that there were so many ex-smokers in his community studies—in which he analyzed how smokers regulated their nicotine levels when smoking in a laboratory. This led Schachter to conclude that nicotine addiction is a physical dependence that cannot be overcome: "Virtually all long-term smokers are addicted"—which at that time meant to him that if they tried to quit, their bodies would rebel and drive them back to cigarettes. Schachter continued, "Many, perhaps all, exceptions to an addiction model can be understood in terms of such notions as self-control, concern with health, restraints, and so on." Schachter's last caveat covers a lot of ground. What exceptions is he talking about, by the way? In his nicotine addiction articles, he mentions one example—that Orthodox Jews who are addicted to cigarettes quit smoking "without a qualm" on the Sabbath. [24]

How is it that Orthodox Jews can overcome chemical dependence so readily for the entire Sabbath day when it is the first twenty-four hours during which people feel withdrawal pangs most intensely? The answer would appear to be that Orthodox Jews' devotion to God and Jewish tradition is greater than their urge for tobacco. Indeed, this is the problem with all laboratory research on addiction, especially with that conducted on animals. While cocaine addiction may indeed look irresistible in the confines of a cage or in a study designed purely to test the chemical properties of a substance, organisms in real environments survey a larger range of choices, many of which have greater meaning to them in the long run than does simple enjoyment of a drug high or the discomfort of ridding one's system of a drug. Indeed, even in the most extreme cases of addiction, the decisive factor is the values that addicts have or do not have that either defeat or maintain the addiction.

Somehow this story doesn't appeal to scientists, however, because these values that combat addiction—like God, health, self-control, a desire for the good opinion of others—have been around forever and don't constitute scientific-seeming discoveries. Yet time and again the tales of quitting addictions that people tell us are ones that express a special meaning they assign to quitting the addiction in their value system. Sometimes the alternative values that free the addict have been suppressed and await reactivation. After all, people have sometimes engaged in their addictions daily (in the case of smoking, for example) for decades. Stories about people's "moments of truth" are nearly always descriptions of the reawakening of such dormant values.

## UNCLE OZZIE QUITS SMOKING

My favorite example of the values that cause a person to quit smoking is my uncle Oscar. Ozzie, a union activist, smoked three packs a day and more from the age of eighteen until a fateful day when, in his forties, he went to lunch with his regular cronies. On this day in 1960, cigarette prices had gone up a nickel. As Ozzie put the extra coin in the machine, a coworker said: "Look at Oscar; why, if they raised the price of cigarettes to a dollar, he'd pay up. Those tobacco companies have him by the balls." Ozzie looked at the man (so he told me later) and said, "You're right. I'm going to quit." His friend, who also smoked, then asked, "Can I have your cigarettes?" Ozzie replied, "What, and throw away the money I just spent?" After he smoked that pack, however, Ozzie never smoked again. (He is now an active seventy-four-year-old.)

Why did my uncle quit that day? It's hard to say. He claims that in that time and place (he worked on a General Electric assembly line, and all of his coworkers smoked), he had never once thought about quitting. But I think I know something about the underlying values that made him quit. For Ozzie to be told—and more important, to believe—that his behavior meant he was a sucker to American tobacco conglomerates was equivalent to his realizing he was under the control of those he hated most, and that his union activism (indeed, his entire life) was being compromised. Imagine if a Jewish smoker discovered that the Nazis owned the companies that made cigarettes and were trying to addict all Jews! This is something like the reaction my uncle had.

I often jokingly summarize this story for addiction audiences by saying, "This story makes clear that the best way to quit smoking is to become a communist." Of course, the joke is that only for a very strong anticompany, pro-union activist like my uncle could a sense of servitude to the capitalist system serve as the motivation to quit smoking. But my facetious claim is really quite close to the common claim that the best way to get everyone to quit drinking is to force them to join AA. AA works for those with salient religious values, who place God in the middle of their decisions, and who favor group confessionals. Others often think AA rituals are foolish, even offensive—just as they would if we made them join the Communist Party. (Several people have now sued to reverse state regulations requiring them to attend AA on the grounds that these violate their religious freedom.)

# Overcoming Cravings and Avoiding Relapse

Not only must addicts select a moment to quit, but they must then remain unaddicted, resisting all impulses to return to habits that filled their lives for years and decades. Really, that so many people successfully quit addictions is quite a remarkable phenomenon. When addicts who successfully avoid relapse are interviewed, they describe a number of conscious policies they pursue. Frequently they reorganize their lives around new friends and activities and separate themselves from their former drug-associated involvements. In this regard, those who quit smoking are more constrained than are those who quit heroin, since most smokers are probably not going to get divorced, move, or change jobs in order to overcome nicotine addiction. On the other hand, many smokers probably already face pressures from family and at work to quit that they can now harness to maintain their resolve to stay off cigarettes.

Therapies for treating addiction emphasize the cravings that drive an addict to relapse and that the therapies often claim are irresistible. (This is the justification for nicotine gums, for example, which reduce such craving.) Untreated former addicts, on the other hand, describe a variety of psychological ploys they use to reinterpret their cravings in a negative light so that these urges lose their power. Instead of the global kinds of "cognitive therapies" favored by psychologists, untreated addicts tend to select idiosyncratic techniques that have special meaning for them. Patrick Biernacki detailed this process in relation to heroin addicts who quit drugs without treatment in his book *Pathways from Heroin Addiction*. The addicts Biernacki interviewed resisted cravings by placing thoughts they had about resuming narcotics use in a negative context and "then doing non-drug-related things":

> What people think about, and do, instead of fulfilling the cravings for drugs are intimately associated with the social worlds they are participating in and their related identities and perspectives. For example, some people who have broken their drug addiction become very health conscious and concerned about their physical well-being. When these people experience drug cravings, they may place the thoughts about using drugs in a negative context by thinking about one of the physical illnesses—perhaps hepatitis—that plague illicit addicts. . . .
>
> It is important to note that the processes of negative contexting and the supplanting of thoughts of reusing addictive drugs are not the same as those involved in psychological "therapies" that attempt to desensitize or decondition people to cues that have come to be associated with drug use, withdrawal distress, or illness. Rather, the processes involve an active reinterpretation of cues and the replacement of them with thoughts that are inextricably related to the identities and perspectives that are emerging and being pursued in the more total life scheme of the person.[25]

In other words, people are not passive victims of the addictive urges or cues that occur in their bodies or in their lives; they select not only the settings in which to live nonaddicted lives, but also the reactions they have to the urges they experience to return to their addictions. The methods they use are in keeping with their values and the people they see themselves as having become.

Consider this story, for example, about an addict quite far along in this process of redefining his "urges" to use drugs. Jerry, a heroin addict since adolescence, spent his early adulthood in and out of prison in the Bronx. After leaving prison for the third time, he thought, "I have to change something." As a way of saying good-bye to this life, he went out and shot up for another weekend. Then he moved to Connecticut, went to school—he was illiterate when he started—and secured a master's degree in social work. Years later, after he married and became a local figure in the therapy field, Jerry suffered a severe burn in his kitchen and was hospitalized. At his release, he was given an unlimited prescription for the narcotic Percodan. After his pain ceased, Jerry mused that as an addict, he would have found any number of excuses to continue filling the prescription. Perhaps he even entertained the possibility of doing so. Instead, he thought how much he would have to change—losing the respect he had built up, deserting his family, letting his house and life go to ruin—to return to drugs, and he simply let the prescription lapse.[26]

Treatments that emphasize abstinence in the belief that addictions are diseases argue that addicts may never again consume their drug of choice—or any drug—in a controlled manner. Thus, a single drink is the equivalent of a month-long binge for the AA member. Those who don't undergo therapy are less likely to believe the adage "one drink, one drunk" or to behave in this way, however. In a study comparing treated and untreated heroin addicts who stayed clean, sociologist Dan Waldorf found the major difference between the two groups was that untreated former addicts often did take a narcotic again without relapsing. (Recall that this was typical for the returned Vietnam veteran addicts.) Indeed, many former addicts Waldorf studied intentionally tried heroin after quitting to prove to themselves they were no longer addicted and that they could choose not to resume their habits.[27]

In a study of "untreated smoking cessation," University of Washington psychologist Alan Marlatt found that successful quitters frequently did smoke again after quitting, perhaps at a party or a bar.[28] However, unlike those who relapsed after such an experience, those who remained free of their nicotine addictions did not overreact to their slips. Instead, the reformed smokers learned from such incidents either to avoid certain situations in the future or else to come forearmed with a plan of action the next time they were likely to be around smokers or otherwise face the temptation to smoke. Based on findings such as these, Marlatt has developed a theory of relapse prevention that *convinces* addicts and alcoholics of the *opposite* of the AA message: that even after they have consumed a single drink or cigarette, they have the power—and the obligation—to desist. The biggest problem with the disease model, as Marlatt sees it, is that it leads addicts to interpret relapses as proof that they are powerless in the face of their addictions.

# What Is This Thing Called Self-Efficacy?

Are addicts themselves responsible for not returning to drugs, or alcohol, or cigarettes, or the like? If addicts do slip, will they resume their addiction where they left off, or will they regain their equilibrium and carry on without it? The primary question is, with whom does the power to resist addiction lie? The answer has serious implications for the incidence, the remission, and the prevention of addiction.

Stanford psychologist Albert Bandura has presented the psychological theory of *self-efficacy*—the feeling that people can control the outcomes in life that matter to them. According to Bandura, whenever psychotherapy succeeds, it does so by enhancing people's sense of self-efficacy. As we have seen, people who think of themselves as alcoholics are more likely to drink excessively when they drink, even when they actually are not drinking alcohol but only *believe* they are. This finding suggests that those most easily influenced and least likely to believe they can regulate themselves are most likely to fill the rolls of addicts. If, on the other hand, people believe that they can control their lives, they are better able to control the drugs they use or do not use.

In addition, those with lower self-efficacy probably require more outside support to remain sober when they encounter problems and attribute any improvements they make to the group or the treatment or whatever external remedy was sold them as the answer to their problem. They then often *equate* their sobriety or improvement with the treatment, both to themselves and to the outside world. Others do not approach their problems in this way and fail from the AA perspective to show proper humility and contrition. Let's return to the alcoholics that Tuchfeld interviewed, the ones who solved their own drinking problems:

The one thing I could never do is go into formal rehab. For me to ask somebody else to help with self-made problems, I'd rather drink myself to death.

I'd never consider going to a doctor or minister for help. Good Lord, no! That would make me drink twice as much. I'm the kind of person who has to do things on his own.

But as far as I was concerned, AA was absolutely of no attraction to me, absolutely not.

I would sit there and listen to their stories . . . and I couldn't fit myself into their patterns.

I have always considered myself a fairly strong person, in that I could do whatever I wanted to do, and I didn't feel that I needed anybody to help me. I still feel about the same way. . . . It seems to me that the person needs to have it within himself, be strong enough to handle his own problems. . . . You have got to have some inner strength, some of your own strength in resources that you can call up in yourself.

While AA regards these as typical cases of denial, we might instead inquire whether there are advantages to people deciding that their cure is their own, both to create and to maintain. Following the publication of *The Natural History of Alcoholism*, Dr. George Vaillant sent me additional data to those he reported in his book about alcoholics who were in remission. Of those who quit drinking on their own, *none* of the twenty-one men followed up since the end of the study were abusing alcohol. (Twelve had gone ten or more years without a drink, four had abstained for three to ten years, and five men drank less than once a month.) Of the twenty-two men Vaillant followed up who had relied on AA to abstain, only *five* had gone for ten or more years without a drink, six had gone for three to ten years, four had gone one to two years, two drank less than once a month, and *five* continued to abuse alcohol. *Relapse was more common for the AA group:* 81 percent of those who quit on their own either had abstained for ten or more years or drank infrequently, compared with the 32 percent of those who relied on AA who fall in these categories (see table 2).

Although this analysis involves only a small number of cases, the data support the argument that those who believe their cure is dependent on a particular therapy or group show the least stability in resolving their problems and most readily give up and go back to

**Table 2**
**Follow-up Data from George Vaillant's**
**Life Study of Alcoholism**[29]

| | | AA Reliance | |
|---|---|---|---|
| | *Abstaining without AA* | *10–100 meetings* | *100–2,000 meetings* |
| number with at least 5 more years follow-up | n = 21 | n = 13 | n = 9 |
| 10 + years abstinent | 12 (57%) | 2 (15%) | 3 (33%) |
| 3–10 years abstinent | 4 (19%) | 3 (23%) | 3 (33%) |
| 1–2 years abstinent | 0 | 3 (23%) | 1 (11%) |
| less than 1 drink/month | 5 (24%) | 1 (8%) | 1 (11%) |
| continued alcohol abuse | 0 | 4 (31%) | 1 (11%) |

drinking. It is youthful members of AA and other groups who are most vulnerable if they adopt such a view of themselves, their problems, and the groups they join. It may be possible to convince young people they are lifetime addicts who cannot hope to control their behavior, drinking or otherwise, without the constant presence of AA or therapy in their lives. What remains to be seen is whether as many people will mature out of AA reliance as do so from drug and alcohol dependence.

# One Danger of Therapy—
# Forestalling a New Self-Image

Various arguments can be made for therapy—that even if it produces no greater cure rate than does natural remission in the case of addiction and alcoholism, and even if many people succeed without it, therapy nonetheless can speed the process or perhaps help some who

## THE YOUNGEST ADDICT OF THEM ALL

*People* magazine had as its cover girl on January 16, 1989, the youngest addict it had ever depicted, Drew Barrymore.[30] The cover read: "A star of 'E.T.' at 7, she started drinking at 9, smoking pot at 10 and using cocaine at 12. [The cover didn't mention that she smoked cigarettes "constantly" at 9½.] Now 13 and in therapy, she hopes to help other girls (and their parents) by telling the cautionary tale of her tormented childhood." Barrymore's father was an alcoholic and drug abuser who hadn't seen his daughter in seven years; her mother was in the dark about Drew's life. While preteenager Drew was attending discos and drinking and taking drugs, her mother felt, "I had to give her time and space. I began to lose perspective on what was going on with Drew."

Her mother and a "recovering" friend forced Drew to enter treatment when Drew was 10½. She then went on location to make a film where, although she didn't drink or take drugs, she spent late nights at gambling casinos. Soon afterward she relapsed, entered a hospital, and stayed off alcohol and drugs for eighty-eight days. Drew relapsed next when someone offered her cocaine in the ladies' room of a New York nightclub while she was waiting for her "ex-boyfriend." "After taking a quick hit, I started shaking, knowing that I had just blown all the sober days I was proud of. . . . I figured as long as I'd stepped over the line, I might as well go all out"; she immediately bought more cocaine. After Drew stole her mother's credit card to get a flight to L.A., her mother hired two private detectives to kidnap Drew and return her to treatment.

The article described the all-day structure of the treatment program—school, "then group therapy, then counseling, then more group therapy, dinner, and therapy groups with the patients and their families." At first, Drew only pretended she was serious when she confessed she was an alcoholic and an addict. "But gradually, as I looked over the way I'd been behaving and feeling, I realized that

I have a very addictive personality. Friends say the two best words to describe me are obsessive and compulsive." Now she is ready to help others, knowing "I'm Drew, and I'm an addict-alcoholic." The thirteen-year-old has "been sober for three months, two weeks and five days."

The *People* article included a standard column from an expert, Derek Miller, a psychiatrist who runs a hospital program for juvenile alcoholics and drug abusers. He made clear that "although there is nothing available clinically to test for genetic dependence, . . . parents should be very careful to keep their children off all alcohol if there is a history of either alcoholism or biologically based depression in the family." Barrymore's family tree, of course, includes a number of alcoholics. (If her alcoholism was inherited, were her cigarette smoking and cocaine addiction inherited, too?) Although Dr. Miller warned, "Abstinence is the key to all treatment," he cautioned, "the younger the adolescents, the harder it is for them to understand they have a problem."

Thus this psychiatric expert presents all the standard bromides that lay the groundwork for Drew's future relapses. For example, we see that Drew is primed to go on a binge the minute she goes off the treatment regimen, including having so much as a sip of wine. Meanwhile, one can only wonder who would think this very troubled girl—as the article presents her—is in a position to advise anyone else. Before she approaches anything like a cure for her own problems, she needs to develop better coping mechanisms, a more mature self-awareness, and a reasonable, productive life-style for a young adolescent.

---

could not be helped otherwise. These are legitimate considerations that merit empirical investigation. But simply asserting them—even with the support of people who feel very strongly that this was the case for them—does not prove them. I have already described the case of the man who quit smoking after joining Smokenders but whose three colleagues in that endeavor returned to smoking. When confronted with information that many millions of smokers quit on their own, he sputtered, "Anyone who tries to quit on their own is a fool, or crazy."

For this man, belief in his program is tantamount in his mind to continued abstinence from cigarettes. Whether this is the case or not is probably a useless debate—the man isn't smoking and he's better off in most, or perhaps all, ways. But there are also costs to be calculated. His irrationality is a cost. He also may be more likely to relapse to smoking than someone who does not hold the same beliefs. In contrast, people who outgrow addictions without becoming wedded to a particular philosophy are under most circumstances less fragile and susceptible to relapse. They also have the opportunity to develop the self-image of "regular person"—a person with a normal range of problems, but not one ready to go off the deep end of addiction at the slightest provocation.

In a previous section, we reviewed the case of the former heroin addict, Jerry, who voluntarily stopped his prescription for a narcotic painkiller. For this man, returning to drug addiction was almost an impossibility; in order to do so, he would have had to go back to being an entirely different person from the one he had become. Typically, this kind of total elimination of an addict identity takes many years. It isn't a direct outcome of a stay in a hospital or a period of therapy, but rather results from years and decades of lived experience with a new identity. In a 1987 study published in the *Journal of Studies on Alcohol*, two Swedish physicians studied hospitalized alcoholics at least fifteen years (and on average more than twenty years) following their hospitalization for severe alcohol dependence. Most of the men who had achieved remission were social drinkers rather than abstainers; this was particularly true for those who had achieved good social adjustment.[31]

Most of these former alcoholics had completely transcended their previous alcoholic identities. They now considered themselves—and acted like—ordinary social drinkers. This level of remission requires that addicts and alcoholics unlearn old habits; that they establish new life patterns, including relationships and work and leisure activities; and that they adjust their self-image so that they see themselves as having gone beyond the role of recovering alcoholic. Like former heroin addict Jerry, the person may understand his former addicted self, but he now conceives of himself as having an entirely new range of possibilities and obligations.

Disease-based therapy entirely rejects this possibility. Such therapy sometimes even disallows the possibility that the person can survive without constant attendance in the therapy program, let alone that the person can drink again or otherwise escape a permanent addict identity. This limited view of addicts, and of human beings, may be useful during peak periods of addiction and self-destructive behavior. But it is not appropriate for the large body of substance abusers and other types of addicts, a majority of whom can have fuller lives when they cease thinking of themselves exclusively as recovering addicts.

# What Does Therapy Accomplish?

George Vaillant, as I have mentioned, represents a remarkable phenomenon. His own data—and clinical experience—indicate that it is inaccurate and useless to deal with alcoholism as a disease. Yet as a doctor and supporter of AA, all his work is a defense of the medical approach to alcoholism. Vaillant argues as follows: "alcoholism is not, strictly speaking, a disease. . . . [But] calling alcoholism a disease . . . is a useful device both to persuade the alcoholic to admit his alcoholism and to provide a ticket for admission into the health-care system."[32] This, despite Vaillant's stated view about alcoholism treatment that "in the long run, it is ineffective." Indeed, Vaillant makes clear in his research that the alcoholics he treated did no better than untreated alcoholics.

It might seem strange to read about natural remission from a principal defender of the medical treatment of alcoholism. Yet in his book's summary chapters recommending how therapists and physicians should help alcoholics, Vaillant cautions primarily of the need to "learn to facilitate natural healing processes" and "how *not to interfere* with the recovery process." As Vaillant makes clear *twice* in his book's closing pages (including the very last page): "If treatment as we currently understand it does not seem more effective than natural healing processes, then we need to understand those natural healing processes."[33] Vaillant recommends that we do this by observing how alcoholics so often cure themselves, although in his book,

Vaillant does not review a single case of an alcoholic who successfully quit or cut back drinking on his own—even though this group forms the majority of his cases.

What light can we shed on the natural healing process Vaillant urges as the most important topic for study and utilization in the alcoholism field? We have seen across the range of addictions that it takes both intrapsychic change—or a reconceptualization of who you are, what is good for you, and how you wish to live—and real-life changes to bring off quitting an addiction. Therapy succeeds when it helps with these very concrete but global chores—helping the person to see the addiction in a new light while developing life resources to a point where the person can do without whatever rewards he or she once sought from the addiction. Even when people turn to therapy, however, they must ultimately accomplish these things for themselves.

In chapter 3, we discussed the work of William Miller and Reid Hester, who evaluated every available controlled study of alcoholism treatment. As Miller and Hester indicated, the research "is gratifyingly consistent. The results of well-controlled studies in this area have seldom contradicted one another. . . . Certain methods have a very good track record, working well across a wide range of populations and settings. Others seem to have little therapeutic value, and are rather consistently found to yield little impact on drinking behavior. . . ." Yet these are the standard treatments in American alcoholism programs, as shown in table 3.

These authors' survey identified two general types of effective therapy—therapy that either changes the attractiveness of the involvement, such as aversion therapies—and therapy that enhances the individual's ability to deal with negative emotions or to get positive results and reinforcement in life. Following are descriptions of the effective treatments listed in table 3:

• *Aversion therapies* have traditionally involved administering chemicals that induce vomiting or applying other painful stimuli when an alcoholic is drinking, so that the alcoholic associates drinking with these unpleasant sensations. However, behavioral therapy in which the drinker learns to associate nauseating imagery with drinking (called "covert sensitization") has been shown to be as effective as chemical or electric-shock aversion techniques and is much more

### Table 3
### Supported Versus Standard Alcoholism Treatment Methods[34]

| Treatment methods currently supported by controlled outcome research | Treatment methods currently employed as standard practice in alcoholism programs |
| --- | --- |
| Aversion therapies | Alcoholics Anonymous |
| Behavioral self-control training | Alcoholism education |
| Community reinforcement approach | Confrontation |
| Marital and family therapy | Disulfiram (Antabuse) |
| Social skills training | Group therapy |
| Stress management | Individual counseling |

palatable. Antabuse (disulfiram), the most popular chemical therapy, is not an aversion technique but a drug the alcoholic continues to take to prevent him from drinking.

• *Behavioral self-control training* (also called controlled-drinking therapy) teaches drinkers self-administered techniques for moderating their drinking. Although such therapy is common in Scandinavia and Britain (and perhaps even more so in southern European countries), it has been completely rejected in the United States. Yet *not a single comparative study* has found abstinence treatment to be better than controlled-drinking therapy for any group of alcoholics.[35]

• *The community reinforcement approach* combines job and marital interventions designed to increase people's skill in dealing with problems at work and home while making it more costly for them to drink—for example, encouraging wives to lock husbands out of the house when they return drunk. At the same time, alcoholics are taught a time-out procedure during which they reassess their feelings and coping options whenever they're stressed or otherwise likely to drink.

• *Marital and family therapy* does not refer here to therapies in which family members learn that alcoholism is a disease and that they play a role in the alcoholic's "denial" because they are "enablers." Instead, effective family therapy examines actual interaction patterns—for example, a husband who only expresses his anger when drunk—in favor of offering constructive techniques for coping with family stress and communication issues.

• *Social skills training* teaches alcoholics assertiveness and communications skills so they can express their feelings directly and interact with others in a straightforward and effective manner.

• *Stress management* teaches relaxation skills and primes people to assess problems in a nonanxious way and to figure out the best available options for dealing with a situation.

In the final analysis, what works in all these effective therapies is identical to what works for people who improve their lives without therapy: a strong desire to change; learning to accept and cope with negative feelings and experiences; development of enough life resources to facilitate change; improved work, personal, and family dealings; a changed view of the attractiveness of the addiction brought on by a combination of maturity, feedback from others, and negative associations with the addiction in terms of the person's larger values. The scientific research reinforces a very straightforward and logical view of how people quit drinking or otherwise eliminate addiction; that is, the science of addiction is a science of common sense and human coping. The best thing people can do to solve or prevent addiction is to learn to control their destinies, to find social and work rewards, and to minimize—or at least to bring within controllable limits—stress and fear, including their fear of the addiction.

# 8

# Our Confusion over Law, Morality, and Addiction

S AMPLE NEWS items:

### DEFENDANT IN MASS SLAYING
### IS GUILTY OF REDUCED CHARGE

A Brooklyn man described in testimony as a drug dealer and cocaine addict was acquitted of murder yesterday but convicted on reduced charges of manslaughter in the killings of 10 people [all of whom were shot in the head at point blank range] in a Brooklyn apartment last year.

In interviews after court had adjourned, some jurors said that they were persuaded Mr. Thomas had intended to kill the eight children and two women he found in the apartment, but they believed he had acted under extreme emotional distress and the influence of drugs. . . . "It was the drugs," the jury foreman said.[1]

*

### JERSEY COURT DISBARS 2 LAWYERS
### IN MISUSE OF MONEY OF CLIENTS

The New Jersey Supreme Court today disbarred four lawyers who said their alcoholism or drug addiction had caused them to misappropriate clients' funds. The state's highest court said that although the state's public policy recognizes alcoholism as a disease, disbarment was warranted, *not as a punishment* but for the protection of the public (emphasis added).[2]

*

## Compulsive Gambling May Be a Handicap, and a Shield from Firing

So suggested a federal court in Philadelphia in a case involving an FBI agent who lost $2,000 in Atlantic City, gambling federal funds he was given for an undercover assignment. He went into a treatment program, attends Gamblers Anonymous meetings and stopped gambling. But he was fired because of the incident. The judge rejected an FBI argument that it didn't discriminate by firing the agent for misusing the funds.[3]

*

## Deaver Is Sentenced to Suspended Term and $10,000 Fine

"I believe, as the jury [which convicted Deaver] obviously did, that Michael Deaver knew his answers were false," the judge said. "Mr. Deaver remains as accountable as anyone, afflicted [with alcoholism] or not, for having testified untruthfully." But Judge Jackson said he was still swayed by defense arguments that Mr. Deaver's alcoholism may have been a factor in the perjury.[4]

*

## Battered Women Who Kill

Ewing argues that most of these women kill to prevent their batterers from destroying them psychologically. This innovative theory of psychological self-defense would considerably broaden the legal definition of self-defense and provide a new legal justification for many homicides by battered women.[5]

*

## Can Companies Refuse to Hire Drug Abusers?

Unbelievably, it is easier to refuse to hire the occasional drug and alcohol user than the addict because the occasional user is not a member of the handicapped class and does not receive federal protection.[6]

Almost daily, newspapers carry stories involving drugged and alcoholic behavior, as well as behavior resulting from more esoteric diseases. And we are confounded over how to react to the stories or deal with the misconduct. A drunk Kentuckian drives a truck the wrong way on a highway and kills twenty-seven people—mostly teenagers. Prosecutors ask for twenty-seven murder sentences. About the same time, however, Oprah Winfrey interviews convicted drunk drivers who explain they *must* drink excessively—one woman said if she *didn't* take a drink, she would die—and must be treated for their disease of alcoholism. Cocaine addicts are regularly pulled in for treatment of their drug dependence—even if, as with Dwight Gooden, their drug use is sporadic and incidental. At the same time, we observe gang killings nightly on TV. A gang member is interviewed: "I didn't care about nothing but getting high—stealing, killing someone, or dying myself; it didn't matter to me."

Yet the models of addiction and violence promoted by television news stories and educational specials (like the PBS *Mind* series)— that claim that addiction means that people can't control their behavior and that violence is often the result of uncontrollable neurochemical forces—are completely wrong. To be totally ignorant about the new "scientific" ideas about addiction and violence and to think that people who commit crimes when addicted or who hurt others are simply criminals is actually to be far closer to the truth as revealed both in research and in effective social policy than is the purportedly scientific viewpoint. Nonetheless, anyone who maintains today that people who take drugs, steal, and kill are morally defective is typically held up as an example of ignorance and prejudice and of failure to comprehend the real nature of the behavioral or brain diseases involved.

As this book has made clear, rather than determining people's conduct, substance use is the *result* of what people believe, value, and want. We have entirely put the moral cart before the horse. And even as we make this fundamental mistake, we rail against the way people use drugs and drink and how they act when intoxicated. But we no longer have a moral basis on which to disapprove of or respond to their misbehavior. We ourselves have given them their defense: they were blinded by their disease of alcoholism or drug dependence. At the same as we condone easy, irrational, and dangerous defenses for crime, we also erroneously tell people that the authorities know when they are addicted and how to cure them. Thus, we compel people to be treated for their behavior, even when the behavior violates no laws.

At the one extreme, we defend murderers based on their alcoholism, use of drugs, premenstrual tension, TV addiction, post-Vietnam trauma, love addiction, junk-food addiction, and the like. Mothers who kill newborn children are offered an ironclad legal excuse—they were in a foul mood because of postpartum depression. We remand for alcoholism or addiction treatment people who steal and kill. At the other extreme, we take adolescents from their schools and homes when they have been taking drugs and force them into coercive boot-camp groups that hound them into acknowledging they are addicts. We tell company employees that they are alcoholics and that, unless they seek treatment—which means making a lifelong statement about themselves—they will be fired.

One example of the substitution of addiction myths for legal rights and moral responsibility has been the series of cases in which smokers sue tobacco companies for addicting them and causing their resulting health problems (or a surviving spouse may sue the company for killing the smoker). Since the smokers are addicted, the legal argument is, they cannot help smoking until they kill themselves. Please don't mistake my message: tobacco companies with their own sleight-of-hand pseudoscience and promotion of addiction are *not* models of moral behavior that I endorse. But to use the force of the law to defend and explain the choices of addicted smokers—those incapable of regulating their behavior based on moral and health judgments—is an abomination. That most people don't start smoking and that 40 million smokers have quit indicates that society has no business compensating those who decide to start and who then don't quit.

In my description of smokers, I intentionally use the language of volition. We have no better language—no language more accurate, more useful, or more morally sound—for describing behavior connected with compulsions to misbehave. What are we to make of television programs that interview rapists or others who have led bizarre sex lives and who then claim, "When I had this urge [for sex] nothing else mattered; I would do anything"? To accept this logic is to subvert the basis of civilized behavior. Moreover, we deny the value and strength of the most important of all determinants of behavior—social norms and our commitment to accept them. *The selling of the idea of addiction is a major contributor to the undermining of moral values and behavior in our era.*

# Child and Wife Abuse—Cultures of Violence

The concept promoted in the increasingly evident cases of wife and child abuse is that these are diseaselike problems that have always been rampant and whose ubiquity has only recently been recognized. And of course, testimony given in thousands of congressional hearings, court cases, television shows, and educational programs is that child and wife abuse are totally unrelated to social class, race, religion, or people's values. *Not an iota of systematic data supports any of these contentions, which are now standard wisdom.* And as I have consistently shown, ignorance can never form the basis for useful remedies for any type of problem.

A number of authors have fought the diseasing of child and wife abuse. Leroy Pelton, a researcher for the New Jersey Division of Youth and Family Services, notes that "every national study of officially reported incidents of child neglect and abuse has indicated that the preponderance of the reports involves families from the lowest socioeconomic levels." Of course, the argument is, middle-class families *disguise* their abuse of their children, and that is why we simply miss the obvious. Actually, Pelton points out, the more severe the abuse, the less likely it is to be hidden, yet the discrepancy in reports of child and family abuse between middle-class and underprivileged Americans becomes *greater* the more severely the child or family member is hurt, up to and including being killed.

Pelton seeks to explain why "proponents of the myth of classlessness" persevere with so "little substance for their beliefs . . . in the face of evidence that child abuse and neglect, especially in their most severe forms, occur disproportionately among the lower socioeconomic classes."

The mundane problems of poverty and poverty-related hazards hold less fascination . . . ; concrete approaches to these problems appear to be less glamorous professionally than psychologizing about the poor and prescribing the latest fashion in psychotherapy. Although concrete services are the ones most attractive to prospective lower-class consumers, they are the services that are least appealing to the middle-class helping professional. . . .

Thus the myth serves several functions. It supports the prestigious and fascinating psychodynamic medical-model approach and, by dis-associating the problems from poverty, accords distinct and separate status to child abuse and neglect specialists. . . . Both [the] professional and politician, each for his own reasons, are disinclined to see the problems as poverty-related—the former to increase his chances of gaining funding for a medical-model approach, the latter to increase his own chances of getting a bill passed and thus appearing to be aggressively dealing with the phenomenon of child "battering," which the public already perceives as a "sickness."[7]

The "classless" myth of family abuse is most successfully pro-mulgated through sensationalistic and highly selective reporting—exactly the kind of distortion proponents claim causes most of us to miss the fact that our middle-class neighbors are beating their chil-dren and wives. The much-publicized case of Charlotte Fedders is one we hear a great deal about, in good part because of Fedders's book, *Shattered Dreams.* Fedders was beaten by her six-foot-ten-inch husband, John, chief enforcement officer for the Securities and Ex-change Commission—who even punched his wife in the stomach when she was pregnant. As repugnant as this crime is and as highly placed the perpetrator, it does nothing to refute the data indicating that far fewer middle-class husbands hit their wives than those in lower social-economic groups.

To acknowledge such realities is, of course, to invite the criticism that one is a social bigot. In fact, it is a form of racism and classism that we *ignore* revelations of child abuse or wife beating when they occur in groups other than the middle class, and only consider it noteworthy when a highly placed figure like John Fedders is in-volved. The same phenomenon appears in the case of child abuse. Here the most highly publicized case in recent history is that of Joel Steinberg—the attorney accused of murdering his adopted daughter, Lisa. Yet in New York City, 103 children died from parental abuse or neglect in 1987—or an average of two a week—nearly all in lower-social-class or ghetto neighborhoods.[8] This number rose to *126* deaths of children in 1988.[9] For the most part, we ignore these killings.

Social workers and police in agencies that deal directly with do-mestic violence are less persuaded of its classlessness than the therapists and experts whose opinions we read in the papers. At the time of the Steinberg trial, the *New York Times* typically announced an epidemic of wife and child abuse, "a pattern that crosses racial and socioeconomic lines." At the tail end of the article, Edmund Stubbing, a New York City policeman who works for the Victims Services Agency, reported that the city received 350,000 calls a year reporting fights between husbands and wives. In one Bronx precinct with a population of 120,000, 15 percent of households called police about domestic violence. The *Times* reported that "to Mr. Stubbing and city police and court officials, there is a strong correlation between poverty and domestic violence, but most outside experts say wife and child abuse cut fairly evenly across racial and socioeconomic lines. Those with money are better able to avoid public disclosure than the poor, these experts say."[10]

The "outside experts" the newspaper article referred to are the empire builders in the treatment industry Pelton describes. Those who actually conduct research on the issue agree fully with policeman Stubbing. National surveys and other research provide a consistent description of the people and families in which family violence is likely to occur:

> If one had to come up with a profile of the prototypical abusive parent, it would be a single parent who was young (under thirty), had been married for less than ten years, had his or her first child before the age of eighteen, and was unemployed or employed part-time. If he or she worked, it would be at a manual labor job. . . . Stressful life circumstances are the hallmark of the violent family.

The sociologists who wrote this, Richard Gelles and Murray Straus, found that it is the disadvantaged of both races who have more violent households. They find no difference in the rates of child abuse by blacks and whites nationwide: "While blacks . . . encounter economic problems and life stresses at greater rates than whites, they also were more involved in family and community activities than white families."[11] In black ghettos where family structure and community have been destroyed, obviously, these inhibitions to family violence will be less apparent.

Not all middle-class people avoid household violence, and there is abuse in middle-class households. And of course, while abuse is more common in underprivileged environments, the majority of parents everywhere do not consistently abuse their children. Indeed, in ways that we have seen throughout this book, family violence is worst in households in which all other types of antisocial disruptions occur. For example, the most systematic abuse of women occurs in homes where problem drinking and drug abuse are more common— "almost half of all couples who engage in conjugal or parental violence report that it is associated with drinking by the one who is violent, by the victim, or both."

Gelles and Straus, however, are at pains to make clear that alcohol and drug abuse do not "cause" family violence. It is more accurate to say that households predisposed toward violence are also those predisposed toward abuse of drugs and alcohol and all other types of social problems. For example, "across the board, children from violent homes are more likely to have personal troubles—temper tantrums, trouble making friends, school problems—failing grades, discipline problems, and aggressive and violent flare-ups with family members and people outside the home. These children are three to four times more likely than children from nonviolent homes to engage in illegal acts—vandalism, stealing, alcohol, drugs—and to be arrested." This does not describe child abuse as a hidden phenomenon but as part of an overall complex of problems that cannot be hidden because it has so many unavoidable manifestations.

Why are we always trying to convince those of us who live in peaceful neighborhoods—who know people who don't smoke and never get drunk, whose children behave themselves and do well in school, and whom we have never seen abuse their children—that we probably reside in hidden hotbeds of alcoholism and domestic violence? The extreme position is that *anybody* is equally likely to beat his or her child to death or to allow the child to die through neglect. This is patently absurd to any reasonable person. Yet the constant voicing of such myths has the effect of desensitizing us to the crime and the violence of hurting children. If it is an illness, then we should be less disapproving of it, after all. In this way, the disease approach once again makes the behavior we hate more likely! To put it simply, people who feel most strongly that it is evil to brutalize a child and that adults who do so are reprehensible are those least likely to perpetrate, participate in, or tolerate such violence.

And of course, when middle-class people do act out of expected character by brutalizing their families or committing incest, they are the *most* likely candidates to be diagnosed as being diseased and to be treated, as was the character Ted Danson played in the 1984 TV film about incest, *Something about Amelia*. Obviously, nice people who act this way can't be in their right minds; unlike the ghettoized individuals who commit similar crimes, these middle-class family assailants *must* be ill. As Jay Ruby, a Temple University professor, noted about the film, "When you portray a case of incest in which the father at the end is just a little bit confused and sorry for what he did, it reduces these problems to something like running a red light."[12] Three researchers, on the other hand, noted that the single most important facet of successful programs for dealing with family violence was "holding the violent person personally responsible for his or her violent actions and stressing that he or she is not powerless to stop it." Effective therapies for family abuse make completely clear that "physical violence and emotional abuse is not appropriate or excused."[13]

## The Battered Woman Syndrome and Other Psychological Defenses for Killing Spouses

In several prominent trials, women have been defended for killing their husbands on the grounds that their husbands beat them. However, they didn't usually kill their husbands during a violent confrontation, when they were actually defending themselves from attack (the standard basis for a self-defense plea). Instead, expert psychological and psychiatric witnesses have presented the argument that these women had lost the ordinary self-protective mechanisms that would have enabled them to leave a violent husband. Instead, they remained tied into the relationship until their only way of extricating themselves was to kill the man. This defense, entitled the battered wife (or, more appropriately, "battered woman") syndrome, has become the standard plea in cases where a woman kills her abusive husband.

The pioneering case of this defense involved Francine Hughes and was depicted in the NBC movie *The Burning Bed*, based on the book of the same name. (The TV movie, starring Farrah Fawcett, got the highest Nielsen ratings of the 1984 TV season.) Hughes, who set her sleeping husband on fire in 1977 after twelve years of an abusive marriage, was exonerated by a jury on the grounds that she was temporarily insane. *The Burning Bed* created sympathy for Francine Hughes but did not support the solutions sometimes proposed for wife abuse. For example, Francine and her husband Mickey had actually received a great deal of counseling from social welfare agencies that had intervened in this troubled marriage. We must also remember that Hughes *did* leave her husband several times, only to return to him voluntarily. In other words, the relationship involved a mutual attraction, even while each partner deeply resented the other. And despite the happy picture of Fawcett celebrating the outcome of her trial at the end of the TV film, the real-life Francine Hughes has continued to lead a troubled and debilitated life.

Concerned professionals and women's groups that support battered-wife pleas for women who kill their husbands are not helping women like Hughes as much as they think. It goes without saying that women—like everyone else—have a right to defend themselves when they feel their lives are threatened. And it is *obligatory* that the police and penal authorities restrain batterers who indicate they plan to kill a spouse who has turned them in (just as we can't allow witnesses in organized crime trials to be murdered). It is even more important, in ascending order of preference, that women feel empowered enough to leave relationships that become abusive, that they not enter relationships with abusive men in the first place, and that society work to reduce family abuse and violence generally. However, none of these aims is furthered by regarding women who are beaten up as sufferers of a psychological syndrome or even as victims of pervasive male violence perpetrated on female victims.

Marital violence most often occurs when both partners are parts of subcultures that offer them few ways to express themselves and where people frequently hurt one another. The legal system can help the women, children, and men in these relationships up to a point by acting decisively after the violence explodes. Even then, we have horrifying tales of men who are ordered out of their homes by the courts but return at some point to kill their wives, often then com-

mitting suicide themselves. Neither trials nor psychological counseling can affect the underlying conditions of such relationships. And
political support for abused women who strike out at abusive spouses
is a far cry by itself from enabling people to avoid violence or create
positive lives.

The book *Violent Men, Violent Couples* discusses the development
of the family violence field.[14] Its three authors had previously written
*The Family Secret*, an early exploration of wife beating that advocated
shelters for battered women. In their later book, the authors describe
the progression from women's shelters to counseling for male abusers
to a family systems approach for violent families. The need to involve
husbands in therapeutic efforts was prompted by the simple realization that shelters cannot deal with all the problems in communities
like the Bronx, where 15 percent of families may call the police to
quell domestic violence in a given year. At the same time, simply
blaming men for the violence accomplishes little, especially since
many of the women choose to return to their husbands. Furthermore,
research shows that *women* perpetrate violence as well as receive it—
against both their children and their spouses. Violent families are
often locked into an escalating cycle of violence by both partners.

The first national survey on family violence, conducted by Murray
Straus and his colleagues in 1976, found that one in six (17 percent)
wives said their husbands had struck them sometime during their
marriage.[15] In the previous year, one in twenty-two (4 percent) had
been physically abused. The average battered wife is abused three
times a year. Are these data reliable? In previous interview surveys,
these investigators found that people readily unburdened themselves
about the details of violence in their families. Moreover, the incidence
of domestic violence Straus and his colleagues reported was higher
than previous estimates. This research team also found, however,
that 4.5 percent of husbands reported violent attacks by their wives.
An article written by one of the team, Suzanne Steinmetz, claiming
battery of husbands was actually more likely to go unreported than
wife abuse was attacked by women's group leaders.[16]

That both spouses often perpetrate violence in violent families
supports the view of violence as a family—rather than an individual—problem. On the other hand, in the large majority of cases
violence by women against men is provoked by husbands' violence.
The argument that violence is provoked by the spouse was effective

## FAMOUS CASES OF CHILD AND WIFE ABUSE

The case of Joel Steinberg, who allegedly beat his "adopted" six-year-old daughter Lisa to death, is another middle-class instance of family violence that has gained tremendous public attention. Hedda Nussbaum, Steinberg's mate, testified for the prosecution that Steinberg had beaten her severely and that, in her resulting emotional state, she had allowed him to beat Lisa repeatedly and had been unable to call for help on the night the comatose Lisa lay dying. Nussbaum became a heroine to some people, and groups that applaud battered-women defenses spoke out strongly for her. During the trial, however, testimony was introduced that Nussbaum had also beaten Lisa, that she had smoked cocaine, and that she had calmly lied to the authorities about what had happened to Lisa. Since Nussbaum was not on trial, but only testifying against her former lover, she could walk free after the trial. Hedda's physical freedom contrasts starkly with the life Lisa will never know.

Steinberg pleaded not guilty to killing Lisa, although after much testimony about the madhouse he and Hedda lived in, Steinberg's attorneys moved to introduce an insanity plea based on Steinberg's cocaine-induced paranoia. Clearly, Steinberg's behavior was not that of an ordinary human being—testimony was presented that Steinberg had beaten Lisa because he thought she was staring at and "hypnotizing" him, that he had turned Lisa's comatose body over to Nussbaum the night Lisa died and then left for dinner, that when he returned he had ordered Nussbaum to smoke cocaine with him, and that he had appeared unconcerned when told at the hospital that his daughter had died. Indeed, Steinberg refused to allow his attorneys to rely on the insanity plea at the beginning of the trial, as they wanted to do.[17] Nonetheless, jurors indicated that they couldn't vote to convict Steinberg of murder because "There was doubt about Mr. Steinberg's awareness during twelve critical hours— hours when the battered child lay on a bathroom floor after the fatal blows were struck—because of testimony that he had been using cocaine for days."[18] If an insanity plea had been fully presented and accepted, Lisa might have been "proved" to have been in the hands of two incompetent adults, neither of whom was responsible as they smoked cocaine together while Lisa's life ebbed away.

During the Steinberg trial, another abused child died in one of the 126 such cases that occurred in 1988. Five-year-old Jessica Cortez was found dead with "numerous bruises over her entire body, her face and head, a broken left arm, a possible skull fracture, a two-inch ulcerated scar on her lip, and bruises to her sexual area."[19] The actual cause of Jessica's death turned out to be a broken neck. Charged with the murder were the girl's mother, Abigail Cortez, and her live-in male companion, the fourth man with whom she had had children. Two of her former lovers were currently in prison, and Cortez no longer had contact with two of her five children. Returning to the scene of the murder to investigate, police found nine-year-old Nicky (Jessica's brother) hiding in a closet. Both the boy's legs were fractured, he had eight other broken bones, and bruises covered his body.

The apartment in which Jessica lived was said to be the scene of frequent drug episodes as well as violent beatings. Abigail Cortez told reporters that her companion had frequently beaten her along with the children, and her attorney immediately drew a parallel between this and the Steinberg-Nussbaum case and said he would present a battered woman defense.

---

in Francine Hughes's trial. However, the same argument has also been effectively presented by *men* under similar circumstances—when the other person is dead and not able to defend himself or herself in court. In 1977, Richard Herrin bashed in twenty-year-old Bonnie Garland's skull with a hammer when she told him she wanted to date other men. Herrin pleaded not guilty to second-degree murder due to a mental disease, and the Catholic community at Yale University (where both Garland and Herrin were students) leaped to Herrin's defense, portraying him as a Mexican American adrift on an Ivy League campus. Herrin ultimately received a manslaughter sentence.

As psychiatrist Willard Gaylin points out in his book on the case, *The Killing of Bonnie Garland*, the victim was not alive to testify, leaving only the killer to describe his distraught emotional state and to enlist the sympathy of the trial audience. The trial also gave Herrin the chance to blame Garland for causing the anguish and resulting mental state that led him to kill her. Perhaps the ultimate transfer of guilt of this sort occurred at the trial of Steven Steinberg for slaying his wife Elana. Steinberg claimed he stabbed his wife twenty-six times while he was sleepwalking, driven to distraction as he was by his wife's incessant nagging. (He initially claimed burglars had invaded their home and murdered his wife.) This so-called Jewish-American princess defense was successful, and the killer was acquitted of murder and freed.[20]

By muddying the moral picture in this way, the host of psychological and disease defenses for killing serves primarily to desensitize us to killing and loss of life and to provide elaborate frames for the same old reasons people have always had for killing one another. If we as citizens and as a society want to display mercy and excuse emotional killings by people who are relatives, friends, or lovers of their victims (the majority of killers), we may indeed decide to do so. But we can then hardly deplore these crimes and complain about the high incidence of such killing. Once again, we have caught ourselves in the dilemma of psychologizing and diseasing crime while bitterly resenting the fruits of the crime. And well-meaning professional organizations, I fear, will not find that explicating and excusing the emotional states that cause love partners to kill one another will lead to fewer such crimes and victims.

To show just how deluded is our disease excuse-making—how political on the one hand and how devoid of therapeutic meaning on the other—consider an effort by the American Psychiatric Association to enter three new diseases into the revision of the third edition of its *Diagnostic and Statistical Manual of Mental Disorders (DSM-III)*. The three were: masochistic personality (typical of women who stay in abusive relationships); rapism (the disorder that propels men to rape); and premenstrual syndrome (which has also been used as a defense in trials of women who have killed their husbands). The objection brought against masochism by those active in the establishment of the battered woman syndrome was that it blames women who stay in abusive relationships rather than the situation itself or the abusive men. Rapism, on the other hand, was seen to excuse violent sex crimes against women.[21]

Eventually, Masochistic Personality Disorder was changed to Self-Defeating Personality Disorder and included, along with Premenstrual Syndrome or PMS (called Late Luteal Phase Dysphoric Disorder), in the 1987 revision of *DSM-III (DSM-III-R)* as a "proposed diagnostic category needing further study." Rapism was excluded from *DSM-III-R* altogether. Post-Traumatic Stress Disorder (an important example of which is post-Vietnam stress) is, on the other hand, a full-fledged syndrome in *DSM-III-R*, while postpartum depression was not included in *DSM-III-R* as a diagnostic category. Postpartum depression has nonetheless been used as a defense in an increasing number of cases where women kill their children.

# What Is It Called When Middle-Class Women Kill Their Children?

There are some crimes so horrible that their commission is their own defense. Such is the case of the man described in the news story at the beginning of this chapter who systematically shot eight children in the head, along with one of their mothers and another woman. Who else is capable of such a crime, people naturally react, except someone crazed with drugs? The protypical crime that serves as its own defense is the mother who kills her own infant child. This is especially true when the woman is white and middle class. No sane person could kill her own children, and therefore, in this perfect crime, committing it excuses you from responsibility and punishment. Such a defense for killing your own children has now been formalized as postpartum depression. In one memorable episode of the *Larry King Show*, King interviewed a woman who had successfully used this defense when tried for drowning her child, along with a man whose wife had been imprisoned for killing their child. King and his two guests insisted that the authorities must be blind to fail to understand the nature of this new disease.

In New York, this defense succeeded for the pediatric nurse who admitted suffocating two of her newborn babies and trying to kill a third but who was acquitted of murder by a New York City jury: "The jury verdict was the first in New York to absolve a mother charged with murdering her children on the ground that she suffered from a psychosis caused by severe postpartum depression."[22] In this case, the disease was required to explain why, in addition to killing her children, this mother disguised the killings and then proceeded to have more children. Following on the New York case, a California judge set aside a jury conviction of murder in the case of "a 24-year-old woman who had argued that she was suffering from 'baby blues' [or postpartum psychosis] when she ran her automobile over her infant son and then left the body in a trash can." Following the judge's decision, the woman's "family applauded and cheered."[23]

The irony cannot be missed. As we become more and more worried about the epidemic of child abuse, we then excuse mothers who murder their children because the women suffer from a disease. At the same time, as with all the other new diseases described here, professionals in the field claim that postpartum depression is rampant yet unrecognized, that as many as a third of mothers undergo PPD, and that we need to recognize PPD's frequent occurrence and cope with it and treat it (although postpartum *psychosis*, which is when mothers kill their children, is as yet thought to be rare). How do most mothers overcome their exhaustion and depression after bearing children sufficiently to avoid hurting them? We seem to be working against the essence of parenting, in which people for the better part control their mood swings and tolerate their discomfort as a condition for having and nurturing children.

# Some Random Defenses for Murder, Crime, and Being in a Bad Mood

Obviously, once we have discovered that PMS and postpartum depression cause people to kill lovers, husbands, and children, the door is opened for just about any negative experience to justify just about any subsequent misbehavior. One prominent example of this trend is post-Vietnam trauma, which has become a major growth industry in research, treatment, and the law. We might wonder how so many people who returned from World War II and the Korean War failed to become alcoholics, criminals, and family abusers. Of course, neither did the large majority of those who returned from combat in Vietnam act this way. Nonetheless, in 1985 the *New York Times* reported:

> The war in Vietnam, which ended for the United States a decade ago, is being recalled with increasing frequency and vividness in court-rooms around the country as veterans charged with crimes cite their traumatic Vietnam experiences as their prime defense. In the past five years, hundreds of Vietnam veterans . . . have said they should not be held accountable for such crimes as murder, rape and drug dealing.[24]

In 1988, CBS aired a TV special, *The Wall Within* (with Dan Rather as moderator), that revealed a million veterans suffered from the disease of post-traumatic stress. The men with this disease in-terviewed for the program included one who had almost killed his mother, one who spent years on prescribed drugs, one who defends his mountain home with a gun. The reviewer in *People* was not entirely persuaded by the program. "I'm not quite as easily convinced as CBS was that the syndrome is so widespread and so simply di-agnosed and that Vietnam is its sole cause. Certainly the Holocaust, World War II and the Korean War could have caused at least as many traumas, yet they have never been so readily blamed." Then the reviewer relented: "There is still an important and touching story here, further evidence that the tragedy of Vietnam is not over yet."[25]

It is important to reflect on the Vietnam trauma (or Post-Traumatic Stress Disorder, in *DSM-III-R*) defense. It maintains that stressful events that take place in adulthood can cause crimes, both violent (such as murder) and premeditated (such as running drugs), com-mitted literally decades after the experience. Indeed, it is hard *not* to imagine someone in a violent subculture, one in which killing and drug dealing are more likely to occur, who cannot cite some deep trauma—from parental abuse to abandonment to witnessing brutal crimes—in his or her defense. In short, we have opened up violence as an excuse for perpetual violence without, however, showing any societal tendency to reduce violence or the conditions that lead to it. Clearly, the only way to eliminate the reactions experienced by Vietnam veterans is to avoid wars like Vietnam. Nonetheless, murder and family abuse in ghettos continue unabated, and we certainly wish to reserve the right to send young Americans into war again.

Defenses for murder have now been based on bad diet and eating junk foods (used notably by former San Francisco city supervisor Dan White, who shot and killed Mayor George Moscone and gay supervisor Harvey Milk), watching too much television, and taking medications or ceasing to take them. (Shana Alexander argued in her book, *Very Much a Lady*, that Jean Harris killed diet doctor Herman Tarnower because she was withdrawing from her amphetamine addiction.) It *is* true that people who do all these things are more likely to commit murder. *People* magazine's 1987 two-part cover story on Mark David Chapman—John Lennon's killer—described how Chapman spent the days and nights before murdering Lennon aimlessly eating junk food and watching television in his hotel room. Indeed, the inability to find meaning in his life and the tendency to express himself instead through violence were the hallmarks of Chapman's insanity, leading him in turn to drugs, charismatic Christianity, and murder.

Although Shana Alexander laid out Jean Harris's defense for killing Herman Tarnower based on drug and love addiction, Jean Harris herself did not rely on these defenses at her trial, and as a result she was convicted of murdering Tarnower. Since the trial, Harris has sought to have her case reheard on the grounds that she did not take advantage of these ready pleas. Similarly, Joel Steinberg might sometime claim that he was too psychotic or still so much under the residual influence of drugs to accept an insanity defense at his trial. All of this suggests some future point when no one can ever be convicted of a crime, since everyone has some kind of disease defense for their actions, and those who cannot mount a defense based on some disease will, ipso facto, be obviously mentally incompetent to stand trial!

It is also important to reflect on what these various defenses for misconduct and mayhem tell us about our attitudes toward taking responsibility for ourselves and others. PMS and postpartum depression are explanations for why we mistreat those closest to us because we feel bad. These defenses seem to describe a completely self-gratifying universe where a bad mood or sexual urges are grounds for maiming or molesting children, and where the law and psychiatry try to justify societywide failures at the exercise of self-control. In the 1988 film *Distant Thunder*, John Lithgow portrayed a veteran who hasn't contacted his son for years—and can't deal with the child when they do meet. The film expects viewers to empathize with a man too preoccupied with his feelings to act like a father on the grounds of the character's Vietnam trauma and to examine their own souls if they are so inhumane as to react to Lithgow as an immature whiner.

The hallmark of a civilized society is that people learn to restrain their impulses in line with the needs of their communities, neighbors, and families—a basis for civilized dealings that psychology and psychiatry paradoxically are now systematically undermining. We are in the process of rejecting the idea that people can be responsible for their behavior when they are in a bad mood. We often see that how we word things reflects how we experience them. What does it mean to call people "suicide victims" and to say others suffer from "alcohol abuse" rather than saying that they have killed themselves or abuse alcohol (or, better still, that they drink too much)? Misusing the language in these neo-Orwellian disease formulations is the surest sign that we are deceiving ourselves in preparation for living in a desolate social universe that we decry but cannot change.

## Treatment as Punishment

Addiction interacts with the law in another way besides allowing criminals to beat their raps. From the other side, the *majority* of referrals to treatment for alcohol and drugs are involuntary, ordered either by the courts, through employee assistance programs that insist that an employee undergo treatment or else lose a job, or through school counseling interventions that confront children with a variety of coercive techniques. People are then compelled in these programs to declare themselves addicts or alcoholics and to modify their behavior well beyond the punishments they might have been meted out had they simply been convicted. For example, DWIs in many states today are forced to undergo treatment, and the condition for maintaining their license or staying out of jail is to stay entirely alcohol free, for which they may be tested for periods ranging from months to years.

The large majority of those arrested for drunk driving, however, do not come close to manifesting the symptoms of clinical alcoholism.[26] As a result, a person who may have deserved some sort of punishment is now declared incapable of drinking and may be penalized *years later* if he or she should even drink occasionally or moderately. Nightmarish situations like the following result:

Dawne Green had much that troubled her last week. Her baby wasn't due until October 5, but she was showing signs of early labor; a state-sponsored agency decided she had an alcohol problem, even though she says she doesn't drink anymore. . . . The net result was that her driver's license had been suspended indefinitely although she hasn't committed a traffic violation in 16 months. And still to come was word on whether she might be arrested for violating a state mandate. . . .

Green never disputed that she was intoxicated when she was arrested for drunk driving in Middlesex County on August 29, 1984. . . .In December 1985, Green's license was restored. In April, she was ordered by the Intoxicated Driver Resource Center (IDRC) to report to the county center for testing and to bring $50 to cover costs. She complied, and "that's where my problems began."

"They handed me a 100-question test, showed me some slides and then sat me down and said I had an alcohol problem," she said. "I said, 'How could I?' Except for the time I was arrested, I rarely drank more than a couple of glasses of beer or wine and that was only a couple of times a month. And since I got pregnant, I haven't touched alcohol at all," Green added. "Listen, I know I did wrong the night I got stopped, but since then my driving record is clean. . . ."

Green said she attended an initial session at the Family Service Agency of Princeton, but balked when informed she would be required to attend 18 weeks of counseling sessions at $20 per session. "I paid for my mistake and I don't think it's fair to keep after me for a problem I had one night two years ago. . . . [Yet] every time I questioned anything, they told me if I didn't cooperate I would get my license suspended and be sent to jail."

Green asked for an outside second opinion on the alcohol-problem designation, a request that is handled by the local IDRC. Middlesex IDRC Director Erwin Michel refused: "I had several reasons to believe she had a problem and needed counseling. I stand by my decision."[27]

In chapter 5, we saw that addiction treatment has expanded rapidly by the coercive recruitment of patients, particularly involving the young. A case that illustrates the 1984ish potential of these trends in "therapy" is that of Fred Collins. Collins was treated in the well-known Straight, Inc. drug program. A college student, Collins was confined against his will and subjected to twenty-four hour surveillance, isolation from outside friends and family, hazing verging on physical violence, and a continuous bombardment of data about his chemical dependence—all based on Collins's admission that he used marijuana from time to time. Collins escaped by jumping out of a window and eventually was awarded $220,000 by a jury for false imprisonment. Straight, Inc., however, refused to acknowledge guilt and defended itself on the grounds of Collins's drug dependence, and Nancy Reagan and government officials continue to praise and support the program.[28]

A couple was awarded $1 million by a Minneapolis jury when authorities forced them into an alcoholism treatment program after their daughter testified that they frequently drank and fought; she later testified that she had said this only because her parents were too strict and she thought she would have more freedom in a foster home. The parents were Scottish immigrants, which could have contributed both to the differences in the parents' and child's views of drinking and to their different attitudes about parental strictness.[29] Are these cases extreme? While CompCare and other treatment groups always say any individual cases of inappropriate and coercive treatment are aberrations, even an industry consultant for the National Association for Alcoholism Treatment Programs revealed, "I'm afraid this happens far more often than people in the field want to admit; it's something of a scandal."[30]

We are now entering a period when compulsory drug and alcohol testing and treatment will alter the lives of all our children, if not most of us. President Reagan sought to implement widespread drug testing in the federal government, while the Presidential Commission on Organized Crime recommended "a widespread national program to test most working Americans for drug use," with the federal government withholding "contracts to private employers that do not begin drug testing programs."[31] There is broad support for drug testing in the belief that some sacrifice of personal freedoms is demanded in the face of massive drug abuse in the United States. In an August 1986 poll, three-quarters of workers said they are willing to be tested, while 18 percent said drugs were the most important problem facing America (compared with 2 percent who said this in April 1986).[32]

Thus far, however, large-scale drug testing has not revealed that epidemic proportions of Americans abuse drugs at work. By the end of 1988, 8,064 of the Department of Transportation's 100,000 workers had been tested for drug use. Tests of sixty-one workers (less than 1 percent of those tested) indicated drug use, and four workers (fewer than five one-hundredths of one percent) were dismissed as a result of drug testing.[33] Naturally, if any of these one in two thousand workers who was fired had been driving a train, we might be glad that he or she was found out. However, we may also wonder if transportation companies don't have any other means of making sure intoxicated drivers don't pilot vehicles. For example, Exxon hardly needed drug testing to determine that the captain of the Exxon Valdez (the tanker involved in the massive Alaskan oil spill in March, 1989) presented an unacceptable risk, since he had previously lost his driver's license for drunk driving and had been visibly drunk on the job. Companies will need to continue to rely on these methods, since drug testing programs are very expensive, can only be administered sporadically, and have a long lag time before anything can be done about a drug-using driver. Before the government began testing transportation workers, Colorado representative Patricia Schroeder reported that an extensive House Subcommittee on Civil Service study of drug testing of federal employees showed the tests would "be costly and useless."[34]

## Drug Testing as Therapy

Drug testing is now generally combined with treatment and with guarantees that people cannot be fired because they have a disease-type disability (such as alcoholism). In other words, a drunken pilot or train engineer may be placed in treatment once he or she is discovered to be endangering people's lives on the job. Given the record of success that treatment programs have shown, does this reassure you as a potential passenger on a vehicle piloted by a person who has been irresponsible enough to come to work intoxicated? For

## ONLY THE EXCEPTIONAL COLLEGE ATHLETE OBJECTS TO BEING TESTED

When the NCAA instituted mandatory drug testing in 1986, the ACLU's legal director for the state of Washington advertised to find one athlete at the University of Washington to challenge the program; none would. Eventually, a handful of athletes nationwide did contest their drug testing. Simone LeVant, a Stanford swimmer, got a Santa Clara County Superior Court judge in California to rule that the testing violated the California constitution. LeVant was thus the only swimmer at the 1987 NCAA championships who did not undergo testing. Andy Geiger, the athletic director of Stanford, stated, "We don't think it's right that athletes are the only people to be selected out of the study body to be drug tested."[35] (Apparently, Geiger would prefer testing *all* students.) Although Geiger opposed testing, he told LeVant that he and Stanford couldn't help her.

Among the few other athletes who challenged the tests were cross-country runners at the University of Colorado and Northeastern University. When the Northeastern runner refused to be tested, Massachusetts Supreme Court justice Francis O'Connor declared, "What right does he have to play athletics?"[36] A sardonic article in the *New York Times* entitled "Sportsman of the Decade?" reviewed the case of Colorado runner David Dreyden.[37] "Derdeyn [sic] is not a football or basketball player . . . and those who believe in his chance for immortality are civil rights lawyers. . . . Dreyden is a 28-year-old sophomore (he spent four years in the Army) with long red hair, a scraggly beard and a Willie Nelson–style bandanna headband." The article noted that Dreyden was not a typical student of the 1980s but was, "at least in appearance, every inch a throwback to the 60's. Appropriately enough."

At the end of 1987, another Santa Clara County Superior Court judge ruled that the NCAA's program violated constitutional rights of privacy, saying, "The paradox of this testing program is that an accused criminal of the most serious crimes is afforded more rights than our athletic heroes." Despite such judicial rulings, Michigan basketball coach Bill Frieder said, "I'm in favor of testing—I don't give a damn about constitutional rights when I'm coaching." Digger Phelps, Notre Dame's basketball coach, asserted, "When drugs are out of control in society, somebody has to be a role model." The NCAA's testing program revealed 34 positives out of 3,511 athletes tested (less than 1 percent). Two-thirds of these positives were for steroids; all the drug-using athletes were football or men's basketball players—none of them runners (like Dreyden) or swimmers (like LeVant).[38]

---

example, Joseph Hazelwood had undergone treatment before running the Exxon Valdez aground.

In this approach, both in the courts and in company programs, the system considers irresponsible drug use and drinking as signs of "chemical dependence" and, in fact, deals most harshly—through jail sentences and firings—with people who insist they are not out of control of their drug use. Everyone, no matter how well they perform at work, must undergo urine tests and show no signs of drug (and sometimes alcohol) use, while those who cannot perform their work due to drug or alcohol use are excused from work to receive treatment. It seems we will entirely reverse what were once ordinary standards of behavior: the person who does his or her job but who drinks or takes a drug off-site will be penalized, while the one who can't perform on the job is excused on the grounds that he or she has a disease.

In 1988, almost half of the Fortune 500 companies routinely employed mandatory drug tests. They did so because, as a survey of Fortune 1,000 executives and public officials indicates, they now overwhelmingly (79 percent) recognize that substance abuse is a "significant or very significant problem in their organizations." This is a substantial change, according to Lee I. Dogoloff, executive director of the American Council for Drug Education, who says, "Five years ago, many of them didn't know they had a problem." In the midst of this boosterism over substance abuse programs in business, the survey asked seventy human resources executives whether their existing substance abuse programs did any good.

> The overwhelming majority saw few results from these programs. In the survey, 87 percent reported little or no change in absenteeism since the programs began and 90 percent saw little or no change in productivity ratings.

While this analysis might make some stop short about the advisability of widespread testing and treatment programs, this *New York Times* business section article blithely proceeded to recount the cost of drug abuse on absenteeism and productivity in the workplace and the need for employee assistance managers to gather the support of top-level management for expanding these programs.[39]

Federal law has now been enacted that penalizes people for possession of even small quantities of drugs (the so-called zero-tolerance policy). The act also denies drug users access to federal programs and loans, as well as administering fines and confiscating drug users' property. The zero-tolerance approach ignores the de facto acceptance by law enforcement agencies in major cities that it is simply impossible to prosecute most drug users because drug use in inner-city neighborhoods is so rampant. Under the current laws, New York state reported in January 1988 that those incarcerated for possessing and selling drugs had become the largest single category of prison inmate.[40] Paradoxically, at exactly the same time that more people are put in jail for using drugs, more people in jail for robbery, rape, and other felonies are being diverted to drug treatment rather than serving ordinary sentences. "As prison and jail populations swell beyond capacity, cities and states are increasingly using drug tests to identify the worst criminal offenders, and using treatment of drug abuse to alter their criminal behavior."[41]

The 1988 federal drug act for the first time incorporates significant treatment proposals in antidrug legislation. When treatment becomes part of law, people who are suspected of drug use or who test positive for drugs are forced to undergo drug treatment. Mark Gold, the Fair Oaks physician who treated John Phillips, reviews such laws approvingly: "Such statutes should declare unequivocally that use of the drug is unlawful and will be punished with increasingly stiff sentences. . . . Appropriate mandatory treatment should be a key requirement along with supervised probation."[42] The major impact of this legislation will be to enlarge the number of Americans treated for addiction—primarily people whose occasional use least resembles the compulsive use originally claimed to justify treating addiction as a medical ailment.

The invasion of personal freedom represented by drug testing is now regularly excused on the grounds that its purpose is therapeutic and not punitive, and that it is used simply to help those who have the medical problem of drug abuse. In 1986, one New Jersey school board instituted testing because, it said, drug abuse was epidemic in the school district. A state judge declared the board's universal drug-testing program unconstitutional, since he felt that the five percent of the student body that had sought substance abuse treatment did not justify testing all students. The judge declared that "the constitutional proscription against unreasonable search and seizure is not limited to only those who are suspected of criminal behavior." But at what percentage would universal testing have been justified—10 percent, 15 percent? In the world as envisioned by this school board and bought by increasing majorities of Americans, the failure of some to perform their work or to remain free of drugs or crime means that all Americans should have their bodily processes regularly monitored by the authorities.

The lawyer for the school board indicated that the school board would appeal—"We've been authorized by the Board of Education to go as far as the U.S. Supreme Court." Predictably, the lawyer and the board claim that the testing program is required by the medical nature of the problem. The appeal will "emphasize the argument that drug use was a medical condition. 'We want to prove that it's an illness,' he said, 'just like diabetes, cancer or AIDS.' "[43] In other words, testing is being done just as it might for a cholera outbreak. Here is the essence of the diseasing of America, where we consider ourselves out of control *as a nation*. We now accept that without military intervention at our borders, overseas actions against Third World nations that grow drugs, universal drug testing, and coerced treatment, we would simply drown in our drug use.

The complaint most often lodged by those who object to drug testing is the inaccuracy of the tests. But what if a technological advance permitted each American to be fitted with a sensor that would set off an alarm at police headquarters if the person ever consumed a drug? All of the justifications for drug testing would still hold, and we would have an airtight method that assured instantaneous, perfect detection. If we take seriously the view that people can no longer be expected to regulate or resist drug use on their own, then this approach makes complete sense. With all objections on the grounds of constitutional civil liberties overcome, the issue becomes purely one of perfecting the technology.

It could be said that we have already lost the war on drugs when so many believe that Americans simply cannot be expected to make sensible decisions about what they put in their bodies. In terms of this vision, self-regulation has proved impossible for Americans, who must now be treated or threatened out of their personal preferences for using drugs or alcohol. Otherwise, we believe, Americans simply cannot be expected to do the right thing or to preserve their health. The price we pay for this worldview, against which there is surprisingly little opposition, is subversion of the American tradition of respect for the freedom and dignity of the individual. We might also extend this new approach of bureaucratic regulation of personal behavior to such areas as eating and children's television viewing—addictive activities of which we are also clearly out of control as a nation. And will this new world of behavioral regulation, brought about by our humanitarian impulses and medical advances, be a world worth living in?

# 9

# How We Lost Control of
# Our World

In worrying about legendary maniacs, we ignore real threats. . . .
In addition, the urban legends foster fear and mistrust, jeopard-
izing our sense of community. Once people believe that their
world contains dangerous maniacs, they are likely to withdraw
into the safety of privacy and anonymity.

—Joel Best, "The Myth of the Halloween Sadist"[1]

I hate it as I'd hate a little drug habit fastened on my nerves. Its
influence is the same but more insidious than a drug would be,
more demoralizing. As feeling fear makes one afraid, feeling more
fear makes one more afraid.

—Mary MacLane, *I, Mary MacLane*

THE PARADOX of the American addiction treatment industry is
the tremendous growth it maintains without demonstrating that
it works. In the case of alcoholism, the treatment industry first
convinced us that alcoholism is a major problem and now persuades
us that the problem is ubiquitous. This problem augmentation—
and not any evidence the industry has offered that it can stem alcoholism or treat it effectively—serves as the justification for the
entire industry. The alcoholism industry thus presents a model of
growth for any other industry that would carve out a niche in the
mental health marketplace. The drug abuse industry is another case
of the success of futility. We have spent successive fortunes on campaigns against drug use—yet inner-city addiction and drug degra-

dation achieved their major gains in urban ghettos only *after* we targeted drug abuse as a major social problem.

The addiction treatment industry is an expression of larger trends in American society. The principal trend has been our failure to stanch every social problem associated with the underclass that has evolved in the United States. Rather than address the fundamental social issues underlying ghetto deterioration, addiction policies speak to primarily middle-class anxieties. Problems rooted in ghetto life, in addition to substance abuse, include violence, childhood obesity, and the poor health of the fetus and newborn in America relative to every other industrialized nation in the world. And although these problems are worst in the ghetto, middle-class America also suffers from a version of each problem more severe than those found in other economically advanced countries.

Moreover, the addiction industry expresses the sense of loss of control we have developed as a society, an anxiety brought on by our utter incapacity to alter the trends over which we are so distraught. We have simply proved incapable of identifying correctly the sources of our most dire problems, and our tendency instead is to respond to our anxieties. Our fears themselves have now absorbed our attention to the point where they endanger our individual mental health and our health as a society. Our fears for our children, among other fears, affect us so much that we can no longer carry on a community life in the United States. Yet the failure of community leads to greater alienation, health problems, and the kind of violent and addictive relationships we examined in the previous chapter. Americans as a group now share some of the traits said to characterize mental illness, such as a terror at something nameless that we cannot shake.

# Is the United States Worse Off Than It Used to Be, or Than the Rest of the World?

In order to get a handle on our social problems, we need to evaluate how bad these problems are, compared with America in the past and compared with the rest of the world. When our terror becomes unmanageable, we need to examine its realistic basis; perhaps the problem about which we are concerned has actually improved over time or isn't as bad as it is in other places. I believe that we badly overstate some of our problems, especially alcoholism and drug abuse, as well as such newfound problems as PMS and postpartum depression.

From the other side, I think we suffer more than we realize from a lack of sense of community and from our failure as a society to attack social problems. I believe that we *are* creating problems for ourselves—many related to addiction—and that more and more Americans feel themselves in the throes of one or several such compulsions. As we have seen, deciding one is addicted is a complicated process, entailing that one see oneself as being out of control of one's habits. And Americans do seem to feel that they are more out of control of their lives than they have felt in the past. This loss of control—despite all claims about the discovery of new biological causes of menstrual discomfort and genetic sources of alcoholism, depression, anxiety, and other conditions—is principally a social and psychological phenomenon.

Problems that we may overstate—and that have a large subjective element to them—are drug addiction and alcoholism. The signs are complicated, however. Americans' drinking has decreased in recent years, and it comes nowhere near the high per-capita levels of colonial and postcolonial America or of many European countries (like Belgium) that nonetheless do not consider alcoholism a serious problem. Americans use less cocaine and narcotics per capita today than they did at the turn of this century (when Coca-Cola contained a *substantial* dosage of cocaine, and when narcotics could be bought everywhere at drugstores and from street medicine salesmen). As we approach 1990, middle-class Americans use less cocaine than they did in the early 1980s, and kids are smoking less marijuana than they did in the 1970s. Drug experimentation in the United States is fairly common, although compulsive drug use is rare among high school and especially college students and is far from common in the average American community.

Despite the overall decline in alcohol consumption, drunkenness generally continues at a high level among adolescents and young adults in America. Ghetto, minority communities—particularly such minorities as Native Americans, Eskimos, Hispanics, and blacks—

have a high incidence of alcoholism. Furthermore, drug abuse—especially of the most destructive, antisocial kind—is rampant in urban black and Hispanic communities. Runaway addiction in our inner cities, combined with smaller pockets of middle-class abusers, places our overall addiction rates far ahead of those for all European nations, even those—such as Holland, England, and Sweden—that have witnessed increased drug addiction in the 1970s and 1980s. For example, cocaine abuse did not become widespread in Europe (as many originally predicted), and crack use is still practically unknown there. As in the case of heroin, cocaine abuse will lag far behind in Europe for years, and then will follow the American lead in only a far milder way.

Thus, we see a mixed picture of high levels of drug use and drinking in some communities and in some groups of young people, combined with most young people maturing out and most middle-class communities becoming more abstemious. Overall, Americans do not drink and consume narcotics or cocaine as much as they have done at peak levels in the past. *Despite* these data, however, more Americans—and particularly young Americans—either declare themselves or are declared by others to be drug- or alcohol-dependent. For example, although alcohol consumption in the United States declined between 1977 and 1987, AA membership doubled during that period. (AA's census figure for the U.S. in 1987 was 775,000; its estimated 1988 census figure is 850,000.) Furthermore, a government epidemiologist declares, this paradox will persist: "Despite moderating per capita alcohol consumption nationwide, the treatment of alcoholism and other chemical dependencies will remain a growth industry well into the foreseeable future."[2]

## Two Things *Are* Worse in America— Obesity and Violence

Unlike the ambiguous cases of alcohol and drugs, which large parts of the American population rely on less, one behavioral/addictive problem is clearly growing worse. This is obesity, the appetitive behavior that—particularly for the young—may be the most out of control. It is odd that exactly at this time, the scientific community is beginning to accept the view that obesity is inherited.[3] Yet several

## THE DECLINE OF A BLACK COMMUNITY

As we saw previously, cocaine use has dropped overall but has increased in the inner city. This jump in ghetto usage of cocaine has been of the most potent forms of the drug, used in the most addictive style, and is accompanied by the greatest violence. While middle-class users do shop for crack in inner cities, their usage patterns are typically more moderate and less often accompanied by the violence, addictiveness, and social disintegration that mark inner-city drug use.

One example of this process is the District of Columbia. Over the past two years in Washington, an intense police crackdown has led to a rate of twenty-one drug-related arrests per thousand D.C. residents. Nonetheless, drug use and related crime have increased, and constitute 60 percent of all crime in the city. The district prison is the most crowded in the United States; its population has increased 50 percent in the last five years, and a hundred more prisoners enter the system each month than leave it. Treatment facilities are likewise overloaded, and drug users referred to the system regularly leave treatment without completing the program and with no further follow-up. While federal drug expenditures in the 1988 fiscal year amounted to about $1.5 billion to be used for treatment and prevention resources and facilities, this figure translates into only about fifty hospital beds for drug treatment in D.C.—a small percentage of the addicts in the city.[4] Washington, D.C., is today overwhelmed by drugs, and drug-related violence is a constant presence in the lives of inner-city residents. And however extreme D.C. is, it is more or less typical of nearly every major U.S. city with a sizable black ghetto, including Detroit, Philadelphia, Boston, New York, Los Angeles, Providence, Hartford, Chicago, and Omaha.

crucial aspects of obesity cannot readily be explained from a genetic standpoint. For example, obesity is highly related to socioeconomic status (SES). In a study in three Eastern cities, girls from a lower socioeconomic group were obese nine times as often as those from a high SES group.[5] In addition, changing life circumstances—like moving ahead socially or professionally—are associated with weight loss.[6] Finally—and most important of all—obesity has increased dramatically for children:

> Data from four national surveys indicate pronounced increases in the prevalence of pediatric obesity in the United States . . . [including, since the mid-1960s] a 54% increase in the prevalence of obesity among children 6 to 11 years old and a 98% increase in the prevalence of superobesity.[7]

How can the doubling of superobesity in children be explained genetically? Whatever role genes play in obesity seems to have been overridden by a general trend toward fatness in America. What might help to explain this phenomenon is the strong relationship between obesity and television viewing discovered by two researchers at the New England Medical Center, William Dietz and Steven Gortmaker, who have been tracking pediatric obesity. These investigators have shown that television viewing actually *causes* obesity: "Television viewing precedes obesity, even when controlled for confounding variables, . . . the relationship is unidirectional [obesity does not cause TV watching], . . . a dose-response effect occurs [the more TV you watch the fatter you get], and . . . a mechanism exists by which this association can be explained."[8]

Thus we have decided that obesity can't be controlled because it is largely inbred at the same time that childhood obesity has skyrocketed, even as our society is ostensibly undergoing a physical fitness craze. Supposedly, Americans are more concerned with fitness than ever before; yet our kids are fatter than ever before (as well as frequently using drugs and alcohol). We are unable to get a handle on physical fitness for our society as a whole, and our health messages seem not to be reaching most of those with the worst health behaviors. The economic constraints that many Americans face, the decline in regular physical activity, the greater reliance on electronic entertainments, the radical increase in fast-food consumption—all make young people fatter, no matter how many articles about health appear in our magazines and how many health clubs open.

One other area in which the United States is doing worse than other countries—and increasingly so—is our level of violence. In the previous chapter, we saw that one response to wife abuse has been to ease the proscription on wives killing husbands. Instead, we might consider that all this family violence takes place in a very murderous society. The homicide rate in the United States is ten times that of the urban areas of Western Europe. *This* is a worrisome problem, one that presumably could attract as much attention as drug addiction and spouse and child abuse (which, of course, contribute to murder statistics). Moreover, murder is most often committed in the groups among which we noted that family abuse is greatest, like black Americans, although murder is more common among white Americans than among Europeans.[9]

This formula—the problem is greatest for underprivileged Americans, but is nonetheless greater among the rest of us than in comparably advanced, industrial societies—holds for drug abuse, obesity, child abuse, and other problems discussed in this chapter, including infant mortality and teen pregnancy and motherhood. More noteworthy about the United States than any individual social problem, however, is the larger dread that holds us captive when we contemplate our world and our children's world. And this fear is crucial to all our other problems and the possibility that we can find solutions for them.

# We Have Nothing to Fear
# So Much as Fear Itself

A 1987 tract, *When Society Becomes an Addict*, claimed that we live in an addictive world, that our entire society is predicated on addiction and denial, and that therefore we need to implement a massive twelve-step program for *everyone*, making the government a kind of extension of AA. To see addiction everywhere and to decide that what we need is more AA fervor in order to achieve "recovery" as a society is so badly to miss the sources of addiction as to exacerbate what already makes the United States a world leader in addiction. America's problem is not that it *refuses* to see its addictions—it sees *too many*. We fear so many things that already too much of our society's ameliorative energy goes toward warning people against and protecting them from the many addictive dangers we have discovered.

Given how extensive the addiction treatment industry already is, why, then, do we continue to have so much to fear? The problems this book discusses all seem to be worsening, to judge from treatment activity and public service announcements and therapy advertisements. More victims of the various addictions and loss-of-control syndromes—such as gambling, compulsive shopping, PMS, postpartum depression, and, of course, drinking and drug taking—are constantly being treated, yet we become more hysterical about all of these problems as each year goes by. What accounts for the paradox that as we expand our treatment facilities and public responsiveness we perceive our problems as less manageable? The addictive cycle—relying more on something as it brings us less satisfaction and success—does indeed seem to typify our society, but mainly that part of it represented by the addiction treatment industry.

The never-ending cycle of claiming that there is more of a problem than we thought, then investing more resources in combating it, then reassessing the problem as being worse than we originally suspected so that it requires more resources starts, of course, with alcoholism. In 1940, a leading alcoholism expert declared, "Over 100,000 persons are suffering from alcoholism in the U.S. today."[10] In 1946, an expert at Yale claimed that "there are in this country more than a million excessive drinkers."[11] In 1956, the *Quarterly Journal of Studies on Alcohol* estimated there were 5 million alcoholics; in 1965, the National Council on Alcoholism estimated 6.5 million; the NCA raised its estimate in the 1970s to 10 million.[12] By the 1980s, the figure most often quoted was 15 million American alcoholics. In 1986, advertisements for Dennis Wholey's book *The Courage to Change* claimed that "there are 20 million alcoholics in the United States" and that "80 million Americans, one in three, are directly and tragically affected by this insidious disease."

In 1972, the National Institute on Alcohol Abuse and Alcoholism (NIAAA) claimed in its *Annual Report to Congress* that "alcohol abuse and alcoholism drain the United States economy of an estimated $15 billion a year." In 1983, despite millions more in expenditures, the NIAAA estimated the costs of alcoholism to have increased almost eightfold, to $116 billion![13] One would think that such a dismal performance would cause Congress to cut back its mandate for alcoholism treatment and prevention, especially since alcoholism treatment has now become a major private industry. Instead, of course, the federal government continues to increase its expenditures in this area, despite which the National Council on Alcoholism and other alcoholism lobbying groups are predicting a steady rise in the financial toll taken by alcoholism.

Our history of combating drug abuse is no better. Each president since Nixon has had his own war on drugs. Nixon's and Carter's wars concerned primarily heroin, although new drug waves hit American cities after each claimed victory over drugs. Reagan's war, announced in 1982, was directed at cocaine. Yet cocaine supplies are more abundant and cheaper in the United States today than when Reagan's war began. Cocaine and crack addiction has visibly increased in most American cities. Identifying and combating drugs as a major social problem has not eliminated, reduced, or even held the problem at the earlier levels that were deemed unacceptable! By fiscal year 1989 the federal government spent $4 billion in its onslaught against drugs. Because even this massive expenditure had negligible effect, George Bush sought to add to Ronald Reagan's $5 billion request for the 1990 fiscal year, although not as much as the $6.5 billion Congress proposed for its war on drugs. The new federal thrust in combating drugs emphasizes treatment and such new tacks as civil penalties for drug users. At the same time, the money spent to destroy overseas supplies and to interdict drug imports also has increased radically, as has the involvement of the U.S. military—in the form of the Coast Guard and the National Guard—in these efforts.[14]

The self-exacerbation of addictive problems is closely tied to the self-exacerbation of fear. The more we fear a problem, the more we worry and warn people about it, the more instances of the problem we find and the greater our perception of the danger. The process is one of a progressive sense of loss of control; the greater the number of things we discover to be afraid of, each of which individually inspires progressively more fear, the more depressed and frightened we become. Indeed, the reported incidence of both depression and anxiety are increasing, just as more people enter treatment for each and just as we boast of remarkable breakthroughs in treatment for each.[15] What explains this process whereby we claim greater knowledge at the same time as we experience diminishing control in almost every area of behavioral and emotional disease?

## Infant Mortality and Defects

As a case study of our failure to deal successfully with what we identify and treat confidently as a medical problem, let us consider infant mortality, birth defects, and related dangers for the newborn. Drinking and drug taking during pregnancy have been reported since the 1970s as major causes of all these problems. In the mid-1970s, for example, fetal alcohol syndrome (FAS) was identified, and in 1981 the U.S. surgeon general warned that pregnant women should never drink. In 1986, *New York Times* health writer Jane Brody stated, "An estimated 50,000 babies born last year suffered from prenatal alcohol exposure." Brody described FAS as "growth retardation before and after birth . . . facial malformations, including small, widely spaced eyes . . . brain damage, including an abnormally small head and brain" and claimed that "the fetal damage wrought by alcohol occurs independently of the effects of smoking, poor nutrition, poverty, illness and exposure to other drugs."

But, Brody indicated, most cases of prenatal alcohol damage go undetected. "Experts estimate that for every child with FAS, at least 10 others have more subtle and often unrecognized alcohol-caused problems. Indeed, prenatal alcohol exposure may turn out to be the primary cause of learning disabilities and hyperactivity." More chillingly, "there is no known safe level of alcohol intake during pregnancy," and "even a small amount of alcohol consumed at the wrong time may affect fetal development adversely. . . . *Even drinking before pregnancy (as little as one drink a day) may have an untoward result*"[16] (emphasis added). If even drinking casually before a woman becomes pregnant can maim a fetus, it is no wonder that many American mothers have panicked about their drinking! Meanwhile, American concern over drinking during pregnancy has not been matched by that in any European country—and yet virtually all of these countries have better birthing outcomes than the United States.

There are strong reasons to be skeptical about all of Brody's key points. One research team led by British physician Jeremy Wright found *no* cases of FAS among 903 women, although some drank quite heavily during their pregnancy. The authors concluded that FAS "is a rare disease . . . associated with pathologically heavy drinking."[17] Another study, conducted with 1,690 mothers by Roy Hingson and his coworkers at Boston City Hospital, found that "neither level of drinking prior to pregnancy nor during pregnancy was significantly related to infant growth measures, congenital abnormality, or features compatible with the fetal alcohol syndrome."[18] What did predict abnormally low birth weights and other deficiencies reminiscent of FAS were lower maternal weight gain and smoking either marijuana or tobacco. The authors noted "the difficulty in isolating and proclaiming single factors as the cause of abnormal fetal development"; instead, an overall life-style—combining drinking, smoking, and drug use—in most cases seemed to lead to infant abnormality.

Two FAS researchers at Boston University—Henry Rosett, a psychiatrist, and Lyn Weiner, a public health specialist—have disputed warnings that pregnant women must abstain from alcohol. Surveying their own work and that of over four hundred other FAS investigations, Rosett and Weiner found that all cases of FAS occurred among chronic alcoholics who drank heavily during pregnancy. The investigators also found that women can reverse the damage to their fetus from alcohol at any point during pregnancy by cutting back or eliminating drinking. They concluded, "the recommendation that all women should abstain from drinking during pregnancy is not based on scientific evidence."[19]

It might seem that we would wish to scare pregnant women about drinking even the slightest amount of alcohol (as Jane Brody and the AMA do), in order that they not undergo even the slightest risk that comes with drinking. But Rosett and Weiner found, on the contrary, that current FAS education is overly alarmist and stressful to expectant parents. In these researchers' view, the most common problem from drinking during pregnancy today is the stress-related effects that women suffer from their regrets over drinking minute doses of alcohol. The authors have described in interviews, for example, cases where women phone in hotlines hysterical because they inadvertently ate some salad with a wine dressing!

Prenatal care is certainly important for healthy childbirth. Yet our new information on dangers to the fetus and emphasis on abstinence during pregnancy seems not to help us bear healthier children. The larger problem is that the promulgation of FAS information and recommendations that women quit all drinking and drug taking does not affect the women who are most likely to abuse alcohol and drugs. These same women receive little or no prenatal health care, eat worse and take worse care of themselves in every way during pregnancy, and have high rates of infant mortality. Indeed, World Health Organization pediatrician and epidemiologist Marsden Wagner has found that prenatal care improves birth outcomes only up to a certain point. The most crucial factor in successful birthing is, instead, community supports for the expectant mother.[20] America rarely offers such supports, particularly for the highest-risk infants and mothers.

The United States ranks twenty-second among nations in preventing infant mortality, behind not only European nations, Australia, and Japan, but Bermuda and Singapore as well. In the early 1980s, the infant mortality rate declined in the United States as it did in other nations. However, in the mid-1980s, infant mortality leveled off in the United States while remaining substantially above the European rate. At the same time, over the past twenty-five years, physical and mental birth *defects*—of the type some attribute to drug and alcohol use—have *doubled* in the United States. Dr. Mary Grace Kovar, an analyst at the National Center for Health Statistics, remarks, "Regardless of the exact numbers, we are seeing real increases in children with some form of handicap, and this is resulting in a substantial burden to society, a burden that will increase with time."[21]

Both infant mortality and deformed neonates are tied to teenage pregnancy. Teenage childbearing cost the nation $16.6 billion last year. The problem is monumental among black teens (more than half of black children are now born to teenagers) and foreshadows large-scale social failures for this group through the coming decades. Even considering only white Americans, the United States leads industrialized nations in teenage births and abortions. American teens, however, are *not* more sexually active than those in other Western nations: "Overall . . . the lowest rates of teen-age pregnancy were in countries that had liberal attitudes toward sex [and] had easily accessible contraceptive services for young people, with contraceptives being offered free or at low cost and without parental notification."[22]

How is it that we have outdone all other nations in warning expectant mothers about the dangers of drugs and alcohol, and yet we have increasing infant mortality and birth defects? The French do not incessantly warn pregnant women never to drink. Why, then, are their birth outcomes so much better than ours, even given their lower per-capita income and investment in medical technology? We might ask the same question about why we have done so poorly at discouraging teen pregnancies, even while we spend so much more than other nations on efforts to discourage adolescent sexual activity. To analyze our failure to protect newborns from death and deformity, despite gargantuan and expensive medical and public health efforts, is to recapitulate the themes in this book. We fail because:

1. *Disease diagnoses of problems shift the emphasis from social and cultural to individual causes and cures.*
Many of the problems of newborn mortality and defect are localized in the underclass—the mostly minority, ghettoized segments of our society that are immune to all our best warnings and whose lives point them toward drug and alcohol abuse and toward other unhealthy behaviors—particularly during pregnancy and early childhood—that undermine infant, child, and adult health. The underclass is a problem we have been absolutely unable to affect. Indeed, the worsening teen pregnancy problem, particularly in ghettos, guarantees a larger core underclass and even poorer birthing outcomes for the future.

2. *We substitute moralizing for meaningful interventions.*
While Nancy Reagan and others implore teens not to have sex or take drugs or drink, we do nothing to reverse the social conditions associated with these behaviors. Furthermore, the evidence is that those who are already more conflicted about their sexual activity are *more* likely to have unwanted pregnancies. "Unmarried women with negative attitudes toward sex tend to use less reliable methods of birth control—if they use them at all. . . . Women with such negative attitudes seem to have trouble processing information about sex and contraception and often rely on their partner to make decisions about contraception."[23]

*3. While we fail to inform (at least in a way they can use) the least informed, we at the same time alarm the most alarmist and misinform everybody.*

Those who most require advice about drinking—"women who drink heavily and whose children are at greatest risk—are the least responsive to this type of [informational] campaign."[24] Yet many women are in a constant state of anxiety about the impact of their behavior on their unborn infants, "constrained by a multitude of prohibitions that may overwhelm" them. These women are often severely distressed, with negative results for their own health and that of their fetus. They are the callers to fetal alcohol hotlines, hysterical because they ate rum cake unwittingly at a party. As Rosett and Weiner point out, "exaggerating the facts about alcohol and pregnancy blurs the real dangers of heavy drinking. It distracts . . . public health efforts from the target population in greatest need."

*4. We miss the life-style for the trees.*

Women don't maim their unborn children because they are unaware of the dangers of alcohol, just as mothers who abuse drugs are hardly under the impression this could be good for a fetus: "Despite women's awareness of the potential dangers of alcohol use during pregnancy, . . . 20% reported consumption at levels that they themselves defined as 'risk.' " Nor do these women overdrink primarily because they are "alcoholics" who cannot control their drinking. They actually are expressing a worldview, a style of life, that goes beyond individual health warnings and treatment of one type of substance abuse or another. For example, heavy drinking is inextricably related to cigarette smoking and other drug use in the populations most likely to damage their unborn children. These women already receive too many health warnings relative to their capacity to assimilate this information and to translate it into realistic coping and improved health and living conditions.

# But Even the Privileged Are Not Well Off

The failure of the United States to match the safety record of other industrialized nations in birthing and neonatal care extends beyond the poor and underprivileged, however. For the United States is distinctive not only for its uneven distribution of prenatal care and thus the high infant mortality and disability rates among ghettoized and impoverished mothers. The broad middle class of America is oddly ambivalent and anxious about childbirth. We saw, for example, that many middle-class mothers express tremendous fear about their prenatal behavior, including having unwittingly drunk barely detectable amounts of alcohol. Yet Rosett and Weiner indicate that the "stress from preoccupation with possible dangers [to the fetus] may be a greater danger than any of the activities [the mother fears] themselves."

This fearfulness about childbirth and pregnancy seems odd in a nation with the greatest reliance on medical care in the history of the world. Americans have highly technological births. As a rule, even healthy and low-risk births occur in hospitals, under medication, with the mother hooked up to a fetal monitor, and with a high percentage of cesareans. Yet birth outcomes are worse in the United States than in any other Western society, even among economically better-off Americans. For example, the U.S. cesarean rate is double to triple that of every European country with an infant mortality rate lower than that of the United States. Europeans simply don't demand the degree of medical attention to deliver babies that Americans do: every country in Europe with lower perinatal and infant mortality rates than the United States uses midwives as the principal birth attendant for at least 70 percent of births.[25]

The contrast is perhaps greatest between Holland—a country in which 5 percent of births are by cesarean section—and the United States—in which almost a quarter (24.4 percent) of births were cesarean in 1987. Moreover, in Holland, 36 percent of babies are born at home, and most deliveries even on hospital premises are in nonmedical settings in which mothers are attended by midwives and leave after a maximum thirty-six hour stay.[26] Nonetheless (or perhaps as a result), Holland has fewer infant deaths than the United States even when minority women are factored out. Underlying these differences in approach to and outcomes from birthing is an attitudinal difference between Americans and the Dutch. Dutch society anticipates that birthing will be difficult and will involve some pain, but women accept this as a normal part of giving birth.

All this leads to notable differences in the birthing landscapes of the two countries. American women often report anxiety about the aggravation and strain of undergoing vaginal births.[27] While many middle-class Americans enroll in birthing classes to assist them in giving birth naturally (which few manage to do), the Dutch, with far less fanfare, almost uniformly have medically unassisted births with better outcomes. This fact recapitulates the theme of this book— that despite our preoccupation with health and with being psychically liberated, we are increasingly dependent on external agencies and less sure of our ability to manage our own bodies and our lives. Something in our social milieu defeats educational programs purported to encourage parents to be more self-reliant in giving birth, as this goal is constantly undercut by medical advertising claiming advances that make childbirth safer and more comfortable.

## How Dangerous Is Our Children's World?

Anxieties about childbirth are matched by anxieties about raising children in what we see as a very dangerous world. Is the world really a more dangerous place for children today than it was twenty or fifty or one hundred years ago? Children are more likely to be exposed to drugs, although most take drugs only casually and outgrow their drug use. Some groups of adolescents have always drunk— some heavily—but drinking is more widespread among the young than in previous decades. Young people are also sexually active at earlier ages—although since few adolescents get AIDS from heterosexual contact, the most life-disrupting danger from teen sex is premature parenthood. Murder by and against children has risen in recent years, particularly in the inner cities. Suicide is also reported at a higher level, although some argue that this number has not substantially increased for adolescents. All told, accidents, suicide, and murder constitute the three major causes of death among young people. On the other hand, children in the last century certainly died more frequently from illness, as well as from accidents and violent causes overall.

It is not clear that some epidemics from which children are said to be suffering—such as child abuse—are at especially high levels today. For most periods in the history of the world, children did not enjoy a special place of regard, and the young were likely to suffer abuse and neglect of all kinds. More recently, in the United States, it seems unlikely that most people hit their children more than did their own parents—corporal punishment, once a common feature of middle-class homes and schools, has apparently diminished greatly. Covering a more recent period, Murray Straus and his colleagues found in their national surveys that the number of parents who reported violence toward their children *declined by almost half* between 1975 and 1985, from 3.6 percent (36 in a thousand) to 1.9 percent. (Wife abuse also declined in this period, from 3.8 percent to 3.0 percent.)[28] Once again the increases in reported deaths of children from neglect and abuse in the last decade are mainly localized in inner cities.

While some question the Straus group's survey results because they don't believe parents would honestly report abusing their children, it isn't clear why fewer parents would admit abusing their children in one survey compared with another if there were no differences in actual abuse. The researchers think the most likely cause for this decline—since family violence is highly associated with economic downturns and poverty—is that 1985 was a much better year for Americans economically than was 1975. It is also possible that the last ten years have made Americans less approving of family abuse and that this has translated into less abuse.

Although family abuse may be overstated, abuse by parents still far and away constitutes the most abuse against children. When combining the major causes of danger to the young—accidents, suicide, murder, drugs and alcohol, and physical and sexual abuse— we must always remember that the major sources of such harm are the young themselves, their friends and acquaintances, and their parents. It remains a truism of the study of murder, for example, that most killers know their victims, and that a large percentage of victims and killers are relatives or lovers. The Child Welfare League of America, reporting on child sexual abuse, similarly makes clear that such victims are generally abused at home by their parents. While we look outside with fear and dread, the dangers within ourselves and our homes are by far the greatest threats to our health and happiness.

Why do we often prefer to conceptualize our fears as external dangers or dangers beyond our control? This is how we often think about drug abuse, and this approach underlies the entire addiction treatment movement. One example of this externalization in the case of abuse of children is the ubiquitous fear in our society that children's Halloween candy is being poisoned or booby-trapped. Halloween is the occasion for nonstop media warnings about examining minutely every piece of candy the kids bring home (if we let them out at all). Examining "the widespread belief that anonymous sadists give children dangerous treats on Halloween," researchers Joel Best and Gerald Horiuchi examined seventy-six specific incidents reported in the quarter-century between 1958 and 1984. They found no deaths or serious injuries caused by sadists in any of these stories.

Best and Horiuchi did find that two highly publicized reports of deaths that were said to be caused by Halloween treats were in fact cases of abuse closer to home. In 1970, five-year-old Kevin Toston died after eating heroin that he reportedly found in his candy. But investigation revealed that the boy found the heroin he ate in his uncle's house. An even more notorious death was that of eight-year-old Timothy O'Bryan, who died in 1974 after eating a cyanide-laced treat. However, police later found that the boy's father had poisoned the candy. In other stories, children placed a dangerous object in the treat because they wanted to play a prank and had heard so many news warnings about contaminated candy. For the researchers, "Halloween sadism can be viewed as an urban legend, which emerged during the early 1970s to give expression to growing fears about the safety of children, the danger of crime, and other sources of social strain."[29]

Also common among parents is the fear that small children will be kidnapped and/or assaulted by a stranger. Indeed, one version of this fear has organized gangs canvassing shopping centers for unattached children, whom they then spirit off. This, too, appears to be an urban legend. The American Academy of Pediatrics reviewed the status of missing children in the United States, with special reference to kidnappings by strangers. Of all missing children, 95 percent are runaways, while the vast majority of the rest are kidnapped by a parent, usually in a custodial battle. "In 1984," the academy reported, "the Federal Bureau of Investigation had nearly 350,000 reported cases of missing children, but only 67 of these missing children were kidnapped by strangers."[30] Other experts outside the FBI say there may be more children abducted by a stranger than the FBI investigates in a given year. Nonetheless, according to Gelles and Straus, there are perhaps a thousand kidnappings of children by parents for every kidnapping by a stranger.[31]

The relatively small number of children who are kidnapped by strangers are not usually picked up at shopping malls or in front of their homes while playing. One of the sixty-seven children on FBI records in 1984 was Inez Jean Sanders. Inez was abducted at age five when her mother left her with a woman the mother had befriended in a motel in Phoenix, Arizona, while the mother was traveling alone to her parents' home in Florida for ten days in 1980. The kidnapper later abandoned Inez, and five years after the abduction the girl was reunited with her mother.[32] In other words, these kidnappings are frequently associated with high-risk—sometimes extremely high-risk—behavior by a parent. Compare this reality with the warning issued to parents on television and in newspapers by Daniel Travanti about kidnapping: "It can be anybody. You can never tell."

Travanti is used in advertisements for missing children because he played John Walsh, the father of Adam Walsh—a six-year-old boy who *was* kidnapped at a shopping mall in 1981 and murdered by his abductor. This story, made into a TV film in 1983, has had a tremendous impact on American society. The original film described the incredible anxiety and then the pain that Adam's parents experienced, along with the absence of a system for finding a lost child (although Adam in all likelihood would not have been helped by such a system). The Walshes' and Adam's story eventually played a key role in the passage of the Federal Missing Children Act in 1982 and the establishment of the National Center for Missing and Exploited Children.

Material accompanying the *Adam* film claimed that fifty thousand parents would never see their lost children again, creating the impression among many that fifty thousand children had been kidnapped (and perhaps killed) by strangers. In addition, the National Center estimates that between 1.3 million and 1.8 million children are missing. These alarming statistics have been explicitly challenged by the FBI. A news story on NBC's *Nightly News* (the network that showed *Adam*) in 1985 reported the FBI claims that between twenty thousand and fifty thousand children had been missing for a "significant" time. Of all children ever reported missing, 95 percent are discovered within twenty-four hours and many of the rest shortly thereafter.

Since most of the long-term missing are runaways and most of the rest are kidnapped by a noncustodial parent, the program concluded that the probability of a child's being abducted by a stranger is the same as that of being struck by lightning.

But who would object to statistics that make parents, children, and schools more careful in guarding against abduction? In other words, so what if these programs and national centers are alarmist? The contrary position is that, at this point, many people are already intensely worried about the danger of kidnapping. The NBC program interviewed a girl in an Illinois school who thought that "kids were being kidnapped every day" in the neighborhood. In fact, the program reported, no child in the school district had ever been kidnapped. Some very prominent spokespeople oppose the national campaign to fingerprint school children, as one expression of our hysteria over kidnapped children. Dr. Spock, for one, claims that such programs give children morbid fears that are unwarranted, fears that the programs do nothing to reduce.

Overall, we have two contrasting views of the dangers children face. One is expressed by Richard Schoenberger, head of the juvenile section of the Michigan State Police: "We found that the chances of a stranger abducting a child were so minimal [less than 1 percent of missing children in a study conducted by his department], parents should not be tethering their children to the front yard." John Walsh, on the other hand, has declared, "No town is safe—no child is safe—from the sick, sadistic molesters and killers who roam our country at random. This country is littered with mutilated, raped, strangled little children."[33] John Walsh's suffering tells him this is the case. Whether or not our society should act as though this were the case—and the consequences of living by this worldview—may be a different matter.

Whatever the objective dangers of kidnapping today are compared with these of previous eras, children's lives today are unquestionably more circumscribed than they were in the past. Many—if not most—parents consider it unfeasible for children, even teenagers, to take a bus into the city or ride a bike into town on their own. What is lost because of this caution is the idea that children can learn and grow from exploration, independence, and even a degree of risk and adventure. Yet the abilities to manage oneself, to accept the responsibility of independence, and to generate adventure and excitement without behaving antisocially are skills that enable people to avoid drug or alcohol abuse and other addictions. Consider, for example, that today the term *latch-key kids* describes a new social ill. On the other hand, having responsibility for keeping house, watching smaller children, and filling one's time constructively was a common requirement for most farm or immigrant children, many of whom benefited in maturity and self-control from these experiences.

## How Fear of Our Communities *Causes* Our Problems

Although a director of the National Center agrees that the number of lost children identified through fingerprinting is "pretty minuscule," he nonetheless maintains that the program is essential for "focusing parental concern on the danger of abduction." However, scare programs for drugs and crime—as in the case of the lifer's program depicted in the film *Scared Straight* (see chapter 5)—have shown more *negative* results than benefits. According to the chief of the prevention research branch of the National Institute on Drug Abuse (NIDA), "Those programs that use scare tactics, moralizing and information alone may actually have put children at increased risk"—that is, they result in more drug use.[34] It is worth noting that this description applies not only to David Toma's bombastic moralizing but also to the full-page ads that the NIDA itself sponsors under the aegis of the Partnership for a Drug-Free America, like the one of the father mourning in a graveyard because he missed the signs that his child was using drugs.

In the case of prophylactic campaigns about kidnapping and Halloween candy, what suffers most is our feeling of community. These campaigns—and the spirit underlying them—directly attack community life. And *every problem identified in this book is exacerbated by the diminution of our communities*. Even stranger kidnappings are best combated by community efforts. For example, years after schoolboy Etan Patz disappeared on the way to his bus in New York City, a cab driver revealed that he had driven the apparently protesting boy and a man to the train station. The feeling of involvement that would make observers step in under such circumstances is the best guarantee that children will be protected.

Let us return to the Lisa Steinberg case, described in chapter 8. In dealing with family abuse, simply catching and remonstrating with an abusive parent or husband has approximately the same impact as does therapy for abuse, and a significant number of husbands stop beating their wives or children when they are singled out by the community, friends, or the police for their misbehavior. Recall also that Lisa's adoptive mother, Hedda Nussbaum, isolated herself from her family, her job, and her friends as her lover Joel Steinberg's beatings became more severe. With fewer outside people entering their home to notice and comment on Nussbaum's appearance and the strange goings-on in the Steinberg household (such as the filth and disruption), there were no checks on Joel Steinberg's increasingly bizarre behavior.

Having faith that the world is a place amenable to our control and that other people are well-meaning and can be befriended is an essential component of mental health and normal human development. To lose the sense that the world is a good place is to lose something irreplaceable—a loss no amount of therapy can assuage. The violent relationships we examined in the previous chapter are related to this pervasive alienation from people and the environment. Those who are most suspicious of the world around them and unable to be comfortable with other people are those most desperate to latch onto another person—often a completely inappropriate partner or a relationship doomed from its onset to self-destruct. In my book *Love and Addiction*, I showed that the love addict is not someone with the most experience at intimacy; rather, it is the withdrawn and alienated who are most susceptible to forming treacherous, explosive, and self-defeating ties with other people—including their lovers.

## Inspiring Fear

We saw early in this chapter that obesity is an addictive behavior and a health problem that is growing rapidly among children, and that a definitive link has been established between television viewing and obesity. What is it about the act of watching television that increases the risk of addiction, as in the case of obesity? Kids get fatter watching television because it is a sedentary activity that interferes with calorie-burning activities like playing outside. TV view-

## DENYING WHAT GOES ON IN THE HOME

A major point made by the children of alcoholics movement is that the family is forced to deny the abnormality of the drunken parent's actions, thus creating a kind of insane inner family life. The same holds for violent families. We may wonder whether the same kind of denial and insanity holds for families of compulsive eaters, gamblers, shoppers, PMS and depression sufferers, and so on. And what about highly neurotic parents who shout a great deal? Is their behavior accepted as par for the course within the home and denied and hidden from outsiders? For many families, family problems (and denial and insanity) are introduced by the children—for example, when they take drugs. If the mathematics add up to every American having at least one disease, then every family is undergoing some form of denial.

Is the solution, then, to get all these families into treatment along with the diseased member? When the middle-class families whose children abuse drugs and who then join parent support groups finally let down their guards in public to describe their problems, they often for the first time share their fears and anxieties with other families. But being open and sharing feelings could well have improved their family problems long before this point, as they would for practically every family in America. The point is not to organize a group for every variety of family problem; the point is that nearly every American home would be improved by greater contact with other families, by greater community support, by greater intimacy with nonfamily members. This is because, first, families behave better when they are in contact with outsiders. Second, children would have a broader variety of models of family behavior—sometimes better, sometimes worse—to choose from. And third, Americans—like all people—need more emotional support than they are able to get within their immediate families alone.

ing also encourages addiction because it is a passive, consumer-oriented form of entertainment. Indeed, just as excessive eating is a passive form of entertainment built around consumption, so too are excessive drug taking and drinking. The link between watching television and obesity and other addictions is that watching television depletes the child's resources for direct experience and interaction with the environment in favor of vicarious experiences and involvements.

One reason drug addicts and alcoholics welcome their addictions is because they perceive these to be safer than the riskier activities of putting themselves on the line in dealing with the world free of drugs and alcohol. Thus—paradoxically—young drug abusers and drinkers may be more fearful than their non-substance-abusing counterparts, even though they actually court more danger and get into more trouble. There is evidence that people who watch more television are more fearful than others. Research by George Gerbner, dean of the Annenberg School of Communications of the University of Pennsylvania, has shown that heavy television viewers overestimate the number of crimes and other dangers in their environments.[35]

In part, the explanation for the association of fear and television viewing is that children who are more fearful in the first place stay in to watch television more. At the same time, Gerbner hypothesizes, television focuses so much on crime that it convinces viewers that the world is a dangerous place. Thus, regardless of whether the world has become more dangerous in the last quarter-century, television viewing has made it seem that way. Many of our messages to children accomplish the same thing, and it would seem that we have more frightened children today. However, as the example of TV and overeating indicates, our fear-inspiring communications rarely lead to better health or other positive results. Instead of frightening children, what we must actually do to combat obesity and other addictions is to make our children less afraid and more capable of facing their environments, even though these can never be made fully secure and certain.

One test, then, of whether our society can combat drugs and drinking and dangerous love relationships is whether we can make people, especially children, less rather than more fearful. This formidable task is one on which we seem to be losing ground rather than making progress, as we constantly strive to make children more afraid of drugs, as well as a number of other activities. In the United

States today, we have given up on the idea that children—and adults—can be counted on to make decisions on their own about drugs, and instead we dedicate ourselves to an escalating war to eliminate all exposure to drugs. If our goal were to create people competent to deal with their environments and content enough to resist self-destructive temptations, our current efforts would prove we had already lost the war on drugs. If, on the other hand, children welcomed life enough to resist addiction on their own, drug abuse in itself would become a minor problem.

The disease theory of alcoholism and addiction is an elaborate defense mechanism to prevent us from examining those things that—individually and as a society—we fear too much and do not believe we can deal with. One of people's primary purposes in taking drugs and drinking excessively is to eliminate the fears with which they cannot deal realistically. As a society, the fantasy that abusing alcohol and drugs is the result of a disease rather than of misdirected human desire and faulty coping skills is also meant to reassure us. Yet just as with the individual alcoholic or addict, relying on this reassuring fantasy debilitates us for combating the problems from which we recoil. Put simply, we don't have the courage to confront the dilemma that addiction is transmitted through ordinary family and societal processes, including such daily socially sanctioned activities as television viewing and our fearful messages about the outside world. We will never begin to combat addiction effectively until we can examine ourselves and our society and find the sources of addiction within.

## Summary: Loss of Control as a National Theme

In this chapter, I have explained that we have been unable to improve the health of the newborn, despite having the most technologized health care system in the world. I have also discussed how our concerns about the health and safety of our children have become irrational, as have our fears about strangers and about our communities. I have analyzed how our fears stem primarily from our sense of being unable to control our worlds as individuals, as families, and as communities. But what has given us the idea that we are so impotent and helpless? Why have we become enmeshed in dysfunctional, exaggerated fears about our environment? Why have we decided that we—and our children—cannot control even our own emotions and behavior?

Why is it that America has now entered the age of addiction? Why have we become so afraid that addiction is everywhere and that we are out of control of our eating, shopping, lovemaking, gambling, smoking, drug taking, menstrual cramps, feelings after birth, anxieties and depressions, and moods of all kinds? What characterizes modern-day Americans and American society that can possibly explain the out-of-control growth of the experience of being out of control? Let me list what I believe to be the main dimensions of this problem:

1. *We have marketed loss-of-control conceptions to a fare-thee-well.*
We so often believe we have lost control because we are told so constantly about the danger that we will lose control, about the prevalence of loss of control, and about the signs that indicate we have lost control. It is only to be expected that so many people would take up the cues from the media and everywhere else around them that maybe they, too, are out of control of something in their lives, and that this is a disease requiring a kind of medical attention. It is also a natural by-product of the marketing of loss-of-control ideas and treatments that we increasingly see the world as an uncontrollable place.

2. *We are alienated from many of our basic emotional and physical experiences.*
Among technological societies, we in the United States are the most alienated from basic emotional and physical experiences. In our efforts to protect ourselves from accident and assault, we have built up our fears of our physical and social environment to the point that dealing with our fearfulness is frequently our most pressing problem. As a result, we worry incessantly that no matter how sensibly we act, we can be hurt by the world around us, by the people around us, and by our own bodies and behavior.

3. *America is the most medicalized of all societies.*
Americans rely more on medical technology for solutions to both sickness and ordinary life problems than any other society. Ameri-

cans invariably seek more medical treatment, and American doctors and other professionals seek to provide this treatment, whereas Europeans more often allow healing to take its course and recognize that every medical intervention has its own risks. Indeed, Europeans more readily accept that every problem does not have a solution and that life has a good deal of uncertainty and imperfection about it. The American credo, in contrast, is that medicine can ultimately fix everything that is wrong with us.[36] This reliance on medicine extends to our attacks on our largest, most complex social problems.

*4. We are preoccupied with our innermost feelings but are oblivious to how these feelings stem from our social relationships.*
Americans are famous for their self-improvement programs, particularly those geared toward emotional well-being. At times it seems that, as a nation, we are all involved in the constant contemplation of our neuroses. Yet although we spend so much mental energy examining what is wrong with us and our relationships, we refuse to consider how our emotional states and patterns of interacting are linked to social structures like family, work, and community. We prefer to make individual resolutions to change or to consult with private physicians or therapists or to join self-help groups rather than to strive to change our families, our work, and our communities.

*5. Americans are not comfortable in communal arrangements.*
One great paradox in America is that so many of us are willing to join self-help groups and movements, and yet are reluctant to be part of our own communities. Americans live and love isolated suburban existences. We don't meet in pubs, cafés, and boulevards like those in some countries, or join with neighbors or extended families in sharing meals and household space. In fact, "making it" means *not* having to do these things. As a result, for most Americans, the concept of community is moribund. The condo "community" of transients is the model for American life today.

*6. Americans are ambivalent about alcohol, drugs, and intoxication.*
From temperance to Prohibition to the modern drug era, an awful lot of American history has focused on efforts to regulate Americans' pursuit of intoxication. Why is this? Americans are both prudish and idealistic, so that we believe we can be perfect and that intox-

ication and bad behavior should and can be eliminated. At the same time, like people everywhere else, many Americans welcome intoxication. Only for Americans, our drive for intoxication conflicts so greatly with the value we place on self-control. It is, of course, our constant disappointment at failing to live up to this value—a value many cultures don't share—that makes us so preoccupied with loss of control.

7. *Temperance and AA have radically affected the American sensibility.*
The historical facts of temperance, Prohibition, and AA—while they spring from the depths of American culture—have also had a tremendous impact on how we conceptualize our social and personal problems. The mission of temperance adherents and AA proselytizers has been to convey the beliefs that alcoholism is a disease and that alcohol exercises an alluring but destructive power over our bodies and minds—our souls, in fact. And these preachers and businesspeople have done a passionately successful job in selling Americans this view of the world. One of the most successful aspects of this sales job has been the convincing of liberal-minded Americans that it is most humane and helpful to regard drunkenness and other misbehavior as being out of people's control.

8. *Disease conceptions have come to stand for all of our fears.*
We in America congratulate ourselves on discovering so many things that can addict us (a list that grows never-endingly), at the same time that we never gain a sense that we can control the sources of our fears. These two themes interact addictively—that is, more of the one creates more of the other. In this addictive cycle, we feel temporarily relieved when we can claim some unwanted behavior (our own, our children's, a stranger's) is due to some new disease. But the longer-term consequence of this process is to make us more frightened and impotent and more likely to identify new diseases. Addiction then becomes the all-purpose explanation for the control of ourselves and our worlds that constantly eludes us.

# 10

# Creating a World Worth Living In

## *Community, Efficacy, and Values*

Instead of mounting a collective attack on general violence, we are letting it poison our sense of community. . . . We are allowing distrust and paranoia to replace cooperation and determination. Citizens seem to be turning inward, pessimistically adopting a garrison mentality that accepts a certain amount of violence as part of a hopelessly deteriorating situation. This attitude can result in a self-fulfilling prophecy in society at large, . . . [where] people abandon all but the most atomistic strategies for coping with violence ("I have my stun gun. Do you have yours?"). . . .

The fundamental solution for general violence in our society (along with family violence) is to reestablish the sense of community—and the sense of responsibility for the community— that . . . have all but been destroyed in many parts of our society.

—Anson Shupe, William Stacey, and Lonnie Hazlewood[1]

The alcoholism-disease way of thinking leads us to disown our responsibilities to keep each other reasonably sober as a part of the process of keeping each other human. Instead, it encourages us to relinquish our authority for informally constraining each other's drinking behavior to designated "experts" who are all too eager to assume the task.

—Harold Mulford, director of Alcohol Studies
at the University of Iowa[2]

W E HAVE not made a dent in addiction and other problems discussed in this book through all of our expensive therapies, and our gargantuan treatment industry may even exacerbate our addictiveness as a society. Thus, I am amused when some people complain that my work doesn't offer enough therapeutic recommendations, for it is clear that we can never, ever treat away our society's addiction and related problems. Treatment is too piecemeal, occurs too late in the process, is too expensive and labor intensive, addresses crucial life issues only indirectly, and reaches too few of the worst addicts because they are too poor, lead such irregular lives, and don't seek or stay in treatment. Furthermore, we generate at least as many new addicts, alcoholics, and problem lives generally as we cure *using the best of approaches*. And as we have seen, the best approaches are rarely used in the United States.

The only way to actually affect our addiction rates is to bring about basic social change. While such change may be difficult, anything that fails to deal with the real sources of the problem is wasted effort. The few therapies that are effective *succeed because* they work to change real social forces in people's environments. These forces include work opportunities, family and community supports, and the moral and values atmosphere (and rewards and punishments) in people's lives. For example, the three family violence researchers quoted at the beginning of this chapter extract three elements that, they find, characterize all successful family violence programs. These programs:

1. Hold the violent person personally responsible for his or her violent actions and stress that the person is capable of ceasing;

2. Monitor the violent person's behavior;

3. Create a moral atmosphere in counseling sessions that clearly indicates that physical violence and emotional abuse are not appropriate or excusable.

Other programs, such as those that emphasize the uncontrollable, disease-based nature of the person's violence, are not effective. Furthermore, these investigators note, situations in which the abuser gets no therapy can be as successful as good treatment programs. Many men arrested for beating their wives stop their violence as soon as they are discovered and their crime is revealed. (This study contradicts the disease notion that violent spouses will always be violent.) The authors note, "Confronting violent men, who are otherwise of average intelligence, with the inappropriateness—both legal and moral—of their actions seems to work." In other words, strongly impressing the abuser with community standards of behavior serves by itself as effective therapy.

The three points listed by the family violence researchers can be expanded to incorporate three further techniques for reducing family violence:

1. Counseling should enhance people's ability to cope with their environments and to express constructively their feelings and problems.

2. The police and courts must express direct disapproval of violent spouses (including arrest and conviction, as appropriate) while accepting—and demanding—that abusers can change.

3. The local community should help not only violent spouses but all spouses deal with marital and family stress.

In terms of point 3, it is unfortunate that only after abuse takes place do individuals and families get any help for dealing with family stress. In other words, community support generally comes in the form of therapy. It often seems that the best way to gain any emotional sustenance or help with personal problems is to acknowledge we have a disease and are among the walking wounded. Short of attempting suicide or being arrested in possession of drugs, Americans can't seem to attract the concern of their fellow citizens.

## What Works in Alcoholism

As noted above, successful therapy for family violence: (1) holds the individual responsible for his or her behavior, (2) monitors the problem behavior, (3) establishes a moral atmosphere in therapy that clearly disapproves of the behavior, (4) enhances alternative coping mechanisms, (5) applies clear legal sanctions to misbehavior, and (6) relies on community disapproval and support. *Exactly the same therapy works for drugs and alcohol.* Chapter 7 described psychologists William Miller and Reid Hester's review of every "controlled" investigation of alcoholism treatment. (Controlled research is that in which those receiving therapy are compared with a "control" group that receives another treatment or no treatment.) Miller and Hester found that the same types of therapy had time and time again demonstrated their effectiveness: behavioral family therapy, stress management, social skills training, behavioral self-control (also known as con-trolled-drinking) therapy, aversive conditioning, and the community reinforcement approach.

These therapies generally have one of two things in common. They either clearly regulate the problem behavior (controlled-drinking therapy and aversive conditioning), or they enhance the alcoholic's skills for coping with self, others (especially family), and work. Miller and Hester note in particular that "if one were to judge the effec-tiveness of alcoholism treatments based on the strength of scientific support . . . for them, the community reinforcement approach (CRA) would . . . be at the top of the list."[3] CRA relies on the community, but in a different way from therapy groups organized for alcoholics or others that provide a special sense of community and identity linked to the problem condition itself. Instead, CRA makes use of family and community relationships in the natural world of which the alcoholic is already a part.

The CRA program combines problem-solving training, behavioral family therapy, and job skills training. In this way, CRA galvanizes forces in the alcoholic's life to reinforce sobriety and discourage further drinking. For example, the therapy trains a drinker's wife simply to lock the drinker out if he comes home drunk, until he knows unambiguously that his wife refuses to accept the drinking and what will be the consequences if he continues his drunkenness. In a comparison of CRA with standard AA and alcohol-education groups for randomly assigned hospitalized, chronic alcoholic pa-tients, CRA patients drank on 14 percent of days, compared with 79 percent of days for the AA and education groups, while the latter had twelve times the number of unemployed days and spent *fifteen times* the number of days institutionalized. Nonetheless, as Miller and Hester observe, CRA and all the other therapies that work for alcoholism are not employed anywhere in the United States, in favor of the universal use of the ones that don't work.

---

# Therapeutic Communities

To use the phrase *community as therapy* immediately suggests another phrase—*therapeutic community*, the label given to group homes and other communal arrangements under the direction of a staff of therapists. George De Leon, who has evaluated outcomes at Phoenix House, the well-known treatment facility for heroin addicts, describes the addicted person and the aims of the therapeutic community (TC) as follows:

> The problem is the person, not the drug. Addiction is a symptom, not the essence of the disorder. In the TC, chemical detoxification is a condition of entry, not a goal of treatment. . . .
>
> Rather than drug use patterns, individuals are distinguished along dimensions of psychological dysfunction and social deficits. Many clients have never established conventional lifestyles. Vocational and educational problems are marked; middle class mainstream values are either missing or unachievable. Usually these clients emerged from a socially disadvantaged sector, where drug abuse is more a social response than a psychological disturbance. Their TC experience is better termed habilitation, the development of a socially productive, conventional lifestyle for the first time in their lives.
>
> Among clients from more advantaged backgrounds, drug abuse is more directly expressive of psychological disorder or existential malaise, and the word rehabilitation is more suitable. . . .
>
> In the TC's view of recovery, the aim of rehabilitation is global. The primary psychological goal is to change the negative patterns of behavior, thinking and feeling that predispose drug use. . . . Healthy behavioral alternatives to drug use are reinforced by commitment to the values of abstinence; acquiring vocational or educational skills and social productivity is motivated by the values of achievement and self-reliance. Behavioral change is unstable without insight, and insight is insufficient without felt experience.[4]

Charles Winick, a pioneering addiction researcher, examined all of the therapeutic communities in operation for adult heroin addicts in New York City.[5] He found that therapeutic communities retrain their clients in fundamental living skills, including getting a high school diploma, developing basic competencies (like managing a bank account), graded assignments to work, and even personal hygiene. The TCs Winick studied were geared toward success outside the TC—that is, toward allowing the client to function in the real world. For example, all the communities emphasized occupational training and job placement. TCs such as Phoenix House downplay the disease model of addiction. In place of the medical model, Mitchell Rosenthal, director of Phoenix House, emphasizes the inculcation of values:

> In a Phoenix House the teaching of socialization and its consequent morality is made both explicit and emphatic. . . . We regard anti-social, anti-military, amoral and acting-out behavior as "stupid."[6]

A director of the London Phoenix House, David Warner-Holland, makes clear that the responsibility for change remains with the addict:

> We believe it is essential the addict be given ample opportunity to help himself in his own recovery and to assume responsibility for his life. Treatment of the ex-addict as helpless and incapable deprives him of this opportunity and panders to his manipulative and irresponsible behavior.[7]

The underlying philosophy of these TCs is clearly that addicts are doing something wrong, that they should change, and that their problems are due to a combination of their social milieu and their personalities, which they must do something about themselves— very different assumptions from the disease approach and medical treatment. Notice also that the directors of these programs are prepared to use the phrase *ex-addict*—a phrase forbidden to the "recovering" alcoholic in AA. Thus, unlike the Synanon-type groups that have been accused of cultism, Phoenix House and similar TCs have an end point, after which people must leave the group to carry forward their lives on their own.

De Leon's and Winick's evaluations offer substantial evidence of success through TC programs. However, limitations in this research should be noted. Winick's research examined clients before and after treatment, finding great improvement in terms of avoiding prison, working, and staying away from drugs. What brings people to the point of treatment, and whether at that point they could do as much on their own, can't be addressed as it is in controlled research, which randomly assigns clients to different programs or to no-treatment versus treatment. De Leon's research compared those who stay in TC treatment through graduation with those who drop out and found that graduates do far better.[8] Again, comparisons are tricky and can't evaluate addicts seeking other treatment or improving on their own.

Winick, to his credit, notes that "the positive dropout—that is, the person who wishes to leave treatment before graduation and whose immediate goals are constructive ones, such as attending school—should not be regarded as a therapeutic failure but rather as someone to be helped" (that is, encouraged and supported in his or her progress). De Leon, who has been employed by Phoenix House, cannot afford to be so open-minded toward those who quit the program. (Winick is, in contrast, an independent, outside investigator.) Furthermore, the big problem with comparing dropouts with perseverers in the therapeutic community is that one's own failures become one's comparison point! Especially since research "studies agree in revealing a rather high dropout rate in therapeutic communities."

Clearly, I have reservations about programs that teach morals in a militarylike environment that regards "anti-military" attitudes as "stupid" and considers human beings who think they would be better off outside the program as dangerously misguided people who should be restrained. My misgivings multiply the younger the program's inmates are and in the absence of legal justifications for coercing people to enter or stay in treatment that is at times abusive. On the other hand, successful elements in these therapeutic communities for drug addiction absolutely affirm the elements found to work in family abuse cases and in successful alcoholism programs: assuming that the addict *can* change and is responsible for change on his own; *insisting* on change as a moral imperative; developing skills for functioning in the real world; and inculcating values toward constructive and prosocial activity—like work and positive behavior toward the community and other people.

### THE PROBLEM WITH SYNANON

Synanon is a support group for heroin addicts that was established in 1958 by an AA member, Chuck Dederich, in Santa Monica, California. Like AA, Synanon emphasized the requirement of lifetime membership in the organization. For a time in the 1970s, Synanon was a glamour group whose results were thought to be near-miraculous, and Jane Fonda and other Hollywood luminaries raised funds for the organization. Dederich's regime became increasingly irrational and dictatorial, however, and he employed a security force to threaten and assault members who tried to leave the group. In 1980, he was convicted of conspiracy to commit murder after he directed two underlings to place a rattlesnake in the mailbox of an attorney representing dissident Synanon members.

One participant-observer in a number of addict self-help groups developed severe misgivings about the entire therapeutic community process, based in part on the Synanon experience. He noted that most Synanon techniques, including "immediate, harsh criticism for lapses in expected behavior or work performance, authoritarian rule by 'old timers,' and emotional growth by conforming to the unrelenting twenty-four-hour surveillance in the organization, have been adopted by most therapeutic communities in the United States. . . . In retrospect . . ., I must emphasize my belief that therapeutic communities are not the panacea, the easy answer to drug-abuse treatment some . . . have seen them to be. . . . Abuses are so eminently possible because of the inherently authoritarian nature of therapeutic communities."[9]

# The Community as Therapy

It is notable that when we decide to create therapeutic communities or therapy based on community reinforcement, we must first create a community, since these don't exist as is for the addict. Consider, on the other hand, an approach to alcoholism that builds on existing community resources—the now largely defunct Iowa Community Coordinator program. Harold Mulford, in the article quoted at the beginning of this chapter, describes how this community program worked. Begun in Cedar Rapids in 1966, the Iowa program hired a community coordinator in each town to deal with alcoholics. The University of Iowa trained coordinators and monitored the results in each town, providing the coordinators with feedback "to help them learn from and build on their own and others' experiences." Coordinators were not required to have any special background or training. It was "simply expected that they would care about alcoholics, and draw upon their common sense, experience, intuition and empathy to contact people with drinking problems and lend them a helping hand. Their [coordinators'] approach to clients varies depending upon the nature of the case. No two are treated alike." Mulford elaborates on the coordinator's role:

[The coordinator] explains to alcoholics that there is no solution for their problem that anyone can give or sell them. They must get it the old-fashioned way—work for it. Any benefit they get from others' efforts to help them is in proportion to the effort they themselves put into the process. He does nothing to alcoholics, and he does nothing *for* them that he can get them to do for themselves. Nor is his office a place for the community to dump its responsibilities to alcoholics. To encourage widespread community responsibility, he seeks to involve as many other citizens in the alcoholic's recovery as possible.

Serving as a catalyst for natural rehabilitation forces, the coordinator helps alcoholics restore and strengthen social relationships—through job, family, Alcoholics Anonymous, church and social activities. He also helps them use appropriate community services and resources to resolve their medical, legal, financial, religious or other problems.

In 1975, however, the Iowa program was centralized under the State Alcoholism Authority, funded by federal and state funds and directed through federal guidelines according to the orthodox medical model. (Before that, communities themselves had been responsible for paying the coordinator and whatever office rent and expenses he or she needed.) The immediate result was that costs rose at least twofold for each community, while the State Authority's budget increased by a factor of ten. Yet strangely, more alcoholics fell through the cracks, and in the first two years of operation, the new federally and state-organized community programs served half as many new alcoholics as had the old community programs! Mulford explains the cost differential:

> The great cost-effectiveness advantage of the coordinator approach lies in the vastly greater number of persons served at minimal cost. The Washington County center [the one community coordinator program remaining in Iowa—this county turned down the federally funded program] has annually been serving about 250 alcoholics on an annual budget of less than $45,000. That would treat only three or four cases in a nearby hospital-based center, and only one or two in an expensive private clinic.

Thus the $2 billion Americans now spend for alcoholism treatment could fund literally tens of thousands of community and neighborhood coordinators and programs. The alcoholism movement always calls for *more* money to be spent on alcoholism—this is taken as a measure of America's commitment to combating alcoholism, and of its own success. Mulford, in contrast, here describes an actual program, growing out of real community responses, that costs a fraction of the typical medically based programs and that would plow money directly into American communities. However, even under a Republican, Reagan administration—one that gave lip service to voluntarism, returning power to communities, and cost-effective government expenditure—America simply continued to build up its costly and ineffective alcoholism bureaucracy. Ironically, according to Mulford, a personal, community-based response not only is more cost-effective but would succeed better at minimizing drinking problems in the community:

> All of us, including problem drinkers, share responsibility for constraining the problem. Each of us is responsible for restraining his or her own, and everyone else's, drinking behavior. Alcohol excess is a

people problem, not a technological problem. We deceive ourselves to expect to solve the problem with a quick technological fix such as a treatment pill or preventive vaccine. No less deceptive is the costly illusion that we already have an effective treatment.

Mulford's warnings about the dangers of turning over our responsibility for the drinking of those around us is not an abstract concern. The Berkeley Alcohol Research Group (ARG) studied community responses to drinking problems in societies around the world. Robin Room, director of ARG, notes that "we were struck with how much more responsibility . . . [those in developing nations] gave to family and friends in dealing with alcohol problems, and how ready . . . [those in technological societies] were to cede responsibility for these human problems to official agencies or to professionals." Yet anthropologist Dwight Heath has noted that drinking problems—especially the isolated, compulsive drinking that defines alcoholism—are "virtually unknown in most of the world's cultures," particularly in preindustrial cultures.[10] The major exceptions to this, of course, are the indigenous preindustrial communities that have been destroyed by outside forces, as has occurred with Native American and Eskimo societies in the United States.

Room summarizes ARG's cross-cultural findings:

> Studying the period since 1950 in seven industrialized countries [including California in the U.S.] . . . we were struck by the concomitant growth of treatment provisions in all of these countries. The provision of treatment, we felt, became a societal alibi for the dismantling of long-standing structures of control of drinking behavior, both formal and informal.[11]

The institution of modern medical and social services systems for dealing with problems like alcoholism coincides exactly with the removal of the forces most effective in curtailing these problems in the first place.

## Communities and Health

Mulford argues for nothing short of human communities, which he finds to be the best form of "treatment." Community and social support are the key to human beings' ability to function, to overcome problems, to recover from illness, and to avoid sickness—even cancer and the most virulent illnesses. Leonard Sagan, in *The Health of Nations*, discusses why life expectancy in the United States ranks nineteenth among nations—worse even than Spain and Greece.[12] Sagan finds that community supports and the ability to control one's life are the crucial ingredients in life expectancy. Sagan cites historical evidence that community and self-efficacy have been far more important than modern nutrition and antibiotics for prolonging life. He shows through research on the outcomes of medical treatment that the same factors are crucial both for responding well to treatment and for preventing the onset of illness. The same factors, as we saw in chapter 9, determine the success of birthing outcomes.

Homelessness is another area in which research has shown that social supports play a major role, particularly at critical points. The availability of family and community supports often prevents people from becoming homeless in the first place. *After* people become homeless, the predominant social forces tend to reinforce this condition (for example, by breaking up marriages), and it becomes very hard to reintegrate the family into society. Even for the emotionally disturbed homeless, the crucial prognosticators of survival and recovery are the social supports available to them, beginning with family and personal relationships and extending to include work opportunities, stable support groups, and warm places to go to be safe, to sleep, and to build bridges to life. I discussed the case of Joe Rogers (in chapter 1), the founder of the National Mental Health Consumers' Association, who regained his sanity in conjunction with getting married and becoming engaged in community organizations.

Gigantic shelters do nothing for the homeless, insane or otherwise. In fact, we have passed a critical point in many of our cities where we can only respond to the overwhelming need to get people off the street, rather than actually try to help people regain a position in life. In the United States, we first moved people out of large institutions because of the neglect and abuse that characterized these places. However, we failed to put into place even minimal support for the formerly institutionalized people who suddenly reemerged into society. Today, our only response (à la Mayor Koch) is once again to warehouse them, even though they constantly tell us they'd rather stay on the street—as miserable an existence as that is—than enter the dangerous, squalid barracks we wish to send them to. (It was Joyce Brown's preference for the street that, in part, made Mayor Koch decide she was insane.)

How did Americans in early eras deal with insanity, homelessness, and crime, short of institutionalizing people? Colonial America did not have prisons, asylums, or poorhouses.[13] Rather, families did everything they could to help a person avoid losing a home or a farm when he or she couldn't cope and took into their homes those who lost their families through illness or accidental death. Along with the family, the community and church offered help to those who could no longer function independently. For better or worse, those without such community ties were exiled. Yet with practically no public (and certainly no state or federal) infrastructure, eighteenth-century Americans dealt more successfully with every one of the social problems we now call a disease than we currently do.

Today, we certainly would want to help those who were outside the purview of the colonial community. For example, Indians and slaves, who did not experience the same positive community controls and supports, showed frequent alcoholic misbehavior.[14] We also certainly don't want to lock away the insane, as was done in the America of the nineteenth century. The trick is to be able to manage humane caretaking as a society without abrogating more and more family and community initiative and responsibility. Otherwise, we have the never-ending cycle of stretching our resources thin to help all those problematic people who don't make it in our society, while there are more and more such people needing help. The rise in disease treatments for behaviors and emotions is primarily a compensation for our deteriorated community. It is not an answer to this deterioration. Instead, we need to take responsibility for our communities and make them more efficacious. While this is certainly a difficult undertaking, there is no substitute for it.

# Efficacy

Efficacy is the ability to bring about desired goals. The efficacy of a community is its ability to regulate itself and its residents, to care for its less fortunate members, and to create a positive and successful community environment. At the same time, people vary in their

## THE REAL, AS OPPOSED TO THE THERAPEUTIC

American corporations today frequently bring employees together off-campus to participate in "team-building" retreats. These exercises insist on mock confidentiality and intimacy, often including such experiences as having people fall backward into the arms of fellow workers, supposedly creating a sense of mutual trust. The feelings generated by these retreats often dissipate rapidly, however, when workers return to their daily jobs, where intimacy and mutual support may not be the rule. General Electric tried a different approach. During an off-site business meeting, it gave five hundred employees the day off to help construct a homeless shelter for St. Vincent DePaul. In a single day, the group accomplished months of labor in terms of the ordinary construction schedule for the shelter.

Without having to be roused by the usual self-serving exhortations that accompany team-building experiences, employees reckoned the construction experience a positive one: they appreciated being able to do something of value for others; they saw their colleagues in a new light, for they too welcomed the chance to do good; cooperation was required to accomplish a worthwhile goal; and finally, it isn't often that people have a chance to sweat next to one another in real labor. Many likened it to their college and army experiences, where they had formed the closest friendships of their lives. Actually, it was quite like a barn raising—a common community experience in an earlier America.[15]

---

individual senses of self-efficacy, or confidence in themselves and in their ability to regulate different behaviors (eating, drinking, and the like) and to achieve their personal aims. Community efficacy is important for an individual's personal sense of efficacy as well, and individual self-efficacy is enhanced when people believe that their community is responsive to them and concerned with their well-being.

In chapter 6 we saw that self-efficacy is an important determinant of people's susceptibility to addiction. The ways in which communities empower people, therefore, are essential elements in the addiction-proneness of populations, and the loss of community increases the risk of addiction for everyone. For example, in the Sam Shepard play *Fool for Love*, a man and a woman engage in a long, violent struggle for dominance and affection, hurting each other but never achieving emotional satisfaction. The play takes place in a virtual vacuum—the two people have no points of connectedness except with one another. This extreme portrayal of frustrated, addictive love is psychologically accurate, and the kind of mutually self-destructive relationship the play depicts is characteristic of barren, isolated social worlds.[16]

Without the nurturance of family and community, people are more prone to adopt any number of addictions; for example, the high level of addiction in Vietnam was due in good part to soldiers' loss of the supportive social structures they had at home. Soldiers' likelihood of being addicted subsided proportionately when they regained these crucial life props. Likewise, both community involvement and a sense of personal efficacy are central ingredients in young people's mastery of the world and control of their impulses and behavior. It is for this reason that maturity tends to increase young people's social integration and to lower their rates of problem drinking and drug use.

When people fail to outgrow addiction, on the other hand, it is because they are unable either to develop adult skills or to become a part of normal social networks. For example, in Charles Winick's classic study of maturing out, the *minority* of young addicts who remained addicted through adulthood sustained a series of institutional dependencies—on hospitals, treatment centers, and prisons. Therapeutic communities that strive to reverse this dependent role and to inculcate adult values and competencies face a tremendous job. De Leon describes the process as "habilitation, the development of a socially productive, conventional lifestyle for the first time" in addicts' lives. The process of socializing adults requires such a large investment of resources that it can be successfully completed for only a small portion of all those who require it.

Obviously, we will succeed at reducing addiction to the extent that we can prepare children to achieve adulthood through ordinary lived experience rather than in therapeutic communities (and cer-

tainly not in hospitals). Children learn self-efficacy through the en-
couragement of adults like their parents and teachers, combined with
actual practice at developing competencies. Either one alone is inadequate. When they are objects of too much negativity, children
tend to overlook their strengths and to fail to see the qualities they
actually have. On the other hand, it does little good to tell people
that they are funny or good dancers or clever or athletic or whatever
unless they practice these skills until they master them.

One other requirement for this maturational process is an environment that is stable and supportive enough to give children the
space to grow and learn. Inner cities often do not provide such an
environment, and a large percentage of children reared in bombed-
out cityscapes will not have a chance to develop a fully matured
adult outlook and set of competencies. My sense of childhood development among the broad middle class is that parents typically err
today in not having enough faith in children to manage their own
lives and in not giving them enough space for independent activity.
Childhood today is a much more closely managed affair than it was
at any time in the past—there is less and less room for personal
experimentation and learning from one's mistakes. I think it unsur-
prising in this context that more people today believe they are incapable of managing their lives and that some type of remedial
experience—like hospitalization—is becoming a frequent part of
growing up.

## The Myth of Adolescent Maladjustment

Having said this, I do not want to repeat the common mistake of
making adolescence out to be more difficult than it is—and adolescents less competent than they are. A number of recent studies have
pointed out that research is usually skewed toward the maladjusted
young, which has created a myth of the prevalence of adolescent
maladjustment. In fact, as Shirley Feldman—a Stanford psychologist—notes, adolescent development is more peaceful and gradual
than it is usually portrayed.[17] Daniel Offer, a psychiatrist, found in
a worldwide study of teenagers that 80 percent are confident and

well adjusted and have good coping skills.[18] Joseph Adelson, a child development researcher at the University of Michigan, summarizes the results of his and every other piece of systematic research: "the idea of adolescent upheaval and alienation and defiance is a wild exaggeration."[19]

I once attended a presentation by the substance abuse counselor at my local school district. He asked those present to recall how they had felt as adolescents. The counselor then proceeded to write down only the negative comments people gave. As result, the blackboard was filled with comments like "alienated," "alone," "angry," "bitter," "desperate"—even "suicidal"! In this way, this serious young man defined adolescence itself as a disease state. He may have been accurately reflecting his own life and that of the young people he usually spoke to. But his picture of the typical adolescent is so badly biased as to be less than helpful for the majority of children in any school system. The problem is that mental health education in the schools is geared almost exclusively toward the maladjusted. The typical drug and alcohol educational program, for example, features as speakers the kids who have had the worst life problems and who are abnormal in their lack of self-control and their abuse of drugs and alcohol. Most kids—quite appropriately—set themselves apart from these supposed exemplars.

One other aspect of my experience at my local school district meeting is worth relating. The district had a program for taking elementary school children to New York City's Lincoln Center to hear a concert. An unpaid helper who had become involved with the program spoke after the drug counselor did. The woman became transported as she described the value of the music program and of how much it had meant to her—for example, she had never been to Lincoln Center until she took the school children there! The woman soon caught herself, however, and apologized for her enthusiasm. "I realize," she said, "that this program isn't as serious and important as the drug program we just heard about." On the contrary, the introduction of people to experiences with potentially lifetime payoffs in pleasure and appreciation is what education is all about, and it is a commentary on our current concept of education that people apologize for educating children instead of performing therapy on them.

## Protecting Oneself

In chapter 9, we saw that parents often perceive the world as stark and frightening, a view they convey to their children as well. The general tendency of adolescents to be well adjusted and content addresses some of parents' anxieties—generally speaking, children are far better off psychologically than experts and parents suspect. Children may also be better at warding off danger than parents give them credit for. But certainly, if the world holds nearly as much danger as many parents fear, the development of self-protective skills is a high priority for children. Simply frightening children with fear-inspiring messages is not the way to enhance these skills, however. How do children best learn to protect themselves? And from the other direction, what is it about some children that makes them particularly vulnerable to dangerous involvements?

For example, handbooks have been issued that advise children and their parents about how to avoid being molested or kidnapped. One such booklet, entitled "Child Lures" (put out by Ralston Purina), emphasizes that children should be suspicious of strangers and all the tricks they play. However, in a final summary, the booklet indicates that certain children are heavily targeted by molesters. The most susceptible children—according to this pamphlet—are those who appear unkempt, who are often out alone at night, who frequent video arcades, who smoke cigarettes, who come from families in the middle of bitter divorces, from families in which parents are sexually promiscuous, from families where single parents carelessly rely on male friends as caretakers, and from families that have weak values. Clearly, some children's lives predispose them far more to the dangers of molestation. The predisposing factors in this list cover a lot of ground: some may be causal, others parallel outcroppings of under-lying causes.[20] However, the overall tenor of the items should by now be familiar to readers of this book.

Beyond the social and family disadvantages that lay children open to the importunings or assault of strangers, there is the question of educating children to make sensible decisions about the people they meet. Children need to learn how to make distinctions between kind and good strangers and strangers who have bad intentions or who will get them in trouble. Somehow, a person who forms adult in-timacies has to learn similar things. When children form friendships or fall in love, they must know how to decide what kind of people are good for them. Take, for example, the case of Dominique Dunne, who was murdered by her boyfriend, John Sweeney. Dominique's father, the writer Dominick Dunne, described how Sweeney publicly assaulted a professional acquaintance of Dominique's in a jealous rage shortly before the killing.[21] This incident apparently was not atypical.

Or alternatively, Bonnie Garland made a bad decision in becoming as intimate as she did with a very dependent student like Richard Herrin—from a culture perhaps more prone to interpret sexual intimacy as indicating a permanent tie than Bonnie Garland herself felt. This is *not* to place the blame for their deaths on these women themselves. But if not blaming the victims in such cases means that we cannot figure out ways to select lovers and friends that make us happy and keep us healthy (or alive), then we will be forced to assume that the only reasonable possibility is abstinence from intimacy, or arranged marriage, or staying with whichever person we first become connected with, as long as he or she is passable but safe.

Clearly, the answer is to establish firm standards of conduct not only for our children to follow themselves, but that children can apply to others. Children need to be able to recognize and appreciate good qualities in others they would befriend or love. Communicating such standards requires that parents must make tough judgments about proper behavior. These standards are the opposite of those based on disease notions, which mistakenly assume that misbehavior is the result of uncontrollable genes. Fatalistic, disease beliefs are more common among women who end up in Al-Anon as spouses of alcoholics or among abused women even *before* they join such groups or are abused. Short of reeducating every woman who has entered an abusive relationship or who tolerates an alcoholic, our best hope would seemingly be to teach the kind of values and self-respect that cause some women to avoid men like Joel Steinberg in the first place.

# Overcoming Distress and Failure

The inherent resilience of most teens and adults is apparent in their tendency toward normality and in their ability to recognize which sorts of strangers to avoid. More than this, even people from very precarious family and social backgrounds show the ability to rebound from all sorts of trauma. Human recuperative power is a remarkable thing. For example, people often show tremendous resources in overcoming addictions along with a host of other personal problems—including schizophrenia and other emotional disorders. After all, it is true that smokers show little self-control up until the day they quit smoking and don't return to it—whereupon they become paragons of self-control for other people to envy and admire. What is most distressing about current psychological and disease theory is that it attacks—both subtly and directly—this ameliorative, life-seeking impulse that so many people display.

A psychiatric designation has been invented to explain why people can never be whole again after experiencing trauma. This is the post-traumatic stress disorder. The concept of extended trauma is the basis for the belief that adults inevitably require therapy—perhaps for the rest of their lives—if long ago they lived with alcoholic parents, or had an infant die, or were sexually abused, or were in a war zone. It is as if an effort had been undertaken to beat out the last resistance to disease ideologies, where people who *apparently* achieve normality are revealed actually to be suffering from the disease of denial. Thus, not only do disease theories explain away the failure of a small group of people to bounce back from disappointment or tragedy, they strive to expand the number of such failures by working away at the majority who unaccountably recover from life shocks.

Research on shock and trauma survivors suggests it is difficult to undermine human resilience, however. For example, when Surgeon General C. Everett Koop was charged by President Reagan with reviewing the research indicating that abortions caused long-lasting psychological trauma in women, Koop—despite sharing Reagan's anti-abortion stance and despite having an implicit mandate to document such damage—reported that the research did not support this view. Psychologist Ronnie Janoff-Bulman, who investigates how humans cope with significant traumas, finds that

> although some victims of trauma—such as rape, crime or natural
> disaster—develop a far more negative view of the world than before

[their] victimization, a much higher percentage develop a slightly more realistic world view that nonetheless remains essentially positive and retains some illusions about the the world's goodness.[22]

And thank God for that. Otherwise, tragedy and crime would dominate the human spirit. Yet by supporting a vision of the inherent weakness of the human spirit, psychiatric designations and support-group philosophies contribute to our pessimism and depression.

Human resilience—and the opposition that some express toward this resilience as being illusory—is apparent among children of alcoholics. In the first place, it has to be noted that even those studies *devoted* to outlining the genetic transmission of alcoholism—from Goodwin's keynote study on—have found only a minority (in most cases a small minority) who become alcoholics themselves. The majority escape an alcoholic heritage. The Tecumseh, Michigan, epidemiological study discussed in chapter 3 showed that children's chances of doing so are improved when it was the parent of the opposite sex from the child who drank heavily, or when the children—as adults—recall that the heavy-drinking parent manifested drinking problems.[23] The major message here for alcoholics' offspring is that the ability to develop an independent perspective on their parents' drinking problems is what is crucial for escaping an alcoholic inheritance. As one woman with an alcoholic father told me when she received some literature on children of alcoholics, "It would have been helpful for me to know my father's behavior wasn't normal; it *wouldn't* have been helpful for me to hear I was likely to become an alcoholic myself." (This woman drank moderately.)

There is a similar message in the child abuse literature. Have you ever heard people say, "I didn't like how I was treated as a child, and I've made sure not to treat my own children that way"? Two psychologists, Joan Kaufman and Edward Zigler, investigated the likelihood that parents who were abused as children would in turn abuse their own children, as television programs and ads so frequently claim.[24] They noted from the research that "although a history of abuse is more common among parents who maltreat their children, many parents who do not report abusive childhood experiences become abusers and a sizable number of parents who were maltreated as children do not." Since, typically, only the families of abused children are investigated and interviewed, it is often hard to know how many parents who were abused themselves do not carry this behavior forward.

One study cited by Kaufman and Zigler interviewed parents of newborns about the parents' childhood experiences. Among the children from forty-nine sets of parents in which at least one had been abused as a child, nine babies were maltreated. "The rate of inter-generation transmission [of child abuse] in this investigation was [therefore] 18%," or the ratio of 9 to 49. Murray Straus and his colleagues' national survey of family violence also obtained an 18 percent rate of transmission from parent to child.[25] Kaufman and Zigler found the Straus group's figure low because they excluded single parents and focused on abuse of adolescents rather than small children or babies. On the other hand, a study that reported tremendously high rates of parental transmission of abuse, Kaufman and Zigler noted, focused predominantly on single mothers in underprivileged neighborhoods. "The results of this study are more appropriately interpreted as the result of multiple determinants on the etiology of abuse (e.g., history of abuse, poverty, stress, isolation)," rather than of abuse alone.

The researchers concluded, "Although there is some truth to the notion that abuse is cyclical, there are also many factors that diminish the likelihood of abuse being transmitted across generations. Being maltreated as a child puts one at risk for becoming abusive, but the path between the two points is far from direct or inevitable." The important question is what factors prevented parents from perpetuating abuse. In one study, the factors that enabled abused parents not to maltreat their own children were extensive social supports, less ambivalence about being parents, and being "more openly angry about their earlier abuse and better able to give detailed accounts of their experience." In other words, those who developed insight were less likely to repeat the problems they faced as children. Most of those who accomplished this did so without therapy. They were often aided by forming relationships with another adult—"a relative, teacher, minister, friend—who is emotionally nurturing."[26]

Children need to develop an independent perspective and a critical awareness of their parents' misbehavior within alcoholics' families as well. In the Tecumseh community study, adults who recalled their parents as having more drinking problems or whose opposite-sex parent drank beyond the community norm were less likely than average to imitate their parents' drinking patterns. In these cases, parents discredited themselves as models of drinking, and children were more careful to drink healthfully themselves. Anything that allows children to develop such an independent perspective and to be able to recognize and deal with parents' limitations will help children in problem families and in all families. In some cases, it seems that having had some problems as a child *strengthens* children's independence.

The plight of children of alcoholics has been brought to America's attention by a diligent group of clinicians, none of whom has investigated the *incidence* of psychological problems among children of alcoholics—that is, whether such problems are actually greater for these children than for the population at large. Marc Schuckit, a psychiatrist at the University of California at San Diego, compared young male university students and staff who had close alcoholic relatives with a matched group from nonalcoholic families. The two groups did not differ significantly in such personality measures as anxiety and neuroticism.[27] Jeanette Johnson, a researcher at the National Institute on Alcohol Abuse and Alcoholism, has noted that children growing up in an alcoholic household often show a heightened durability. The additional caretaking responsibilities that these "resilient" children of alcoholics take on, Johnson believes, may not be a bad thing and may instead foster competence and maturity.

The founders of the adult children of alcoholics movement have themselves noted many apparently well-adjusted children in alcoholic families. Thus one of the major categories of problems among children of alcoholics emphasized by well-known figures in the field— such as Sharon Wegscheider-Cruse and Claudia Black—is this "hero" or "caretaker" figure. Generally, they are women whose fathers were alcoholics; these outwardly normal—even exceptionally competent—children are in fact depicted as the major victims of alcoholism, since they shoulder their burdens without complaint and fail to acknowledge their suffering. Wegscheider-Cruse relates that such women, when educated about their position within the family constellation, suddenly show a shock of recognition. Joining with others like them affirms their idiosyncratic experiences. But couldn't nearly all of us show similar shocks of recognition about our particular family constellation and unexplored childhood experiences? It might be said that each of us deals with his or her own family dysfunctions in our own ways.

As Donald Goodwin, the pioneering genetics researcher quoted at the beginning of chapter 5, comments, "Adult children of alcoholics are about like adult children of everybody else with a problem." Indeed, the children of alcoholics movement has consciously tried to broaden its appeal by pointing out how often children from nonalcoholic families develop the same problems as children with alcoholic parents. Herbert Gravitz and Julie Bowden prefaced the 1987 revision of their book *Recovery: A Guide for Adult Children of Alcoholics* by taking exactly this argument to its most absurd length:

> Children of alcoholics are but the visible tip of a much larger social iceberg which casts an invisible shadow over as much as 96% of the population. These are the other 'children of trauma'. . . . Not knowing what hit them, and suffering a sourceless sense of pain in childhood, they perpetuate the denial and minimization which encase them in dysfunctional roles, rules and behaviors.

Gravitz and Bowden estimate the number of such children—people—in the United States to be 230 million! One wonders whether the few—4 percent—who do not come from a dysfunctional family or suffer some sort of childhood trauma require a special group because they are so isolated. Actually, the same message would apply to all these people. As Goodwin makes clear in urging people to discount the stigma of being an adult child of an alcoholic, they should "take responsibility for their lives—rather than presenting themselves as helpless victims of fate."[28]

We see in the Tecumseh study of children who do not imitate their parents' drinking problems and the Kaufman and Zigler summary of research on parents who do not repeat their own parents' abusiveness just how often people gain strength and insight through lived experience, even unpleasant and adverse experience. The smaller group who fail to withstand their families' problems, such as drinking problems, come from families that are disturbed in so many ways—socially, economically, and in their family dynamics—that the children cannot gain a firm foothold in a reality that transcends the family maelstrom. However, it isn't accurate to label these children's problems as solely the result of alcoholism; rather, it is the disturbance of the family structure from all directions that prevents the children from emerging as whole adults.

To prevent alcoholism and other problems in children, whether or not their parents have such problems, the fundamental issues remain. The children must be competent to deal with their environments; they must value sobriety and accomplishment; they must be capable of intimacy; and they must find nurturance and support either inside or outside the family. Kaufman and Zigler point out the dangers that result, in contrast, when people decide they are the heirs to some special family trauma, such as a legacy of abusiveness.

> Unqualified acceptance of the intergeneration hypothesis [of child abuse] has had many negative consequences. Adults who were maltreated have been told so many times that they will abuse their children that for some it has become a self-fulfilling prophecy. [From the other direction] many who have broken the cycle are left feeling like walking time bombs. In addition, persistent acceptance of this belief has impeded progress in understanding the etiology of abuse and led to misguided judicial and social policy interventions.

The appropriate interventions would be those that minimize all the other social deprivations—like poverty and ghetto life—that these children are subject to as part and parcel of their being abused (and of their tendency to abuse their own children if such economic and social problems persist for them as adults). In addition, the single factor that best enables abused children to grow into sensible, non-abusive adults is social support—the same thing that helps all people overcome trauma and dysfunction.

## Inculcating Positive Values

While people from stressed or problematic backgrounds can often make good, especially when society offers them the support necessary to do so, it is obviously better for the family to transmit appropriate values and psychological strength directly. After all, most moderate drinkers come from moderate-drinking backgrounds; those from problem drinking backgrounds fight harder to accomplish this. The same is true of practically all other problems discussed in this book.

For the most part, parents play the largest part in producing healthy outlooks in their offspring. The parental role is especially crucial since, as this book has indicated, the values our society currently imposes don't maximize people's chances of making their way in life, avoiding addictions, and developing positive outlooks.

It is because so much weight is placed on parents and their values that we need to make clear how important parents' roles are and at the same time to let them know they are capable of making a difference. Among other dysfunctions traceable to the disease perspective, the fatalistic view that addiction can grab anyone from the family fold—perhaps due to genetic inheritance, perhaps to a chemical accident—severely understates just how crucial familial relationships are. In this way, the very movements that stress that alcoholic families and those with related dysfunctions are the victims of diseases prevent people from shouldering the responsibility for their family dynamics. And the transmission of fundamental values is the most essential of all family responsibilities.

This book has outlined a group of values—of attitudes and outlooks—that are clear antidotes to addiction. Many of them are familiar and are often given lip service. But they are given added weight and importance when we think of them as essential ingredients for creating a world that we will find it worthwhile living in.

*Achievement and competence.* People fall prey to addiction more readily when they lack positive motivation to achieve or work. Children need to learn that accomplishment is important and within their reach, not solely for material rewards, but because people should make positive contributions to the world and other people and because it is satisfying to make such contributions and to mobilize one's skills effectively. Participating with children in constructive activity, like reading, building, or gardening—and encouraging independent activity whenever feasible—are strong precursors to achievement and competence.

*Consciousness and self-awareness.* Addiction is the result of accumulated self-destructive behavior that people ignore, just as unconscious acceptance of any negative syndrome ingrains that habit in people's lives. To be able to think practically and constructively about oneself is the best antidote to *any* failing in one's upbringing, so that learning a sense of critical consciousness means one can avoid potentially all the pitfalls to which one may be exposed. Thinking as an activity—about oneself, about others, about one's environment—is a powerful enterprise. Talking, reading, and reflecting are crucial family interactions, even when the family has problems.

*Energy and activity.* Addiction is passive, and passivity allows any problem to root itself securely in people's lives. An active orientation toward life, relationships, and how one spends time means that children will not fall passive victims to unhealthy relationships—from compulsive TV viewing to sick love affairs. The best route to avoiding or extricating oneself from life's pitfalls and to bringing about the life one desires is for people to know how to go out and get what they want. At the same time, activity that is purposefully pursued is satisfying in a way that time-filling, addictive activity or purely functional work can never be.

*Health.* The greatest harm most people experience is the result of what they do to themselves. People can instead learn to be healthy through learning good health habits—of diet, rest, and exercise—and by gaining a broader sense of the value of their bodies and minds. Self-enhancement, the opposite of self-destruction, is a fundamental outlook whereby people seek opportunities to gain and grow and to reject involvements and people that will diminish or harm them. Indicating to children the potential for the growth of their minds and bodies creates in them a general health-seeking orientation.

*Responsibility and self-regulation.* Addicts fail to regulate themselves; furthermore, they concentrate on their internal states and feelings without concern for the impact of their behavior on the rest of the world. Giving children responsibility, from housework and homework to welcoming guests and conducting themselves properly in public places, is the practice from which lifetime abilities of self-regulation and civic responsibility emerge. If children cannot learn when to eat and when to stop eating and how to take meals with others, for example, they are likely to fight lifelong battles with at least a few of the problems discussed in this book.

*Self-respect.* Addiction is a self-preoccupation that befalls people with little self-regard. Real self-respect is not the result of receiving constant attention; it is the fruit of being appreciated for what one can do well and contribute to oneself and others. In this sense, parents don't have to set out consciously to encourage self-esteem so much as they should simply stay alert to the qualities their children continually develop and express. At the same time, allowing—and insisting—that children make real contributions proves in a natural way how important the children are, so that they don't depend on parents—or anyone else—to make them feel worthwhile.

*Intimacy.* Addiction is an endless effort to overcome the inability to transcend oneself through real engagement with other people. To achieve this kind of genuine intimacy requires all of the values listed here, including even competence at dealing with the world (without which we are susceptible to indiscriminately turning over responsibility for ourselves to other people). More than anything, we need to increase in our society and in our personal lives our opportunities for real contact with others. Supporting our children's efforts and opportunities to be with other people and to carry out their friendships is a fundamental contribution to their lives.

*Community.* This book is a catalogue of the personal and social losses stemming from the disappearance of a sense of community. Community values are at the core of our survival and contentment as individuals and as a nation. To value and uphold—and certainly not to undermine or damage—community property, standards, and safety is not only a public service, it is essential to a well-composed self. When parents perform charitable work or volunteer for worthwhile causes while reaching out to neighbors and friends, they show children that it is important to contribute to the well-being of others.

## Our Own Capacities

The major danger of our disease theories is that they will persuade us that we are all subject to, or already victims of, innumerable, inexorable, lifetime diseases. In popularizing this vision of life, many scientists and therapists seem to be bent on attacking our self- and societal regard and our individual and collective competencies, and to be congratulating themselves for their success in revealing to us how susceptible to debilitating nonphysical diseases we all are. This is surely a strange agenda for people purporting to represent objective knowledge and concern for others—although, as we have seen in official movements of the past, from the Inquisition to the fight against communism as expressed in McCarthyism, human beings can persuade themselves that any forceful point of view based on received opinion is right and good.

The antidote to all of this is to question disease imagery whenever it appears, to gather within ourselves our own strength and sense of what is right, to request that those we deal with do likewise, and to support people in their attempts to contest disease bromides in their own lives. As we have seen, people accomplish this all the time in working out personal resolutions for their problems. These resolutions may be less than the ideal solutions that disease therapies often claim may be achievable, although disease therapies as yet cannot achieve them (and never will). It takes guts to challenge the prevailing wisdom that reveals for us all the things that we cannot hope to control in our lives individually and together. It also takes guts to disapprove of crime and misconduct, from plagiarism to killing, even when cheaters and killers have good explanations for their actions or when they seem contrite. For without being prepared to declare unequivocally that antisocial conduct is bad, we lose the meaning of what is good and right.

In all of this, we need to face up to the fact that our current efforts to respond to people in humane ways—however well meaning— have not brought the benefits we have hoped for. There is still tremendous room for helping people by offering them access to accomplishment and real skills with which to pursue it. But even such help will fail if it does not entail creating genuine communities. Then all our addiction will increase, along with other social problems, while our responses as a society will themselves become more pathological. Science fiction that depicts cities of the future whose denizens live in towers totally sealed off from the streets and rabble below, while interacting only with machines and using advanced neurochemistry to induce feelings like love and fun, is the logical extension of the idea that medicine has a cure when a society ails. As we proceed down this road, we must ask at every step along the way whether we are creating a world worth living in.

# Notes

## Chapter 1

1. C. Holden, "The neglected disease in medical education," *Science* 229(1985):741–742.
2. *Diagnostic and Statistical Manual of Mental Disorders*, 3rd ed. (American Psychiatric Association, 1980).
3. M. Karno et al., "The epidemiology of obsessive-compulsive disorder in five US communities," *Archives of General Psychiatry* 45(1988):1094–99.
4. S. Blakeslee, "8-Year Study Finds 2 Sides to Teen-Age Drug Use," *New York Times*, 21 July 1988, 1, A23.
5. D. B. Heath, "Sociocultural variants in alcoholism," in *Encyclopedic Handbook of Alcoholism*, eds. E. M. Pattison and E. Kaufman (Gardner, 1982), 436.
6. P. M. Boffey, "Gains against cancer since 1950 are overstated, Congress is told." *New York Times*, 16 April 1987, 1, B10.
7. C. G. Moertel, "On lymphokines, cytokines, and breakthroughs," *Journal of the American Medical Association* 256(1986):3141.
8. S. M. Levy, *Behavior and Cancer* (Jossey-Bass, 1987); S. Locke and D. Colligan, *The Healer Within* (Dutton, 1986); R. Ornstein and D. Sobel, *The Healing Brain: A New Perspective on the Brain and Health* (Simon and Schuster, 1987).
9. While the original formulation of the "type A" personality emphasized impatience and preoccupation with work, a more recent formulation sees the essential personality elements that predispose people to heart attack as hostility and cynicism about the intentions of others; see R. B. Williams, Jr., "Psychological factors in coronary heart disease," *Circulation* 76(supplement I)(1987):117–23.
10. V. Berridge and G. Edwards, *Opium and the People: Opiate Use in Nineteenth-Century England* (Yale University Press, 1987), 150.
11. E. S. Vallenstein, *Great and Desperate Cures: The Rise and Decline of Psychosurgery and Other Radical Treatments for Mental Illness* (Basic Books, 1986).
12. Antipsychotic drugs early on consisted of the major tranquilizers, such as chlorpromazine, and still are mainly from the phenothiazine family; antidepressants are principally (MAO) inhibitors and tricyclic (and heterocyclic) antidepressants. Lithium is used for the manias and for manic-depressive or bipolar mental disorders.

13. J. Mervis, "NIMH data points way to effective treatment," American Psychological Association *Monitor*, July 1986, 1, 13.
14. One interesting case of a physician who felt that antidepressant drug treatments were failures and who wrote a best-seller touting the cognitive and environmental therapies that the NIMH clinical trials found to be at least on a par with drug therapies was D. D. Burns, *Feeling Good: The New Mood Therapy* (Morrow, 1980).
15. H. M. Schmeck, Jr., "Schizophrenia focus shifts to dramatic changes in the brain," *New York Times*, 18 March 1986, C1, C3.
16. D. Goleman, "Focus on day-to-day support offers hope to schizophrenics," *New York Times*, 19 March 1986, B12.
17. P. M. Boffey, "Schizophrenia: Insights fail to halt rising toll," *New York Times* 16 March 1986, 1, 32. Copyright 1986 by The New York Times Company. Reprinted with permission.
18. D. Goleman, "Schizophrenia: Early signs found," *New York Times*, 11 December 1984, C1, C16.
19. E. F. Torrey, *Schizophrenia and Civilization* (Aronson, 1979); *Surviving Schizophrenia* (Harper & Row, 1983); *Nowhere to Go: The Tragic Odyssey of the Homeless Mentally Ill* (Harper and Row, 1988).
20. H. M. Schmeck, Jr., "Defective gene tied to form of manic-depressive illness," *New York Times*, 26 February 1987, 1, B7.
21. H. M. Schmeck, Jr., "Schizophrenia study finds strong signs of hereditary cause," *New York Times*, 10 November 1988, 1, B22.
22. J. E. Brody, "Spiders seduced into yielding secrets of web," *New York Times*, 17 September 1985, C7.
23. G. Sonnedecker, "Emergence and concept of the addiction problem," in *Narcotic Drug Addiction Problems*, ed. R. B. Livingston (Public Health Service, 1958), 18.
24. L. Grinspoon and J. B. Bakalar, *Cocaine: A Drug and Its Social Evolution*, rev. ed. (Basic Books, 1985).
25. Berridge and Edwards, *Opium and the People*.
26. D. F. Musto, *The American Disease: Origins of Narcotic Control* (Yale University Press, 1973).
27. Berridge and Edwards, *Opium and the People*, 149.
28. E. M. Brecher, *Licit and Illicit Drugs* (Consumers Union, 1972), 71.
29. J. A. Califano, Jr., *The 1982 Report on Drug Abuse and Alcoholism* (Warner Books, 1982).
30. D. Goleman, "Obsessive disorder: Secret toll is found," *New York Times*, 13 December 1988, C1, C11.

## Chapter 2

1. I. Berkow, "View from the bottom: A long lost season," *New York Times*, 7 April 1986, C12. Copyright 1986 by The New York Times Company. Reprinted with permission.
2. T. Alibrandi, *Young Alcoholics* (CompCare, 1983), 60.

3. H. G. Levine, "The alcohol problem in America: From temperance to alcoholism," *British Journal of Addiction* 79(1984):109–19.

4. H. G. Levine, "The good creature of God and the demon rum," in *Alcohol and Disinhibition*, eds. R. Room and G. Collins (National Institute on Alcohol Abuse and Alcoholism, 1983).

5. W. J. Rorabaugh, *The Alcoholic Republic* (Oxford University Press, 1979).

6. Levine, "Good creature," 127.

7. D. J. Rothman, *The Discovery of the Asylum* (Little, Brown, 1971).

8. H. G. Levine, "The discovery of addiction: Changing conceptions of habitual drunkenness in America," *Journal of Studies on Alcohol* 39(1978):143–174.

9. M. E. Lender and J. K. Martin, *Drinking in America* (Free Press, 1982).

10. J. Kaplan, *Mark Twain and His World* (Crown, 1983).

11. Levine, "Good creature," 130.

12. J. R. Gusfield, *Symbolic Crusade: Status Politics and the American Temperance Movement* (University of Illinois Press, 1963).

13. J. Kobler, *Ardent Spirits: The Rise and Fall of Prohibition* (Putnam, 1973).

14. M. M. Hyman et al., *Drinkers, Drinking, and Alcohol-Related Mortality and Hospitalizations: A Statistical Compendium* (Rutgers Center of Alcohol Studies, 1980).

15. D. Vreeland (with G. Plimpton and C. Hemphill), *D.V.* (Knopf, 1984).

16. N. E. Zinberg and K. M. Fraser, "The role of the social setting in the prevention and treatment of alcoholism," in *The Diagnosis and Treatment of Alcoholism*, 2nd ed., eds. J. H. Mendelson and N. K. Mello (McGraw-Hill, 1985).

17. F. L. Allen, *The Big Change: 1900–1950* (Harper and Row, 1952); A. Churchill, *The Improper Bohemians* (Dutton, 1959); A. Sinclair, *Prohibition: The Era of Excess* (Little, Brown, 1962).

18. D. Cahalan, I. H. Cisin, and H. M. Crossley, *American Drinking Practices* (Rutgers Center of Alcohol Studies, 1969).

19. Alcoholics Anonymous, *The Story of How More than One Hundred Men Have Recovered from Alcoholism* (Works Publishing Company, 1939). The idea that alcoholism is due to an inbred allergy was actually originated by a physician, William Silkworth, who treated Bill Wilson at a New York City sanitarium for alcoholics. Wilson also declared AA's indebtedness to the temperance-era Oxford Groups, from which it got "its ideas of self-examination, acknowledgment of character defects, restitution for harm done, and working with others." See *Alcoholics Anonymous Comes of Age* (Alcoholics Anonymous, 1957), 39. Other works describing the outlooks, backgrounds, and antecedents of Alcoholics Anonymous and its founders include E. Kurtz, *Not God: A History of Alcoholics Anonymous* (Hazelden, 1979) and B. H. Johnson, *The Alcohol Movement in America* (Ph.D. diss., University of Illinois, 1973). The last remarkable work is an encyclopedic reference for the backgrounds, attitudes, and interactions among those who spearheaded the alcoholism movement in America.

20. H. M. Trice and P. M. Roman, "Delabeling, relabeling, and Alcoholics Anonymous," *Social Problems* 17(1970): 538–46.

21. R. Room, "Sociological aspects of the disease concept of alcoholism," in *Alcohol and Drug Problems*, vol. 7, eds. R. G. Smart et al. (Plenum, 1983).

22. W. R. Miller, "Haunted by the *Zeitgeist:* Reflections on contrasting treatment goals and concepts of alcoholism in Europe and the United States," in *Alcohol and Culture,* ed. T. F. Babor (Annals of the New York Academy of Sciences, 1986).

23. D. Cahalan, *Problem Drinkers: A National Survey* (Jossey-Bass, 1970); Cahalan, Cisin, and Crossley, *American Drinking Practices.*

24. R. Room, "Treatment seeking populations and larger realities," in *Alcoholism Treatment in Transition,* eds. G. Edwards and M. Grant (Croom Helm, 1980), 212.

25. G. D. Talbott, in *The Courage to Change,* ed. D. Wholey (Houghton Mifflin, 1984), 19.

26. More accurate accounts than Talbott's of how the estimate of 10,000,000 alcoholics came about—and the whole process of inflating estimates of the prevalence of alcoholism—are described in D. Cahalan, *Understanding America's Drinking Problem* (Jossey-Bass, 1987), 16–19; L. Gross, *How Much Is Too Much?* (Random House, 1985), 119–23; J. R. Gusfield, *The Culture of Public Problems* (University of Chicago, 1981), 55–60; C. Weiner, *The Politics of Alcoholism* (Transaction Books, 1981), 184–85.

27. D. Cahalan and R. Room, *Problem Drinking Among American Men* (Rutgers Center of Alcohol Studies, 1974); W. B. Clark, "Loss of control, heavy drinking and drinking problems in a longitudinal study," *Journal of Studies on Alcohol* 37(1976):1256–90; W. B. Clark and D. Cahalan, "Changes in problem drinking over a four-year span," *Addictive Behaviors* 1(1976):251–60.

28. C. M. Weisner and R. Room, "Financing and ideology in alcohol treatment," *Social Problems* 32(1984):167–84; R. Longabaugh, "Evaluating recovery outcomes," presented at Conference, Program on Alcohol Issues, University of California, San Diego, February 4-6, 1988.

29. C. M. Weisner, "The alcohol treatment system and social control: A study in institutional change," *Journal of Drug Issues* 13(1983):117–33.

30. L. D. Johnston, P. M. O'Malley, and J. G. Bachman, *Use of Licit and Illicit Drugs by America's High School Students, 1975–1984* (National Institute on Drug Abuse, 1985).

31. "Children of alcoholics: Strength in numbers," *New York Times,* 26 February 1986, C1, C10.

## Chapter 3

1. These data are from 1982 and 1987 Gallup polls. The Gallup organization summarized these findings in "Misconceptions about alcoholism succumb to educational efforts," *The Gallup Report No. 265,* October 1987, 24–31.

2. F. Baekeland, L. Lundwall, and B. Kissin, "Methods for the treatment of chronic alcoholism: A critical appraisal," in *Research Advances in Alcohol and Drug Problems,* vol. 2, eds. R. J. Gibbons et al. (Wiley, 1975), 306.

3. R. E. Hagen, R. L. Williams, and E. J. McConnell, "The traffic safety impact of alcohol abuse treatment as an alternative to mandating license controls," *Accident Analysis and Prevention* 11 (1979): 275–91; D. F. Preusser, R. G. Ulmer, and J. R. Adams, "Driver record evaluation of a drinking driver rehabilitation

program," *Journal of Safety Research* 8(1976):98–105; P. M. Salzberg and C. L. Klingberg, "The effectiveness of deferred prosecution for driving while intoxicated," *Journal of Studies on Alcohol* 44(1983):299–306.

4. R. A. Brown, "Conventional education and controlled drinking education courses with convicted drunken drivers," *Behavior Therapy* 11(1980):632–42; S. H. Lovibund, "Use of behavior modification in the reduction of alcohol-related road accidents," in *Applications of Behavior Modification*, eds. T. Thompson and W. S. Dockens III (Academic Press, 1975).

5. "In the matter of Creative Interventions," State of New York Supreme Court, County of Monroe, Decision Index #8700/85.

6. E. Gordis, "Accessible and affordable health care for alcoholism and related problems: Strategy for cost containment," *Journal of Studies on Alcohol* 48(1987):579–85.

7. R. M. Murray et al., "Economics, occupation and genes: A British perspective" (Paper presented at the American Psychopathological Association, New York, March 1986), 1–2.

8. J. R. Milam and K. Ketcham, *Under the Influence: A Guide to the Myths and Realities of Alcoholism* (Bantam Books, 1983), 42.

9. J. Merry, "The 'loss of control' myth," *Lancet* 1(1966): 1257–58; J. Langenbucher and P. E. Nathan, "The 'wet' alcoholic: One drink . . . then what?" in *Identifying and Measuring Alcoholic Personality Characteristics*, ed. W. M. Cox (Jossey-Bass, 1983).

10. G. A. Marlatt, B. Demming, and J. B. Reid, "Loss of control drinking in alcoholics: An experimental analogue," *Journal of Abnormal Psychology* 81(1973):223–41.

11. N. K. Mello and J. H. Mendelson, "A quantitative analysis of drinking patterns in alcoholics," *Archives of General Psychiatry* 25(1971):527–39.

12. G. A. Marlatt, "Alcohol, the magic elixir," in *Stress and Addiction*, eds. E. Gottheil et al. (Brunner/Mazel, 1987).

13. N. K. Mello and J. H. Mendelson, "Drinking patterns during work-contingent and non-contingent alcohol acquisition," *Psychosomatic Medicine* 34(1972):1116–21.

14. G. Bigelow, I. A. Liebson, and R. Griffiths, "Alcoholic drinking: Suppression by a brief time-out procedure," *Behavior Research and Therapy* 12(1974):107–15; M. Cohen, I. A. Liebson, L. A. Faillace, and R. P. Allen, "Moderate drinking by chronic alcoholics: A schedule-dependent phenomenon," *Journal of Nervous and Mental Disorders* 153(1971):434–44.

15. Gallup poll, "Misconceptions."

16. J. Mason, "The body: Alcoholism defined," *Update* (Alcoholism Council of Greater New York), January 1985, 4–5.

17. D. W. Goodwin, F. Schulsinger, L. Hermansen et al. "Alcohol problems in adoptees raised apart from alcoholic biological parents," *Archives of General Psychiatry* 28(1973):238–43.

18. D. W. Goodwin, F. Schulsinger, J. Knop et al. "Alcoholism and depression in adopted-out daughters of alcoholics," *Archives of General Psychiatry* 34(1977):751–55.

19. D. Lester, "Genetic theory: An assessment of the heritability of alcoholism," in *Theories of Alcoholism*, eds. C. D. Chaudron and D. A. Wilkinson (Addiction Research Foundation, 1988); R. M. Murray, C. A. Clifford, and H.M.D. Gurling, "Twin and adoption studies: How good is the evidence for a genetic role?" in *Recent Developments in Alcoholism*, vol. 1, ed. M. Galanter (Plenum, 1983); J. S. Searles, "The role of genetics in the pathogenesis of alcoholism," *Journal of Abnormal Psychology* 97(1988):153–67.

20. A. I. Alterman, J. S. Searles, and J. G. Hall, "Failure to find differences in drinking behavior as a function of familial risk for alcoholism," *Journal of Abnormal Psychology* 98(1989):50–53; J. Knop, D. W. Goodwin, T. W. Teasdale et al., "A Danish prospective study of young males at high risk for alcoholism," and V. E. Pollock, J. Volavka, S. A. Mednick et al., "A prospective study of alcoholism," both in *Longitudinal Research in Alcoholism*, eds. D. W. Goodwin et al. (Kluwer-Nijhoff, 1984).

21. G. E. Vaillant, *The Natural History of Alcoholism* (Harvard University Press, 1983), 106.

22. M. A. Schuckit and V. Rayses, "Ethanol ingestion: Differences in blood acetaldehyde concentrations in relatives of alcoholics and controls," *Science* 213(1979):54–55.

23. S. Peele, "The implications and limitations of genetic models of alcoholism and other addictions," *Journal of Studies on Alcohol* 47(1986):63–73.

24. M. A. Schuckit et al., "Neuropsychological deficits and the risk for alcoholism," *Neuropsychopharmacology* 1(1987):45–53.

25. C. R. Cloninger, M. Bohman, S. Sigvardsson, et al. "Psychopathology in adopted-out children of alcoholics," in *Recent Developments in Alcoholism*, vol. 3, ed. M. Galanter (Plenum 1985).

26. D. Cahalan and R. Room, *Problem Drinking Among American Men* (Rutgers Center of Alcohol Studies, 1974).

27. M. A. Schuckit, "A comparison of anxiety and assertiveness in sons of alcoholics and controls," *Journal of Clinical Psychiatry* 43(1982):238–39; "Extroversion and neuroticism in young men at higher and lower risk for the future development of alcoholism," *American Journal of Psychiatry* 140(1983):1223–24.

28. M. A. Schuckit, "Ethanol-induced changes in body sway in men at high alcoholism risk," *Archives of General Psychiatry* 42(1985):375–79; B. W. Lex, S. E. Lukas, N. E. Greenwald, and J. Mendelson, "Alcohol-induced changes in body sway in women at risk for alcoholism," *Journal of Studies on Alcohol* 49(1988):346–56.

29. C. T. Nagoshi and J. R. Wilson, "Influence of family alcoholism history on alcohol metabolism, sensitivity, and tolerance," *Alcoholism: Clinical and Experimental Research* 11(1987):392–98.

30. R. C. Johnson et al., "Cultural factors as explanations for ethnic group differences in alcohol use in Hawaii," *Journal of Psychoactive Drugs* 19(1987):67–75.

31. M. A. Schuckit, "Subjective responses to alcohol in sons of alcoholics and control subjects," *Archives of General Psychiatry* 41(1984):833.

32. "New insights into alcoholism," *Time*, 25 April 1983, 64, 69.

33. C. R. Cloninger et al., "Inheritance of alcohol abuse," *Archives of General Psychiatry* 38(1981):867.
34. G. D. Talbott, in *The Courage to Change*, ed. D. Wholey (Houghton Mifflin, 1984), 19.
35. Cahalan and Room, *Problem Drinking*.
36. K. M. Fillmore, "Relationships between specific drinking problems in early adulthood and middle age," *Journal of Studies on Alcohol* 36(1975):822–907; M. T. Temple and K. M. Fillmore, "The variability of drinking patterns and problems among young men, age 16–31," *International Journal of Addictions* 20(1986):1595–1620.
37. S. Peele, "What can we expect from treatment of adolescent drug and alcohol abuse?" *Pediatrician* 14(1987):62–69.
38. E. Harburg, D. R. Davis, and R. Caplan, "Parent and offspring alcohol use," *Journal of Studies on Alcohol* 43(1982):497–516.
39. E. Harburg et al., "Familial transmission of alcohol use: II. Imitation and aversion to parent drinking (1960) by adult offspring (1977)," *Journal of Studies on Alcohol*, in press.
40. G. Elal-Lawrence, P. D. Slade, and M. E. Dewey, "Predictors of outcome type in treated problem drinkers," *Journal of Studies on Alcohol* 47(1986):41–47; M. Sanchez-Craig, D. A. Wilkinson, and K. Walker, "Theories and methods for secondary prevention of alcohol problems," in *Treatment and Prevention of Alcohol Problems*, ed. W. M. Cox (Academic Press, 1987).
41. P. Biernacki, *Pathways from Heroin Addiction: Recovery Without Treatment* (Temple University Press, 1986).
42. M. M. Gross, "Psychobiological contributions to the alcohol dependence syndrome," in *Alcohol Related Disabilities*, eds. G. Edwards et al. (World Health Organization, 1977), 121.
43. B. S. Tuchfeld, "Spontaneous remission in alcoholics," *Journal of Studies on Alcohol* 42(1981):626–41.
44. L.R.H. Drew, "Alcoholism as a self-limiting disease," *Quarterly Journal of Studies on Alcohol* 29(1968):956–67.
45. H. A. Mulford, "Rethinking the alcohol problem: A natural processes model," *Journal of Drug Issues* 14(1984):38.
46. Vaillant, *Natural History*, 188–192.
47. A. M. Greeley, W. C. McCready, and G. Theisen, *Ethnic Drinking Subcultures* (Praeger, 1980).
48. B. W. Lex, "Alcohol problems in special populations," in *The Diagnosis and Treatment of Alcoholism*, 2nd ed., eds. J. H. Mendelson and N. K. Mello (McGraw-Hill, 1985), 96–97.
49. S. Abrams, "Denial comes first: Discussing Jewish reaction to chemical dependency," *Cleveland Jewish News*, 27 December 1985, 16; D. Bean, "Jewish addicts admit it: Not-to-worry myth busted," *Cleveland Plain Dealer*, 1 June 1986, 32A.
50. B. Glassner and B. Berg, "How Jews avoid alcohol problems," *American Sociological Review* 45(1980):647–64.

51. B. Glassner and B. Berg, "Social locations and interpretations: How Jews define alcoholism," *Journal of Studies on Alcohol* 45(1984):16–25.
52. M. L. Barnett, "Alcoholism in the Cantonese of New York City," in *Etiology of Chronic Alcoholism*, ed. O. Diethelm (Charles C Thomas, 1955).
53. Vaillant, *Natural History*, 283–84.
54. W. R. Miller and R. K. Hester, "The effectiveness of alcoholism treatment: What research reveals," in *Treating Addictive Behaviors: Processes of Change*, eds. W. R. Miller and N. K. Heather (Plenum, 1986).
55. K. S. Ditman, G. G. Crawford, E. W. Forgy, et al., "A controlled experiment on the use of court probation in the management of the alcohol addict," *American Journal of Psychiatry* 124(1967):160–63.
56. J. M. Brandsma, M. C. Maultsby, and R. J. Walsh, *The Outpatient Treatment of Alcoholism: A Review and Comparative Study* (University Park Press, 1980).
57. M. A. Lieberman, I. D. Yalom, and M. B. Miles, *Encounter Groups* (Basic Books, 1973).
58. W. R. Miller and R. K. Hester, "Inpatient alcoholism treatment: Who benefits?" *American Psychologist* 41(1986):794–805.
59. C. Holden, "Is alcoholism treatment effective?" *Science* 236(1987):20–22.
60. E. Gottheil et al., "Follow-up of abstinent and nonabstinent alcoholics," *American Journal of Psychiatry* 139(1982):564.
61. J. E. Helzer, L. N. Robins, J. R. Taylor, et al. "The extent of long-term moderate drinking among alcoholics discharged from medical and psychiatric treatment facilities," *New England Journal of Medicine* 312(1985):1678–82.
62. J. M. Polich, D. J. Armor, and H. B. Braiker, *The Course of Alcoholism: Four Years After Treatment* (Wiley, 1981).
63. S. Peele, "The cultural context of psychological approaches to alcoholism," *American Psychologist* 39(1984):1337–51.
64. Elal-Lawrence, Slade, and Dewey, "Predictors of outcome type"; N. Heather, S. Rollnick, and M. Winton, "A comparison of objective and subjective measures of alcohol dependence as predictors of relapse following treatment," *British Journal of Clinical Psychology* 22(1983):11–17; J. Orford and A. Keddie, "Abstinence or controlled drinking in clinical practice," *British Journal of Addiction* 81(1986):495–504.
65. Tuchfeld, "Spontaneous remission."
66. G. Edwards et al., "Who goes to Alcoholics Anonymous?" *Lancet* 1(1966):382–84.
67. Peele, "The cultural context."
68. D. J. Armor, J. M. Polich, and H. B. Stambul, *Alcoholism and Treatment* (Wiley, 1978), 232.
69. J. H. Mendelson and N. K. Mello, *Alcohol Use and Abuse in America* (Little, Brown, 1985), 346–47.
70. Vaillant, *Natural History*, 3. Vaillant's source for this quote is S. E. Gitlow, "Alcoholism: A disease," in *Alcoholism: Progress in Research and Treatment*, eds. P. B. Bourne and R. Fox (Academic Press, 1973), 8. The statement is inaccurate, however, in at least one and perhaps more instances. G. R. Vandenbos, acting chief executive officer of the American Psychological Association (APA), wrote

me (29 March 1989) that the APA has never taken the position that alcoholism is a disease and that, in fact, it had explicitly rejected adopting this position. Nonetheless, the National Council on Alcoholism has stated in public documents for a number of years that the APA supports the view that alcoholism is a disease.

## Chapter 4

1. This program was shown on *Today in New York* on 6 November 1985. I was a guest along with Wright, Barbara McCrady of the Rutgers Center of Alcohol Studies, and Nicholas Pace, an internist who works with alcoholics.
2. H. Fingarette, "Alcoholism and self-deception," in *Self-Deception and Self-Understanding*, ed. M. W. Martin (University Press of Kansas, 1985), 60–61. Herbert Fingarette has also written an important book debunking the disease theory of alcoholism: *Heavy Drinking: The Myth of Alcoholism as a Disease* (University of California Press, 1988).
3. J. G. Woititz, "A study of self-esteem in children of alcoholics" (Ph.D. diss., Rutgers University, 1976), 53–55.
4. D. Rudy, *Becoming Alcoholic* (Southern Illinois University Press, 1986).
5. D. W. Goodwin, J. B. Crane, and S. B. Guze, "Alcoholic blackouts," *American Journal of Psychiatry* 126(1969):191–98.
6. C. McCabe, "Are drunks alcoholics?" *San Francisco Chronicle*, 14 November 1977, 41. Reprinted with permission of Chronicle Features, San Francisco.
7. R. Room, "Treatment seeking populations and larger realities," in *Alcoholism Treatment in Transition*, eds. G. Edwards and M. Grant (Croom Helm, 1980).
8. E. Kurtz, *Not God: A History of Alcoholics Anonymous* (Hazelden, 1979).
9. G. McLain as told to J. Marx, "The downfall of a champion," *Sports Illustrated*, 16 March 1987, 62. Reprinted courtesy of *Sports Illustrated* from the March 16, 1987 issue. Copyright 1987, Time Inc. All Rights Reserved.
10. "Gooden tells of cocaine use," *New York Times*, 26 June 1987, D17.
11. J. Gross, "In a mansion, alliances to overcome addiction," *New York Times*, 3 July 1987, B1.
12. J. Durso, "Gooden is focus of concern," *New York Times*, 24 July 1987, B11, B12.
13. M. Chass and M. Goodwin, "Cocaine disrupts baseball from field to front office," *New York Times*, 20 August 1985, 1, B8.
14. P. Messing, "Fidgety Keith tells coke horror story," *New York Post*, 7 September 1985, 1, 42.
15. *Fifty Most Asked Questions About Smoking and Health . . . And the Answers* (American Cancer Society, 1982).
16. S. Peele, "The 'cure' for adolescent drug abuse: Worse than the problem?" *Journal of Counseling and Development* 65(1986):23–24.
17. *AA Surveys Its Membership: A Demographic Report* (Alcoholics Anonymous World Services, 1987).
18. A. Petropoulos, "Compulsive behavior and youth," *Update* (Alcoholism Council of Greater New York), January 1985, 8.

19. G. B. Melton and H. A. Davidson, "Child protection and society," *American Psychologist* 42(1987):172–75.
20. "Hyperactive boys often turn out to be normal," *New York Times*, 2 February 1988, C3.
21. L. Granger and B. Granger, *The Magic Feather: The Truth About "Special Education"* (Dutton, 1986).
22. W. R. Miller, "Haunted by the *Zeitgeist*: Reflections on contrasting treatment goals and concepts of alcoholism in Europe and the United States," in *Alcohol and Culture*, ed. T. F. Babor (New York Academy of Sciences, 1986).
23. "Morris talks his way out of debt," *Louisville Courier-Journal*, 8 July 1988, F2.
24. B. Ford and C. Chase, *The Times of My Life* (Ballantine, 1979).
25. D. Finkle, Review of "Papa John," *New York Times Book Review*, 17 August 1986, 3, 33.
26. *New York Times*, 14 October 1986, 30.
27. M. D. Newcomb and P. M. Bentler, "Substance use and abuse among children and teenagers," *American Psychologist* 44(1989):242–48.
28. C. Creager, "Calling all counselors: Special people, special causes," *Professional Counselor* (January/February 1987), 4.

# Chapter 5

1. V. Berridge and G. Edwards, *Opium and the People: Opiate Use in Nineteenth-Century England* (Yale University Press, 1987), 251.
2. D. Sifford, "A psychiatrist discusses creative writers and alcohol," *Philadelphia Inquirer*, 2 January 1989, C5.
3. "U.S. group helps sex-addict Christians cope with urges," *Toronto Star*, 16 February 1989, 14.
4. J. H. Masserman, "Alcoholism: Disease or dis-ease?" *International Journal of Mental Health* 5(1976):4.
5. J. Orford, *Excessive Appetites: A Psychological View of Addictions* (Wiley, 1985), 89.
6. J. R. Hughes, et al., "Nicotine vs placebo gum in general medical practice," *Journal of the American Medical Association* 261(1989):1300–05; M. Waldholz, "Study questions nicotine gum's ability to help smokers quit over long term," *Wall Street Journal*, 3 March 1989, B2.
7. H. G. Levine, "The good creature of God and the demon rum," in *Alcohol and Disinhibition*, eds. R. Room and G. Collins (National Institute on Alcohol Abuse and Alcoholism, 1983), 130.
8. B. H. Johnson, *The Alcohol Movement in America* (Ph.D. diss., University of Illinois, 1973), 261–62.
9. See the full-page *New York Times* ad on 27 May 1986, C11.
10. "Children of alcoholics: Strength in numbers," *New York Times*, 26 February 1986, C1, C10.
11. "Mental illness is curable," *New York Times*, 27 September 1988, C21.
12. R. Alsop, "Drug and alcohol clinics vie for patients," *Wall Street Journal*, 14 November 1988, B1.
13. *New York Times*, 28 April 1986, A16.

14. Alsop, "Drug and alcohol clinics."

15. *The Star Ledger*, 5 December 1987, 20.

16. C. Holden, "Is alcoholism treatment effective?" *Science* 236(1987):22.

17. Helen Annis, of the Ontario Addiction Research Foundation, quoted in "In-patient care still favored," *U.S. Journal of Drug and Alcohol Dependence*, June 1986, 1, 11.

18. M. Korcok, "Anatomy of a victory: The DRG exemption," *U.S. Journal of Drug and Alcohol Dependence*, January 1984, 3.

19. M. Korcok, "HCFA extends deadline for DRG compliance," *U.S. Journal of Drug and Alcohol Dependence*, June 1986, 1, 16.

20. L. D. Johnston, P. M. O'Malley, and J. G. Bachman, *Use of Licit and Illicit Drugs by America's High School Students, 1975–1984* (National Institute on Drug Abuse, 1985).

21. "Adolescent treatment debate rages," *U.S. Journal of Drug and Alcohol Dependence*, June 1986, 4, 16.

22. J. O. Finckenauer, *Scared Straight! and the Panacea Phenomenon* (Prentice-Hall, 1982).

23. L. Granger and B. Granger, *The Magic Feather: The Truth About "Special Education"* (Dutton, 1986).

24. E. B. Fein, "Parents tell city panel of fears and anger over special education," *New York Times*, 28 November 1984, B4.

25. *New York Times* Fall Education Survey, 11 November 1984, sec. 12.

26. W. E. Schmidt, "Sales of drug are soaring for treatment of hyperactivity," *New York Times*, 5 May 1987, C3.

27. M. Levine, "Learning: Abilities and disabilities," *The Harvard Medical School Health Letter*, September 1984, 3–6.

28. K. J. Hart and T. H. Ollendick, "Prevalence of bulimia in working and university women," *American Journal of Psychiatry* 142(1985):851–54.

29. "Shopping addiction: Abused substance is money," *New York Times*, 16 June 1986, C11.

30. J. Mundis, "A way back from debt," *New York Times Magazine*, 5 January 1986, 22–26.

31. M. Gold, *The Good News About Depression* (Villard Books, 1987).

32. D. V. Sheehan, *The Anxiety Disease and How to Overcome It* (Scribner, 1984).

33. D. A. Regier et al., "One-month prevalence of mental disorders in the United States," *Archives of General Psychiatry* 45(1988):977–86.

34. M. Karno et al., "The epidemiology of obsessive-compulsive disorder in five US communities," *Archives of General Psychiatry* 45(1988):1094–99.

35. "Cyclothymia: When mood swings are dangerous," *McCall's*, August 1987, 87.

36. J. Crewdson, *By Silence Betrayed: Sexual Abuse of Children in America* (Little, Brown, 1988). See "Behind a rise in sexual-abuse reports," 2 March E8, and "Child sex abuse said to rise," 19 March C14, *New York Times*, 1986.

37. M. R. Liebowitz, *The Chemistry of Love* (Little, Brown, 1983); D. Tennov, *Love and Limerence* (Stein and Day, 1979).

38. P. Carnes, *The Sexual Addiction* (CompCare, 1983); The Augustine Fellowship, *Sex and Love Addicts Anonymous* (1986).

39. CompCare advertising pamphlet for a series of workshops for Patrick Carnes, author of *The Sexual Addiction* and *Counseling the Sexual Addict*.

40. L. M. Watkins, "Premenstrual distress gains notice as a chronic issue in the work place," *Wall Street Journal*, 22 January 1986, 31.

41. Letters appeared in *Wall Street Journal*, 12 February 1986, 31. Reprinted with permission of the *Wall Street Journal* © 1989 Dow Jones & Company, Inc. All rights reserved.

# Chapter 6

1. H. Kalant, "Drug research is muddied by sundry dependence concepts" (Paper presented at Annual Meeting of the Canadian Psychological Association, June 1982; described in *Journal* of the Addiction Research Foundation, September 1982, 12).

2. D. Anderson, "Hunter on the hunted," *New York Times*, 27 October 1988, D27.

3. I summarize and reference the host of data on overlapping addictions in *The Meaning of Addiction*. Some popular (but neither theoretically nor empirically grounded) biological theories try to explain all these addictions through the agency of endorphins (opiatelike chemicals produced by the body). For example, perhaps an endorphin deficiency causes the addict to seek pain relief from a range of addictions. This model will *not* explain why a person would both drink and gamble addictively, or drink and smoke—since nicotine is not an analgesic and does not affect the endorphin system. Indeed, even analgesic or depressant drugs operate through totally different routes in the body, so that one biochemical mechanism can never account for addicts' interchangeable or indiscriminate use of alcohol, barbiturates, and narcotics. In Kalant's words, "How do you explain in pharmacological terms that cross-tolerance occurs between alcohol, which does not have specific receptors, and opiates, which do?"

4. N. B. Eddy, "The search for a non-addicting analgesic," in *Narcotic Drug Addiction Problems*, ed. R. B. Livingston (Public Health Service, 1958).

5. H. B. McNamee, N. K. Mello, and J. H. Mendelson, "Experimental analysis of drinking patterns of alcoholics," *American Journal of Psychiatry* 124(1968):1063–69; P. E. Nathan and J. S. O'Brien, "An experimental analysis of the behavior of alcoholics and nonalcoholics during prolonged experimental drinking," *Behavior Therapy* 2(1971):455–76.

6. T. E. Dielman, "Gambling: A social problem," *Journal of Social Issues* 35(1979):36–42.

7. L. N. Robins, J. E. Helzer, M. Hesselbrock, and E. Wish, "Vietnam veterans three years after Vietnam: How our study changed our view of heroin," in *The Yearbook of Substance Use and Abuse*, vol. 2, eds. L. Brill and C. Winick (Human Sciences Press, 1980).

8. R. R. Clayton, "Cocaine use in the United States: In a blizzard or just being snowed?" in *Cocaine Use in America*, eds. N. J. Kozel and E. H. Adams (National Institute on Drug Abuse, 1985).

9. R. Jessor and S. L. Jessor, *Problem Behavior and Psychosocial Development* (Academic Press, 1977).

10. J. Istvan and J. D. Matarazzo, "Tobacco, alcohol, and caffeine use: A review of their interrelationships," *Psychological Bulletin* 95(1984):301–26.

11. O. J. Kalant and H. Kalant, "Death in amphetamine users," in *Research Advances in Alcohol and Drug Problems*, vol. 3, eds. R. J. Gibbins et al. (Wiley, 1976).

12. H. Walker, "Drunk drivers hazardous sober too," *Journal* (Ontario Addiction Research Foundation), March 1986, 2.

13. M. K. Bradstock et al., "Drinking-driving and health lifestyle in the United States," *Journal of Studies on Alcohol* 48(1987):147–52.

14. Associated Press release, "Lions' Rogers out to prove himself," 31 July 1988.

15. R. Ourlian, "Obituaries," *Detroit News*, 23 October 1988, 7B.

16. C. MacAndrew, "What the MAC Scale tells us about men alcoholics," *Journal of Studies on Alcohol* 42(1981):617.

17. H. Hoffman, R. G. Loper, and M. L. Kammeier, "Identifying future alcoholics with MMPI alcoholism scores," *Quarterly Journal of Studies on Alcohol* 35(1974):490–98; M. C. Jones, "Personality correlates and antecedents of drinking patterns in adult males," *Journal of Consulting and Clinical Psychology* 32 (1968):2–12; R. G. Loper, M. L. Kammeier, and H. Hoffman, "MMPI characteristics of college freshman males who later become alcoholics," *Journal of Abnormal Psychology* 82 (1973):159–62; C. MacAndrew, "Toward the psychometric detection of substance misuse in young men," *Journal of Studies on Alcohol* 47(1986):161–66.

18. C. MacAndrew, "Similarities in the self-depictions of female alcoholics and psychiatric outpatients," *Journal of Studies on Alcohol* 47(1986):478–84.

19. G. A. Marlatt, "Alcohol, the magic elixir," in *Stress and Addiction*, eds. E. Gottheil et al. (Brunner/Mazel, 1987); D. J. Rohsenow, "Alcoholics' perceptions of control," in *Identifying and Measuring Alcoholic Personality Characteristics*, ed. W. M. Cox (Jossey-Bass, 1983).

20. K. J. Hart and T. H. Ollendick, "Prevalence of bulimia in working and university women," *American Journal of Psychiatry* 142(1985):851–54.

21. E. R. Oetting and F. Beauvais, "Common elements in youth drug abuse: Peer clusters and other psychosocial factors," in *Visions of Addiction*, ed. S. Peele (Lexington Books, 1987).

22. J. P. Pierce et al., "Trends in cigarette smoking in the United States," *Journal of the American Medical Association* 261(1989):56–60.

23. R. K. Siegel, "Changing patterns of cocaine use," in *Cocaine: Pharmacology, Effects, and Treatment of Abuse*, ed. J. Grabowski (National Institute on Drug Abuse, 1984).

24. P. Erickson et al., *The Steel Drug: Cocaine in Perspective* (Lexington Books, 1987).

25. L. D. Johnston, P. M. O'Malley, and J. G. Bachman, *Drug Use Among American High School Students, College Students, and Other Young Adults: National Trends Through 1985* (National Institute on Drug Abuse, 1986).

26. C. E. Johanson and E. H. Uhlenhuth, "Drug preference and mood in humans: Repeated assessment of d-amphetamine," *Pharmacology, Biochemistry and Behavior* 14(1981):159–63.

27. J. L. Falk, "Drug dependence: Myth or motive?" *Pharmacology, Biochemistry and Behavior* 19(1983):388.

28. P. Kerr, "Rich vs. poor: Drug patterns are diverging," *New York Times*, 30 August 1987, 1, 28.
29. Most information in this box is from B. Woodward, *Wired: The Short Life & Fast Times of John Belushi* (Pocket Books, 1984), although any interpretations are my own.
30. S. Cohen, "Reinforcement and rapid delivery systems: Understanding adverse consequences of cocaine," in *Cocaine Use in America*, eds. N. J. Kozel and E. H. Adams (National Institute on Drug Abuse, 1985), 151, 153.
31. S. W. Sadava, "Interactional theory," in *Psychological Theories of Drinking and Alcoholism*, eds. H. T. Blane and K. E. Leonard (Guilford Press, 1987), 124.
32. D. B. Kandel, "Marijuana users in young adulthood," *Archives of General Psychiatry* 41(1984):200–209.
33. Robins et al., "Vietnam veterans," 222–23.
34. C. MacAndrew and R. B. Edgerton, *Drunken Comportment: A Social Explanation* (Aldine, 1969).
35. P. E. Nathan and B. S. McCrady, "Bases for the use of abstinence as a goal in the behavioral treatment of alcohol abusers," *Drugs & Society* 1(1987):121.
36. G. A. Marlatt, B. Demming, and J. B. Reid, "Loss of control drinking in alcoholics: An experimental analogue," *Journal of Abnormal Psychology* 81(1973):223–41.
37. C. Winick, "Maturing out of narcotic addiction," *Social Problems* 14(1962):6.
38. Robins et al., "Vietnam veterans," 230.
39. Robins et al., "Vietnam veterans," 221.

## Chapter 7

1. J. P. Pierce et al., "Trends in cigarette smoking in the United States," *Journal of the American Medical Association* 261(1989):56–60.
2. L. T. Kozlowski et al., "Comparing tobacco cigarette dependence with other drug dependencies," *Journal of the American Medical Association* 261(1989):898–901.
3. L.R.H. Drew, "Alcoholism as a self-limiting disease," *Quarterly Journal of Studies on Alcohol* 29(1968):956–67; A. M. Ludwig, "Cognitive processes associated with 'spontaneous' recovery from alcoholism," *Journal of Studies on Alcohol* 46(1985):53–58; R. D. Stall, "An examination of spontaneous remission from problem drinking in the Bluegrass region of Kentucky," *Journal of Drug Issues* 13(1983):191–206; B. S. Tuchfeld, "Spontaneous remission in alcoholics," *Journal of Studies on Alcohol* 42(1981):626–41.
4. C. Winick, "Maturing out of narcotic addiction," *Social Problems* 14(1962):1–7.
5. P. Biernacki, *Pathways from Heroin Addiction: Recovery Without Treatment* (Temple University Press, 1986); D. Waldorf, "Natural recovery from opiate addiction," *Journal of Drug Issues* 13(1983):237–80.
6. S. Schachter and J. Rodin, *Obese Humans and Rats* (Erlbaum, 1974).
7. S. Schachter, "Recidivism and self-cure of smoking and obesity," *American Psychologist* 37(1982):436–44.
8. J. A. O'Donnell et al., *Young Men and Drugs* (National Institute on Drug Abuse, 1976).

9. R. Jessor, "Adolescent problem drinking," in *Proceedings of NIAAA-WHO Alcohol Research Seminar* (U.S. Government Printing Office, 1985), 131.

10. D. Goleman, "Pioneering studies find surprisingly high rate of mental ills in young," *New York Times*, 10 January 1989, C1, C9.

11. S. Peele, "What can we expect from treatment of adolescent drug and alcohol abuse?" *Pediatrician* 14(1987):64.

12. C. K. Aldrich, "The clouded crystal ball: A 35-year follow-up of psychiatrists' predictions," *American Journal of Psychiatry* 143(1986):45–49.

13. "Hyperactive boys often turn out to be normal," *New York Times*, 2 February 1988, C3; S. Mannuzza et al., "Hyperactive boys almost grown up: II. Status of subjects without a mental disorder," *Archives of General Psychiatry* 45(1988):13–18.

14. G. M. Barnes, "Alcohol abuse among older persons," *Journal of American Geriatrics Society* 22(1969):244–50.

15. E. L. Gomberg, *Drinking and Problem Drinking Among the Elderly* (Institute of Gerontology, University of Michigan, 1980).

16. R. Stall, "Respondent-independent reasons for change and stability in alcohol consumption as a concomitant of the aging process," in *Anthropology and Epidemiology*, eds. C. R. Janes and R. Stall (Reidel, 1986).

17. D. M. Peterson, F. J. Wittington, and B. P. Payne, *Drugs and the Elderly* (Charles C Thomas, 1979).

18. A. M. Clarfield, "In grandfather's room," *New York Times Magazine*, 15 June 1986, 40.

19. W. Gerin, "(No) accounting for results," *Psychology Today*, August 1982, 32.

20. R. D. Caplan et al., "Relationships of cessation of smoking with job stress, personality, and social support," *Journal of Applied Psychology* 60(1975):211–19.

21. A. Marsh, "Smoking: Habit or choice?" *Population Trends* 37(1984):20.

22. Yes, Cheryl Tiegs used to be chubby; see C. Tiegs with V. Lindner, *The Way to Natural Beauty* (Simon and Schuster, 1980).

23. M. Worden, " 'Silent majority' recover without treatment," *U.S. Journal of Drug and Alcohol Dependence*, September 1980, 5. All quotes by alcoholics from Tuchfeld, "Spontaneous remission."

24. S. Schachter, "Pharmacological and psychological determinants of smoking," *Annals of Internal Medicine* 88(1978):104–114.

25. Biernacki, *Pathways*, 130–31.

26. L. M. Silverstein, J. Edelwich, D. Flanagan, and A. Brodsky, *High on Life: A Story of Addiction and Recovery* (Health Communications, 1981).

27. Waldorf, "Natural recovery."

28. G. A. Marlatt, S. Curry, and J. R. Gordon, "A longitudinal analysis of unaided smoking cessation," *Journal of Consulting and Clinical Psychology* 56(1988):715–20.

29. Dr. Vaillant sent me these data on 4 June 1985. They represent five to seven years of additional follow-up data on those subjects in remission in the research reported in his 1983 book, *The Natural History of Alcoholism*. I am grateful to Dean Daniel C. Tosteson and Associate Dean Eleanor G. Shore of the Harvard Medical School for their help in obtaining these data.

30. "The Secret Drew Barrymore," *People*, January 16, 1989. Used with permission.
31. G. Nordström and M. Berglund, "A prospective study of successful long-term adjustment in alcohol dependence: Social drinking versus abstinence," *Journal of Studies on Alcohol* 48(1987):95–103.
32. T. Hackler, "Sober thoughts on problem drinking," *United Airlines Magazine*, August 1983, 32.
33. G. E. Vaillant, *The Natural History of Alcoholism* (Harvard University Press, 1983), 285, 316.
34. W. R. Miller and R. K. Hester, "The effectiveness of alcoholism treatment: What research reveals," in *Treating Addictive Behaviors: Processes of Change*, eds. W. R. Miller and N. K. Heather (Plenum, 1986).
35. S. Peele, "Why do controlled-drinking outcomes vary by country, by investigator and by era?" *Drug and Alcohol Dependence* 20(1987):173–201.

# Chapter 8

1. J. Rangel, "Defendant in mass slaying is guilty of reduced charge," *New York Times*, 20 July 1985, 9. Copyright 1985 by The New York Times Company. Reprinted with permission.
2. J. F. Sullivan, "Jersey court disbars 4 lawyers in misuse of money of clients," *New York Times* (national ed.), 13 November 1986, 15.
3. "Compulsive gambling may be a handicap, and a shield from firing," *Wall Street Journal*, 21 June 1988, 1.
4. P. Shenon, "Deaver is sentenced to suspended term and $10,000 fine," *New York Times*, 24 September 1988, 1, 7.
5. Book promotion for C. P. Ewing, *Battered Women Who Kill: Psychological Self-Defense as Legal Justification* (Lexington Books, 1987).
6. "Can companies refuse to hire drug abusers?" *The Right Report* (Society of Consumer Affairs Professionals in Business, vol. 3, issue 4, 1988).
7. L. H. Pelton, "Child abuse and neglect: The myth of classlessness," in *The Social Context of Child Abuse and Neglect*, ed. L.H. Pelton (Human Sciences Press, 1981), 31–32.
8. N. Hentoff, "Is it a crime to do nothing?" *Village Voice*, 22 November 1988, 28.
9. R. Levine, "Koch argues city can't totally end fatal child abuse," *New York Times*, 31 December 1988, 1, 27.
10. S. Erlanger, "A widening pattern of abuse exemplified in Steinberg case," *New York Times*, 8 November 1987, 1, 44.
11. R. J. Gelles and M. A. Straus, *Intimate Violence: The Definitive Study of the Causes and Consequences of Abuse in the American Family* (Simon and Schuster, 1988), 85–86.
12. "Something about Amelia," *Psychology Today*, May 1984, 45.
13. A. Shupe, W. A. Stacey, and L. R. Hazlewood, *Violent Men, Violent Couples* (Lexington Books, 1987), 119.
14. Ibid.

15. M. A. Straus, R. J. Gelles, and S. K. Steinmetz, *Behind Closed Doors: Violence in the American Family* (Anchor, 1980).

16. S. K. Steinmetz, "The battered husband syndrome," *Victimology* 2(1978):499–509.

17. R. Sullivan, "Steinberg case has turned Ira London into a celebrity," *New York Times*, 6 January 1988, B1, B9.

18. R. D. McFadden, "The force of the fatal blows persuaded jurors of 'intent,' " *New York Times*, 31 January 1989, 1, B5.

19. D. E. Pitt, "Mother seized in slaying of 5-year-old," *New York Times*, 16 December 1988, B1, B3.

20. S. Frondorf, *Death of a "Jewish American Princess": The True Story of a Victim on Trial* (Villard, 1988).

21. D. Goleman, "New psychiatric syndromes spur protest," *New York Times*, 19 November 1985, C1, C16.

22. R. Sullivan, "Jury, citing mother's condition, absolves her in 2 babies' deaths," *New York Times*, 1 October 1988, 29.

23. "Woman clear in son's killing," *New York Times*, 24 December 1988, 8.

24. D. Margolick, "Many veterans cite trauma of Vietnam in trials," *New York Times*, 13 May 1985, 1, 11.

25. J. Jarvis, "Tube: 'The Wall Within,' " *People*, 1 June 1988, 13.

26. K. M. Fillmore and D. Kelso, "Coercion into alcoholism treatment: Meanings of the disease concept of alcoholism," *Journal of Drug Issues* 17(1987):301–19; E. Vingilis, "Drinking drivers and alcoholics: Are they from the same population?" in *Research Advances in Alcohol and Drug Problems*, vol. 7, eds. R.G. Smart et al. (Plenum, 1983).

27. J. Peet, "Victim of the system: Jersey bureaucrats baffle, hound woman in DWI case," *Sunday Star Ledger*, 28 September 1986, 1, 14.

28. A. S. Trebach, *The Great Drug War* (Macmillan, 1987).

29. D. Phelps, "$1 million awarded to couple committed for alcohol treatment," *Minneapolis Star and Tribune*, 18 December 1982, 1, 11A.

30. M. Worden, "Adolescent treatment on the hot seat," *U.S. Journal of Drug and Alcohol Dependence*, June 1985, 14.

31. J. Brinkley, "U.S. Panel urges testing workers for use of drugs: Broad campaign is seen," *New York Times*, 4 March 1986, 1, A19.

32. A. Clymer, "Public found ready to sacrifice in drug fight," *New York Times*, 2 September 1986, 1, D16.

33. C. Mohr, "Drug test policy caught in snags," *New York Times*, 18 December 1988, 41.

34. C. Culhane, "Drug testing too costly, invasive—study," *U.S. Journal of Drug and Alcohol Dependence*, August 1986, 1.

35. "Injunction granted in drug-test case," *New York Times*, 12 March 1987, D27.

36. "Drug challenges (continued)," *New York Times*, 17 March 1987, D28.

37. "Sportsman of the decade?" *New York Times*, 23 December 1986, B10.

38. B. Newman, "Another NCAA fumble," *Sports Illustrated*, 17 December 1987, 100.

39. M. Freudenheim, "Business and health: Acknowledging substance abuse," *New York Times*, 13 December 1988, D2.
40. R. D. McFadden, "Drug cases top others in prisons," *New York Times*, 5 January 1988, B1, B2.
41. P. Kerr, "Drug tests rising to reduce prison crowding," *New York Times*, 19 January 1988, 1, A23.
42. M. S. Gold, *800-Cocaine* (Bantam, 1984), 70.
43. R. Hanely, "Drug tests by Jersey school are ruled unconstitutional," *New York Times*, 11 December 1986, B7.

## Chapter 9

1. J. Best, "The myth of the Halloween sadist," *Psychology Today*, November 1985, 14–16.
2. John Noble, deputy director of biometry and epidemiology, National Institute on Alcohol Abuse and Alcoholism, quoted in M. Korcok, "Alcohol treatment industry to grow as risk group matures," *U.S. Journal of Drug and Alcohol Dependence*, March 1987, 1.
3. A. J. Stunkard et al., "An adoption study of human obesity," *New England Journal of Medicine* 314(1986):193–98.
4. B. D. Ayres, Jr., "Washington finds drug war is hardest at home," *New York Times*, 9 December 1988, A22.
5. A. J. Stunkard et al., "Influence of social class on obesity and thinness in children," *Journal of the American Medical Association* 221(1972):579–84.
6. F. E. Braddon et al., "Onset of obesity in a 36 year birth cohort study," *British Medical Journal* 293(1986):299–303; P. B. Goldblatt, M. E. Moore, and A. J. Stunkard, "Social factors in obesity," *Journal of the American Medical Association* 192(1965):1039–44.
7. S. L. Gortmaker et al., "Increasing pediatric obesity in the United States," *American Journal of Diseases of Children* 141(1987):535–40.
8. W. H. Dietz and S. L. Gortmaker, "Do we fatten our children at the television set?" *Pediatrics* 75(1985):807–12.
9. J. Katz, *Seductions of Crime* (Basic Books, 1988).
10. Winfred Overholser, chairman of the Executive Committee of the Research Council on Problems of Alcohol, cited in B. H. Johnson, *The Alcohol Movement in America* (Ph.D. diss., University of Illinois, 1973), 247.
11. Raymond McCarthy—although Marty Mann objected to the use of the term *drinking habit*, she had no quarrel with McCarthy's numbers—cited in ibid. 293–95.
12. M. Mann, *Marty Mann Answers Your Questions About Drinking and Alcoholism*, rev. ed. (Holt, Rinehart and Winston, 1981), 3.
13. D. Cahalan, *Understanding America's Drinking Problem* (Jossey-Bass, 1987), 6.
14. B. Weinraub, "Money Bush wants for drug war is less than sought by Congress," *New York Times*, 30 January 1989, 1, A14.

15. David Sheehan's book, *The Anxiety Disease* (Scribner, 1984), argues that anxiety is a medical condition that responds to drug treatment, although sufferers need to learn that anxiety is a lifetime disease that they can never escape; Mark Gold's book, *The Good News About Depression* (Villard, 1987), explains that, although depression is increasing (one out of four people will be struck by it), it can be treated medically with drug therapy.

16. J. Brody, "Personal health," *New York Times*, 15 January 1986, C6. Copyright 1986 by The New York Times Company. Reprinted with permission.

17. J. T. Wright et al., "Alcohol consumption, pregnancy, and low birth-weight," *Lancet* 1(1983):663–65.

18. R. Hingson et al., "Effects of maternal drinking and marijuana use on fetal growth and development," *Pediatrics* 70(1982):539–46.

19. H. L. Rosett and L. Weiner, *Alcohol and the Fetus* (Oxford University Press, 1984).

20. M. Wagner, testimony before the U.S. Commission to Prevent Infant Mortality (International Comparisons Section), United Nations, New York, 1 February 1988.

21. R. D. Lyons, "Physical and mental disabilities in newborns doubled in 25 years," *New York Times*, 18 July 1983, 1, A10.

22. N. Brozan, "U.S. leads industrialized nations in teen-age births and abortions," *New York Times*, 13 March 1985, 1, C7.

23. C. Turkington, "Contraceptives: Why all women don't use them," *APA Monitor* (American Psychological Association), August 1986, 11.

24. Rosett and Weiner, *Alcohol*, 171.

25. Wagner, testimony.

26. C. A. Miller, *Maternal Health and Infant Survival* (National Center for Clinical Infant Programs, 1987).

27. "Hospital says rules reduced cesarean rate," *New York Times*, 8 December 1988, B26.

28. R. J. Gelles and M. A. Straus, *Intimate Violence* (Simon and Schuster, 1988).

29. J. Best and G. T. Horiuchi, "The razor blade in the apple: The social construction of urban legends," *Social Problems* 32(1985):488–99.

30. American Academy of Pediatrics, "Missing children," *Pediatrics* 78(1986):370–72.

31. Gelles and Straus, *Intimate Violence*, 18.

32. "Five years after kidnapping, girl celebrates 10th birthday at home," *New York Times*, 18 February 1986, A20.

33. "Child ID efforts criticized," *Daily Record* (Morris County, N.J.), 7 November 1985, 1 (reprinted from *Denver Post*).

34. "Some school drug efforts faulted," *New York Times*, 17 September 1986, B1, B6.

35. G. Gerbner and L. Gross, "The scary world of TV's heavy viewer," *Psychology Today*, April 1976, 41–45.

36. L. Payer, *Medicine and Culture* (Holt, 1988).

# Chapter 10

1. A. Shupe, W. A. Stacey, and L. R. Hazlewood, *Violent Men, Violent Couples* (Lexington Books, 1987), 132–33.

2. H. Mulford, "Enhancing the natural control of drinking behavior" (Paper presented at conference on Evaluating Recovery Outcomes, University of California, San Diego, Calif., February, 1988) (*Contemporary Drug Problems*, in press).

3. W. R. Miller and R. K. Hester, "The effectiveness of alcoholism treatment: What research reveals," in *Treating Addictive Behaviors: Processes of Change*, eds. W. R. Miller and N. K. Heather (Plenum, 1986), 152.

4. G. De Leon, "The therapeutic community for substance abuse," in *Therapeutic Communities for Addictions*, eds. G. De Leon and J.T. Ziegenfuss, Jr. (Charles C Thomas, 1987).

5. C. Winick, "An empirical assessment of therapeutic communities in New York City," in *The Yearbook of Substance Use and Abuse*, vol. 2, eds. L. Brill and C. Winick (Human Sciences Press, 1980).

6. M. S. Rosenthal, "The Phoenix House therapeutic community," in *Scientific Basis of Drug Dependence*, ed. H. Steinberg (Churchill, 1969), 397, 402.

7. D. Warner-Holland, "The development of 'concept houses' in Great Britain and Southern Ireland, 1967-1976." in *Problems of Drug Abuse in Britain*, ed. D.J. West (Institute of Criminology, 1978).

8. G. De Leon, "The therapeutic community: Status and evaluation," *International Journal of Addictions* 20(1985):823–44.

9. R. S. Weppner, *The Untherapeutic Community* (University of Nebraska Press, 1983), 38, 213.

10. D. B. Heath, "Sociocultural variants in alcoholism," in *Encyclopedic Handbook of Alcoholism*, eds. E. M. Pattison and E. Kaufman (Gardner Press, 1982), 436.

11. R. Room, "Closing statement," *Evaluating Recovery Outcomes* (Proceedings of conference published by Program on Alcohol Issues, University Extension, University of California, San Diego, 1988), 43.

12. L. A. Sagan, *The Health of Nations: True Causes of Sickness and Well-being* (Basic Books, 1987).

13. D. J. Rothman, *The Discovery of the Asylum* (Little, Brown, 1971).

14. M. E. Lender and J. K. Martin, *Drinking in America* (The Free Press, 1982).

15. As shown on CNN, 27 January 1989.

16. S. Peele, "Fools for love," in *The Psychology of Love*, eds. R.J. Sternberg and M.L. Barnes (Yale University Press, 1988).

17. S. S. Feldman and T. M. Gehring, "Changing perspectives of family cohesion and power across adolescence," *Child Development* 59(1988):1034–45.

18. D. Offer, *The Teenage World* (Plenum, 1988).

19. "Adolescence: Hang-ups and rebelliousness are not the norm, an expert says," *Michigan Today*, December 1985, 6–7.

20. K. Wooden, *Child Lures: A Guide to Prevent Abduction* (Ralston Purina Company, 1984).

21. D. Dunne, "Justice: A father's account of the trial of his daughter's killer," *Vanity Fair*, March 1984, 86–106.

22. T. DeAngelis, "In praise of rose-colored specs," *APA Monitor* (American Psychological Association), November 1988, 22.

23. E. Harburg et al., "Familial transmission of alcohol use: II. Imitation and aversion to parent drinking (1960) by adult offspring (1977)," *Journal of Studies on Alcohol*, in press.

24. J. Kaufman and E. Zigler, "Do abused children become abusive parents?" *American Journal of Orthopsychiatry* 57(1987):186–92.

25. M. Straus, "Family patterns and child abuse in a nationally representative sample," *International Journal of Child Abuse and Neglect* 3(1979):213–25.

26. D. Goleman, "Sad legacy of abuse: The search for remedies," *New York Times*, 24 January 1989, C1, C6.

27. M. A. Schuckit, "A comparison of anxiety and assertiveness in sons of alcoholics and controls," *Journal of Clinical Psychiatry* 43(1982):238–39; "Extroversion and neuroticism in young men at higher and lower risk for the future development of alcoholism," *American Journal of Psychiatry* 140(1983):1223–24.

28. D. Sifford, "A psychiatrist discusses creative artists and alcohol," *Philadelphia Inquirer*, 2 January 1989, C5.

# Index

AA. *See* Alcoholics Anonymous

Abortion, overcoming trauma caused by, 278

Abstinence: from alcohol, 38; as treatment goal, 192

Acetaldehyde, alcoholism and, 64

Achievement, as antidote to addiction, 284

Activities: as antidote to addiction, 285; prevention of addiction and, 160–163

*Adam*, 249

Addict(s): as disease victims, 156–158; drawbacks of defining self as, 92–99; recovering, as treatment providers, 106–111; responsibility for change and, 264

Addiction(s): among athletes, 92, 94–99, 107–108, 109, 110–111, 155; benefit of treating as diseases, 116–117; concept of, 22; convincing children of life-long nature of, 103–106; disease concept portrayed in advertising and, 124–125; disease theory of, 3–5, 6–7, 20–29; experience of, 151–153; experiences and, 148–149; how people quit, 182–184; as legal defenses, 203–229; identification in young, 100–103; incidence of, 25, 136; individual and, 146–148; international comparisons of problem of, 232–234; life phases and, 149; life situations predisposing to, 166–168; loss of control and, 255–258; love, 25, 139; nature of, 146–150; outgrowing, 166–168; protection from, 160–163; reasons not to treat as disease, 1–29; self-image and, 99–100; sexual, 25, 139–140; shopping, 136; situation or environment and, 149–150; social and cultural milieu and, 150; social groups and, 159–160; susceptibility to develop, 153–156; values as antidotes to, 283–286; variety of, 2–3. *See also* Alco-holism; Cigarette smoking; Cocaine; Drug abuse; Eating disorders; Heroin addiction

Addiction Research Foundation (ARF) of Ontario, 161

Addiction treatment industry, 4; failure of, 231–232. *See also* Alcoholism treatment; Treatment

Addictive personality, 154–156

Adelson, Joseph, 275

Adolescents: alcohol use among, 51; hospitalization of, 101; myth of maladjustment in, 274–275; prediction of adult maladjustment and, 177–179; predictors of cocaine use among, 153; pregnancy among, 242–244, 246. *See also* Children

*Adult Children of Alcoholics* (Woititz), 88, 123

Adult children of alcoholics: adjustment of, 282–283; disease concept applied to, 123–124; self-esteem of, 88; treatment of, 52

Advertising, disease concept of addictions promoted by, 119, 120, 124–125

*Against the Grain* (Morris), 107

Agoraphobia, 137

Al-Anon, 52, 123

Alateen, 51–52

Alcohol: ambivalence about, 257–258; influence of beliefs on reaction to, 170; use among children, 26, 51, 136

Alcohol abuse. *See* Alcoholism

Alcohol Research Group (ARG), 269

*Alcohol Use and Abuse in America* (Mendelson & Mello), 81–82

Alcoholics: blackouts among, 89; children of, 52, 66, 88, 123–124, 279, 281, 282–283; defining selves as alcoholics, 88–92, 92–99; influence of environment on, 60;

level of intoxication striven for, 59; number needing treatment, 2; recovering, as treatment providers, 106–111; reformed, on lecture circuit, 38–39; self-cure among, 193–194. *See also* Alcoholism; Drinking patterns

Alcoholics Anonymous (AA), 190; acceptance of credo of, 43–46, 90, 112–113; Al-Anon and, 52; Alateen and, 51–52; belief in success of, 73–74; blackouts and, 89; establishment of, 24; impact on attitudes, 258; lack of effectiveness of, 56–58; loss of control and, 59–60; membership of, 234; mimicking, for other disorders, 24–25; view of alcoholism, 24–25; youth as members of, 101

Alcoholism, 31–54, 55–83; AMA's endorsement as disease, 46; antisocial behavior and, 63; attitudes and, 32–43, 53–54, 258; changing drinking patterns and, 31–35; in children, 26, 51; core belief promulgated by alcoholism movement and, 55–56; demographics of, 2, 69–73; denial and, 79–81; in developing countries, 269; effectiveness of treatment approaches for, 76–79; exaggerating dangers for fetal development, 244; extent of need for treatment and, 47; fatalities related to, 41; genetics of, 60–65, 279; incidence of, 136, 238, 269; inevitability of, 85–88; loss of control and, 38, 52–54, 59–60; medical treatment for, 24, 73–79; motivations for, 157–158; natural recovery in, 67; number of persons in treatment for, 49; overstatement of problem of, 233–234; permanence of, 24; as "primary disease," 67–68; progression of, 65–67; researchers not supporting traditional beliefs about, 81–83; seeking help for, 80; sociological view of, 48; tolerance for alcohol and, 63–64. *See also* Adult children of alcoholics; Alcoholics; Alcoholics Anonymous; Drinking patterns; Prohibition

Alcoholism treatment, 115–143; addiction in children and, 128–131; benefit of treating addictions as diseases and, 116–117; for coalcoholics, 52; common diseases and, 135–143; defining childhood behaviors as problems and, 131–133; eating disorders and, 134–135; effectiveness of, 199–202; expanding marketplace of, 46–52; expenditures for, 126–128; extending disease concept beyond alcoholism and, 117–118; increasing expenditures on, 268; self-cure versus, 194–195; selling addiction concept and treatment and, 119–126; successful, 261–263

Aldrich, C. Knight, 179
Alexander, Shana, 220
Allergy, to alcohol, 44
Ambivalence, about alcohol, drugs, and intoxication, 257–258
American Cancer Society, 25
American Medical Association, endorsement of alcoholism as disease, 46
American Temperance Society, 37
Amish, manic-depressive disorders among, 19
Amphetamines, 119; rejection of, 162
Analgesics, nonaddictive, search for, 151
Anorexia, incidence of, 25
Antabuse (disulfiram), 201
Antisaloon movement, 32
Antisocial behavior: alcoholism and, 63; in men, as disease, 138
Anxiety, incidence of, 25, 136–137
ARF. *See* Addiction Research Foundation of Ontario
ARG. *See* Alcohol Research Group
Armstrong, Edward, 115
Athletes: addiction among, 92, 94–99, 107–108, 109, 110–111, 155; drug testing and, 225–226
Attitudes: alcoholism and, 32–35; ambivalent, toward alcohol, drugs, and intoxication, 257–258; toward drinking, changing, 53–54; toward drinking, in colonial America, 35–40; toward drinking, Prohibition and, 40–43; impact of temperance and AA on, 258
Aversion therapies, 200–201
Aykroyd, Dan, 165

Bandura, Albert, 193
Barnett, Milton, 72
Barrymore, Drew, 124, 196–197
Battered woman syndrome, 138–139; as legal defense for murder, 211–215
*Bed Time Story* (Robinson), 122
Behavior: defining as problem, in children, 131–133; as disease, 20–29; disease conceptions and, 26–27; drunken, social determination of, 169–170
Behavioral self-control training, 201, 261–263
Belushi, John, 164–165
Berra, Dale, 97
Berridge, Virginia, 22, 115
Best, Joel, 231, 248
Betty Ford Center, 33–34
Bias, Len, 128
Biernacki, Patrick, 191
Big Book, 45
Birney, Meredith Baxter, 121

Birth defects, failure to reduce, 240–244
Black, Claudia, 281
Blackouts, among alcoholics, 89
Boggs, Billie. *See* Brown, Joyce
Bowden, Julie, 282
Brandsma, Jeffrey, 75
Brecher, Edward, 23
Bremner, Steven S., 141
Brodsky, Archie, 140
Brody, Jane, 240
Brown, John Y., 186
Brown, Joyce, 16–17, 182, 271
Bukowski, Charles, 173
Bulimia: incidence of, 25, 134–135; social groups and, 159
Burnett, Carol, 102–103
*Burning Bed, The,* 212
"Burnout," among treatment providers, 106–104
Bush, George, 239

Cabell, Enos, 97, 98, 177
Caesar, Sid, 123
*Cagney and Lacey,* 121
Cahalan, Don, 47, 65, 69
Califano, Joseph, 23
Canada, prohibition in, 43
Cancer, 8; failures in dealing with, 8, 9; origin and growth of, 9–10
Carels, Ed, 129
Carter, Billy, 123
Carter, Jimmy, 239
*CBS Evening News,* 50; hospitalization of children portrayed by, 128–129
Cesarean rate, international comparison of, 245
Chapman, Mark David, 220
*Cheers,* 121
Child abuse: decline in, 246–247; as disease, 138; incidence of, 26, 246–247; legal defenses for, 207–211; overcoming trauma of, 279–280
Child Welfare League of America, 247
Child-rearing, drinking in women and, 181–182
Children: addiction for life and, 103–106; alcohol and drug education and, 34; alcohol use among, 26, 51, 136; of alcoholics, 52, 66, 88, 123–124, 279, 281, 282–283; awareness of parental misbehavior and, 280–281; dangerous world and, 246–251; defining behaviors as problems in, 131–133; development of addictions in, 149; establishing standards of conduct for, 277–267; fingerprinting, 250; healthy, parents' role in producing, 284; identification as addicts, 100–103; kidnapping of, 248–250; latch-key, 251;

learning disabilities in, 26, 102–105, 130–133, 179; learning of self-efficacy in, 273–274; legal defense for killing of, 215–218; obesity in, 236; self-protection in, 276–277; as targets for disease diagnoses, 26; treatment of, 102–103, 128–133. *See also* Adolescents; Adult children of alcoholics
Chinatown, drinking patterns in, 72
Cicero, 179
Cigarette smoking: adolescent cocaine use and, 153; defining as addiction, 117–118; incidence of, 25, 136; suing tobacco companies for health problems related to, 206. *See also* Smoking cessation
Clayton, Richard, 153
*Clean and Sober,* 73, 124
Cloninger, Robert, 63, 65
Coalcoholism, 25; treatment for, 52
Cocaine: declining use of, 233; epidemic of, 162; ghetto usage of, 235; incidence of use of, 161; John Belushi's use of, 164–165; multiple substance abuse and, 160; predictors of adolescents' use of, 153; reducing use without treatment, 161–162; as substitute for morphine, 151; values and, 166; war against, 239
Codependence, 25; as disease, 123–124; treatment for, 52
Collins, Fred, 223
Collins, Judy, 124
*Come Back Little Sheba,* 120
Community: deteriorated, treatment as compensation for, 271; efficacy of, 271–274; fear of, problems caused by, 251–252; reluctance to be part of, 257; as therapy, 267–269. *See also* Therapeutic communities
Community feeling, 251–252; as antidote to addiction, 286; extension of life spans and, 10
Community reinforcement approach (CRA), 201–194, 262–263; for alcoholism, 76
Community support: for families, 253; health related to, 269–271
CompCare, 50–51, 140, 223–215; advertising by, 124; involuntary hospitalization of children and, 128–129
Competence: as antidote to addiction, 284; disease theory versus, 286–287
Conduct problems: in adolescents, 178. *See also* Behavior
Confrontation therapy, 95; for alcoholism, 75
Consciousness, as antidote to addiction, 284–285
Control. *See* Self-efficacy

Controlled-drinking therapy, 201, 261–263
Corporations, team building in, 272
Cortez, Abigail, 217
Cortez, Jessica, 217
Cortez, Nicky, 217
Cost. *See* Expenditures
*Courage to Change, The* (Wholey), 123, 238
CRA. *See* Community reinforcement
approach
Crack. *See* Cocaine
Cravings, overcoming, 190–192
Creative Interventions, 58
Crime: increase in homicide and, 237; legal
defenses for, 203–229
Cultural beliefs, addiction and, 169–171
Cyclothymia, 138

Damon, Janet, 136
Danson, Ted, 121, 211
Darrow, Clarence, 32
*Days of Wine and Roses, The*, 120
De Leon, George, 263, 264–265, 273
De Niro, Robert, 164
Death, leading causes of, 8
Debtors Anonymous, 136
Dederich, Chuck, 266
Demographics: of alcoholism, 69–73. *See
also* Socioeconomic status
Denial, alcoholism and, 79–81, 90
Department of Transportation, drug test-
ing and, 224
Depression: drinking to relieve, 157; fail-
ure of treatment of, 14; incidence of, 25,
136–137; postpartum, 25, 138, 215, 218,
221
Developing countries: incidence of drink-
ing problems in, 269; relative lack of
addictions in, 8
*Diagnostic and Statistical Manual of Mental
Disorders (DSM-III)*, 14, 17, 216–217
Dietz, William, 236
Disease(s): addictions as, 3–5, 6–7, 20–29;
behavior as, 20–29; eating disorders as,
134–135; environmental approach to, 8–
9; epidemiological view of, 10–11; as
failures of human agency, 9–11; learning
disabilities as, 132–133; mental, 5–6;
physical, 5; "primary," alcoholism as,
67–68; searches for agents of, 7–9; true,
5–7
Disease advertising, 120
*Disease Concept of Alcoholism* (Jellinek), 72
Disease model: of addiction, 3–5; of alcoholism, AMA's endorsement of, 46; benefits for treatment industry, 116–117;
competencies versus, 286–287; fear and,
258–248, 255; inevitability of alcoholism

and, 85–88; problems associated with,
26–27; tautological nature of, 146
*Distant Thunder*, 221
District of Columbia, growing cocaine use
in, 235
Disulfiram (Antabuse), 201
Ditman, Keith, 75
*Divided Self, The* (Laing), 13
Dogoloff, Lee I., 227
*Dottie*, 137
Drew, Les, 67
Dreyden, David, 225
Drinking patterns: among adolescents, 246;
changing, 31–35; in elderly persons,
180; international comparison of, 233–
234; during Prohibition, 41–42. *See also*
Alcoholics; Alcoholism
Dropouts, from therapeutic communities,
265
Drug(s): advertising of, creating addictions
and, 119; ambivalence about, 257–258;
attention deficits and, 133; effects on
spiders' webs, 20; experience as basis of
addiction to, 151; federal law against
possession of, 227; hyperactivity and,
131, 133; making children fearful of,
254–255; use by elderly persons, 181.
*See also specific drugs*
Drug abuse: in children, 26; failure of war
on, 239–229; overstatement of problem
of, 233–234; prediction of, 177–179. *See
also* Cocaine; Heroin addiction;
Marijuana
Drug testing: college athletes and, 225–
226; compulsory, 223–224; inaccuracy
of, 229; in schools, 228; as therapy,
226–229
Drug therapy, for mental illness, 14–15
Drunk driving arrests: coercive treatment
and, 50, 222–223
Drunken behavior, social determination of,
169–170
Dryer, Fred, 145
DSM-III. *See Diagnostic and Statistical Man-
ual of Mental Disorders*
Dukakis, Kitty, 2, 49, 93–94, 119
Dukakis, Michael, 93
Dunne, Dominick, 277
Dunne, Dominique, 277
Dyslexia, as disease, 132

EAPs. *See* Employee assistance programs
Eating disorders: defined as diseases, 134–
135; incidence of, 25, 134–135; social
groups and, 159. *See also* Obesity
Economy, family violence and, 247–237
Edgerton, Robert, 169

Education: on alcohol and drug abuse, in schools, 34; special, for learning disabilities, 130–131
Edwards, Griffith, 22, 80, 115
Efficacy: of community, 271–274. *See also* Self-efficacy
Elderly people, addiction in, 179–182
Emotion(s), links to social structures, 257
Emotional disorders. *See* Mental illness; *specific disorders*
Employee assistance programs (EAPs), 50
Employment, reducing addictions and, 162
Energy, as antidote for addiction, 285
Environment: influence on alcoholics, 60; learning self-efficacy and, 274; predisposing to addictions, 167–168
Environmental approach, to disease, 8–9
Epidemiological view, 10–11
Epstein, Cynthia Fuchs, 142
Ethnic groups, drinking patterns among, 69, 70–72
Europe, prohibition in, 43
Expenditures: on addiction treatment, 126–128; on alcoholism treatment, 238–239, 268; on finding cure for cancer, 9; on war on drugs, 239
Experience(s): addiction and, 148–149; of addiction, 151–153
Exxon Valdez, 224

Failure, overcoming, 277–283
Fair Oaks Hospital, 125–126
Falk, John, 162
Falwell, Jerry, 123
Family: community support and, 253; extension of life spans and, 10; influences on mental illness, 17
*Family Secret, The* (Shupe, Stacey, & Hazlewood), 213
Family therapy, 201–202
*Family Ties*, 121
Family violence: economy and, 247; incidence of, 213; successful treatment programs for, 260–261. *See also* Child abuse; Spouse abuse
*Fantasia*, drinking portrayed in, 33
FAS. *See* Fetal alcohol syndrome
Fear: contribution of disease model to, 258–248; creation of, 252, 254–255; loss of control and, 255–258; problems created by, 237–240, 251–252
Fedders, Charlotte, 208–209
Fedders, John, 208, 209
Federal Missing Children Act, 249
Feldman, Shirley, 274
Fetal alcohol syndrome (FAS), 240–242
Fillmore, Kaye, 66, 89

Finckenauer, Edward, 129
Fingarette, Herbert, 86
Fingerprinting, of school children, 250
Fisher, Carrie, 124
Fisk, Carlton, 31
Flush, in Orientals, 64
Fonda, Jane, 134, 266
*Fool for Love* (Shepard), 273
Ford, Betty, 2, 49, 82, 107, 108, 109, 122, 128
Foucault, Michel, 12
Frieder, Bill, 226

Gambling: development of addiction to, 152–153; extension of disease model to, 21; incidence of, 25, 136
Garland, Bonnie, 215–216, 277
Gaylin, Willard, 216
Geiger, Andy, 225
Gelles, Richard, 209, 210, 249
Gender differences, in incidence of alcoholism, 70–71
General Electric, 272
Genetics: of alcoholism, 60–65, 279; compulsions other than alcoholism and, 136; of schizophrenia, 19
Gerbner, George, 254
Gless, Sharon, 121
Gold, Mark, 110, 137, 228
Goldman, Albert, 157
Gomberg, Edith, 180
Gooden, Dwight, 92, 94–95, 205
Goodwin, Donald, 61, 115, 282
Gordis, Enoch, 58
Gordon, Barbara, 122
Gortmaker, Steven, 236
Gottheil, Edward, 77
Granger, Bill, 105
Granger, Lori, 105
Grant, Ulysses S., 39, 169
Gravitz, Herbert, 282
Great Depression, 42
Greeley, Andrew, 69
Green, Agnes, 130–131
Green, Dawne, 222–223
Gross, Milton, 67
Group counseling, for alcoholism, 75

Habilitation, 273
Halloween candy, poisoning of, 248
Hamilton, Carrie, 103
Harris, Jean, 220–212
Harris, Ruth, 55
Hazelden, 140
Hazlewood, Lonnie, 259
Health: as antidote to addiction, 285; birth defects and, 241–244; of children, par-

ents' role in, 284; as impetus for change, 186–187; infant mortality and, in United States, 240, 242–244; smoking and, 206; social supports and, 269–271

*Health Consequences of Smoking: Nicotine Addiction, The*, 175

*Health of Nations, The* (Sagan), 10–11, 270

Heart disease, failures in dealing with, 8

Heath, Dwight, 8, 269

Heckler, Margaret, 128

*Help Yourself Diet Plan: The One That Worked for Me* (Pinkham), 122

Helzer, John, 77, 78, 153, 167–168

Hemingway, Margaux, 124

Henderson, Thomas "Hollywood," 98, 99, 109, 110–111, 124

Henningfield, Jack, 163

Hernandez, Keith, 96, 97, 98

Heroin: as nonaddictive substitute for morphine, 151; war against, 239

Heroin addiction: "maturing out" and, 170; therapeutic communities and, 264–265; use of other drugs and, 154–155

Herrin, Richard, 215–216, 277

Hester, Reid, 75, 76, 200, 262

*Hill Street Blues*, 121

Hingson, Roy, 241

Holden, William, 186

Holland, Al, 97

Holland, cesarian rate in, 245

Homelessness, social supports and, 270

Homicide: battered woman syndrome as legal defense for, 211–215; increase in, 237

Horiuchi, Gerald, 248

Hornstein, Sylvia, 141

Hospitalization, of young people, 50, 128–129

*How to Stop the One You Love from Drinking* (Pinkham), 122

Howe, Steve, 97, 98

*Huckleberry Finn* (Twain), 39

Hughes, Francine, 212, 215

Hughes, John, 118

Hughes, Mickey, 212

Hyperactivity, Ritalin and, 131, 133

*I'm Dancing as Fast as I Can* (Gordon), 122

Immigrants, drinking patterns among, 32

Individual, nature of addiction and, 146–148

Infant mortality, failure to reduce, in United States, 240, 242–244

Intemperance, concept of, 38

Interleukin, 9

Intimate relationships: as antidote to addiction, 286; diseased, 139

Intoxication: ambivalence about, 257–258. *See also* Drunken behavior

Iowa Community Coordinator program, 267

Jabbar, Kareem Abdul, 83, 110

Jacovsky, Marilyn, 136

Janoff–Bulman, Ronnie, 278

Jellinek, Elvin, 45, 72, 82, 89

Jessor, Richard, 153, 177

Jessor, Shirley, 153

Jews: alcoholism among, 71; lack of smoking on Sabbath among, 188

Johnson, Jeanette, 281

Kalant, Harold, 145

Kandel, Denise, 167

Kansas, prohibition in, 43

Kaufman, Joan, 279, 280, 282, 283

*Keeping Secrets* (Somers), 124

Kendell, R.E., 58

Kennedy, Joan, 82

Kidnapping, 248–250

*Killing of Bonnie Garland, The* (Gaylin), 216

Koch, Edward, 16, 130, 182, 271

Koop, C. Everett, 278

Kovar, Mary Grace, 242

Laing, R.D., 13, 17

*Larry King Show*, 217

Latch-key kids, 251

Late Luteal Phase Dysphoric Disorder, 217

Learning disabilities, 26; defining as disease, 132–133; permanence of, 102–105; prevalence of adult problems and, 179; special education programs and, 130–131

Legal defense: addictions as, 203–229; diseases as, 27

Legal sanctions, effectiveness against alcoholism, 57

Lennon, John, 220

Lester, David, 62

LeVant, Simone, 225

Levine, Melvin, 132–133

Lewis, Jerry, 186

Lex, Barbara, 70

Lexington, Kentucky public health hospital, 23

Life expectancies: extension of, 10–11; in United States, 8

Life expectancy, community support and control of one's life and, 270

*Life Extension* (Pearson & Shaw), 61

Life phases: addiction and, 149; quitting addictions and, 183

Lifer's Juvenile Awareness Program, 129–130

Lincoln, Abraham, 169

Lithgow, John, 221

*Lives of John Lennon, The* (Goldman), 157

*Lost Weekend, The*, 46, 47, 90–91, 120

Love addictions, 139; incidence of, 25

*Love and Addiction* (Peele & Brodsky), 140, 145

MAC scale, 157

MacAndrew, Craig, 157–153, 169

McCabe, Charles, 90

*McCall's* magazine, cyclothymia described in, 138

McLain, Gary, 91–92, 99

MacLane, Mary, 231

*Madness and Civilization* (Foucault), 12

*Magic Feather, The* (Granger & Granger), 105

Manic-depressive disorders, among Amish, 19

Mann, Marty, 45, 46, 119–120

Mannuzza, Salvatore, 179

Mantle, Mickey, 33

Marijuana: adolescent cocaine use and, 153; declining use of, 233

Marital therapy, 201–202

Marlatt, Alan, 59, 170, 192

Martin, Steve, 99–97

Masochistic personality, 216–217

Masserman, Jules, 117

Maturing out, 173–176, 273; heroin addiction and, 170

*Meaning of Addiction, The* (Peele), 145

Media: creation of addiction treatment industry and, 119–125; drinking portrayed in, 33, 34; drug users portrayed by, 161; problems associated with television viewing and, 236, 252, 254–255

Medical treatment: coercive nature of, 27; as cure for emotional problems, 11–20; failure of, 26–27; U.S. reliance on, 256–257

Medicare, reimbursement for alcoholism treatment under, 127–128

Mello, Nancy, 59, 81–82

Melton, Gary, 102

Mendelson, Jack, 59, 81–82

Mental illness, 5–6; definition of, 12–13; *DSM-III* categories of, 14; environmental approach to, 8–9; family influences on, 17; search for medical cure for, 11–20. *See also specific disorders*

Mental states, onset and remission of illnesses and, 10

Merrel/Dow Pharmaceuticals, 118

Michel, Erwin, 223

Middle class: addictions in, 2, 150; killing one's own children and, 215–218; prenatal care and, 245

Milam, James, 59, 63, 70

Milk, Harvey, 220

Miller, Derek, 197

Miller, William, 75, 76, 200, 262

Minelli, Liza, 33

Mississippi, prohibition in, 43

Moore, Mary Tyler, 33

Morris, Eugene "Mercury," 107

Moscone, George, 220

Motivations, for drinking, 157–158

Mulford, Harold, 67, 259, 267, 268, 269

Murder. *See* Homicide

*Murphy Brown*, 121

*Murphy's Law*, 121

Murray, Henry, 29

Murray, Robin, 58, 62

Musto, David, 22, 162

*Myth of Mental Illness, The* (Szasz), 13

NACoA. *See* National Association for Children of Alcoholics

Narcotics: development of addiction concept and, 22–23. *See also specific drugs*

Nash, Graham, 124

Nathan, Peter, 170

Nation, Carry, 40

Nation, David, 40

National Anti-Saloon League, 40

National Association for Children of Alcoholics (NACoA), 52, 123

National Center for Missing and Exploited Children, 249

National Council on Alcoholism (NCA), 24, 45; disease concept of alcoholism and, 119, 120

National Council on Compulsive Gamblers, 25

National Institute of Mental Health (NIMH), 26, 137

National Institute on Alcohol Abuse and Alcoholism (NIAAA), 34, 46; costs of alcoholism estimated by, 238–239

National Institute on Drug Abuse (NIDA), 163, 251

National Mental Health Consumers' Association, 18, 270

*Natural History of Alcoholism, The* (Vaillant), 24, 68, 175

*NBC Nightly News*, missing children and, 249

NCA. *See* National Council on Alcoholism

*New York Times*: drug testing and, 227; on

schizophrenia, 19–20; stories about co-
caine use in, 163, 166
NIAAA. *See* National Institute on Alcohol
Abuse and Alcoholism
Nicorette gum, 118
NIDA. *See* National Institute on Drug
Abuse
Nidetch, Jean, 187
NIMH. *See* National Institute of Mental
Health
Nixon, Richard, 239
Norwood, Robin, 139
Nussbaum, Hedda, 139, 214, 215, 252

Obesity: defining as addiction, 118, 119;
growing problem of, 234, 236–237; inci-
dence of, 25; related to television view-
ing, 236, 252, 254. *See also* Eating
disorders
O'Bryan, Timothy, 248
Obsessive-compulsive disorder (OCD),
137; incidence of, 26, 137
OCD. *See* Obsessive-compulsive disorder
O'Connor, Francis, 225
O'Donnell, Jack, 177
Oetting, Eugene, 159, 155
Offer, Daniel, 274
Oklahoma, prohibition in, 43
Ono, Yoko, 157
Oppositional problems, in adolescents, 178
"Oriental flush," 64
Orton Society, 132
*Our Town* (Wilder), 31
Overeaters Anonymous, 118
Overeating: quitting, 176. *See also* Obesity
Oxford Group, 38

*Papa John* (Phillips), 109
Parents, role in producing healthy off-
spring, 284
Parker, Dave, 96, 97–95
Partnership for a Drug-Free America, 251
*Pathways from Heroin Addiction* (Biernacki),
191
Patz, Etan, 251
Pauley, Jane, 175
Pearson, Durk, 61
Peck, Scott, 78
Peele, Stanton, 140, 145, 178
Pelton, Leroy, 207
Personality: addictive, 154–156; continuity
of, 177; masochistic, 215; onset and re-
mission of illnesses and, 10
Peters, Bernadette, 143
Phelps, Digger, 226–217
*Phil Donahue Show*, 18
Phillips, John, 109–110

Phillips, MacKenzie, 109, 110
Phoenix House, 263, 264
Physical diseases, 5, 8–10
Pinkham, Mary Ellen, 122–123
PMS. *See* Premenstrual syndrome
Pop, Iggy, 173
Porter, Darrel, 98–99
Post-Traumatic Stress Disorder, 138, 217,
219–220, 278
Postpartum depression (PPD), 138, 217;
incidence of, 25; as legal defense, 217–
218, 221
Powerlessness, addicts' feelings of, 158
PPD. *See* Postpartum depression
Pregnancy: prenatal care and, 244–246;
teenage, 242–244, 246
Premenstrual syndrome (PMS), 138, 217;
incidence of, 25; as legal defense, 221;
pervasiveness of, 141–142
Prenatal care, socioeconomic status and,
244–246
Presidential Commission on Organized
Crime, drug testing and, 224
"Prison awareness" programs, 129–130
Privacy, drug testing and, 225–226
*Professional Counselor*, 111
*Professional Update* magazine, 138
Prohibition, 32; effects and aftereffects of,
40–43; in other countries, 43; repeal of,
42
Prohibition Party, 40
Prosocial activities, prevention of addiction
and, 160–163
Psychotherapy, failure of, 14–15
Publishing, portrayal of addictions as dis-
eases by, 122–123
Punishment, treatment as, 221–226
Pursch, Joseph, 51, 128

Quinones, Nathan, 130

Rand Report, 82
Rapism, 217
Rather, Dan, 219
Reagan, Nancy, 223, 243
Reagan, Ronald, 224, 239, 278
Recovery. *See* Addiction treatment indus-
try; Alcoholism treatment; Spontaneous
recovery; Treatment
*Recovery: A Guide for Adult Children of Alco-
holics* (Gravitz & Bowden), 282
Recuperation, human capacity for, 277–
283
Regan, Riley, 127
Relapse, 116–117; among AA participants,
194; avoiding, 190–192

Responsibility: as antidote for addiction, 285–275; for change, of addict, 264
Richardson, Micheal Ray, 98
Ritalin, hyperactivity and, 131, 133
*Road Not Taken, The* (Peck), 78
Robards, Jason, 123
Robins, Lee, 153, 154–155, 167–168, 171
Robinson, Jill, 122
Rodin, Judith, 176
Rogers, Don, 155
Rogers, Joe, 18, 270
Rogers, Reggie, 155
Room, Robin, 47, 49, 69, 91, 269
Rosenthal, Mitchell, 264
Rosett, Henry, 241, 244
*Roxanne*, 99
Ruby, Jay, 211
Rudy, David, 89
Rush, Benjamin, 37, 54
Ruth, Babe, 33

Sagan, Leonard, 10–11, 270
*St. Elsewhere*, 121
Salaries, of treatment staff, 106
Sanders, Inez Jean, 249
Sanderson, Derek, 98, 107–108, 109
*Scared Straight!*, 129, 251
*Scared Straight! Ten Years Later*, 129
Schachter, Stanley, 176, 187–188
Schizophrenia: biology of, 15; failure of treatment of, 14, 15–20; genetic basis of, 19
Schoenberger, Richard, 250
Schools: alcohol and drug education in, 34; drug testing in, 228
Schroeder, Patricia, 224
Schuckit, Marc, 63, 65, 281
Schwartz, Ira, 129
Scurry, Rod, 97
Segal, George, 121
Self-awareness, as antidote to addiction, 284–285
Self-cure, 173–176; treatment versus, 194–195, 197–199
Self-Defeating Personality Disorder, 217
Self-efficacy, 193–195; community and, 273–274; sense of, extension of life spans and, 10–11
Self-esteem: as antidote to addiction, 285–286; of children of alcoholics, 88
Self-image: addicted, 99–100; conversion in AA and, 112–113; danger of therapy and, 195, 197–199; quitting addictions to protect, 185–186
Self-protection, in children, 276–277
Self-regulation, as antidote to addiction, 285–275

SES. *See* Socioeconomic status
Severinson, Doc, 123
Sexaholics Anonymous, 139
Sex differences, in incidence of alcoholism, 70–71
Sexual activity, among adolescents, 246
Sexual addictions, 139–140; incidence of, 25
*Shattered Dreams* (Fedders), 208
*Shattered Spirits*, 121
Shaw, Sandra, 61
Sheehan, David, 137
Shelters, for homeless, 270
Shepard, Sam, 273
Shopping addiction, incidence of, 136
Shupe, Anson, 259
*Sid and Nancy*, 156
Siegel, Ronald, 161
Slick, Grace, 123
Smith, Cathy, 164
Smith, Lonnie, 96–97
Smith, Robert, 43
Smithers Alcoholism Center, 95
Smokenders program, 100
Smoking. *See* Cigarette smoking
Smoking cessation, 189–190; difficulty of, 174–175; disease model and, 117–118; health as impetus for, 186–187; independent, 25; Nicorette gum and, 118; Smokenders program and, 100; treatment versus self-cure and, 197–198
Social change, need for, 260
Social conditions, infant mortality and defects and, 243
Social groups, addiction and, 159–160
Social skills training, 202
Social supports: family and, 253; health and, 269–271
Socioeconomic status (SES): development of addictions and, 2, 150, 160; family violence and, 207–211; infant mortality and defects and, 243; killing one's own children and, 215–218; obesity and, 236; prenatal care and, 244–246; reducing addictions and, 162
Sociological viewpoint, alcoholism and, 48
Somers, Suzanne, 124
*Something About Amelia*, 211
Speakeasies, 41
Special education programs, for learning disabilities, 130–131
Spiders' webs, effects of drugs on, 20
Spontaneous recovery, 173–176; in alcoholism, 67; from heroin addiction, 170, 173–176; from schizophrenia, 16–17
Spouse abuse: battered woman syndrome as legal defense for murder and, 211–

215; as disease, 138; legal defenses for, 207–211; successful treatment of, 260–261

Stacey, William, 259

Stall, Ron, 180

Steinberg, Elana, 216

Steinberg, Joel, 209, 214–215, 220, 252

Steinberg, Lisa, 209, 214–215

Steinberg, Steven, 216

Steinmetz, Suzanne, 213–214

Straight Inc., 51, 223

Straus, Murray, 209, 210, 213, 247, 249, 280

Stress, post-traumatic, 138, 215, 219–220, 278

Stress management, 202

Stroke, failures in dealing with, 8

Strong, Curtis, 96

Stubbing, Edmund, 209

Suicide, among adolescents, 246

Sunday, Billy, 41

Superobesity, increase in, 236

Surgeon General's report, on cigarette smoking, 175

Sweeney, John, 277

Synanon, 266

Szasz, Thomas, 13, 17

Talbott, G. Douglas, 24–25, 47, 65

Tarcher, Jeremy, 186

Tarnower, Herman, 220

Taylor, Elizabeth, 33, 49

Taylor, Lawrence, 98, 124

Team building, in corporations, 272

Television, portrayal of addictions as diseases by, 120–122

Television viewing: fear associated with, 254–255; obesity related to, 236, 252, 254

Temperance movement, 32, 37–39, 40; impact on attitudes, 258; in other countries, 43

Therapeutic communities, 263–269; positive dropouts from, 265; self-efficacy and, 273

*Times of My Life, The* (Ford), 122

Toma, David, 34, 107, 121–122

Torrey, E. Fuller, 18

Toston, Kevin, 248

"Tough love," 102–103

Trauma: caused by abortion, 278; overcoming, 277–283

Travanti, Daniel, 249

Treatment: of children, 102–103, 128–133; coercive, 221–226; drug testing as, 226–227; effectiveness of, 199–202; expenditures on, 126–128, 238–239, 268; former

addicts as treatment staff and, 106–111; medical, 26–27, 256–257; psychotherapeutic, failure of, 14–15; as punishment, 221–226; quitting addictions without, 173–176; self-cure versus, 194–195, 197–199; successful, for family violence, 260–261. *See also* Addiction treatment industry; Alcoholism treatment

Treatment facilities, for alcoholism, 49, 126; for drug abuse, 235

Truancy, adolescent cocaine use and, 153

Tuchfeld, Barry, 67, 80, 185, 193

Twain, Mark, 39

*Under the Influence* (Milam), 59, 63, 70

United States: cesarean rate in, 245; colonial, attitudes toward drinking in, 35–40; colonial, community supports in, 271; increasing homicide rate in, 237; increasing problem of obesity in, 234, 236–237; leading causes of death in, 8; problems created by fear of addiction in, 237–240

*Update* magazine, 101

Upper class, development of addictions in, 150

Utah, Ritalin use in, 131

Vaillant, George, 24, 63, 65, 67–68, 69, 73–74, 82, 99, 162, 167, 175, 194, 199

Values, 163–166; as impetus to change, 187–188; positive, inculcating, 264, 283–286; preventing addiction, 165

*Very Much a Lady* (Alexander), 220

Vicious, Sid, 156

Vietnam War: development of addiction and, 149–150, 153, 167–168, 171; post-traumatic stress and, 138, 217, 219–220, 278

Violence: growing problem of, 237–227. *See also* Child abuse; Family violence; Spouse abuse

*Violent Men, Violent Couples* (Shupe, Stacey, & Hazlewood), 213

Vreeland, Diana, 41–42

Wagner, Florence, 142

Wagner, Marsden, 242

Waldorf, Dan, 192

*Wall Street Journal*, PMS discussed in, 141–142

*Wall Within, The*, 219

Walsh, Adam, 249

Walsh, John, 249, 250

Warner-Holland, David, 264

Washingtonians, 38, 44; failure of, 45

Wegscheider-Cruse, Sharon, 52, 281

Weiner, Lyn, 241, 244

Weisner, Constance, 49
*When Society Becomes an Addict*, 237
White, Dan, 220
Wholey, Dennis, 123, 238
Wiggins, Alan, 97
Wilder, Thornton, 31
Williams, Robin, 164
Wilson, Bill, 43
Winfrey, Oprah, 18, 205
Winick, Charles, 170, 175, 264–265, 273
Witt, Peter, 20
Woititz, Janet, 88, 123

*Women Who Love Too Much* (Norwood), 139
Women's Christian Temperance Union, 38, 40
Wright, Jeremy, 240–241
Wright, Monica, 85–86, 109, 181

Yale Center of Alcohol Studies, 45

Zero-tolerance policy, 227
Zigler, Edward, 279, 280, 282, 283
Zinberg, Norman, 42

# About the Author

STANTON PEELE, PH.D., a leading figure in the addictions field, has won the Mark Keller Award from the Rutgers Center for Alcohol Studies and the Lindesmith Award from the Drug Policy Foundation. He is the author of the classic *Love and Addiction* and *The Truth About Addiction and Recovery*.